An Unsafe F

An Unsafe Bet?

The Dangerous Rise of Gambling and the Debate We Should be Having

Jim Orford

Alcohol, Drugs, Gambling & Addiction Research Group
School of Psychology, The University of Birmingham, Edgbaston,
Birmingham B15 2TT, UK

WILEY-BLACKWELL

A John Wiley & Sons, Ltd., Publication

This edition first published 2011
© 2011 John Wiley & Sons Ltd

Wiley-Blackwell is an imprint of John Wiley & Sons, formed by the merger of Wiley's global Scientific, Technical, and Medical business with Blackwell Publishing.

Registered Office
John Wiley & Sons Ltd, The Atrium, Southern Gate, Chichester, West Sussex, PO19 8SQ, UK

Editorial Offices
The Atrium, Southern Gate, Chichester, West Sussex, PO19 8SQ, UK
9600 Garsington Road, Oxford, OX4 2DQ, UK
350 Main Street, Malden, MA 02148-5020, USA

For details of our global editorial offices, for customer services, and for information about how to apply for permission to reuse the copyright material in this book please see our website at www.wiley.com/wiley-blackwell.

The right of Jim Orford to be identified as the author of this work has been asserted in accordance with the UK Copyright, Designs and Patents Act 1988.

Library of Congress Cataloging-in-Publication Data

Orford, Jim.
    An unsafe bet? : the dangerous rise of gambling and the debate we should be having / Jim Orford.
       p.   cm.
    Includes bibliographical references and index.
    ISBN 978-0-470-66119-2 (cloth) – ISBN 978-0-470-66120-8 (pbk.)   1. Gambling.
 2. Compulsive gambling.   I. Title.
    HV6710.O74   2010
    363.4'2–dc22   2010027834

This book is published in the following electronic formats: eBook [9780470973066]; Wiley Online Library [9780470972977]

A catalogue record for this book is available from the British Library.

Typeset in 10/12pt Minion by Aptara Inc., New Delhi, India.
Printed in Singapore by Ho Printing Singapore Pte Ltd

01   2011

Contents

Preface

I have written this book because I thought it was needed. I am continually surprised how little challenge there has been to the dramatic liberalisation of the gambling laws and the expansion of opportunities for gambling that have taken place in quite a short period of years. That must surely be attributed to lobbying for expansion by the gambling industry, the desperation of governments to cash in on the proceeds whilst not appreciating the threat that gambling expansion poses for public health, and the absence of well-informed public debate about the issues. I have been horrified, also, by the complicity of those who should be in a position to mount a challenge: practitioners, academics, and their organisations, who are active in the field. As a clinical and research psychologist I have heard directly from people about the destructive potential of gambling. Like countless numbers of people in the past, in the present and no doubt in the future, I have also witnessed the dangers of gambling at close hand in my own personal life. In this book I have tried to summarise the argument that: opportunities for gambling have been growing fast; gambling is dangerous because it can be addictive; the place of gambling in society is controversial; and there is a failure to challenge gambling expansion and to engage in the kind of debate we should be having. I hope it will make a contribution to raising awareness of the issues and stimulating debate.

Part I sets the scene by summarising facts about the expansion of gambling in the late twentieth and beginning of the twenty-first centuries. Chapter 1 takes a global perspective, briefly summarising gambling in three regions: Australia, New Zealand and East Asia; North America; and Europe. References to different countries recur throughout the book and my main line of reasoning – that gambling is dangerous and that not to challenge its expansion represents a serious shortcoming – applies to many countries besides my own. Britain is my main concern, however, and a number of chapters focus on the situation in Britain. Chapter 2 is one of those, summarising some of the facts about the legislative and regulatory gambling framework in Britain and the gambling habits of its citizens.

Part II is all about addiction and is applicable wherever gambling takes place. It is divided into three chapters. Chapter 3 summarises the accumulated evidence for the statement that gambling is dangerous, and that it is so because it has the potential for addiction. Chapter 4 summarises modern addiction theory, within which gambling addiction fits as a core example. Chapter 5 considers the question of why some people are more at risk than others, and the highly politicised question of whether the fault lies principally in characteristics of people's personalities or in the availability and nature of the gambling product itself.

Part III considers gambling as a matter of controversy. The three chapters that make up this part of the book consider the contested nature of gambling from three different perspectives. Chapter 6 offers the reader a 'discourse analysis' of what people have said and written about the topic, identifying 11 different ways of viewing gambling, some old, some new, some negative about gambling and others supportive of its expansion. Chapter 7 considers public attitudes to gambling, drawing particularly on some results of the British Gambling Prevalence Survey, finding attitudes to be remarkably negative. Chapter 8 examines the way in which some economists have attempted to carry out a cost-benefit analysis of gambling for society – a methodology which turns out to be fraught and inconclusive.

Part IV looks directly at our failure to challenge the growth of gambling despite its dangerousness. Chapter 9 puts the spotlight on governments and their complicity with an expansionist gambling industry. Chapter 10 broadens the focus to include others who have joined the government – industry consensus and therefore failed to mount a challenge. Chapter 11 summarises the book's argument, points to areas of complacency about gambling growth and makes a number of recommendations about the regulation of gambling. Some of my recommendations will strike some readers as radical or extreme. But in fact there are many different ways of managing gambling to be found in different countries around the world and each of my recommendations is for something that already occurs somewhere or which has been seriously debated.

My interest in gambling as an addiction goes back a number of years to my time as a researcher at the Addiction Research Unit in London in the late 1960s and early 1970s. Although I alone am responsible for the content of the present book, I owe a great debt to stimulating collaborations with colleagues in London in those days, later with colleagues in the NHS and at the University in Exeter, and most recently with fellow researchers in the Alcohol, Drugs, Gambling and Addiction Research Group at the University of Birmingham and with colleagues at the National Centre for Social Research (NatCen) in London, who carried out British Gambling Prevalence Surveys in 1999/2000, 2006/07 and 2009/10. Special thanks, as always, are reserved for Pat Evans who, as our Birmingham University research group secretary, has expertly turned my dictating into a deliverable manuscript.

Thanks for permission to reproduce previously published material are due to Koninklijke BRILL NV., Leiden, The Netherlands (table 1.2), Springer Science+Business Media (figure 3.1), Elsevier Ltd (figure 4.2), Wiley-Blackwell (figure 4.3) and Taylor and Francis Ltd (figures 5.2 and 10.2 and tables 9.1, 9.4, 9.5 and 10.2).

Section I
Gambling is Growing

The Extraordinary International Growth of Gambling

The pros and cons of gambling are a matter of dispute. Historically that state-ment has always been true and its continuing truth is becoming more and more evident as the early years of the twenty-first century go by. As I hope to make clear, the gambling controversy is an important one for society and for individual citizens and their families. There is one thing about which every-one is agreed however; that the last years of the twentieth century saw a quite staggering liberalisation and expansion of opportunities to gamble around the world. Although regulations governing gambling vary markedly from country to country, and even from state to state within a country, expansionary in-dustry pressure and the temptation for governments to raise money through gambling have been felt almost everywhere. We have seen 'an unprecedented de regulation of gambling in numerous jurisdictions throughout the world'.[1] By the end of the twentieth century gambling had become a 'global player' in the economies of many countries.[2] The figures for numbers of electronic gambling machines (EGMs), expenditure on playing machines or on gambling generally, and the amount of tax collected by governments from gambling activities – and the increases in those figures in just one or two decades – are truly aston-ishing. Some of those figures are shown in Table 1.1.

In this chapter let us look at what has been happening in three regions of the world where statistics on gambling have been collected.

Australia, New Zealand and East Asia

Australia

One country in particular stands out as an object lesson to the rest of the world, illustrating the dangers of gambling expansion. There will be occasion to refer

An Unsafe Bet? The Dangerous Rise of Gambling and the Debate We Should be Having   By Jim Orford
© 2011 John Wiley & Sons, Ltd

Table 1.1 Indications of the size of the gambling market worldwide and how rapidly it has grown: some examples

Australia[3]

  Total staked or wagered: Aus \$95bn in 1999. Net expenditure on gambling: Aus \$11bn (up from 4.5bn a decade earlier), representing 3.5% of household disposable income (up from 2% a decade earlier).

New Zealand[4]

  Total net expenditure on the four main forms of gambling (sports betting, lotteries, casinos, EGMs): NZ \$2bn in 2003/04 (up from 570m a decade earlier). Total number of non-casino EGMs: 25,000 in 2003 (up from 7,000 a decade earlier).

China[5]

  Total lottery sales: equivalent US \$10.5bn in 2006 (up from 2m two decades earlier).

USA[6]

  Total wagered on all forms of commercial gambling: over \$0.5tn in 2000. Total net expenditure: over \$60bn in 2000 (up from a.\$10bn two decades earlier).

Canada[7]

  Gross revenue from gambling in 2004: C\$12.5bn. Average adult expenditure on gambling: C\$600 (up from \$150 a decade earlier). Percentage of provincial governments' income from all gambling revenues: 3.8% in 2004 (up from 2.1% a decade earlier).

Germany[8]

  Total gambling turnover 26bn euros in 2005. Government revenue from gambling 4.3bn euros in 2005 (up from 0.7bn in 1970 and 1.5bn in 1980).

Italy[9]

  Total gambling expenditure 35bn euros in 2006 (up from 8bn, relative to 2006 prices, in 1993). In 18 months up to 2000, 800,000 video poker machines were installed with a turnover of more than 20bn euros.

to it often in the present book. That country is Australia. Not only have several of the Australian states brought in very liberal gambling regimes, with rapid expansion of gambling machines in particular, but also, on account of the concern that this has aroused, more research has been done and more written about gambling in Australia than in most other places. One of the most thorough and comprehensive reports on gambling and its effects in an individual country was the Australian Productivity Commission report of 1999. The report began by saying, '. . . even by Australian standards, the recent proliferation of gambling opportunities and the growth in the gambling industries have been remarkable'.[10]

  Much of that remarkable growth was attributable to legalisation and rapid growth in the numbers of gambling machines, or what are commonly known in Australia as 'poker machines' or simply 'pokies'. They are much more sophisticated than the simpler types of gambling machine that used to be the norm in Britain and elsewhere. Fully electronic, controlled by buttons or touch-screens, they enable people to bet on multiple lines (20 lines is not uncommon) and using multiple credits (or multiples of the nominal denomination of the machine). Each machine is capable of consuming in excess of AU $1,000 an hour.[11] One estimate is that the number of EGMs in Australia rose in the decade prior to the Productivity Commission report from around 70,000 to approximately 190,000.[12] Ninety per cent of these machines existed in easily accessible locations, such as in bars, hotels and clubs.

As one commentator put it, gambling proliferated in Australia, 'despite having already been one of the world's most heavily gambling provisioned nations'.[13] The figures in the table show how the total expenditure of Australians on gambling rose between the 1980s and the end of the century, not just in billions of dollars but also in very real terms as an average percentage of disposable household income. In fact, so prominent a feature of the Australian economy was gambling in the 1990s that by the second half of the decade it was contributing over 10% of total state and territory tax revenues.[14] By 2003 gross gaming revenues in Australia were equivalent to 1.9% of gross domestic product, considerably in excess of comparable figures for countries such as New Zealand, Canada and the USA and the European Union.[15]

One of the features of the new gambling scene is its mind-boggling complexity. Even those who make a special study of the subject find it difficult to keep abreast of what is going on in one country, let alone internationally. Australia provides a good example of that complexity, as it does of so many features of modern gambling. Gambling legislation is partly a matter for the Australian national government and partly under the control of the individual states and territories. Hence, by the beginning of the new century the number of non-casino EGMs per thousand adults varied widely, from zero in Western Australia where they were only permitted in Perth's one casino, to New South Wales (NSW) and the Australian Capital Territory with concentrations of more than 20 machines per thousand adults and per capita annual expenditures on EGMs of getting on for 1,000 Australian dollars.[16] What happened in the state of Victoria provides a good example, repeated around the world, of the difficulty of holding the line against gambling expansion when gambling is more easily available in other jurisdictions nearby. An inquiry in the 1980s, influenced by what was seen in NSW, had recommended against the introduction of gambling machines but in the end a deciding factor was the obvious leakage of potential gambling revenue over the border into NSW where there were a number of very large social clubs with many poker machines and large parking areas for coaches.[17] EGMs were legalised in Victoria in 1991 and by 1993 there were over 200 local gambling venues – half local pubs and half licensed social clubs – with over 13,000 poker machines.[18] At around the same time legislation was passed permitting the setting up of a casino; the Melbourne casino opened in 1994 with 130 gaming tables and 1,200 EGMs, the latter number rising later to the legal maximum of 2,500.

Although the state of Victoria was relatively late legalising EGMs compared to its neighbour New South Wales, and has a lower number of them per head of population, gambling in Victoria has been particularly carefully studied thanks to the development there of a well thought out public health campaign on the subject of gambling.[19] Interestingly, the piece of legislation that allowed for EGMs was called the Gaming Machine Control Act, and it offers us a very good example of a jurisdiction responding to the need to monitor and regulate a kind of product which carries dangers. It provided for just two operators (Tattersall's and Tabcorp) who were required to operate a centralised monitoring system that enabled all machines to be monitored 24 hours a day, recording all games played, amounts wagered, prizes paid and cash retained, thus providing security, aiding the operators in marketing decisions, and accessible to government regulators for financial control and auditing.[20] As in most other Australian states and territories, caps were placed on the number of EGMs permitted overall or within particular localities. By the end of the century, non-casino machines had been capped at 30,000, equivalent to eight for every 1,000 adults, lower than figures for some other parts of Australia but high by international standards.[21]

Australia's gambling is of interest well beyond its shores for yet another reason. As well as having an indigenous, Aboriginal, population whose poorer average health, compared to most Australians, is a continuing cause for concern, Australia also has a large immigrant population. Many recent immigrants have come to Australia from Asian countries such as China and Thailand and special studies have been made of the gambling of members of those immigrant groups in cities such as Melbourne and Brisbane.[22] Gambling in the Northern Territory is of special interest because indigenous Australians constitute 30% of the NT population. Until 1996 gambling machines in the territory were restricted to the two casinos, in Darwin and Alice Springs. Thereafter machine gambling became much more accessible in hotels and clubs, particularly to those living in smaller urban centres. Although only one third of the indigenous NT population lives in urban centres, visits from rural communities to urban centres are frequent, and gambling – both card gambling and commercial gambling – is a worry for many indigenous Australians.[23]

Although gambling machines have figured large in the expanding gambling scene, machines by no means exhaust the possibilities for gambling in Australia. Horse race gambling, for example, has been transformed in Australia from a small-scale local social activity to become part of a huge global gambling industry as part of the booming sports betting industry. Races such as the Melbourne Cup have become major international events, races have been re-scheduled to maximise betting opportunities across national and international time zones, and bettors around the world can place their bets by telephone or online. For Australia this serves as a kind of export industry since sports betting is not legal in some other countries. For example CANBET, located in Canberra, makes almost all its money from betting on college football in the USA where such betting is illegal; and CENTREBET, an internet sports bookmaker in the Northern Territory, was reported to be attracting 80% of its clientele from overseas, 20% in the USA.[24]

As we shall see, the different ways in which countries have attempted to reg-ulate, or in some cases not regulate, online gambling, has become a prominent feature of the complexity that is so characteristic of the world of gambling. Australian federal law permits online sports betting, poker, games of skill and lotteries but not keno-style games, scratch tickets or instant lotteries, and, illogically perhaps, does not permit Australian residents themselves to gamble at its government-licensed online casino.[25]

New Zealand

A similar transformation occurred during the same era in New Zealand. In the late 1980s the country saw the introduction of a national lottery, a scratch lottery (Instant Kiwi) and the licensing of EGMs in clubs and hotels.[26] New Zealand had no casinos prior to 1995. In 2000/2001 its government undertook a comprehensive review of gambling and in September 2003 the parliament passed its new Gambling Act. A spokesman for the New Zealand Department of Internal Affairs described the Act as a regulatory one which turned the tide of gambling expansion, prohibiting the licensing of any more casinos and any expansion of opportunities for gambling within existing casinos, bringing about a reduction in the number of venues where EGMs could be played outside casinos, and a slight fall in overall expansion of the four main forms of gambling – betting on horse and dog races and other sports, lottery products, casino gambling, and non-casino EGMs.[27] The only online gambling permitted is sports betting operated by the Racing Board and lotteries run by the Lotteries Commission. Otherwise operating online gambling in New Zealand is illegal.[28] Phillida Bunkle, formerly New Zealand consumer affairs minister, speaking at a conference held in London in October 2007, was much less sanguine about the 2003 Act, believing that it had done little to reverse the expansion that had occurred and that it had not been in response to public demand.

As in Australia, special concern has been expressed about the exposure to gambling of indigenous and immigrant groups, including Maori, Pacific Islanders and immigrants from Asian countries.[29] There is evidence that Maori people spend more per head on gambling than New Zealanders of European heritage even though Maori median incomes are roughly half that of non-Maori.[30]

China, Thailand and Japan

The pressure to legalise and expand gambling has also been felt in East and South-East Asia and in Japan. All forms of gambling were illegal in China from 1949 until the state lottery commenced in 1987. All other forms of gambling remain illegal. The state runs two types of lottery, a welfare lottery which raises money for civil projects such as building old people's homes, and a sports lottery which has raised money for, amongst other things, the 2008 Olympic Games. According to two researchers based in China, the Chinese authorities officially regard the lotteries as charitable giving rather than gambling: tickets are 'issued' rather than 'sold' and winnings are viewed as incentives for donation rather than as prizes. The price of a single game is small but, as elsewhere, maximum prizes are 'life-changingly' large. Although, expressed in terms of per capita expenditure, the Chinese lottery is small compared to many other national lotteries, it has become a prominent aspect of China's social life.[31]

Macau constitutes a special case having long had a casino industry with a murky reputation run by a single private operator and enjoying a monopoly on casino gambling in the whole region. It came under Chinese rule in 1999 and was allowed to retain a casino industry opened up to private international competition.[32] Like Las Vegas in the USA and Sun City in the Johannesburg area of South Africa, once casino gambling spread at the end of the twentieth century and its regional monopoly was broken, Macau has had to reinvent itself as a general tourist destination rather than simply a gambling location.[33]

Thailand is another Asian country where only the government lottery has been legal, although it is generally recognised that underground lotteries are popular with lower-income groups and that sports betting, particularly on football, is common amongst middle and higher income groups.[34] In 2008 the Thai Prime Minister announced the intention to end the ban on casino gambling: five casinos were to be built in holiday resorts in order to compete in the tourist market with Macau, Malaysia and Singapore. The latter was due to open its first gaming resort in 2009.[35] For similar reasons new or expanded casino industries are to be found in South Korea and the Philippines and the same is being considered in Taiwan.[36]

In Japan casinos as exist elsewhere are not legal but at one time it was thought that the country had the largest number of gambling machines of any country in the world.[37] Japanese gambling machines are a mixture of the kind of 'slot' or 'fruit' machines familiar in other countries, and a game known as pachinko – a kind of vertical pinball game which has been very popular in Japan and elsewhere in south-east Asia. Winnings were in the form of prizes which could only be exchanged for money with dealers operating outside the 'pachinko parlour'. Since new-style machines were introduced in Japan in 1981, their numbers have increased and they are now reported to outnumber the traditional machines.[38] Although some viewed traditional pachinko as harmless entertainment, others viewed it as being much like other forms of gambling machine playing. Only those aged 18 or over were allowed to enter a pachinko parlour.[39] The parlours are ubiquitous in Japan and according to one estimate the amount of money spent in them per head of the Japanese population was greater in 2004 than the amount USAmericans spent annually on all types of gambling taken together.[40]

North America

The USA

Similarly, in the USA the growth of gambling has been extraordinary. In the mid-1970s gambling of any kind was legal in only a few states, but by the new millennium gambling in some form was legal in all but three. Revenues grew by almost 1,600% between 1976 and 1998, and the size of the industry grew ten-fold. More money was being spent – meaning wagers less winnings – on gambling than on all live events such as concerts and plays, all film shows in theatres, all spectator sports and all forms of recorded music combined; and more on gambling than on children's toys.[41] The gambling industry had become a major force, employing more than half a million people. The growth of casinos – mostly in a few years between 1989 and 1996 – from a few isolated sites like Las Vegas, thence to riverboats (or in some cases located on the Gulf Coast on larger stationary barges), and from there to urban areas, combined with separate legislation allowing Native USAmerican tribes to operate casinos, has been a prominent feature.[42] Casino gambling has figured much larger in the recent expansion of gambling in the USA, and in policy debates in that country, than have EGMs outside of casinos, which are much less common than in Australia, New Zealand and Europe, or sports betting shops which are commonly found in the UK and elsewhere in Europe but which are generally prohibited in the USA.[43]

However, as in other countries there has been a 'ratcheting up' effect generally as a result of competition between different forms of gambling and different legislatures, heightened during periods of economic slowdown and recession when state governments found themselves particularly strapped for money.[44] The authorisation of gambling machines at race tracks has been another trend, purportedly in order to provide the racing industry in one state with a level playing field in which to compete against other newly authorised forms of gambling and to give it a competitive edge over race tracks in other states. This has had the effect of creating what some have called 'racinos', where the presence of gambling machines has transformed race tracks into de facto casinos with a high proportion of total revenues being generated by machines rather than race betting.[45]

Just like Australia, the USA embraces different states that have dealt with gambling in very different ways. Four years into the new millennium commercial casinos were permitted in only 11 of the states and tribal casinos in 25.[46] That has inevitably led to the same kind of cross-border effects that were found between New South Wales and Victoria in Australia. Inter-state competition in the USA is illustrated by the case of neighbours Iowa, Illinois and Mississippi. Iowa was the first state to allow riverboat casinos. The first opened in 1991 with strict limits of five dollars a bet and losses of 200 dollars per excursion. Within a year the neighbouring states had legislated for riverboat gambling without such restrictions and with a larger number of available games. By 1994 Iowa had, as a result, removed its limits, expanded permitted hours of operation, legalised new games and eliminated restrictions on the amount of boat space devoted to gambling, at the same time responding to lobbying by the racing industry by lowering taxes on race gambling and allowing EGMs at the tracks.[47] New York State is another example. Surrounded by successful casino gambling venues in Atlantic City, Connecticut and in Ontario, Canada, and further motivated by economic slowdown and concern over the economic consequences of the September 2001 attacks in New York City, the state authorised six new tribal casinos in October that year and machine gambling at eight racetracks.[48] There have, however, been some reverses, such as local elections in 1996 reversing the legal status of video poker machines in half the parishes in Louisiana, and authorisation for such machines in South Carolina being allowed to expire in 2000.[49] Ohio's voters also rejected casino gambling but the state borders on a number of others, such as Michigan, West Virginia, Indiana and New York, where there is legal casino gambling, and the extensive casino facilities in Atlantic City in New Jersey are only a few hours away.[50]

The growth of state-sponsored lotteries has also been part of the picture. The first of the modern era was New Hampshire's, begun in 1963. But only three states had lotteries by the end of the 1960s, and it was the 1970s, 80s and early 90s that saw the take-up of lotteries by the majority of states. A few others inaugurated lotteries in the first few years of the new century, leaving by 2005 only eight states without them. As with lotteries in other countries, such as Britain, inauguration was usually followed by moves towards bigger prizes and more frequent draws.[51] Examining these trends as examples of the diffusion of innovations, analysis suggests that having neighbouring states already with lotteries was a significant factor – an example of what might be called 'external diffusion'.[52] In the case of casinos, having a neighbouring state already with a riverboat casino was a positive factor, but a neighbouring state with a land casino appears to have operated in the reverse direction, perhaps because of the unsavoury image that may still attach to casinos – other than riverboat casinos that may have benefited from a more romantic image. There is also evidence for 'internal diffusion': a state that already had a lottery was significantly more likely to legalise casino gambling. Interestingly, the existence of horse race gambling in the state appears to have operated in the opposite direction, a factor that may be attributable to lobbying against casino gambling by a threatened horse racing industry. The development of racinos may have served to reduce such opposition.

The USA has been one of the most prohibitionist countries over online gambling. In October 2006 the federal government passed the Internet Gambling Prohibition and Enforcement Act which effectively made it illegal for US firms to provide internet gambling, and possibly, although it remains contentious, for foreign firms to provide online gambling for US citizens.[53] As a result, at least one online betting firm chief executive was arrested, PartyGaming dropped out of the FTSE 100 index and British internet companies lost billions in value in a few weeks.[54] The World Trade Organisation ruled that prohibition was illegal and discriminatory towards foreign firms.[55]

Canada

Neighbouring Canada has shared the growth in gambling experienced by the USA and other countries but at the same time illustrates the differences that exist in the detail of how gambling has developed and been regulated in different countries. Casinos spread rapidly in the 1990s, but in Canada they are either indigenous First Nations' Casinos[56] or are provincial government owned or operated by a single provider on behalf of the province.[57] The 1990s, following a crucial piece of legislation in 1985 which gave provinces exclusive control over gambling and legalised machine gambling,[58] also saw many provinces expand their lottery products, including the controversial Video Lottery Terminals (VLTs), in the form of machines available in bars and taverns. British Columbia was an exception in Canada in not legalising VLTs.[59] Added to the more familiar 'slot'-type gambling machines, lottery ticket centres, permanent casinos, racetracks and 'teletheatres' (for off-track betting), plus temporary casinos, bingo, raffles and other activities, one estimate was that in 2004 there were over 120,000 places where a legal bet could be placed in Canada. One study estimated that, by then, Canadians were spending more on legal, government-operated gambling than they were on clothing, shoes and medicines combined.[60]

Consistent with the provincial government operation of gambling in Canada, it is the provincial operators, such as the Atlantic Lottery Corporation and the British Columbia Corporation, which began providing online sports and lottery betting in 2004. Canadian law has been interpreted as meaning that such online gambling provision is legal provided it is only patronised by residents of the province providing the site. Some indigenous groups have asserted that they are sovereign nations able to pass their own gambling law. For example, the Kahnawake First Nation in Quebec has been hosting internet gambling sites since 1999–2000 and is now one of the world's largest online gambling hosts, with over 300 sites offering all forms of internet gambling.[61]

Europe

The *Study of Gambling Services in the Internal Market of the European Union*[62] provides a fairly comprehensive picture of gambling in the EU in 2003, including data from countries that joined the Union in 2004. A selection of the findings is shown in Table 1.2. Lotteries alone constituted nearly half of the gambling market. Casinos, non-casino EGMs and betting each made up 15–20 per cent. Compared to the USA, casinos had a relatively small share but gambling machines outside casinos a relatively large one. Betting contributed a similar amount and bingo a significant but lesser proportion. Casinos, at least in limited numbers, had been legal before the Second World War in some countries, including Germany, Austria, France and Italy. Other European countries such as the Netherlands, Spain and Luxembourg authorised casinos in the 1970s and others such as Switzerland, Sweden and Belgium followed in the 1990s. Switzerland is a good example of a country that has responded to pressure to move in the direction of a freer commercial casino market. In 2001, partly aimed at encouraging tourism and reversing the flow of gamblers and their money across the border into neighbouring countries where there had been more opportunities for casino gambling, concessions were granted for

Table 1.2 Gross gaming revenues, in millions of euros, by country and sector – European Union 2003[62] (reproduced with permission from Eadington, in Coryn et al., 2008, p.76)

	Total	Casinos	Lottery	Gaming machines	Betting services	Bingo services
Austria	894	218	595	0	81	n/a
Belgium	679	47	486	137	9	0
Cyprus	73	0	34	0	39	n/a
Czech Republic	593	66	109	347	34	2
Denmark	830	44	429	221	96	40
Estonia	25	18	7	n/a	n/a	n/a
Finland	1241	22	485	571	157	6
France	7603	2546	3085	0	1972	n/a
Germany	8421	959	4991	2335	136	n/a
Greece	1068	89	474	0	505	0
Hungary	580	37	278	236	24	6
Ireland	1144	0	265	243	609	27
Italy	6205	617	4502	0	975	111
Latvia	67	7	4	53	1	1
Lithuania	41	14	25	1	2	n/a
Luxembourg	97	78	19	n/a	n/a	n/a
Malta	114	23	24	0	66	1
Netherlands	2065	699	783	564	18	n/a
Poland	432	45	295	53	38	2
Portugal	1434	301	802	201	11	120
Slovakia	216	95	71	50	1	n/a
Slovenia	264	193	38	33	n/a	n/a
Spain	4887	321	1126	2550	62	827
Sweden	1583	125	664	224	507	63
United Kingdom	10972	950	3390	1859	3526	1248
Totals	51527	7514	22981	9675	8867	2455
Percent of total	100.0%	14.6%	44.6%	18.8%	17.2%	4.8%

22 casinos in cities and tourist areas throughout the country.[63] European casinos have mostly been much smaller than the mega-casino complexes to be found, for example, in Australia, the USA, South Africa and Macau, although larger resort casinos are at the planning stages in European countries such as Spain and Slovenia.[64]

The size of the 'remote gambling' European market (including gambling accessed by computer, phone or interactive television), estimated separately, was calculated to be of the order of 5% of the size of the rest of the gambling market. A survey of remote gambling operators in the European Union suggested that betting services, accessed remotely, might be constituting over half of all remote gambling revenues, casino games approximately another third and virtual gambling machines much of the rest, with smaller amounts attributable to bingo, internet poker and lottery products.[65]

Take the Netherlands as one example. Like Britain and most other Western European countries, gambling of certain types, such as lotteries and horse and other sports betting, was already legal, but the last quarter of the twentieth century saw – as in most other countries – the appearance of new forms of gambling and an expansion of overall gambling provision and expenditure.[66] Casinos were legalised in the mid-1970s, EGMs outside casinos in the mid-1980s and scratchcards in the mid-1990s. At the time of writing, providing or participating in internet gambling remains illegal. The Netherlands is also a good example of the ambivalence which surrounds gambling and the question of how tightly controlled it should be. In almost all European countries, particularly in Scandinavian countries, part or all of gambling provision has been controlled by government in the form of state monopolies or concessions to one or a small number of suppliers. Despite the recent expansion of gambling and pressures towards a free market, gambling in the Netherlands has remained governed by the Gambling Act of 1964 under which the commercial exploitation of gambling is mostly illegal, with all profits from gambling continuing to go to good causes or taxes. That applies, for example, to all casinos, which operate under the brand name and uniform house style of *Holland Casino*. The single exception consists of EGMs outside casinos – of which there were approximately 43,000 in gambling arcades and other locations such as bars and restaurants in 2004 – which are allowed to be operated commercially. At the peak of the 'golden years' for slot machine entrepreneurs in the 1990s, machines were turning over in the region of 1bn euros, after which regulations were tightened in response to widespread concern about the dangers of machines and in some cases successful local opposition.[67]

In 2003 gambling revenues in the Netherlands, excluding remote gambling, just topped 2bn euros. Large sectors, for a relatively small country, were casinos – exceeded in size, as the table shows, only by Germany, the UK and, well out in front, France – the lottery sector – taking fifth place behind clear leaders Germany and Italy, followed by the UK, Spain and Portugal – and the gambling machine sector, where the Netherlands followed the front runners Spain, Germany, the UK and Finland.[68] In 2009 a new Gambling Act for the Netherlands was expected and it remains to be seen how successful that country will be in preserving its control over gambling in the face of continued pressures for further liberalisation and expansion.

A number of European countries have been accused by gambling operators of restricting cross-border gambling trade in contravention of the free-trading rules of the European Union. The Netherlands is one case in point. France is another country that has tried to prevent gambling providers, registered elsewhere, from offering services to its nationals. The French Government has been accused of inconsistency, encouraging and benefiting financially as it does from French lottery, casino and sports gambling. There have been many legal battles, both within individual countries and at the European Court of Justice. Just one continuing case is that of an online bookmaker registered in Malta wishing to provide betting for French internet users, a service which in France has been the exclusive right of the *Pari Mutuel Urbain*. Other

countries that have had complaints received against them at the European
Commission include Greece, Germany, Italy, Denmark, Belgium, Sweden and
Finland.[69]

Gambling has also been growing in Eastern European countries and in
Russia.[70] Amongst European Union accession countries, highest gambling revenues have been recorded in the Czech Republic, where EGMs, many located in
bars and by train and bus stations, make up the biggest sector, and in Hungary
where various lottery and other numbers games run by a state monopoly, and
EGMs operated by a large number of commercial companies, are the largest
sectors.[71] Hungary provides a good example of the explosion of gambling that
occurred in most of the former Soviet bloc countries that underwent rapid transition after 1989. Prior to that date gambling had been confined to a national
lottery in which the drawing of goods rather than money prizes had played a
large part, some scratch tickets sold by hawkers and some betting at horse racing
tracks. Apart from the lottery, the general image of gambling was a negative one,
and all other forms of gambling were illegal. Between 1988 and 2005 there was
a rapid extension of the range of lotteries, other number games and scratchcard
games offered via the state monopoly. During the decade of the 1990s, the
number of companies operating EGMs expanded ten-fold, reaching over 1,000
in number, operating between them more than 30,000 machines. Betting and
casinos – the latter only starting in 2001 – constitute smaller gambling sectors.
Altogether, gambling revenue increased four-fold in the decade between 1995
and 2005, reaching 890 million euros by the latter date.

The proliferation of EGMs in widespread locations outside casinos has been
one of the most noticeable features of the European expansion of gambling of
recent decades. Different European countries have dealt with them in different
ways.[72] Some, such as France, Austria and Portugal have been more like the
USA in prohibiting gambling machines outside casinos altogether. Others, such
as Italy and Poland, have attempted to ban them or have considered doing so.
Spain and Switzerland are two other European countries, besides the Netherlands, that found it necessary to put the rapid and uncontrolled expansion of
gambling machines into reverse and to tighten up on legislation. In Spain gambling was on a small scale and mostly illegal until 1977. EGMs were legalised in
1981 and had become widely accessible within a very few years, with nearly half
a million machines installed in leisure centres, casinos, bingo halls and almost
every bar and restaurant in the country.[73] By the end of the 1980s it had been
recognised that EGMs had been introduced too hastily, with little appreciation
of their impact and few controls on their availability. New legislation was introduced in the early 1990s which reduced the numbers, speed of operation
and attractiveness of machines. That appeared to have an immediate effect on
the amount being spent on EGMs but in 2005 the EGM sector remained a
large one in Spain with nearly a quarter of a million machines and total expenditure of over ten billion euros. Switzerland, cited earlier as a country that
chose to expand casino provision, phased out EGMs outside casinos completely,
over a five-year period ending in 2005.[74] Scandinavian countries are amongst
others where concern has been expressed about what many have seen as an

over-liberal policy that has allowed uncontrolled expansion.[75] In Sweden machines were banned between 1979 and 1996.

Despite the efforts of a number of countries to preserve state controls on gambling and even in some cases to put into reverse the rise in gambling availability, most predictions are that European gambling is set on continued growth. Much depends, however, on how disputes about free trading across EU member country boundaries are resolved. If individual countries are able to preserve a degree of protection from foreign operators then, according to at least one expert prediction, gross non-remote gambling revenues will continue to increase moderately year by year. If, on the other hand, courts rule that such protections are illegal and cross-border gambling trade increases considerably, then expansion could be much greater – perhaps of the order of 50% over a seven-year period. If there were complete harmonisation, growth might be even greater.[76] In the case of remote gambling, the years 2000 and 2001 witnessed massive growth, slowing in the following years. Even allowing for that de-escalation, however, one prediction was for an 85% growth between 2003 and 2012, with perhaps 20–30% of revenue coming from cross-border trade.[77]

Finally, before turning to look in more detail at British gambling in the next chapter, the point needs to be made that, global though it may appear to be, the recent explosion of gambling has not taken place everywhere. Some countries, Islamic ones in particular, but also Israel, are ones where there is general opposition to gambling and where gambling is illegal.[78] Turkey is one of the few countries to have moved in a direction opposite to the general expansionary trend, making casinos illegal in 1998.[79] It is sometimes stated that gambling is universal and has always been so. But that statement has been challenged by a careful review of historical and anthropological evidence which suggests that there may have been swathes of the globe, particularly in most of South America, southern Africa and Australia, where gambling was absent or at least very uncommon prior to colonisation.[80]

Chapter summary

What have we learnt from this quick, and inevitably quite superficial, tour of recent gambling around the world? The main conclusions would appear to be the following.

The last two decades of the twentieth century and the first few years of the twenty-first saw *a remarkable growth in the provision of gambling in many countries*, including Australia and New Zealand, the US and Canada and most European countries. In a number of countries new legislation was passed which encouraged gambling expansion by removing pre-existing regulatory restraints. There is evidence from a number of countries that the percentage of disposable income that citizens spent on gambling increased greatly; and that taxation on gambling contributed an increasing proportion of country, state and provincial government revenue. Reducing restraints on the provision of gambling and creating a free market in gambling was seen by governments as consistent with free trade principles. Encouraging tourism, and in some cases exporting remote forms of gambling to other countries, were often amongst the motives for gambling expansion.

Internationally, *the way gambling is provided and regulated varies greatly.* There are many countries where all or most forms of gambling are illegal. In those countries where much gambling is legal, the degree of government control varies: in some countries national or regional governments have monopoly control over lottery provision and in others the government controls most gambling. Laws in different jurisdictions have encouraged certain forms of gambling more than others; for example, casino gambling in the USA and France and non-casino machine gambling in Australia, Japan, Spain and a number of other European countries. Countries have been required to respond rapidly with legislation regarding online gambling and have done so with very different degrees of restriction. There is no one, single way of regulating gambling which governments are inevitably required to follow.

Because they are motivated to capture gambling taxes *there is pressure on governments to legalise forms of gambling which are available to their citizens elsewhere* – in neighbouring countries or regions or, in the case of online gambling, globally. The diffusion of legalised gambling from one Australian state to another, and from one US state to another, is a good example. Diffusion can also occur internally as a result of competition between different sectors of the gambling industry. These processes of diffusion result in a 'ratcheting up' effect on gambling provision generally.

There has been *an accompanying trend towards gambling becoming more accessible and more diverse.* 'Convenience gambling' in the form of electronic gambling machines available outside casinos in venues such as bars and clubs is one of the most notable aspect of that trend; the rise of online gambling is another. At the same time there has been a trend towards a greater diversity of gambling provision at a single venue. The diversification of sports betting, once the virtually exclusive domain of horse race betting, is one example. So-called 'racinos', created by the introduction of EGMs at race tracks in the USA, is another.

The widespread international expansion of gambling has been *accompanied by continued consciousness of the need to monitor and control gambling* because of its potential dangerousness for citizens. In some countries with large indigenous and immigrant populations, those groups have been considered particularly at risk. There are examples from many countries of actions being taken to restrict the numbers of gambling outlets, particularly the numbers of EGMs. Several states in Australia and some in the USA, New Zealand and several European countries including The Netherlands, Spain and Switzerland, are examples of it having been found necessary to put into reverse the previous expansion of provision of EGMs.

2

The Rise of Gambling in Britain

1960–2005: a period of dramatic change in gambling policy

In Britain, all gambling, with the exception of the National Lottery and spread betting, is covered by the Gambling Act 2005. It replaced most of the previous legislation, including the 1968 Gaming Act which was the most important piece of prior legislation and which had set the tone for British gambling in the last decades of the twentieth century. It would be difficult to over state the change. One British law professor has described it as 'a dramatic shift in policy'.[1] In fact the 2005 Act was the culmination of changes in government attitudes towards gambling and growing gambling industry pressure for change which had been taking place throughout the 1970s, 80s and 90s. The 1960s had been a difficult decade for British gambling. The long-awaited legalisation, in 1960, of most forms of gambling, after over half a century of virtual prohibition on all forms except betting on horse races at the track, had inadvertently allowed for a much greater proliferation of casinos than had been anticipated, along with a good deal of associated criminal activity. The Act of 1968 was a response. The 1,200 casinos in operation at the end of that decade fell immediately to only 120, a number that remained virtually unchanged for the following three decades.[2] With that problem solved, a long period of complacency ensued during which the scene was set for the dramatic liberalisation of gambling which was to take place around the turn of the new millennium.

A key event during that period, seen with hindsight to have been much more important than it appeared to be at the time, was the 1976–78 Royal Commission on Gambling, chaired by Lord Rothschild. It concluded that the legalisation of gambling had been successful, that it was being well

An Unsafe Bet? The Dangerous Rise of Gambling and the Debate We Should be Having   By Jim Orford
© 2011 John Wiley & Sons, Ltd

regulated, and that some relaxation of the regulations was warranted. Notably, the Commission was not greatly exercised by concern about the dangers
of addiction to gambling. Knowledge about problem gambling was still very
thin and rudimentary at that time and it is only more recently that the potential addictiveness of gambling has started to receive the attention it deserves
(it is the subject of Section II of the present book). The Commission's report
encouraged the Home Office to ease, little by little, its attitude to tight regulation and was in keeping with the gradual move during those years towards
a view of gambling as a normal activity and a set of products that could be
made available in an unexceptional commercial environment.[3] An Amendment Act in 1984, plus occasional 'statutory instruments', allowed relaxations
such as inter-track tote betting on greyhound races, relaxation of controls on
bingo advertising and the removal of a number of relaxations on betting offices, including, contrary to the Commission's recommendations as it happens,
the TV broadcasting of live or recorded racing and other sports events.[4] The
gradual lifting of restrictions on gambling should be seen, not in isolation of
course, but as part of the general policy, pursued by both Conservative and
Labour governments of that era, to reduce restrictions on business generally.
A number of changes in gambling regulations, all apparently small and, like
the Rothschild Commission report, exciting little media and public attention,
were made possible by the 1994 Deregulation and Contracting Out Act which
allowed the government to relax, by statutory instrument and without further
primary legislation, some of the controls on all forms of business including
gambling.

The start of the National Lottery and its effects on the rest of gambling

It was the start-up of the National Lottery (NL) that was probably the most
significant event of that period, however, and certainly the one that commanded
greatest public attention. Public lotteries had been popular in the past for
raising funds for such public works as London's water supply or the building
of the British Museum, but they had been illegal since 1826. The Rothschild
Commission had recommended the restoration of a National Lottery. The first
weekly Lotto game was held in November 1994 and the first National Lottery
Instants scratchcard game was introduced in March 1995. The NL was successful
beyond all expectations. Total sales in 1995–96 exceeded £5 billion and sales
reached a peak of £5.5 billion in 1997–98.[5] Sales declined thereafter in line with
the experience in other countries where it has been found that 'lottery fatigue'
sets in after initial enthusiasm. This puts the government, the lottery regulator
and the monopoly supplier, *Camelot*, in an invidious position. Charged with
maximising the money raised for good causes but also with minimising the
encouragement of excessive playing by people who might be vulnerable, the
promoters of the nation's own lottery are caught in a paradoxical position
which, as we shall see, is common to all promoters of a potentially dangerous
activity such as gambling who claim to be operating in a socially responsible

way. The response to falling sales is inevitably to devise new games, invent ones that may be more attractive and to make it possible to play NL games more frequently. This runs the risk of converting what was intended as a harmless form of leisure pursuit, initially sold to the nation as 'tasteful and beyond reproach'[6] and hardly 'gambling' at all, into something that begins to have some of the characteristics of 'harder' forms of commercial gambling.[7] A second, mid-week, Lotto draw was introduced in February 1997, and a further game, *Thunderball*, arrived in June 1999, weekly to start with and then bi-weekly from October 2002. Further games such as *Hotpicks* and *Daily Play* followed. *Lotto Extra* allows jackpot prizes that are not won to rollover to increase the size of the jackpot prize the following week (up to a maximum of £50 million after which it must be shared out to second prize winners). *Instants*, renamed *Scratchcards* in 2003, has included well over a hundred different games with several on the market at any one time.[8]

The effect of the NL on the rest of the gambling industry was overwhelmingly one of stimulation: to use an expression employed by a number of commentators, the effect was one of 'ratcheting-up' gambling across the board.[9] This effect might have been anticipated but was not. According to David Miers, another of Britain's law professors who has made a special study of gambling, the government failed to recognise the implications of its 'promotion of a national and massively advertised new gambling opportunity offering prizes far in excess of those available elsewhere'. The effect was that other sectors of the commercial gambling market were driven to seek the same relaxations of the rules under which they were operating.[10]

In the last years of the century regulations were eased in almost all gambling sectors. The Gaming Board, which seems to have had a very comfortable relationship with the gambling industry in those years, generally agreed with everything that was being proposed. In the betting sector, for example, Sunday racing with on- and off-course betting was introduced, the provision of non-alcoholic drinks and snacks in betting shops was permitted for the first time and betting shop windows were now allowed to be clear and to display advertising. Particularly significant were moves towards the diversification of forms of gambling allowed in betting offices – not just an increase in the range of sporting events on which it was possible to bet, but also the permitting of jackpot gaming machines and fixed odds betting games.[11]

In the casino sector changes were introduced that made application for casino membership easier. Opening hours and hours during which alcoholic drinks could be sold were extended. Some limited advertising in newspapers, magazines and elsewhere, giving factual information about casinos, was permitted. Significant was the fact that debit cards could now be used for purchasing tokens. Other important changes were those that extended the variety of forms of gambling available, often in a way that was likely to increase the dangerousness of gambling.[12] 'Casino stud poker' and 'super pan 9' were new games introduced in 1995, and at the turn of the century other games were being proposed such as 'casino brag' (a three-card game played against the bank), 'big six' (a spin-the-wheel game) and 'sicbo' (in which betting takes place on the outcome of three dice being thrown). Other variations being proposed included a simplified version of roulette, a change to the layout of the dice table to allow additional bets and an accumulator jackpot feature to be added to casino stud poker. Even more significant was the proposal for electronic terminals for playing roulette positioned away from the table where the game was being played. The permitted number of jackpot slot machines allowed in a casino was also increased.[13] But it was also clear that the casino sector aspired to much greater things, including a much larger number of gambling machines – which in casinos in other countries such as France and the USA were considerably more profitable than the casino table games themselves – and the much greater development of the casino as a leisure centre with a wide range of entertainment and dining facilities alongside the gambling.[14]

At the same time the gaming machine sector was itself proposing changes; for example, to remove the requirement that machines could only accept payment for a single play, that machines be allowed to accept bank notes and cards, and removal of the requirement that a machine pay out before accumulated winnings could be replayed.[15] In the bingo sector, also, there were changes in the direction of derestriction – for example, the use of debit cards, abolition of controls on amounts that could be charged per two-hour period, abolition of the requirement to give licensing justices 14 days notice of any alterations to charges, permission for bingo clubs to install both low stake/low prize gambling machines and up to four jackpot machines, an extension of Sunday opening hours, and a permitted increase in maximum bingo prizes including removing limits on prizes for 'multiple bingo' (played across the country at several clubs simultaneously).[16] Unlike the bingo sector, which thrived in the years following the inauguration of the NL,[17] the football pools, with its long-held monopoly as a popular, long-odds form of gambling, declined markedly in popularity after the start of the NL, despite also succeeding in arguing for some changes in the direction of liberalisation such as a reduction in permitted age of participation to 16, newsagents being allowed to collect stakes and the introduction of jackpots and rollovers.[18]

The final decades of the twentieth century, and particularly the final years of the last decade, were ones in which the growth aspirations of the gambling industry were greatly encouraged by government inclinations in the direction of deregulation and the competitive stimulation provided by the start up of the NL. Underlying all the individual pieces of deregulation was the emerging philosophy that the way gambling was provided should be according to free market principles and it was that philosophy that governed the thinking of the Gambling Review Body which reported in 2001. That represented a complete turnaround in the official way of thinking about gambling that had previously prevailed. The view that had taken shape throughout the twentieth century, and which was finally enshrined in the successful 1968 Act, was that gambling should be permitted but not encouraged. It was acknowledged that there was a certain demand for gambling and that it was sensible that the demand should be met and that it was not wise to try to prohibit gambling altogether. At the same time, gambling promoters were not allowed to stimulate demand, for example by advertising or by setting up gambling facilities where there was no existing evidence of demand. A key principle was that gambling should only be meeting 'unstimulated demand', and proposals for new casinos and bingo clubs would be denied unless they could provide evidence of demand – the so-called 'demand test'. Casinos, for example, were only allowed in certain 'permitted areas' – 52 of them, each with 1969 populations over 125,000 – and if one already existed in an area it was unlikely that any proposal for another would be successful.[19]

The Gaming Board responded to the change in government thinking and pressure from the industry for deregulation by agreeing to depart from the previous rules. In 1994 the Board referred to the strict regulations they were operating under as 'outdated, intrusive and unnecessary'[20] and in 1999 it agreed to change its policy of objecting to the award of a new casino licence in a permitted area where another casino already existed.[21] Professor Miers made a very significant remark, and one with which the present author agrees, when he wrote that these very significant changes were '. . . not driven by any perceived substantial change in the level of consumer demand, but by supply-side self-interest'.[22] It was in that changed climate that the Home Office in 1999 asked for a complete review of gambling in Britain and for recommendations for legislative changes. The latter, it was understood, would be in a derestricting direction.

The 2001 report of the Gambling Review Body: gambling firms hit the jackpot

The Gambling Review Body, as it was termed, reported in July 2001, not to the Home Office which had set it up, but to the Department for Culture, Media and Sport (DCMS).[23] It made no fewer than 176 separate recommendations. The report had been eagerly awaited by everyone with a professional interest in gambling in Britain, and it was generally assumed that its recommendations would shortly enter into law, as indeed turned out to be the case. Under the chairmanship of Sir Alan Budd, a former senior Treasury civil servant and known freemarket sympathiser, it had been asked to take a thorough new look at all aspects of gambling (except the NL which the government protects from market forces). The switch of lead government department while the review was being carried out, from the Home Office, with its concern with crime and regulation, to DCMS, responsible for sport and leisure, was itself a good illustration of the profound change in government thinking about gambling.[24]

Almost all the recommendations of the review were in the direction of removing restrictions on gambling and it was widely recognised in the press for what it was. *The Daily Express* described it as a 'radical overhaul' and a 'sweeping aside of restrictions', *The Daily Telegraph* a 'liberalisation', and *The Guardian* the 'first big shake-up since 1968, lifting many restrictions'. *The Independent* suggested the report read like a 'bookie's wish list', and a report in *The Mirror* stated 'Gambling firms hit the jackpot yesterday'. The Chief Executive of *Gala Leisure*, quoted in *The Daily Mail*, saw the report as providing a 'terrific opportunity' which would end 'ludicrous anomalies'. In the same paper the Managing Director of *Leisure Parcs* was reported as saying, 'This is about unlimited stakes and prizes. You could walk in off the street and £1 could make you millions'.

The list of new freedoms for gambling promotion suggested by the review report was a long one. It included the abolition of the previous restriction of casinos to a limited number of permitted areas and the abolition of the rule that a new member of a casino was required to wait 24 hours before playing. A greater variety of games would be permitted in casinos and bingo halls, and bingo would also be allowed unlimited stakes and prizes and multiple games and rollovers. Perhaps most significant of all were the recommendations that the advertising of gambling would be permitted and that the prohibition on British-based online gambling sites should be removed. But the vision that excited most press attention at the time was that Britain might, under the new proposals, become for the first time host to Las Vegas-style casino gaming resorts, later to be termed 'regional casinos'. The existing law, which tightly constrained where a casino might be opened and what activities were permitted within it, did not permit that kind of place, containing both casino table games and rows of gambling machines which offer unlimited prizes – a type of machine not then permitted in the UK – as well as a range of other entertainment, dining, drinking and other facilities. The papers were full of the prospect that Blackpool on the north-west coast would be the first such resort in Britain. Almost all of them referred to the town, some at great length, often accompanied by photographs, drawings or cartoons depicting the iconic Blackpool tower and the seafront and proposed casino developments such as Pharaoh's Palace. The town was said to have been in decline for some years, with a high rate of unemployment, a slump in the hotel trade and an increase in drunkenness and crime generally. In *The Independent* a local council spokesperson was quoting as saying that it was 'the only solution to hauling Blackpool out of its downturn'.

In fact, change in British gambling policy had been continuously taking place throughout the twentieth century. Broadly speaking the change had been from one in which the anti-gambling movement was powerful at the beginning of the century to one in which liberalisation was predominant by the century's end.[25] Although any attempt to divide a whole century of policy change into discrete stages is bound to be an over-simplification, the century and a bit between the Street Betting Act of 1906 and the present day may conveniently be thought of as containing three fairly distinct periods in British gambling policy – see Table 2.1. Although some forms of gambling were legal in the first period, off-course cash race betting, betting offices and large public lotteries were illegal and this period was one that had many elements of prohibition where gambling was concerned. The 1960 Betting and Gaming Act brought a decisive end to that phase and Britain entered the second period, one characterised by a policy under which gambling was permitted, tolerated but not encouraged. Exactly when that gave way to the present era of liberalisation is a matter for debate but many believe that it was the National Lottery Act of 1993 which gave official blessing to gambling as a thoroughly approved of form of leisure activity – although

Table 2.1   Three phases of British gambling policy, 1906–2007

Phase 1 – Partial prohibition, gradually challenged

1906	Street Betting Act	Acceptance of bets on streets and in other public places made illegal
1923	Select Committee on Betting Duty	Accepted the principle of legal, regulated gambling; concluded a betting tax was practicable
1933	Royal Commission on Lotteries and Betting	Argued that prohibitions on gambling should be minimal but thought betting offices should remain illegal
1934	Betting and Lotteries Act	Legalised private and small public lotteries
1951	Royal Commission on Betting, Lotteries and Gaming	Recommended that bookmakers could accept cash bets in licensed premises; but that gaming machines be illegal
1956	Small Lotteries and Gaming Act	Introduced societies' lotteries for charitable or sporting purposes

Phase 2 – Gambling permitted, tolerated, but not encouraged

1960	Betting and Gaming Act	Legalised almost all forms of gambling including commercial gaming clubs, licensed betting offices, and gambling machines in a wide variety of venues
1968	Gaming Act	Brought in controls on casinos; established the Gaming Board
1975	Lotteries Act	Allowed local authorities to conduct good cause lotteries
1978	Royal Commission on Gambling	Recommended the setting up of a National Lottery; and removal of some of the restrictions on betting offices

Phase 3 – The era of gambling liberalisation

1993	National Lottery Act	Made provision for the setting up of a National Lottery (which begins operating in 1994)
2001	Gambling Review Body reported to the Department for Culture, Media and Sport	Recommended abolishing the principle of unstimulated demand for casinos and other gambling establishments; the legalising of larger prizes; tighter controls on machines; and the setting up of a Gambling Commission
2002	Department for Culture, Media and Sport publishes its proposals for liberalisation in *A Safe Bet for Success*	
2005	A new Gambling Act is passed	
2007	The new Act comes fully into effect	

the government tried to argue at the time that the NL would not really be gambling at all – and made it inevitable that policy regarding all forms of gambling would need to be reviewed and the whole field liberalised.

The fundamental change that took place in British gambling between the 1960s and the 2000s moved the country from a position in which gambling was acknowledged to exist and permitted, but was constrained and not encouraged, to one in which, whilst being closely regulated, gambling is otherwise left to market forces to determine. By implication and in practice, therefore, gambling is now encouraged. It will be a principal argument later in the book that this altered gambling regime puts government in a position which is awkward and difficult to defend. If, as will be shown in later chapters, gambling is associated with serious harms for individuals, families and society, and furthermore is something that the majority of citizens view with suspicion, then the government is bound to be treading a very thin line. Having turned its back on the former regime of limited tolerance, it is now committed to encouraging a vibrant, innovating and expanding gambling industry. It also becomes, of course, increasingly dependent on its own revenue derived from gambling. Government is therefore likely to be seen as promoting gambling-related harms and not doing enough to protect its citizens or to reflect public opinion.

British gambling in the early twenty-first century: more varied, more accessible

Although deregulation had been moving on in the years leading up to the report of the Gambling Review Body, it was their report in 2001 and the subsequent 2005 Gambling Act, which came fully into operation in September 2007, that represented the culmination of that process and marked clearly the new era in British gambling. What, then, does gambling in Britain look like following those major landmark events? One way of putting it would be to say that, fuelled by freemarket competition, plus fast-moving technological change and innovation, it is increasingly varied and rapidly changing. It would be equally accurate to say that the new regulatory regime is highly complex and difficult to fathom. The Act runs to 362 sections, 18 schedules and includes over 100 pages of explanatory notes.[26] On top of that, before the Act could be fully operational, much of the detail remained to be filled in by the Department for Culture, Media and Sport, by the Gambling Commission, which replaced the Gaming Board as the principal regulator in October 2005, and by local authorities. The result is a highly complex set of rules and regulations. In the opinion of one of the country's legal experts, Professor Light, the huge volume of secondary material to be produced, 'together with the arcane nature of some of the Act's provision, leaves much scope for interpretation and confusion'.[27]

It is hard enough for those who have been directly involved in lobbying, drafting and consulting to follow it all. As will be discussed later, there are many aspects of the new regime which will directly affect members of the public in their general role as citizens, in special roles such as those of parents, or as consumers of gambling products. It is the case, however, that, apart from prominent publicity over the question of whether there should be large regional casinos, and if so where in Britain they should be located, there has been little opportunity for the public to learn about the changes, much of the detail of which is highly obscure and complicated to understand. There is a real concern that, the regulations being so complicated, it will be difficult to communicate the detail to everyone who needs to know – including adult players, young people, parents, publicans, club officials, police, to name just a few.

Increasing tolerance and liberalisation of gambling has not merely been a matter of lifting restraints on already existing forms of gambling, but in addition it has brought new forms of gambling to add to the old, and increasing sophistication in those forms of gambling that were already well known. That has resulted in a number of trends which may not be immediately apparent to most citizens but which are likely to render gambling more dangerous than it was. Part of this trend is the proliferation of opportunities to gamble which have been described by some as 'convenience gambling'.[28] The widespread siting of gambling machines in amusement arcades, pubs, motorway service stations and elsewhere in Britain following the 1960 Act is perhaps the best example. Another part of the trend is a gradual move from non-continuous forms of gambling – generally thought to be 'softer' and less dangerous – to opportunities for continuous play – the 'harder' or more dangerous forms.[29] The transformation of British betting shops since they became legal in 1960 is a very good example. The inauguration of new, 'midweek' NL games allows even that form of gambling, generally considered one of the less dangerous, to be played more frequently. An insidious part of the trend is the way in which the distinction between the supposedly softer and harder forms of gambling may be becoming blurred, and, furthermore, how more and less dangerous forms of gambling, previously kept rather separate, may increasingly be provided in the same location.

Gambling machines

Let us look at some of the complexity of modern British gambling, starting with 'fruit', 'slot' and other machines – referred to collectively as electronic gambling machines, or EGMs. Table 2.2 shows how difficult it is for anyone thinking of installing a machine on their premises, let alone for a member of the public, to understand the differences between the different categories of machine and which types in what numbers are legal in what settings. In fact the Gambling Act allows for four categories of machine, with sub-categories, differing in permitted sizes of stakes and prizes. Although, under the new Act, machines of any kind would no longer be permitted in some premises where they had

An Unsafe Bet?

Table 2.2 Gambling machines allowed in Britain under the 2005 Gambling Act (as at January 2010)[32]

Category	Maximum stake[a]	Maximum prize[a]	Allowed in
A	Unlimited	Unlimited	Regional casino[b]
B1	£2	£4,000	Any casino
B2[c]	£15 per stake £100 per game	£500	Any casino Betting premises[d]
B3	£1	£500	All the above Bingo premises[e] Adult gaming centres[e]
B4	£1	£250	All the above Clubs and institutes[f]
C	£1	£70	All the above Pubs and bars[g] Licensed family entertainment centres[h]
D	10p[i]	£5[i]	All the above Unlicensed family entertainment centres and travelling fares[j]

[a] Maximum stakes and prizes are not fixed in the Act but can be changed in regulations set by the Secretary of State
[b] At the time of writing no regional casino has been authorised in Britain
[c] Formerly known as Fixed Odds Betting Terminals (FOBTs)
[d] A total of four machines allowed of any category B2 to D
[e] A total of four machines of categories B3 and B4 allowed plus any number of C and D
[f] A total of three machines allowed of any category B4 to D
[g] A total of two machines of categories C or D plus more by permit only
[h] Any number of machines of categories C and D allowed
[i] Non-cash stakes and prizes of slightly higher values are also allowed
[j] Any number of category D machines allowed

been incidental to the main business being conducted, such as takeaway food shops, mini cab and taxi offices and other non-arcade and unlicensed premises, they remain in other places where gambling is not the main business, such as motorway service and train stations, and, most significantly, in public houses.[30] Contrary to two of the principles expounded in the Gambling Review Report, the report did not recommend the removal of gambling machines from pubs. This is out of line with the Gambling Review Body's principle that opportunities to mix gambling and the consumption of alcohol on the same premises should be kept as few as possible, and certainly contrary to their desire to minimise what it called 'ambient gambling', that is gambling incidental to the main activities conducted on the premises in question. Social clubs are another site of controversy. Responding to great pressure from such clubs, many of them party political ones, the government overruled the Gambling Review Report recommendation and allowed machines in clubs to have jackpots of £250.[31] In general the move has been in the direction of allowing a larger number of machines, and machines of higher category.

Machine categories D, B2 and A deserve special note here. Category D machines have been one of the most controversial aspects of the 2005 legislation for the simple reason that Britain, uniquely amongst countries that have a systematic set of gambling regulations in place, continues to allow children of any age to play such machines. Britain stands entirely alone on this. Not surprisingly, therefore, the Gambling Review Body (GRB) expressed great unease on this issue. Being persuaded that machine gambling could be particularly dangerous for young people, their inclination was clearly to prohibit all kinds of machines for under 18 year olds.

> Although we have concluded that children should be at liberty to enter, what we have termed, family entertainment centres, we remain uneasy about encouraging children to gamble. Most will come to no harm, but some will. . . if we were creating the regulations for the first time, we would certainly recommend that no gaming machines should be played by under 18s[33]

They were doubtful about the argument put forward by the British Amusement Catering Trades Association (BACTA), who represent gambling machine manufacturers, that banning under 18s from playing arcade machines would have a devastating effect on the seaside resort business. Nor did they accept the argument of BACTA and others that low stake/low prize machines were trivial and should not be regarded as gambling at all. In the end, however, the GRB, by their own admission subjected to considerable pressure by the gambling industry which was particularly desperate to retain its profits from seaside arcades, drew short of prohibiting children from gambling in certain arcades or parts of arcades – often, but not only, at the seaside.

In fact, their final recommendation ran counter to another of their basic principles, that gambling should be restricted to people of 18 years of age or over (16 in the exceptional case of lotteries). It has been argued by the gambling industry, and was accepted as part of the government's thinking, that category D machines can be distinguished from other categories of machine. In fact until recently – and still colloquially – they were not referred to as gambling machines at all but rather as one class of 'amusements with prizes'! The distinction really does not stand up to scrutiny. A category D machine is in all essential respects just like any other gambling machine except for its lower maximum stakes and prizes. It is unlikely to be the absolute size of stakes and prizes that is of importance since what appears to an adult to be a small stake or prize is likely to be seen very differently by a child or by a young person on a very small income from pocket money or a part-time job. Referring to category D or low stake/low prize machines as 'amusements' and the arcades in which they are situated as 'family entertainment centres' relies on and helps to perpetuate confusion between play, which is at worst harmless and at best enhancing of child development, and exposure to a potentially dangerous activity which constitutes a threat to development.

At the other end of the scale, category A machines do not yet exist at all in Britain. With unlimited stakes and prizes, they would be introduced into Britain for the first time and would be confined to the so-called 'regional casinos'. Regional casinos would be casinos on the Las Vegas model, of a kind yet unknown to Britain, and which turned out to be the single most controversial aspect of the Gambling Bill (see below). At the time of writing the decision has been taken not to go ahead with any such facility for the time being. Those concerned about problem gambling are therefore much relieved that the line has for the moment been held against the introduction of category A machines.

Fixed odds betting machines and the changed nature of betting shops

Category B2 is a new one which became necessary as a result of one of the most recent innovations on the British gambling scene. In fact it is a good example of how the gambling industry is always trying to think up something new and attractive, in the process setting a further challenge for the gambling regulators. When the Gambling Review Body was deliberating at the turn of the century this type of machine was a newcomer. Officially known then – and still referred to by most people – as fixed odds betting terminals (FOBTs) or fixed odds betting machines (FOBMs), they started to appear in high street betting shops. They are machines on which can be played fixed odds and betting games. Some of the first such games offered in betting shops looked very much like lotteries, and *Camelot* raised objections. In fact, unlike a lottery, the size of winnings is fixed and is not dependent on the number of winning players.[34] FOBMs can now offer a variety of pure-chance games including virtual forms of bingo and what look just like casino games, such as roulette. Hence casino operators also raised objections. As a result they are now regulated as if they were gambling machines – which of course they are – and under the new regulations a betting office is allowed to install four gambling machines in total, including any FOBMs. Because of their large maximum stake of £100 they might be seen as lying somewhere between machine categories A and B,[35] and have now officially been categorised as B2 machines. The Department for Culture, Media and Sport has recognised that they 'risk seriously increasing problem gambling'.[36] The view of Mike Atherton, journalist and former test cricketer, in his well-informed book *Gambling*, is that FOBMs '. . . have changed the face of high-street bookmaking. They have enabled the bookie to bypass laws that for years prevented them from hosting casino-style games'.[37] By redesignating FOBMs as B2 category gambling machines, and withdrawing initial objections to the siting of them in betting shops, the government and its gambling regulator have legitimised this new form of gambling and contributed to its normalisation as part of the accepted, modern gambling scene. This is a perfect example of how gambling opportunities have snowballed. It was argued that they were not offering casino games because they were machine controlled; also fixed odds and a large maximum stake made it look as if they were suitable for a venue previously dedicated to horse race and other sports betting. The fact of the matter is that they have been responsible for one of the shifts in the direction of mixing different forms of gambling and increasing the scope of gambling forms available at a single location.

As previously mentioned, betting offices had already been allowed to extend the sports and other events on which they could lay bets, to use the telephone and internet to receive bets, to provide commentaries on sporting events from around the world, to advertise more freely and to modernise their premises. The 2005 Act formalised these changes by bringing bookmakers under the statutory regulator, the new Gambling Commission, for the first time; by abolishing the demand criterion for setting up new betting shops; and permitting evening opening, up to 10.00 pm, throughout the year (this had been allowed for the summer months for some years).[38] All of which was likely to 'facilitate increased spend from existing gamblers and attract new gamblers'.[39]

Casinos

Although the new regime has liberalised gambling across the board, it is the opening up of possibilities for new casinos that has aroused most media attention and controversy. Table 2.3 describes the three types of casino that could be licensed under the 2005 Act (plus those licensed earlier). In fact, although the third type is referred to as 'small', most British casinos in existence prior to 2005 were smaller still. Under a provision of the Act they will be allowed to continue to operate but such casinos would not be granted a licence if they were newly trying to start up now.[40] The minimum size requirements for new casinos

Table 2.3   Types of casino that can be licensed in Britain under the 2005 Gambling Act[41]

Regional casino
Must have a minimum of 40 gaming tables and will be permitted 25 machines for each gaming table available for play i.e. a machine/table ratio of 25:1. Will need 50 tables to qualify for the maximum allowed 1250 machines.

Large casinos
Must have at least one gaming table. Permitted five machines for each gaming table available for play, i.e. a machine/table ratio of 5:1. Will need 30 tables to qualify for the maximum allowed 150 machines.

Small casinos
Must have at least one gaming table. Will be permitted two machines per gaming table available for play, i.e. a machine/table ratio of 2:1. Must have 40 tables to qualify for the maximum allowed 80 machines.

Existing '1968' casinos (i.e. licensed under provisions of the earlier, 1968, legislation)
Allowed no more than 20 category B machines. No machine/table ratio applies. Can opt to have no category B machines but unlimited category C and D machines.

reflects the anxiety that continues to be felt about the danger of proliferation of large numbers of small casinos, as happened in the 1960s prior to the passing of the 1968 Gaming Act.

Specifications of the ratio of gambling machines to tables for playing casino games such as roulette and blackjack are a prominent feature of the new casino licensing requirements, as Table 2.3 clearly shows. The reason for that is straightforward. In the well-known large casino resorts around the world – such as Las Vegas in the USA, Sun City in South Africa, in Macao in east Asia, on the Queensland coast in Australia, and in some other European countries – gambling machines, numbering in their hundreds, greatly outnumber gaming tables and are much the more profitable. These casinos are of a type sometimes referred to as 'international-style' casinos, of a kind hitherto quite unknown in Britain.[42] Although the 120 or so existing casinos is a larger number than existed in almost all other European countries, the British casinos were very different kinds of establishments, more in the nature of private clubs catering to a small specialised market.[43] Outside of the few relatively opulent London casinos catering largely for rich overseas visitors, the clientele of most British casinos was said by the 1978 Royal Commission – perhaps complacently – to be made up of local people 'who play for comparatively modest stakes in comparatively modest surroundings'.[44]

The three types of casino now to be permitted therefore represent a compromise between the introduction of a completely free market and a wish to preserve something of the previous, rather unique British approach. In the event, opposition to what the government was proposing has, at least for the moment, limited the change still further. In order to pass the Act in the 'washup' period just before the 2005 general election, the government was forced to restrict the number of regional casinos to a maximum of eight (the extraordinary original suggestion had been for 40) and finally to just one, plus an 'initial limit' of eight 'large' and eight 'small' casinos.[45] The government had also had to agree to set up an independent Casino Advisory Panel to advise where the 17 new casinos should be located. It was the location of the proposed single regional casino that proved most controversial and embarrassing to the government. The Millennium Dome in London was one of the 27 applicants. The government was finally forced to concede, under the Freedom of Information Act, that prominent members of the government had been meeting with a US businessman who had a stake in the Dome and who also had business dealings with one of the members of the Casino Advisory Panel. In the end, instead of recommending the Dome, or the seaside town of Blackpool, long considered the front runner with a strong case on the grounds of need for regeneration (one of the selection criteria), the panel recommended Manchester City Council's proposal to site the regional casino in a relatively poor part of inner Manchester, one of Britain's very largest provincial cities. This brought down a storm of criticism from many sources, including the Bishop of Manchester, predicting that the personal, family and community harms would outweigh any gains for Manchester and its people. The ability to monitor the social and economic impacts was a second criterion for selection of a location for the regional casino, and it was widely believed that this criterion was not met by the Manchester proposal. The House of Lords wanted it looked at again, and after a review ordered by the new Prime Minister any idea of a regional casino in Britain was shelved for the time being.

Meanwhile local authorities in 16 areas across the country were given permission to issue licences for the other two types of casino. They will add to the 140 operating at the April 2006 cut-off date, after which new licences could not be granted under the 1968 Act, plus some others awaiting the outcome of applications. Informed estimates were that the total number of British casinos might rise to a total of around 200 – more than a 40% increase.[46] In addition, the new-style premises will offer more in the way of facilities, including other forms of gambling such as betting, and in the case of the 'large' casinos, bingo as well.[47] The government's 2002 White Paper *A Safe Bet for Success* suggested that the aim was that visiting a casino would be easier and 'a more complete leisure experience, potentially appealing to a far wider range of customers'.[48] As one legal expert has suggested, 'As a result of these measures, there will be significantly amplified opportunity for casino gambling in Britain. . . it is clearly envisaged that people who have not visited a casino before will be encouraged to do so'.[49]

Betting exchanges: a revolution in betting

Probably just as significant as new-style gambling machines and larger casinos, and an indication of the way the internet has been used to increase access to gambling, is another new development – the so-called 'betting exchanges'. These allow individuals to bet against one another, using the internet, through facilities offered by the operator of the betting exchange. The latter, of which *Betfair* is the most successful and best known, have been called 'bet brokers' by the Horse Race Betting Levy Board and 'betting intermediaries' in the 2005 Act. They extract a commission from the winner, and are now subject to taxation, but the odds decided upon and the settling up afterwards are left to the individual betting participants. In his book Atherton refers to this as a 'revolution' in betting.[50] In some ways it can be seen as a remarkable return to the original nature of gambling in which individuals bet against one another without the need for the services of a bookmaker. Indeed it represents a serious challenge to traditional bookmaking and may put smaller bookmakers out of business. Even *William Hill* announced their intention to hedge bets with a betting exchange rather than with on-course bookmakers.[51] The interesting thing is that a punter now has the choice of 'backing' a horse to win (assuming the event is a horse race), as would normally be done with a bookmaker, or 'laying' a horse to lose, as a bookmaker does. The two parties can suggest whatever odds they wish and once they have been put in touch and odds agreed, the bet is on. The one who lays the bet is therefore acting as a kind of bookmaker but, much to the annoyance of the Association of British Bookmakers, escapes both taxation and regulation.[52] *Betfair* has been enormously successful. It did £100,000 worth of business in its first six weeks in 2000, and by 2005 was turning over £50 million a week, with revenues of nearly £70 million and profits of £13 million.[53] In 2003 it was awarded the Queen's Award for Enterprise. Race fixing has always been, and continues to be, a threat in the horse racing world and betting exchanges probably increase that threat.[54] As Atherton puts it, the fact that anyone can now make money from a horse losing is 'potential dynamite for owners, trainers and the like',[55] although *Betfair* argues that they can provide a trail of bets more easily than a highstreet bookmaker, and they now have agreements with the Jockey Club and the Football Association to monitor and report unusual betting patterns.

Bingo was liberalised

Although it has attracted much less attention, bingo playing has also been liberalised. In addition to the changes, referred to earlier, that had already been taking place, under the new Act unlimited prizes and rollovers, and unlimited linked games, can be offered, regulations allow increased stakes, advertising rules are relaxed and up to four category B3 gambling machines are permitted.[56] Very indicative of the way things are changing is the scrapping of the demand test for setting up new bingo clubs, along with the need to be a member of a bingo club in order to play – parallel changes to those brought in for casinos. From the 1960s, when bingo clubs were first legalised, they became very popular as safe and congenial social clubs, particularly for working-class women, many of whom did not consider bingo to be a form of gambling at all.[57] It was generally considered that, gambling though bingo undoubtedly was, it did not expose participants to the temptations of 'hard gambling', and according to the Gaming Board it was appropriate to take 'a benevolent view of bingo provided it remained a neighbourly form of gaming played for modest stakes. . .'.[58] The various changes to bingo must pose a threat to that view. Meanwhile from a commercial point of view bingo clubs, which had diminished in number in the 1990s and early 2000s, but increased in size, were threatened by the possibility that bingo in casinos, permitted under the 2005 Act, might take away their business. There was a possibility that bingo clubs might be forced to close or to convert to casinos.[59]

Internet gambling

The clearest example of the way in which technology is transforming gambling is of course internet gambling, otherwise referred to as 'online gambling', simply 'e-gambling', or 'remote gambling' – although the latter term is usually taken to refer to any participation in gambling that does not involve face-to-face contact between the punter and the operator – using phone, computer or interactive television for example. The more restricted term 'internet gambling' also includes both (i) using the internet to communicate indirectly with an operator in order, for example, to place a bet on a real horse race or to purchase a ticket for a real lottery, and (ii) playing a *virtual* game such as poker or roulette or playing a virtual gaming machine on the internet. The former was mostly perfectly legal prior to the 2005 Act. It is the latter – internet gambling on virtual games – that has been so controversial and the regulation of which is particularly problematic. It is generally agreed that the opportunities for fraud are so great that some form of regulation that protects the public is essential. What particularly exercised the Gaming Board and the British Government as the twentieth century reached its close was the march that was being stolen in this field by other jurisdictions, such as those in the Caribbean, notably Antigua, the states of Australia, Gibraltar, the Isles of Man and Alderney in the UK, South Africa, parts of Canada, and elsewhere, which permitted internet gambling sites to operate based in their countries.[60] For those countries it could be seen as a kind of cyber-tourism,[61] whereas for countries like Britain it seemed to represent a threat to its own nationals from lax regulation and, perhaps bearing most heavily, loss of potential British business opportunity, tax revenue and export earnings. The Gaming Board put the marketplace argument clearly in their report for the year 2000[62]:

> . . . there is a need to act quickly if a valuable commercial opportunity is not to be missed for ever. Such a missed opportunity would conflict with the government's stated aim of making Britain a leader in e-commerce.

The Gambling Review Body was particularly challenged by the question of online gambling. Overall their view was that it '. . . should be seen as just another way of delivering a service',[63] and they recommended that it should be licensed and regulated by the new Gambling Commission. It did recommend that players should be carefully identified to prevent under-age playing and money laundering, that players should be enabled to set maximum stakes and limits, and to self-ban (self-banning or self-exclusion is discussed more fully in Chapter 3), and that clocks and counting systems should be regularly and clearly displayed on the screen in order to keep players informed of how long they had been playing and how much they had won or lost. But at the end of the day the government's decision to permit internet virtual gambling from UK-based sites for the first time, under the 2005 Act, '. . . is as much to do with enhancing its own financial position as it is with protecting the uninitiated or the vulnerable from compromising their own'.[64]

In practice, because virtual remote gambling is a global industry, whether operators will choose to site themselves in Britain or elsewhere, and whether players will choose to use British-based sites or others, is difficult to predict. The operators will doubtless be looking to balance the credibility that might come with Gambling Commission licensing and freedom to advertise in Britain against the cost and burden of conforming to regulations plus the level of taxation being imposed on them.[65] It has been suggested that operators might be looking for a tax rate of around 2–3% rather than the 15% actually set by the March 2007 budget.[66] The latest information available to me when writing this book was for 2007–8, showing that most virtual internet gambling sites available to British citizens were based elsewhere, particularly in the small Channel Island of Alderney, in Gibraltar, on the Isle of Man and in Malta.[67]

Where the internet site is based is probably of less interest to players themselves. What is clear are the enormous number of internet gambling sites now available and their ease of access for anyone who has an internet connection at home, including sections of the population – including women and young people – who might not have been attracted to the places where gambling had been available in the past.[68] As Mark Griffiths, the UK's leading authority on internet gambling and on gambling amongst young people, puts it, now 'everyone has a casino in the home'.[69] If the aim of the British Government, when it decided to go for the most liberal option of legalising all internet gambling for British operators and players, was to make sure that Britain was at the forefront of the expansion of online gambling, then it appears to be succeeding. According to one review published in 2007, just over 100 online gambling sites were operating in the UK, a number only exceeded by Costa Rica, Antigua and Barbuda, Kahnawake Mohawk Territory in Quebec, Curacao and Gibraltar. The highest volume of online transactions was recorded in the UK.[70] A report by the Department for Culture, Media and Sport in 2006 estimated that there were approximately a million regular online gamblers in Britain, making up nearly one third of Europe's 3.3 million regular online gamblers.[71] Again, one of the special concerns is the ease of access for children and young people. One study, published in 2004, of 30 UK internet gambling providers, found that only half made meaningful efforts to verify a player's age.[72] Another found that a 16 year old with a debit card was able to place bets online on 30 out of 37 UK sites that were tested.[73] A survey, reported in 2007, of over 8,000 12–15 year olds, reported that 8% had played the National Lottery game on the internet. Some had played free games that were available online, but 18% reported that the system allowed them to register, 16% played with their parents, 10% had used a parent's online National Lottery account with the parent's permission, and 7% had used a parent's account without permission.[74] There are the same difficulties in regulating internet-provided gambling as there are with other potentially dangerous internet offerings such as internet pornography[75] and there is similar concern about lack of responsible practices.[76]

Spread betting

Spread betting is a special case. It is another late twentieth-century newcomer which illustrates yet again the rapidly changing nature of gambling and the dangers and uncertainties associated with the expansion of gambling. At the same time it illustrates something else, which is the ever-present question about what constitutes gambling and what distinguishes one form of gambling from another. The question arises in the case of spread betting because, although in recent variants involving betting on all manner of sporting events, it is without doubt gambling, its origins lie in stock market trading. Whether the latter itself constitutes gambling has always been an interesting question, and to most people the answer has been that most of the time it is not – although opinions on that may have changed as more and more evidence of rash and irresponsible financial trading becomes public. But in 1974 a former merchant banker set up *IG Index* (IG standing for Investors Gold) which in effect enabled punters to bet on whether the price of gold would rise or fall. What was offered was not a fixed-odds bet but rather a *spread* bet. The example Atherton gives is *IG Index* offering gold at 150–155 per ounce (the US dollar price of gold). If the gambler decides to buy (go long) at £10 for every one dollar movement, £10 would be made for every rise in price above 155, but £10 would be lost for every fall in price below 155. If the decision, on the other hand, was to sell (go short) at £10, then £10 would be made for every one dollar movement below 150 and £10 lost for every rise in price above 150.[77] It can be seen from that simple example that the wider the 'spread' offered, the less advantageous it is to the gambler. More importantly it can be seen that, unlike what happens in all other forms of gambling, where the player loses no more than the stake, in spread betting wins and losses are determined by the degree to which the player gets the bet right or wrong. Not only did other firms, such as *City Index* and *Cantor Index*, join *IG Index*, with more and more people betting on the stock markets in this way, but *Sporting Index*, offering spread betting on sport, followed shortly,[78] and even *Spreadfair*, the spread betting version of *Betfair*.[79] Cricket is an ideal sport for spread betting because of the wide variation in the number of runs that a team might score in an innings or the number of runs that can be scored by an individual batsman. But in practice the possibilities are endless – it is possible to bet on the number of corner kicks, minutes elapsing before the first goal or the number of yellow cards shown in a football match, or indeed on any countable variable pertaining to any sport.[80]

In law, unlike all other forms of commercial gambling, spread betting is a contract for differences and, if conducted commercially, is a 'contractually based investment'. Despite the inroads it has made in the world of sports betting, and reflecting its origins in stock market trading, it is regulated by the Financial Services Authority under the Financial Services and Markets Act 2000, and is completely outside the 2005 Gambling Act and regulation by the Gambling Commission.[81]

Other lotteries

One of the things that makes gambling such as fascinating field of study, but which at the same time makes it over-complicated for the public to understand and treacherous for the unwary, is its diversity. One of the odd corners of the British gambling field, for example, consists of the rules governing what gambling games can be played in pubs, with what stakes and for what prizes – of renewed interest since the rise in popularity of poker. Another relates to the kind of lotteries, other than the NL, that are permitted in law. One of the intriguing aspects here is the way in which the law has struggled with the distinctions between lotteries, which are defined as games of pure chance and where the size of winnings depends on the number of winners (unlike in fixed-odds betting), other forms of gambling in which there is an element of skill, and prize competitions which are not considered gambling at all. The question of 'when is a competition not a competition' is highlighted by supposed competitions which would in effect be lotteries were it not for the posing of a spurious question such as 'What is the capital of France?' The history of the skill versus chance debate is a long one. For example, a test case that set a precedent for many years was settled in 1903 when the High Court ruled against the owner of a general grocer's shop frequented by children, who claimed that a machine installed in the shop involved the exercise of skill. It required the player to operate a simple spring-lever to project a coin to the top of the machine from whence it fell into one of a number of compartments, one of which was a 'win'. A prosecution was brought against the shopkeeper on the grounds that no skill was involved and that the odds favoured the shopkeeper. The latter's argument was that, with practice, a player would acquire familiarity with the strength of the spring and hence be able to exert some control over the final destination of the coin![82] Then as now machine manufacturers were inventive, developing machines which offered clearer opportunity to exercise some skill, for example by having the player actively move the coin-receiving cups from side to side by means of a lever rather than the coin falling into one of a number of stationary cups. In another famous test case in British law the civil court judge held that such a machine was lawful because it involved 'more than a mere scintilla of skill', and the decision was upheld by the Court of Appeal.[83]

Following the 2005 Act there are now six different types of lottery which are either eligible for obtaining lottery operating licences or which are exempt from the requirement to hold such a licence[84] – society, remote, local authority, incidental non-commercial, private society, work or residential, and customer lotteries.[85] Whereas local authority lotteries had virtually fallen into disuse by the first years of the new century, the amount of money raised by societies' lotteries had risen sharply since the start of the NL.[86] These various kinds of lottery are permitted on the assumption that they are relatively 'soft' forms of gambling, like the NL relatively harmless and constituting ways of raising money for good causes. But in order to keep it that way, and to protect the NL from competition, it has been considered necessary to keep careful limits on them, for example in terms of the frequency of play and size of stakes. Even so, in this relatively obscure and little publicised part of the gambling field, deregulation has been the order of the day. To the previously existing types of permitted lottery, the 2005 Act added small lotteries that could be run by a business provided they were open only to customers on the business premises. It permitted society and local authority lotteries to have rollovers, and percentage limits on expenses and prizes as a proportion of proceeds were removed, as were absolute limits on ticket prices. Remote lotteries and the selling of tickets by machine were permitted. The bar on money prizes for small lotteries was lifted. Some have voiced concern that as restrictions are eased there is the danger that such lotteries, traditionally thought of as a soft form of gambling, might take on some of the features of harder forms of gambling.[87]

Advertising

Whether, and to what extent and how, gambling products should be advertised is a particularly sensitive issue. The general ban on gambling advertising was an important feature in the traditional policy of social regulation pursued in Britain from the 1960s until the early 1990s. Once the decision had been taken to introduce a National Lottery, '. . . it followed that. . . the traditional policy would be compromised'.[88] Prominent advertising on public hoardings, on television or at sporting events attended by all ages now brings the general British public, most of whom gamble if at all only on the NL, in contact with the diverse world of gambling with which they might not otherwise be personally familiar. Instead of being tucked away out of sight where only the most motivated will find it, the ways in which different forms of gambling may now be advertised, following the 2005 Act, puts gambling much more clearly in the public arena. Since the odds are stacked in favour of gambling promoters being the winners, and most players lose most of the time, it might be said that any gambling advertising is almost bound to be misleading. At the very least a strong case can be made for outlawing any advertising of gambling that creates the impression that the odds on winning are better than they actually are. In fact it has been suggested that since in effect the odds constitute the 'price' of the gambling product, advertisements should always carry information about what the odds are.[89] In the case of the NL the promoter is governed by the basic principle that the chances of winning should not be misrepresented, that a person's financial anxieties should not be exploited, that excessive or reckless playing should not be encouraged, that playing should not be presented as an alternative to work, that advertising should not target the young, and that it should not link the Lottery with the sale of alcohol or drugs or with betting and gaming.[90]

Gambling contracts now enforceable by law

A final feature of modern gambling is one that might be considered to be of interest only to lawyers,[91] but which in fact provides a vital indication of the way in which the government has acquiesced in a fundamental change in the way in which gambling is officially regarded and regulated. I refer here to the question of whether gambling debts should be, like other debts, enforceable by law. Ever since the Gaming Act of 1845, the agreement that a gambler entered into by betting with another gambler or a gambling promoter was not considered to be a legal contract; if the debtor did not wish to pay up there was nothing in law that the creditor could do about it. Gambling was in that sense viewed as outwith the law. Needless to say, however, promoters had their ways of enforcing payment of gambling debts. For example casinos often used the threat of force and the Jockey Club named and shamed defaulters by publicly posting information about the non-payment of debts.[92] Even after the legalisation of off-course betting in 1960, that position, consistent with the principle that gambling should not be encouraged, remained unchanged. It is only with the passing of the 2005 Gambling Act, following the recommendations of the Gambling Review Body, that the gambling relationship is now seen as a contractual one, with contracts legally recognised and enforceable. Along with the passing of lead government responsibility to the Department for Culture, Media and Sport, this is as clear an indication as any that gambling is now officially viewed as an ordinary commodity and that suppliers and consumers should be able to rely on the law to enforce the decisions they have made.[93]

The colossal British gambling industry

Britain now has as much gambling diversity on offer as almost anywhere. Taken altogether its gambling industry is now colossal. By the end of the twentieth century, a detailed estimate of the total annual amount wagered on all forms of gambling in the whole of the UK in 1998 was £42 billion, producing a gross yield – in other words, after winnings have been paid out – of £7.3 billion.[94] By 2006/07, the Gambling Commission estimated that total gambling industry turnover was £84 billion with a gross gambling yield of £9.9 billion.[95] Table 2.4 shows a breakdown according to the different gambling sectors based on information for the year 2008. Perhaps particularly notable is the large and apparently growing size of the betting sector, and the continued prominence in the figures of the National Lottery, gambling machines – an estimated quarter of a million machines in the UK – and casino gambling, plus now remote gambling which hardly featured at all a decade earlier.

Who gambles? Results of the 2006/07 British Gambling Prevalence Survey

At the time of writing the best up-to-date data on British gambling habits was to be found in the results of the British Gambling Prevalence Survey which was carried out by a top British survey organisation, the National Centre for Social Research (NatCen), between September 2006 and March 2007. The method used was to draw a representative sample of over 10,000 private addresses in England, Scotland and Wales. Questionnaires were given to, or left for, every person 16 years of age and above, and a field worker either waited while they were completed or returned later to collect them. Up to five calls were made to an address if necessary. What were the results? One major purpose of the survey was to estimate the prevalence of problem gambling, but we shall leave those results until the whole idea of gambling addiction has been introduced in Chapter 3. For now we shall look at some of the results about the proportions of people who take part in the different types of gambling.

Table 2.4 The size of the British gambling industry (figures are in £millions, for the calendar year 2008 unless otherwise stated)[96]

Gambling sector	Size
National Lottery	1,360[a]
Other lotteries	93[b] (April 08 – March 09)
Betting (mostly off course betting, but also on course and pools betting including football pools)	1,897[c]
Gambling machines in betting shops	1,138[c]
Bingo	1,703[d]
Gambling machines in bingo clubs	214[c]
Casino table games (takings from gambling machines in casinos not included)	479[e] (April 08 – March 09)
Gambling machines in arcades	489[c]
Remote gambling	896[f]

[a] Returns to good causes after deducting prizes and expenses
[b] Balance after deduction of prizes and expenses
[c] Gross profit
[d] Gross sales
[e] House win
[f] Gross yield for remote betting, bingo and casino gambling; may be an underestimate due to incomplete returns

Table 2.5 summarises the results of asking the survey respondents about the different forms of gambling they had engaged in in the last 12 months. The table is a large one, partly because gambling habits are very different for men and women and it is necessary to show the results for the two sexes separately, but more particularly because the list of the forms of gambling available to people in Britain in the year before the survey is a long one. After much discussion with a range of knowledgeable people, including representatives of the gambling industry itself, and after preliminary testing and piloting, the 16 forms of gambling shown in the table were included. This itself is staggering, showing as it does how many different ways of gambling are now legally available to people in Britain. What the list also indicates is the growing diversity of gambling opportunities and the growing complexity of the field. In fact the 2006/07 survey was the second of its kind, the first having been carried out, also by NatCen, seven years earlier in 1999/2000. At that time only 11 forms of gambling were asked about. In the year prior to the earlier survey, back in the closing years of the twentieth century, forms of gambling such as FOBMs, online betting with a bookmaker, and virtual gaming, betting exchanges, and spreadbetting, either

Table 2.5   British Gambling Prevalence Survey 2006/07: percentages of men and women reporting having engaged in each of 16 forms of gambling in the last 12 months[97]

Gambling activity	Men %	Women %
1 Tickets for the National Lottery Draw (not including scratchcards)	59	56
2 Scratchcards, including National Lottery scratchcard games played online (but not newspaper or magazine scratchcards)	19	20
3 Tickets for any <u>other</u> lottery including charity lotteries (but not the Irish or other international lotteries or buying raffle tickets)	12	12
4 The football pools (not including betting on football matches with a bookmaker)	5	2
5 Bingo cards or tickets (not including newspaper bingo tickets or bingo played online)	4	10
6 Fruit/slot machines (not including quiz machines)	19	10
7 Virtual gaming machines <u>in a bookmaker's</u> to bet on virtual roulette, keno, bingo, etc. (not including quiz machines)	4	1
8 Table games (roulette, cards or dice) <u>in a casino</u> (not including poker or casino games played online)	6	2
9 Online gambling like playing poker, bingo, slot machine-style games or casino games <u>for money</u>, including gambling online through a computer, mobile phone, or interactive TV (but not bets made with online bookmakers or betting exchanges)	4	1
10 Online betting <u>with a bookmaker</u> on any event or sport including betting online through a computer, mobile phone or interactive TV (but not bets made with a betting exchange or spread-betting)	6	1
11 Betting exchange – this is where you lay or back bets against other people using a betting exchange. There is no bookmaker to determine the odds. This is sometimes called 'peer to peer' betting	2	<0.5
12 Betting on horse races <u>in a bookmaker's, by phone or at the track</u>, including tote betting and betting on virtual horse races shown in a bookmaker's (but not bets made with online bookmakers or betting exchanges)	22	13
13 Betting on dog races <u>in a bookmaker's, by phone or at the track</u> including tote betting and betting on virtual dog races shown in a bookmaker's (but not bets made with online bookmakers or betting exchanges)	7	3
14 Betting on any other event or sport <u>in a bookmaker's by phone or at the venue</u> (not including bets made with online bookmakers or betting exchanges, or spread-betting)	10	3
15 Spread-betting – In spread-betting you bet that the outcome of an event will be higher or lower than the bookmaker's prediction. The amount you win or lose depends on how right or wrong you are	1	<0.5
16 Private betting, playing cards or games for money with friends, family or colleagues	15	6

had not been invented or were so new that they were not considered worthy of inclusion. The table shows the 16 forms of gambling which appeared in the questionnaire. Note how it was necessary to add instructions to most of the items in order to help respondents distinguish one form of gambling from another. Again this tells its own story. Developments in communications technology and the inventiveness of the gambling industry, plus the liberalisation introduced by the 2005 Act – making it much easier, for example, to offer a number of different forms of gambling at the same venue – have had the result that distinctions between different forms of gambling are now harder to draw, with resulting confusion for all, except for those who are very well informed about latest developments.

Turning to the results themselves, there were a number of interesting findings. The first is the overall percentage (68%) of people who reported that they had engaged in any form of gambling at any time in the previous 12 months. This suggests that a surprisingly large minority, very nearly a third of all British adults, are total abstainers when it comes to gambling. The second notable result, perhaps not surprising, is that the NL is far and away the most commonly engaged in form of gambling. Not only does it beat all the other forms by a long chalk in terms of numbers who have played at all in the last 12 months, but it is one of only two forms where over half who engage in it at all said that they did so at least once a week – football pools being the other. All other forms of gambling appeared to be minority and mostly infrequent activities. This was particularly the case for the five new forms of gambling – although interestingly enough relatively high proportions of the small minorities who reported engaging in those new forms of gambling were doing so quite frequently (for example 21% of the 200 or so people who said they had done any online gambling in the last 12 months reported doing so at least twice a week). But even those ways of gambling that had been around for some time appeared to be engaged in by minorities and mostly infrequently. Scratchcards, betting on horse races, using 'slot' EGMs and playing lotteries other than the NL, are the only forms where the past year percentage of players exceeded 10%, and in all those cases more than half of those who did play said they did so less than once a month. Despite all the media attention and controversy that surrounds casinos, the proportion who said they had done any playing of casino table games in a casino was a mere 4% and three-quarters of those said they had done so less than once a month. Even if all the ways in which it is possible to bet with a bookmaker are combined – on horses, dogs, other events or sports, and online with a bookmaker – the proportion of the population involved in the last 12 months rises only to 22%. Similarly, if the three different forms of online gambling are combined – online betting with a bookmaker, gambling on virtual games online and using a betting exchange — the equivalent figure is only 6%.

Some people who gamble confine themselves to a single kind of gambling activity. That was true, for example, for a third of those who said they had gambled on the NL draw in the last 12 months and for 1 in 12 of those who had played bingo. Other people engage in a wider variety of forms of gambling. In fact 14% of the national sample had gambled on four or more types of activity in the last year. Taking part in as many as four different forms of gambling may be a good indication of a quite serious commitment to gambling and from here on I shall refer to this group as 'multiple-interest gamblers'.

This was a general population sample and therefore included a whole cross-section of adults of both sexes and all ages, financial circumstances and lifestyles. Once the sample is broken down, it becomes possible to see sub-groups who do more gambling than others. For a start Table 2.5 already shows an interesting pattern by sex. Gambling has traditionally been thought of as more of a male preserve and so it still seems to be in Britain for most of the forms of gambling, including the newer ones. The exceptions are the NL, other lotteries and scratchcards, where there are virtually no sex differences – interestingly enough the very forms of gambling that are sometimes thought of as hardly 'gambling' at all – and bingo, the sole form of gambling where the female rate substantially exceeds the male. Men were twice as likely as women to be multiple-interest gamblers.

By age there were clear differences. Most forms of gambling were most common among 25–34 year olds, with lower participation rates for 16–24 year olds and declining participation after age 34, reaching lowest participation rates for those aged 75 years and older. But the pattern is different for different forms of gambling. At the younger end, the 16–24 year olds were the highest participants in the last year for private betting, online gambling and use of fixed odds betting machines and they used 'slot' EGMs and betting exchanges just as much as 25–34 year olds. Beyond age 34 there was a rapid drop-off in use of EGMs, all forms of betting with bookmakers (except on horse races), private betting, casino table game betting, use of FOBMs, betting exchanges and spread betting. In contrast, use of lotteries other than the NL, football pools and bingo were well maintained even up to the oldest age group. The proportion of multiple-interest gamblers was at its highest amongst 25–34 year olds. The numbers of total abstainers from gambling were highest at the two ends of the age distribution: over 40% amongst both 16–24 year olds and those aged 75 and over.

Although the numbers of Black and minority ethnic (BME) group respondents was comparatively small, there seemed to be a strong ethnic group effect, with participation in all forms of gambling lower for BME groups than for the majority White group. Participation was lowest overall, and consistently for all gambling forms, for the Black or Black British group. Rates were also low for the Asian or Asian British group – less than half gambling on any activity in the last year – but with an indication that rates might be similar to the White rate for some of the newer forms of gambling such as spread betting, online gambling and use of FOBMs. It was a limitation that the numbers did not allow separate analyses of people from different ethnic groups whose orientation to gambling may be very different – for example, Indian, Pakistani, Bangladeshi and Chinese groups.

Those who had gambled at all in the last seven days were asked some detailed questions about where they had gambled and with what result. Most of the results about where people gambled were unsurprising but some are worth noting. One is the importance of using betting shop premises for gambling – at least for men, since the forms of gambling available there remained very male dominated. Not only was the betting shop by far the most popular venue for horse and dog racing and other sports betting (although a quarter of all dog race bettors had bet at the track), but a quarter of all football pools bettors and almost a tenth of all EGM players reported conducting their gambling there as well. Another point to note is the ubiquity of gambling machines which were played in a wider variety of locations than was the case for any other form of gambling, pubs being the most popular location, with 'amusement' arcades or centres, social clubs, bingo halls and betting offices also being popular. Pubs were also a popular venue for private betting: a fifth of all private bettors bet in pubs. Private betting, in terms of venue, is otherwise a form of gambling unlike any other, with the most popular locations being the person's own home, someone else's home or via the person's place of work.

Of its kind the British Gambling Prevalence Survey was undoubtedly a particularly good one. There is, however, always a question about whether people answer such surveys honestly and accurately. But the survey was completely anonymous, questions were carefully worded and piloted, and there is no particular reason to think that most of the results are inaccurate. More serious is the question of whether systematic bias is introduced by the inevitable fact that some people who are approached decline to complete the questionnaire. Taking into consideration the fact that contact could only be made with a proportion of chosen households (63%), and once contact had been made not all eligible adults completed a questionnaire (81% did so), the overall response rate was calculated to be 52%. That response rate represents a huge amount of work and there is no doubt that without such a professional organisation behind the survey, the response rate would have been nothing like as high as it was. But, since 48% were non-responders, it does raise serious questions about the limitations of such surveys. For example, are the heaviest gamblers more likely to be represented amongst the group that declines? There is in fact no way of knowing the answer to that question, although many who are familiar with the issues involved believe quite strongly that being a heavy gambler reduces the likelihood that the person would be available when the field worker calls and, if the person is at home, makes it less likely that he or she will be inclined to complete the survey. On the other hand, field workers reported some people declining because they said they had no interest in gambling. These questions about sample bias become more important the larger the proportion of people approached who do not complete the survey. This is becoming more of a problem since all survey organisations report that people are becoming more reluctant to take part in such exercises. It is particularly important for gambling surveys in Britain since the government has said it will support such a survey every three years from now on as part of its commitment to monitor the effects of the 2005 Gambling Act (the results of the 2009/2010 survey are due out in late 2010). The same issues apply in the many other European countries that are seeing the need to conduct national gambling prevalence studies.[98]

Chapter summary

The last half of the twentieth century witnessed a marked change in British gambling policy in the direction of liberalisation. The move was from one of partial prohibition, via one of tight regulation in which gambling was permitted but not encouraged following the relevant Acts of the 1960s, to one in which the free market provision of gambling was encouraged and regulated. The change was gradual but was given a strong boost by the inauguration of the country's National Lottery in 1994, and was consolidated by the report of the Gambling Review Body in 2001 leading to the new Gambling Act of 2005. The lead Government department changed, significantly, from the Home Office to the Department for Culture, Media and Sport. The overwhelmingly liberalising provisions of the 2005 Act were welcomed by the gambling industry which is now colossal in size in Britain and more diverse than almost anywhere else. Besides its National Lottery, Britain has large and innovating betting, gambling machine, casino and bingo sectors, as well as one of the most liberal sets of internet gambling regulations in the world, and new forms of gambling such as fixed odds betting machines (FOBMs), betting exchanges and spread betting. Gambling is now more freely advertised and gambling contracts are now legally enforceable.

A snapshot of British gambling at the end of that half-century of change is provided by the results of the British Gambling Prevalence Survey carried out in 2006/07. Only just over two-thirds of the population were estimated to have gambled at all in the previous 12 months, leaving about a third of the population who are total abstainers when it comes to gambling. The National Lottery is the only form of gambling engaged in by more than 50%. No other form of gambling was engaged in by as much as a quarter of the population and the percentages engaging in some of the forms of gambling that have given rise to concern, such as FOBMs, online virtual gambling, playing table games in a casino, using a betting exchange and spread betting, lay between 1 and 5%. Liberalisation of the gambling laws has not yet resulted in Britain becoming in general a nation of gamblers. The danger is that our natural resistance to gambling will be worn down as time goes on – a theme we shall return to in Section IV. Meanwhile, as Chapter 3 documents, certain sub-groups of the population are at greater risk from gambling problems than others.

Section II

Gambling is Dangerous

3

Gambling Addiction

Even after sound evidence for the smoking – cancer link was starting to accumulate, and surveys were showing that as much as half of all smokers would prefer to stop smoking, the idea that tobacco was addictive was vehemently resisted by the tobacco industry. In fact, it is only necessary to go back a few decades further to find a time when even health experts were dismissive of the idea that something so popular and widely accepted as smoking could be compared to a 'drug' and thought to be addictive. In the 1920s one German pharmacologist wrote of smoking as '... an enjoyment which man is free to renounce and when he indulges in it he experiences its benevolent effects on his spiritual life...',[1] and one prominent psychoanalyst thought that 'most of the fanatical opponents of tobacco that I have known were all bad neurotics'.[2] Particularly strange to our ears now is the statement, again from the 1920s, of Sir Humphrey Rolleston, whose famous report on opiate drugs at that time was highly significant in influencing British drug policy. On smoking he stated, 'That smoking produces a craving... is undoubted, but it can seldom be accurately described as overpowering... To regard tobacco as a drug of addiction is all very well in a humorous sense, but it is hardly accurate'.[3] It was really not until the 1970s that the experts began to win the argument that tobacco use was an addiction, or what the World Health Organisation was now calling 'dependence'. Even then, a number of further decades would need to pass before the proportion of the population who were smokers in a country like the UK had dropped sufficiently and opinion had swung far enough that policy changes such as banning cigarette advertising and smoking in enclosed public spaces would win political support. Back in the 1970s it was still possible to say, '... smokers almost all over the world can now enjoy their habit with the tacit

An Unsafe Bet? The Dangerous Rise of Gambling and the Debate We Should be Having   By Jim Orford
© 2011 John Wiley & Sons, Ltd

approval of their government, vigorous encouragement of the tobacco industry, absolution of their church and the resigned silence of their physicians'.[4]

Early recognition of compulsive gambling

Thirty years later an equivalent statement is true of gambling. But in the meantime, as gambling has been liberalised, recognition has grown that it can be dangerous and can significantly harm people's lives. It is now much more widely recognised than it once was that gambling can get out of control and that for some people it comes to constitute a very real problem. 'Problem gambling' is now very much a part of gambling policy debates. That was not the case at the time when the 1976–78 Royal Commission on Gambling, chaired by Lord Rothschild, concluded that gambling regulation was working well in the UK and that some relaxation of restrictions on gambling could be lifted. The dangers of 'compulsive gambling' – the preferred term at the time – were given short shrift. Not so a quarter of a century later when the Gambling Review Body included in its report a substantial chapter on problem gambling.[5]

There are many continuing misunderstandings and disputes about the nature of problem gambling and its importance for policy, but of its sheer existence there is now little disagreement. Ample evidence of the destruction that out-of-control gambling can wreak on a person's personal life is provided by numerous clinical case studies, surveys of Gamblers Anonymous members, and other studies involving in-depth interviews with individuals who have experienced problems with their gambling.[6] They make it clear how excessive gambling can lead to debts, stealing, deceiving and lying, arguments, even violence, and the breakdown of relationships, as well as personal depression and suicidal feelings. That general picture can be brought to life by providing some quotations from individual people who have figured in such case studies and research projects. The first comes from a comparatively early report from British clinicians who provided case summaries to illustrate their new work with compulsive gamblers in the 1960s.

He had gambled in 'betting shops' for more than 2 years and had lost over £1,200. Initially he ascribed his gambling mainly to boredom, but he had recently gambled to repay his debts, which exceeded £100. His usual practice was to spend all his salary . . . in a betting shop on Saturdays. He invariably reinvested his winnings on horses and returned home with nothing so that his wife and children went without food, clothes and fuel . . . Matters came to a head when he put his own money and the complete pay packet of a sick friend (who had asked him to collect his pay) on one horse and lost £40. This resulted in 18 months probation. His gambling had been causing serious marital difficulties and was affecting the health of his wife and his eldest son. He was referred for treatment by his doctor.[7]

The second example, published in 1998, is from an Australian study of gambling and suicide based on examination of a coroner's office records:

> ...on the 20th October...Mr...a 34 year old married Vietnamese engineer was found hanging in the garage by his neighbour. According to the Police investigation report, Mrs...stated that her husband had lost approximately $13,000 in three lots of $3,000, $4,000 and $6,000 at the casino over the nine months prior to his death. This resulted in marital friction, with his wife being forced to take out a loan to cover their commitments...Bank records revealed that on the 5th October he withdrew $500 from an ATM at the casino, on the 9th he withdrew and lost $1,000 and on the 11th absented himself from work and withdrew another $240 at the casino's ATM. He made a further withdrawal of $700 but it was unclear where this was spent. The remaining balance in his joint account was $7.00 on the evening of his death...While [there] may potentially be compounding factors [such as job stress], it was considered that gambling and financial problems were of paramount importance in his death.[8]

The third example is that of a woman who gave an interview as part of a study which included people identified as probable problem gamblers in the 1999/2000 British Gambling Prevalence Study:

> When you start spending every spare penny you've got, when you start deceiving, cheating and lying, that's when it becomes a problem...I had bank loans, credit cards debts...any credit I could get hold of and built up £1,000 in debt. They started chasing me and there was no way I could pay all the arrears as I was only on £60 a week...The downside of it is that I'm nearly 40 years old and I've got nothing...it's ruined relationships, because rather than go out with friends I go gambling. It's just ruined friendships...I started lying as to where I was going...purely so nobody would find out what I was doing.[9]

But the trouble that individual gamblers can get into through the excessiveness of their gambling has been wellknown for much longer. The difference is that in the past it was even more difficult than it is now to make sense of what was happening because the idea of addiction was not well understood and was certainly not applied to a behaviour such as gambling. In his book *Better Betting With a Decent Feller: Bookmaking, Betting and the British Working Class, 1750–1990*, Carl Chinn, well-known local broadcaster and lecturer and professor of local history at the University of Birmingham, writing about Britain in the first half of the twentieth century, stated: '...it is likely that each community could point to families and individuals demoralized by the activity, and it is not surprising that many working-class people viewed any form of betting as disreputable'.[10] That is an important statement of recognition of the harm that gambling can cause because it comes from someone who was at pains in his book to correct what he saw as a prejudiced view towards working-class gambling and particularly towards the often maligned bookmakers, such as his own father.

The dangers of gambling have been well represented in English fiction, including Graham Greene's *Brighton Rock* and Walter Greenwood's *Love on the Dole* in the 1930s;[11] and in films, including, from 1949, *The Great Sinner*, loosely based on Dostoevsky's nineteenth-century novel *The Gambler*.[12] Reference is often made to Dostoevsky as one of the most famous compulsive gamblers of all time: his own letters and those of his second wife Anna provided psychoanalysts with ample evidence of that.[13] In fact, some psychiatrists and psychoanalysts, early in the twentieth century, recognised that gambling could take a compulsive form decades before that became more widely recognised. Their idea of 'manias' – dipsomania and nymphomania were others – was a forerunner of the more modern concept of addiction. But we can go back still further. An article in the *American Journal of Psychology* in 1902[14] contains a number of descriptions of gambling which indicate how excessive and disease-like it could become.

An often cited, much earlier, source is the book *Liber de Ludo Aleae* – A Book on the Games of Chance – written in 1525 by Jerome Cardano, the controversial Renaissance physician, astrologer, mathematician and writer. He described his gambling addiction and appears to have been ahead of his time in recognising the danger that gambling could become 'a settled habit' amounting to an illness:

> During many years I have played not on and off but, I am ashamed to say, every day. Thereby I have lost my self-esteem, my worldly goods and my time . . . Even if gambling is altogether evil, still, on account of the very many large numbers that play, it would seem to be a natural evil. For that reason, it ought to be discussed by medical doctors like one of those incurable diseases . . . The greatest advantage in gambling comes from not playing at all, there are so many difficulties and so many possibilities of loss that there is nothing better than not to play at all.[15]

In the present day one of the clearest signs that gambling can become seriously out of control is the scale of the gambling self-help movement. The fact that people in large numbers have felt the need to get together with others to support each other in overcoming their addiction to gambling is amongst the strongest evidence that gambling can be very dangerous. The model was the highly successful Alcoholics Anonymous with its programme of 12 steps for members to follow. Based on the same programme, but with an even greater emphasis on the financial side of the problem – for example, Step 3 requires members to make a searching and fearless moral *and financial* inventory of themselves – Gamblers Anonymous (GA) originated in the USA in 1957, growing from just 16 chapters in 1960 to around 600 by the late 1980s.[16] It came to Northern Ireland in 1962 and from there to mainland Britain two years later and by the late 1990s it was estimated there were around 200 GA meetings each week in Britain and Ireland together.[17] By then it had spread to at least a dozen other countries.[18] GA's sister organisation, GamAnon, caters for partners, parents and other family members and friends of compulsive gamblers. Because statutory health services have been so slow to recognise gambling addiction, and research

Table 3.1 Compulsive gambling: The Gamblers Anonymous 20 questions[20]

1	Have you ever lost time from work due to gambling?
2	Has gambling made your life unhappy?
3	Has gambling affected your reputation?
4	Have you ever felt remorse after gambling?
5	Have you ever gambled to get money to pay debts or to otherwise solve financial difficulties?
6	Did gambling ever cause a decrease in your ambition or efficiency?
7	After losing did you feel that you must return as soon as possible and win back your losses?
8	After a win have you had a strong urge to return and win more?
9	Have you often gambled until your last penny was gone?
10	Have you ever borrowed to finance your gambling?
11	Have you ever sold any real or personal property to finance your gambling?
12	Are you reluctant to use 'gambling money' for normal expenditures?
13	Has gambling ever made you careless of the welfare of your family?
14	Have you ever gambled longer than you had planned?
15	Have you ever gambled to escape worry or trouble?
16	Have you ever committed, or considered committing, an illegal act to finance your gambling?
17	Has gambling ever caused you to have difficult in sleeping?
18	Did arguments, disappointment, or frustrations ever create within you an urge to gamble?
19	Have you ever had an urge to celebrate any good fortune by a few hours of gambling?
20	Have you ever considered self-destruction as a result of your gambling?

on the subject has been difficult and slow to develop, studies of GA members, for example in the USA, Canada and Scotland, have played an important role in describing in detail the experiences of individuals whose gambling has got out of hand.[19]

On the basis of their collective experience, GA developed a list of 20 questions, shown in Table 3.1, to help people self-diagnose compulsive gambling. The list gives a good indication of the ways in which GA members had found that excessive gambling could harm them psychologically and socially.[21] A crucial event in establishing the disease-like nature of problem gambling, however, was the inclusion by the American Psychiatric Association of 'pathological gambling' in its Diagnostic and Statistical Manual (DSM) of mental disorders. It was included for the first time in the third edition of the manual (DSM-III) in 1980. The World Health Organisation followed by including it in its International Classification of Diseases (ICD) although the DSM has remained the more influential internationally. It has gone through two revisions since then (DSM-III Revised and DSM-IV) and at the time of writing DSM-V has been in preparation for some time.[22]

The strange phenomenon of self-exclusion

A feature of the world of problem gambling, which illustrates well the addictive nature of gambling, is the strange phenomenon of self-exclusion.[23] It seems to have originated in the procedures that casino operators have long used for evicting unruly or unwanted clients. But more recently such procedures have evolved into gambling industry policies for assisting gamblers to exclude *themselves* from a gambling venue if they believe they have problems controlling their gambling and wish to be helped to resist the temptation to gamble there in the future. The first formally constituted self-exclusion programme was instituted in Manitoba, Canada, in 1989 when the province's first permanent casino was established. Since then similar programmes have been initiated in other Canadian provinces, several states of the USA and in other countries including Australia, South Africa, Poland, France, Switzerland, the Netherlands and the UK. Industry figures for 2008/09 showed there to have been no fewer than 65,000 self-exclusions in Britain, 45,000 in connection with remote and 20,000 non-remote gambling.[24] Even though individuals may appear more than once, these figures are remarkable. Although family members or other concerned individuals might initiate an agreement that an operator ban a gambler from entry to the premises, it is nearly always the gambler him or herself who takes the initiative. The period of exclusion varies. In one study, of patrons of casinos in Quebec, Canada, two-thirds had opted for 12 months self-exclusion or less but a quarter had agreed to five years, and in another study, of several thousand Australian gamblers, the average period of self-exclusion was 1.7 years.[25] Another study, in the state of Missouri, USA, asked self-excluders about their main reasons for joining the programme. About half cited gaining control over their gambling, a third because they needed help, and between 15 and 25% because they had 'hit rock bottom', on the advice of others or in order to save their marriages. Around 5% stated that they opted for self-exclusion in order to prevent suicide.[26]

In Missouri alone the number of applications for self-exclusion rose from just 19 in 1996 to more than 7,000 in 2004. In that US state there exists a formal procedure whereby individuals seeking self-exclusion need to complete an application at one of three state-administered offices or at one of 11 casinos in order to be placed on a 'dissociated persons list' administered by the Missouri Gaming Commission.[27] There has even been a proposal that all casinos should have 'self-exclusion educators' whose responsibilities would include providing information, advice and referral for counselling to anyone who wishes to self-exclude.[28] Even the providers of the British National Lottery have tried, with limited success, to introduce the option of self-exclusion for mobile phone lottery players.[29]

The point about self-exclusion for the present discussion is not whether it works – although many believe it can be a very helpful aid in countering problematic gambling – but rather its great significance in illustrating just what sort of 'disease' it is that Cardano, and all the clinicians and Gamblers Anonymous members who came later, have been on about. There will be more about this in the following chapter. But for now, suffice it to say that what the phenomenon of self-exclusion illustrates so pointedly is that a person addicted to gambling is in the grip of a particularly distressing and troubling conflict. The habit that has developed is so strong and the inclination so difficult to resist, that simple self-control and the normal exercise of willpower are not enough. Special measures need to be taken. It is not unlike a problem drinker taking prescribed antabuse daily – a special way of bolstering resolve in the face of another difficult-to-control form of consumption –, a medication which reacts with any alcohol that might subsequently be taken, making the drinker feel very unwell. Although self-exclusion may seem like an extreme measure, it is really only one of a number of attempts at self-control which are familiar to anyone who has tried to conquer a gambling problem. Deliberately avoiding going out with much money or with a credit card, not buying a paper with racing pages, or going home a long way round in order to avoid the betting shop or amusement arcade, are other common and less dramatic strategies that are used.[30]

What the phenomenon of self-exclusion shows us very clearly is that gambling is no ordinary commodity. It is a dangerous form of consumption that can trap people to the point where they have to take special steps to reduce the harm it is causing.

Gambling addiction is a problem for families

In all discussions about addiction there has been an unfortunate tendency to neglect the majority of individuals who experience addiction at first hand. I refer here to the close family members – parents, partners, children and others – who live under the same roof as, or whose lives are otherwise very closely bound up with, someone who is personally suffering from an addiction. That neglect of the family impact of addiction is partly due to the very individualistic approach that western health care generally takes towards illness and its treatment, and party to the negative, even blaming, approaches to family members that have been adopted in the past by practitioners and academics when discussing addiction – for example, in the past wives were often blamed for their husbands' alcohol addiction and parents continue often to be blamed for their children's drug addiction.[31] It is not surprising that the same has happened in the case of gambling. One commentator from the USA referred to family members of problem gamblers as 'a group with no discursive voice'[32] and a Canadian review of problem gambling and its impact on families began by saying: 'Most of these theories [of problem gambling] focus on the problem gambler with little or peripheral attention given to the family'.[33]

One estimate was that each problem gambler affects between 10 and 17 other people, including family members and co-workers.[34] The massive report of the Australian Productivity Commission,[35] in its comprehensive assessment of the costs and benefits of gambling to Australian society, concluded, on the basis of a survey of clients in counselling, that on average a single problem gambler adversely affected seven other people. In most surveys the issue of family impact is ignored but the 2006/07 British Gambling Prevalence Survey took a small step in the right direction by including a single question on the subject. The question was: *In the last 12 months, has any close relative of yours (including partner) had a gambling problem?* In this representative British sample, 2.4% answered that question in the affirmative,[36] which is roughly four times the percentage who were themselves identified as problem gamblers according to their answers to problem gambling screening questions (see below). Although there are other possible ways of interpreting the figures, one conclusion is that approximately four people are affected on average by each person with a gambling problem.

Two books from the USA, written in the 1980s, became modern classics in the problem gambling literature. One, entitled *When Luck Runs Out*, included a chapter on compulsive gambling and the family, including the following statement:

> It is the nature of emotional disorders that when one member of the family is afflicted, the effects are felt by all the others. There are few, however, in which the impact is felt with such severity as in the case of compulsive gambling.[37]

The other, *The Chase*, which was based on lengthy interviews with 50 compulsive gamblers, included a focus on what the author referred to as an 'exploitative' financial relationship with the gambler's family. This included using entertainment money, money from part-time jobs and overtime money, borrowing from parents or in-laws, lying to the gambler's partner about the true extent of his (all of the gamblers in that study were men) earnings, using as excuses 'bills' or 'deductions' from wages which in reality did not exist, 'borrowing' from family resources such as savings and life insurance, selling or pawning his own or family members' possessions, hiding loans, and when all else failed, using money required by the family for essentials.[38]

The Canadian review, referred to above, listed the following as the most common problems reported by family members of problem gamblers: the loss of household or personal money; arguments, anger and violence; lies and deception; neglect of family; negatively affected relationships; poor communications; and confusion of family roles and responsibilities.[39] In a national survey carried out for the Australian Productivity Commission, those respondents identified as problem gamblers reported, at a far higher rate than others, that arguments had occurred in their families and that they had not had enough time for their families. In a complementary survey of clients at Australian counselling agencies, over two-thirds believed there had been an adverse effect of their gambling on their partners, just under two-thirds on parents, over half on friends, over half on children and just under a third on colleagues. Effects on partners were rated as particularly serious. One of the earliest clinical accounts of compulsive gambling from the 1960s cited the following wife:

> Over the last few years we have had a monster living with our family – a monster in the shape of a 'fruit-machine'. Practically every penny my husband earned went into that machine and while it consumed, we starved. He was obsessed by it. Frequently we were without food, fuel and light.[40]

An in-depth interview study of problem gamblers in Britain also found them referring to the impact of their gambling on others as one of the main downsides to their gambling. They talked primarily about rows with family members and partners about time and money they had spent gambling. The way in which gambling had disrupted or led to breakdown in relationships was also referred to, as one of the men who was interviewed explained:

> At that point I was just constantly chasing my tail and feeling low...I was coming home after gambling and creating arguments with my wife, upsetting my boys...it was because of the torment that I was lashing out on my wife and the boys because I knew I didn't have any money to give my wife, to pay for bills that came in.[41]

Those who, as affected family members, have had such first hand experiences are more likely than others to be against the spread of opportunities for gambling, for example the opening of new casinos in their areas.[42] An example is Roy Hattersley, former Deputy Leader of the British Labour Party, who, following the 2001 report of the Gambling Review Body in Britain, which suggested wholesale liberalisation of gambling, wrote:

> My grandfather was hugely intelligent, brave and handsome. Gambling ruined his life and the life of his family...Will the sort of society which allows unrestricted gambling encourage the standards and values we want to inculcate into our children and grandchildren?...Respect of the individual requires us to allow men and women to make their own mistakes. But, in a civilised society, there is no freedom to exploit others and no liberty to destroy families.[43]

There has been a small number of studies based on interviews with family members who have lived with close relatives addicted to gambling.[44] For example, a series of studies of wives of male problem gamblers in the USA in the 1980s gave ample evidence of the stress that they were under as a result. They found that wives commonly reported feelings of anger and resentment, depression, loneliness or isolation from their husbands, feelings of helplessness and confusion and several physical symptoms such as severe headaches, bowel irregularities, feelings of faintness or dizziness, hypertension and breathing irregularities. Furthermore, wives reported unsatisfactory sexual relationships during the worst of their spouses' gambling and nearly all wives reported having considered separation from their gambling husbands.[45] Particularly sad is the guilt that many spouses described because they thought they might be the reason for their partners' gambling problems and/or because, despite their efforts, they were unable to do anything to stop the behaviour.[46]

In a later English study of 16 close family members, Mya Krishnan and I focused on the dilemmas which partners and parents faced when having a close relative with such a problem. These dilemmas, and the ways in which families had tried to cope, are actually very similar to those described by family members whose relatives have other types of addiction problems such as addiction to alcohol or drugs.[47] For a start, recognising that an accumulation of family problems can be attributed to a partner's or son's or daughter's excessive gambling is not straightforward and often takes some time. Once the problem is recognised it is still quite unclear to family members what they should do about it. One of the first things family members try is to discuss the matter openly, but family members often explained that they were unable to do so because the gambler was rarely at home or because, when they tried to discuss the problem, the gambler denied that there was any problem at all, refused to talk about the subject or simply reacted angrily to any mention of his or her gambling. Family members try to support their gambling relatives in a wide variety of ways. In some cases attempts are made to help the gambler give up gambling. Such actions include attending Gamblers Anonymous meetings with the gambler or travelling to meetings in order to provide moral support, cutting out newspaper articles or mentioning TV programmes regarding gambling, or simply providing general support for the gambler in his or her quest to give up gambling. Inevitably one of the things that family members try to do is to reassert some degree of control over family life, which appears to be getting out of control. Trying to exercise control over family finances, perhaps by refusing to give or lend money or by taking complete control of household or business finances, is naturally one of the most common strategies.

Some of the things that family members do are misunderstood by professionals and others who do not fully appreciate the circumstances they are under. Some of these ways of coping may appear to outsiders to be over-tolerant; for example, paying off the gambler's debts or fines in the hope of giving him or her a fresh start; allowing the gambler to take money from them without their permission or lending him or her money in the fear that if they didn't then the gambler would turn to criminal behaviour; or simply forgiving and forgetting when the gambler had stolen from them.

The fact that family members face such dilemmas, mostly without any recognition or support, and sometimes facing misunderstanding and criticism from others, illustrates how serious the problem of gambling addiction can be and how its effects 'ripple out' to affect many more people than just the addicted gambler him or herself. In that sense it is truly a family and social problem. Although lip service is often paid to that point, in practice help for affected family members is scarcely available. In our study parents and partners were often able to refer to positive aspects of support, particularly emotional support, that they had received from friends and family. On the other hand, family members frequently mentioned their dismay at the fact that, whilst people had been helpful and supportive in the past, they were now losing patience. In other cases family members commented on a general lack of support for them in trying to cope with the situation and often reported that they felt alone in trying to deal with the problem.[48]

As has been the case with other forms of addiction, particular concern has been expressed about the risks to children of parental problem gambling. Again there have been a few studies that are relevant here, but not many.[49] An aspect of these children's experience that is often described is the neglect that can occur because of the addicted parent's preoccupation with the object of his or her addiction. Children may not know when a parent will return from a gambling trip, and when at home a parent preoccupied with gambling may still be unavailable to the child. The way in which a child's safety can be jeopardised has also been described. For example, children may be left alone or unsupervised at home, in parked cars or in dangerous public locations while a parent gambles.

The studies that have been done have found children typically reporting inconsistency in relationships with their parents, a sense of loss in relation to the problem gambling parent, and sometimes material losses, often financial, which themselves can affect their education and social lives. They may find themselves caught in an uncomfortable or inappropriate position in the family, taking on the role of peacemaker, scapegoat, carer, or simply being caught up in the middle of family tension and arguments. Like other affected family members they describe feelings of being rejected, anger, hurt, confusion, helplessness, anxiety, guilt and depression. They too are at risk from stress-related illnesses, including asthma, allergies, headaches and stomach problems. School work can be affected and a high proportion are found to have significant behavioural or adjustment problems, including truancy, running away from home, involvement in crime and an early and/or excessive engagement in alcohol, drug or gambling-related behaviours. In one comparative study of teenage students in a number of southern Californian public high schools, those who reported one or both parents being problem gamblers were significantly more likely than other children to say that their teen years were unhappy, to say that they typically reacted to rejection by 'pretending I didn't care', to rate themselves as insecure, depressed, anxious and unhappy, and to admit to having made suicide attempts.[50] All these childhood accompaniments to parental problem gambling can be found in almost identical form in the somewhat larger professional and academic literature on the experiences of children of problem drinking parents.[51] These are almost certainly the effects, not of parental gambling specifically, but of living in a home disrupted by the preoccupation of one parent with the object of his or her addiction and the family discord which such an addiction creates around it.

Adolescents, women and senior citizens

Adolescents are a high-risk group for problem gambling

It might be thought that gambling addiction was primarily an adult problem, but that is far from being so. Indeed it turns out to be the case that the special vulnerability of adolescents to compulsive gambling is one of the better established facts in the problem gambling field. It is machine gambling that has caused most of the juvenile problems. As long ago as the 1930s the British police were warning of the dangers of gambling machines. The Chief Constable of the Metropolitan Police told a parliamentary committee in 1932 that 'by far the most troublesome form of gaming [in] recent years is the automatic gaming machine of the 'fruit' variety'.[52] But it was following the permissive British legislation of the 1960s, which allowed gambling machines to be located in a wide variety of public settings easily accessible to young people, that teachers, parents, the police and others really started to notice the way in which excessive machine gambling gave rise to adolescent behavioural and emotional problems and family disruption. One of the first relevant studies, carried out by a British psychiatrist, was a survey of the head teachers of 30 secondary schools in four London boroughs. Head teachers were particularly worried if there were amusement arcades housing largish numbers of machines in the neighbourhood of their schools. One head teacher was quoted as saying:

> Once the habit is established, there is a serious interference with school work and truancy often occurs. This leads to a situation in which the children even resort to extortion, in order to continue to play on the machines. This has led to violence in the playground. Often, the most serious effects are on the home. Parents are distraught because money is stolen from the family and from friends. Ultimately, domestic relationships are eroded because all sense of trust is lost, as a consequence of the incessant stealing and lying.[53]

Psychologists and social scientists then started to interview and observe young people in and around arcades and to find out from the young people themselves just how addictive machines could be. A number of those studies were carried out by Mark Griffiths, now of Nottingham Trent University. He talked to young people who believed they had already been addicted to gambling in their early teens, experiencing a constant need to play and to spend all their own, and often others', money at every opportunity, leaving them in debt and wishing that they could stop but finding it difficult to do so. Fruit machines were described by these young people in terms such as 'dead leg' or 'life-destroyers', which should be banned.[54] From one of those studies comes this quotation from a young man whom Griffiths called David:

> If I wasn't actually gambling I was spending the rest of my time working out clever little schemes to obtain money to feed my habit . . . I sold a great deal of my possessions to subsidise my 'fruit-machine' addiction . . . This led me to selling my motorbike after owning it for just three months. The four hundred pounds that I received for the bike lasted just a day . . . During four years of compulsive gambling I think I missed about six or seven days of playing fruit machines . . . I ate, slept and breathed gambling machines . . . All I can remember is living in a trance for four years . . . I lost a great deal of childhood with my parents and only sister which I can never replace. I still get very depressed when I think of the amounts I stole from family and close friends which are totally unrepayable.[55]

The special vulnerability of young people to problem gambling has been confirmed in a number of studies carried out in several other European countries and the USA and Canada.[56] Several writers from those countries have commented on the hidden nature of much adolescent problem gambling, the likelihood that the problem has grown as opportunities to gamble have increased, and the continued and surprising neglect of the problem.[57] Some have compared prevalence rates of adolescent problem gambling with rates of alcohol and drug misuse in young people, which of course has attracted far more attention.[58] In the largest British study of teenage gambling, carried out in the late 1990s, one interesting finding was the high proportion of 12–15 year olds in schools in England and Wales who said they had felt bad in the past year about the amount that they had gambled on fruit machines (22%). That figure was very similar to the proportions who said they had felt bad about the amount of alcohol they had drunk or the number of cigarettes smoked (23% and 19% respectively), and was considerably greater than the numbers who had felt bad about the amount of drugs they had taken (8%).[59]

We saw in Chapter 2 how the British Government, controversially, has continued to allow children and young people to play certain types of gambling machine, and that is an aspect of policy we shall return to in the final section of this book.

Women: a new vulnerable group

Gambling has tended to be male dominated, both in the sense that men have done more gambling in the past and more often found themselves in trouble with it, and in the sense that ideas about gambling and research on the matter has tended to focus on male participants.[60] That situation has been changing. As Rachel Volberg, one of the most experienced gambling survey researchers, has pointed out, women were much less likely than men to participate in forms of gambling that were illegal or which had an unsavoury reputation, preferring the safer and more congenial activities such as playing bingo or having a modest lottery bet. Writing about the USA, women's gambling, as she puts it, 'has started to look more like the gambling done by men' as the availability of legal gambling has grown and gambling has become more normalised.[61] One research group in Australia, particularly concerned about the growth of machine gambling in the state of Victoria, referred to a 'feminisation' of gambling that had occurred along with its normalisation. Theirs was a rare study that focused on women gamblers, in this case recruited in machine gambling venues, in local shopping complexes, or from recreational areas of the university. They identified some women who were spending considerable amounts of time and money on machine playing, gambling more money than they intended, chasing their losses, feeling guilty about it, experiencing criticism from others about their gambling, arguing with others over money used to gamble, and 'borrowing' from housekeeping money to support their gambling habit.[62] It has been noticed that women have been promoted as the new consumers of EGMs in Australia and that some gambling websites are explicitly directed towards women players.[63] The vulnerability of women in some minority cultural groups such as Vietnamese, Chinese and Greek women in the state of Victoria, has also been noted.[64]

Differences remain, however – at least in Britain – in the forms of gambling preferred by women and men, the greater scope of men's gambling compared to women's and the larger average amounts of money that men spend on gambling.[65] It has also been suggested that women and men might be motivated to gamble by different factors[66] and that there may be lifecycle gender differences, with women being proportionately more likely to take up gambling as mature adults, and more often as a means of escape from life stresses and difficulties, including relationship problems.[67] It has also been suggested that women gamblers may be additionally stigmatised by society, receive less sympathy from their families and feel more shame and embarrassment.[68]

Although the larger number of people in touch with services that provide help for people with gambling problems are men, anonymous surveys have been showing very sizeable minorities of problem gamblers, and occasionally even a majority, to be women. One review of 18 studies carried out in the USA found the median percentage of women among problem and 'pathological' gamblers to be 38%.[69] It may be the case, furthermore, that some of the questions used to detect problem gambling may be based on a male stereotype and therefore be less sensitive to forms of gambling problems experienced by women. For example, in the 2006/07 British survey, whereas men were more likely than women to endorse each and every one of the problem gambling questions, women were relatively much more likely to answer affirmatively that they had 'gambled to escape from problems or when you are feeling depressed, anxious or bad about yourself' or that they had 'made unsuccessful attempts to control, cut back or stop gambling', and proportionately much *less* likely to agree that they had 'felt your gambling has caused financial problems for you or your household' or 'felt that you might have a problem with gambling'.

The following statement given to a North American research study illustrates the problems caused to one woman:

> In all honesty, I started going out gambling when my husband was drunk so we wouldn't fight. By that time, my older kids were old enough to take care of the little ones. I started out on the nickel slot machines and progressed to the dollar machines. At first I allowed myself only so much money. And the money I had gave me the time – time away, time not to think, time not to worry. Then I went to a casino where you could write checks. You didn't have to go to the bank machine or anywhere else for money. And that's how I did most of my damage, writing checks.[70]

And the following, from a teenage girl, is from one of Griffiths' studies of 'former adolescent fruit-machine addicts':

> ... any dinner, bus fare money went into fruit machines during school hours. When I started my full time job ... as a cashier, my weekly wages (£75) went ... in a few hours. I needed more money therefore I stole from the cash till ... I am now going to court.[71]

An example of a piece of research which focused on the dangers for women of internet gambling was an interview study of 25 women who had been frequent internet gamblers.[72] Most had had gambling problems according to their answers to a problem gambling inventory. The problem gamblers described having been preoccupied with gambling on the internet, and having amassed debts ranging from £3,000 to £100,000. Relationships had been affected due to secrecy, lies, stealing, neglect of time with children and neglect of partners; and there had been effects on the women's own health, both physical – partially due to neglecting diet – and psychological – several had made suicide attempts and all had experienced feelings such as shame and failure. The research team concluded that it was too early to judge whether the availability of internet gambling would result in increased gambling and problem gambling in women. But their interviewees drew their attention to a number of features of internet gambling which they thought had made it easier for them to become addicted and more difficult to give it up. Some had progressed to problem gambling within only a few weeks of starting to gamble on the internet, raising the question of whether progression to addiction is quicker in the case of online gambling than for other forms of gambling. Amongst the factors mentioned were: the fact that it provided an activity for those at home, including those who might be particularly vulnerable on account of family commitments, or due to being off work sick, unemployed or agoraphobic; the absence of stigma and the fact that it was something that could be done in secret; the fact that it could be good for a relatively inexperienced gambler who might be encouraged initially by simply playing for points before progressing to playing for real money; the possibility of socialising safely through forums and chat rooms; the ease of spending money when it isn't real money in your hand that you are spending; the possibilities for playing multiple games simultaneously; and the relative lack of external checks or controls – it was easy to hide the fact that one had been logged on to a gambling site; and constant pop-ups and emails encouraging gambling which made it harder to give up. But the most obvious factor was the sheer accessibility of internet gambling, day or night:

> I think it was maybe just about access. You know, I could play for 24 hours at a time without even having to get dressed, without even having to go out, it was brilliant it was . . . And there's so few controls . . . It's just far too easy, you know, just to log onto a site.
>
> I don't think I would have got into the gambling side of poker without it actually being online . . . I think it's because I enjoyed it, because it was so easy to do, it was online . . . it's so immediate and it's just always there . . . And the fact that you can access it at any time is good . . . You can get up at two, three in the morning and again, you know, any time of the day you can play.

Don't forget senior citizens

Older people are another group who are not normally associated with gambling – indeed the 2006/07 British prevalence survey confirmed that they are a relatively low gambling group – and their gambling has rarely been a focus of study. A few studies have now started to appear and there is some evidence, from Australia, New Zealand and the USA, that when older people gamble, there may be amongst them a particularly vulnerable group – those on modest, fixed incomes, who are now without a partner and relatively socially isolated, and who have access to play on gambling machines, either because they are accessible in their immediate vicinity, because they have their own transport or because they go on organised day trips to a casino.[73] One of the most thorough studies was carried out with those in their 60s and over who were attending one of a number of clubs, in Brisbane, Queensland, where they played gambling machines. The most popular reasons they gave for gambling were to support the club, to win money and to make friends and socialise. But a third or more said they played machines in order to reduce boredom and similar proportions reported isolation as a motivation for gambling and to 'forget problems when . . . depressed or stressed'. One in seven stated that they played machines to reduce suffering from pain.[74]

Assessing the prevalence of problem gambling

It is difficult to arrive at a valid figure for the numbers of people who have gambling problems. Because such difficulties, like others which involve excessive behaviour or over-consumption, are ones that people typically fall into gradually, often over an extended period of time, it is difficult to be at all precise about when behaviour that is frequent, heavy or habitual has crossed a threshold and become a definite problem. Many people may remain for long periods of time in a 'grey area',[75] somewhere between non-problematic gambling and gambling that clearly constitutes a problem. Whilst some clinicians and epidemiologists believe that 'pathological gamblers' are a distinct group, qualitatively different from others, it is probably true to say that most people who have studied the matter carefully are of the view that problem gambling lies on a continuum, with all shades of problem, from slight to severe, represented. A very important conclusion follows from that assumption, and it is one that is generally not faced up to by policy makers. If problem gambling lies on a continuum, then any attempt to put a single figure on the number of people in the population with gambling problems is bound to be arbitrary: it depends entirely on where the threshold is placed along the continuum.

That rather fundamental, but mostly unacknowledged, difficulty is compounded by the likely way in which the population is distributed along the problem continuum. As I have tried to illustrate in Figure 3.1, the shape of the distribution is not flat, or bi-modal, but is almost certainly strongly skewed towards the severe problem end of the continuum. Skewed distribution curves, like the ones shown in the figure, are ubiquitous in the realms of economics (personal incomes for example), geography (sizes of towns and cities or lengths of rivers, for example) and human behaviour. This particularly applies to behaviours that have a propensity to get out of hand and become excessive.

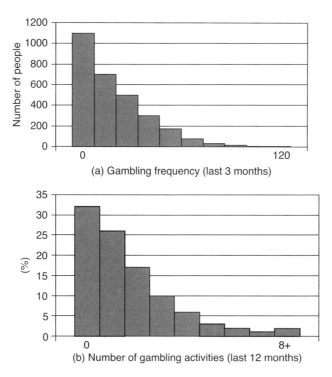

Figure 3.1   Examples of skewed gambling distribution curves[76] a) Norwegian data on gambling frequency; (reproduced with permission from Lund, 2008) b) The numbers of different types of gambling engaged in during the last 12 months according to the results of the 2006/07 British Gambling Prevalence Survey

Researchers have been familiar for some time with skewed frequency distribution curves for alcohol consumption for example: the majority of people in most populations drink relatively moderately but as one moves to the right along the curve we find an ever-decreasing proportion of people who drink more and more excessively compared to the norm. Only in the tail of the curve do we find people whose drinking is so deviant that the problematic nature of their drinking is clear to everyone. It would be very surprising indeed if the extent of involvement in gambling was not distributed in the population according to this skewed distribution law. The figure shows some Norwegian results on gambling frequency and British results on the numbers of different types of gambling activity that people engage in.

The conclusion one has to draw is again one that policy makers, in their enthusiasm for a single prevalence estimate for problem gambling, have probably not appreciated or have chosen to ignore. Because the distribution curve falls away towards the severe end, it follows that those at the most clearly problematic end of the continuum are actually outnumbered by those whose behaviour is less deviant. The grey area turns out to be rather large. If it is reasonable to think of some people having a slight degree of addiction to gambling, others addiction of moderate degree, and yet others a severe addiction, then in all likelihood it is the first of those three groups that is the most numerous and the third the smallest. Any attempt to draw a single line, above which we define people as problem gamblers, is therefore not only arbitrary but actually leaves out of account the majority of people who are experiencing some degree of gambling addiction, albeit less severe. A number of attempts have been made to at least acknowledge this problem conceptually; for example, by referring to the more severe 'pathological gambling' and the less severe 'problem gambling' or 'at-risk gambling'.

None of that has stopped the search for an estimate of *the* prevalence of problem gambling. Of course that is understandable. Government wants a yardstick for planning treatment services and monitoring the effects of policy changes (sceptics might say in the hope that they can raise gambling revenue without having to spend much on treatment); advocates for problem gamblers and their families want evidence that can be used in their campaigns for treatment and prevention; and gambling promoters hope for evidence that gambling problems are confined to such a small minority that no interference in the promotion and expansion of gambling is justified.

The generally accepted way of arriving at a prevalence estimate is to ask a representative sample of the population to answer a series of standard questions each of which addresses a different facet of a gambling problem. From the Gamblers Anonymous 20 questions onwards there has been a large number of such sets of questions. Since none is perfect, for the British Gambling Prevalence Survey (BGPS) in 2006/07 two sets of questions were used, one based on the DSM-IV criteria and the other the Canadian Problem Gambling Severity Index (PGSI).[77] The two scales, although rather similar in a number of ways, are based on somewhat different assumptions. The ten DSM questions are based on a clinical diagnostic model: each question is designed to reflect one of the American Psychiatric Association's criteria for making a diagnosis of pathological gambling. The nine items of the more recently devised Canadian PGSI are based on the idea of a continuum of problem gambling. Whereas the DSM-based scale results in a tally of the number of 'symptoms' (out of ten) that an individual declares, the PGSI, which is becoming popular internationally, produces a broader range of scores (up to a maximum of 27). It may reasonably be asked by what process the criteria and questions that constitute these scales are chosen. That could take us into a long and technical discussion. Suffice it to say here that the process draws on a consensus of expert opinion followed by a lot of hard and detailed work to arrive at a set of standard questions that reflect different aspects of what is known about problem gambling, that avoid too much redundancy, but that at the same time result in a set of questions that cohere (i.e. they are assessing a single construct not several unrelated ones), and are sufficiently straightforward to be understandable to a wide range of people in different regions and countries (and which are suitable for translation into other languages). The resulting scales are designed to be high on sensitivity (i.e. they avoid false negatives as far as is possible) and on specificity (i.e. they avoid false positives).

It is often argued that, however sound such sets of questions may be from a psychometric point of view, the fact remains that they require people not only to recognise that they have these elements of problem gambling but also that they are prepared to admit to them in the course of a survey. Whilst that is undeniable, it can also be pointed out that a set of nine or ten well chosen and tested questions, administered in a standard format in an anonymous survey, is likely to be much more sensitive than simply asking a person whether he or she has a gambling problem – which produces a much lower estimate of prevalence.

There still remains, of course, the problem of setting the cut-off points – which at the end of the day are bound to be arbitrary – for defining problem gambling. This is a matter of standard international convention, based on a consensus of expert opinion, and is an area of some controversy. For the 2006/07 British survey we adopted the convention for the DSM-based scale, which has been used by many, but not all, researchers, that affirmative answers to three or more of the ten questions were indicative of a gambling problem. In the case of the PGSI the following classification suggested by the originators was used: problem gambler (a score of eight or more), moderate risk gambler (between three and seven), low risk gambler (one or two) and non-problem gambler (zero).

The results for Britain in 2006/07 are summarised in Table 3.2. How one interprets those results depends very much on one's point of view. In some quarters the overall population estimated adult prevalence of around 0.5–0.6% has been interpreted as indicating that problem gambling is on a small scale, confined to a 'tiny minority' of people who are, so the argument goes, perhaps in any case specially vulnerable personalities. That interpretation fits nicely with a view of gambling as a normal, largely unproblematic, leisure activity to which people in the modern world are entitled to have access without too much constraint, where the freedoms of the majority should not be limited by consideration for the weaknesses of a minority, and where enterprise and innovation in the provision of gambling should be as freely encouraged as in any other sphere (see Chapter 6 on Gambling Discourses).

There is of course a quite other way of looking at this. First, a 12-month prevalence of 0.5–0.6% is in public health terms substantial (questions were asked in relation to the 'last 12 months': if questions had been asked about a longer period of time, or even about a person's lifetime up to the present, as is sometimes done, then the figure would obviously have been higher). Table 3.3 lists just a few of the many other conditions, each of which has given rise to a

Table 3.2 Estimates of the 12 months, prevalence of problem gambling amongst British adults in 2006/07[78]

Estimate 1, according to the ten questions based on the DSM-IV diagnostic criteria
0.6% (confidence interval 0.5–0.8%) or between 236,500 and 378,000 adults

Estimate 2, according to the nine questions of the Canadian PGSI
0.5% (confidence interval 0.4–0.8%) or between 189,000 and 378,000 adults

Table 3.3   Other conditions with comparable
prevalence which give rise to public concern[79]

e.g. drug misuse
schizophrenia
motor neurone disease
Parkinson's disease
Autism

substantial public health concern, and which have prevalence rates of a similar
order or lower. The figures translate into around 300,000 Britons aged 16 years
or over – a sizeable number by any reckoning. Bear in mind, also, that 0.5–0.6
is the percentage of the whole adult population including senior citizens who
are much less likely than others to gamble, members of certain ethnic minority
groups who are forbidden by their religion to gamble, as well as most of the
rest of the population who either had been engaged in no gambling at all in
the previous year or who had been confining their gambling to the National
Lottery. The percentage of those who did any gambling in the last year who
scored as problem gamblers was higher, 0.8–0.9%, and if the figure is calculated
excluding those who only gambled on the NL draw, it becomes 1.2–1.3%.

Once we start to look at sub-groups then we begin to identify sectors of the
population who appeared to be particularly at risk. For a start, men had a much
higher prevalence than women, and particularly young men aged between 16
and 34. Table 3.4 shows some of the sub-groups with higher prevalence rates.
This strongly suggests that risk for problem gambling is far more than just
a question of vulnerable personalities but is at least partly to do with social
and demographic groups to which people belong. This is something to which
we shall return in Chapter 5. Another issue that we shall need to return to is
the way in which rates of problem gambling vary according to the kinds of
gambling that people engage in. Rates are very uneven: for example, those who
bet on fixed odds betting machines (a comparatively small group, who tend to
engage in other forms of gambling as well) had a much higher rate of problem
gambling than those (a larger number) who bet on horse races (11.2% versus
1.7% according to the DSM scale).

Another important point that has been made is that prevalence rates, which
give equal weight to everyone in the whole population, do not in themselves
answer a somewhat different question, which is: What proportion of all the
gambling that takes place, say in a 12-month period, can be said to be of a
compulsive or problematic kind? Or, to put it another way: What proportion of
the nation's gambling is being carried out by individuals who themselves have
gambling problems? Because of the skewed frequency distribution of gambling,
as shown earlier in Figure 3.1, it is evident that the heaviest consumers consume
much more than their fair share of the product, in this case gambling. A small
insight into this was provided by an interesting survey of British casino patrons
carried out by Susan Fisher in the mid-1990s.[81] The survey was commissioned
by five of the largest British casino firms and took place in a representative

Table 3.4 Selected sub-groups of the British adult population which have higher than average problem gambling prevalence rates[80]

Sub-group	Prevalence %	Total size of the sub-group in the sample*
Those who have gambled at all in the last year	0.9	5622
Younger men (aged 16–34) who have gambled at all in the last year	2.4	680
Those who gambled at all in the last week	1.3	3644
Those who, in the last year, gambled on:		
slot machines	2.6	1139
horse races (excl. online)	1.7	1470
dog races (excl. online)	5.2	404
online	7.4	191
table games in a casino	5.2	298
private betting	2.3	796
Those who gambled on four or more gambling activities in the last year	3.0	1149
Those who gambled two days/week or more on at least one activity last year	2.9	1228
Those who rate their general health as only fair or as bad/very bad	1.4	1789
Current cigarette smokers	1.4	1904
Those consuming 15 or more units of alcohol at least one day last week	2.4	462
Those who had a parent whose gambling was a problem	3.3	230
Those who said they started gambling at age 15 or younger	1.6	1003

*unweighted figures

sample of 40 casinos in London and the provinces. Over 1,000 people were interviewed, of whom no fewer than 16% scored as problem gamblers on a DSM-based scale similar to the one used in the national surveys. That is a staggeringly high percentage and considerably higher than the 5–6% of last year casino visitors who scored as problem gamblers on the DSM scale in each of the two national surveys. The explanation for the discrepancy lies, of course, in the fact that regular, and therefore more likely to be problematic, casino gamblers were present in the casinos in relatively large numbers when the interviews were carried out. The same is probably true of any gambling venue: those present at any moment include disproportionate numbers of those with gambling problems.

Others have tried to estimate what contribution problem gamblers make to the total volume of gambling that takes place, basing their estimates on the amounts that people say they spend on gambling. Australian estimates, based on the careful calculations carried out for the very comprehensive 1999 Australian Productivity Commission report, and confirmed by other studies since then, are that approximately one third of all national gambling profits comes from the pockets of problem gamblers,[82] and a Finnish estimate based on survey findings produced an almost identical figure.[83]

Some, especially spokespeople for sectors of the gambling industry, have argued that Britain's problem gambling rate is low compared to other countries and that this goes to show how responsible British gambling promoters are, and that regulations on gambling are quite sufficient as they are and probably should be lightened as time goes on. But the figures from around the world hardly show that. Although it does appear that rates are higher in the USA and Australia, and in a number of Asian cities that have had a reputation for relatively easy access to gambling, figures from other European countries that have carried out surveys and from Canada and New Zealand have produced rather similar estimates to the British ones.[84] Comparison is in any case difficult because it is not always the same set of problem gambling questions that have been asked and, furthermore, the margin of error around the prevalence estimate (the confidence interval) is usually quite wide, so differences between country estimates need to be substantial before we can have confidence that the differences are real ones.

Lastly, and very importantly, it needs to be pointed out that the BGPS was an adult survey, leaving out under 16 year olds. Adolescents, as discussed earlier, are equally if not more at risk than adults. The best estimate of the adolescent prevalence of problem gambling in Britain comes from a survey of nearly 10,000 12–15 year olds from over 100 schools in England and Wales.[85] Carried out by the same Susan Fisher who conducted the casino study referred to earlier, it used a junior version of the DSM-based scale and produced a prevalence rate of no less than 5.6%. This is a figure several times the estimated adult prevalence, but is very close to figures produced in similar adolescent surveys carried out in other countries.[86] It may even be a slight underestimate because only fruit-machine and scratchcard gambling were asked about. There may have been another biasing effect – of unknown proportions – because the survey was carried out in the schools during school time and hence any pupil who truanted that day could not be included. Since truancy is known to be correlated with gambling this may have been a further factor leading to an underestimate of prevalence.

Exactly the same kind of argument is used by some of those who remain sceptical about the value of prevalence estimates based on surveys such as the BGPS which inevitably have a sizeable refusal or non-response rate. The National Centre for Social Research, which carried out the BGPS, has looked very carefully at the question of non-response and the possibility of bias.[87] In some cases it is possible to make a correction. For example, young men, who tend to gamble more than other groups, also have a higher survey non-response rate. But because it is known from national figures how many young men there should be in the sample, it is possible to give greater weight to the survey replies of those young men who do take part and hence to slightly correct the prevalence rate upwards to compensate for the lack of those young men who did not take part. But that can only be done in the case of a few variables such as sex and age. How can one correct, for example, for the fact that the survey researchers had less success with households living in flats rather than houses, and in relatively deprived rather than better-off areas? At the end of the day there is really no way of knowing whether those who cannot be contacted, compared to those who are reached, are more or less heavy or problematic gamblers. It could work either way. As already mentioned in the previous chapter, survey researchers reported some people declining to take part on the grounds that they were not gamblers and therefore had no interest in completing the survey. On the other hand, those who are at all familiar with problem gambling are bound to wonder whether people with severe gambling problems are more likely than other people to be away from home or otherwise unavailable or disinclined to take part when the researcher calls. Those living away from home, including anyone who is in hospital or prison at the time of the survey, is necessarily excluded. In the case of prisoners there is evidence that prevalence of problem gambling is high compared to the rest of the population, for both men and women prisoners. The latest evidence comes from a pilot study of 200 prisoners at one British male prison. Using the PGSI, the rate of problem gambling was found to be no less than 14%, with a further 17% scoring in the moderate risk group – figures far in excess of those found in the British general population.[88] All in all, some take the view that prevalence estimates are inevitably underestimates. But there is no way of knowing for sure.

Chapter summary

As was the case for tobacco addiction, *the world has been slow to appreciate the addictive properties of gambling.* That individuals could develop an addiction to gambling was recognised by some Victorian novelists, a few early twentieth-century psychiatrists and occasionally in autobiographical writings from earlier centuries. But it was in the 1960s that a number of clinicians started to describe compulsive gambling amongst their patients, head teachers started to express concern about their pupils' addiction to machine gambling, and Gamblers Anonymous arose in the USA and started to spread to other countries. Pathological gambling was recognised by the American Psychiatric Association in 1980. The chapter took a brief look at the strange phenomenon of self-exclusion from gambling venues. The fact that gamblers in large numbers have sought to exclude themselves from gambling, and have sought the help of gambling providers in doing so, illustrates very well the fact that gambling is no ordinary commodity but is addictive and therefore highly dangerous.

The largest group of people who know about gambling addiction at first hand – *partners, parents, children, and other affected family members – have been even more neglected* than have problem gamblers themselves. What knowledge there is about family effects shows gambling addiction to be highly corrosive of family health and the well-being of family members. The chapter also considered adolescence as a time of high risk for gambling problems; women as a group increasingly at risk due to the 'feminisation' of gambling; and older people, also, as a group whose vulnerability to problem gambling should not be under-estimated.

Gambling addiction lies on a continuum. Those in the 'grey area', whose level of addiction is moderate, are more numerous than those whose addiction is severe. Any dividing line, above which people might be said to be 'problem gamblers', is bound to be arbitrary, but that does not stop researchers and their backers from attempting to put a figure on the prevalence of problem gambling. Based on a consensus about where the threshold might best be placed, the 2006/07 British Gambling Prevalence Survey estimated the 12-months adult prevalence of problem gambling to be 0.5–0.6% of the whole population (or 0.8–0.9% of all those who had done any gambling at all in the last 12 months), or *a total of just over 300,000 adults with gambling problems*. These are large numbers in public health terms. The estimate is lower than figures for the USA and Australia and similar to those from other European countries and from Canada and New Zealand. The figures provide minimum estimates of risk. It is possible that those with gambling problems are more likely than others to be missed in such surveys. Certain sub-groups of the population, such as young men and those who gamble frequently or on several types of gambling, have much higher prevalence rates. *Surveys of adolescents suggest a prevalence of problem gambling several times higher than that of adults.* Surveys carried out in gambling venues, and estimates based on the distribution of spending on gambling in the population, suggest that those with gambling problems contribute up to a third of all gambling profits.

In this chapter evidence from a number of sources has been adduced to show that gambling can be addictive. But, it might be asked, how can that be the case? Addiction to alcohol, tobacco and other strong drugs is all very well, but in the case of gambling no substance is ingested. The following chapter sets out the view of addiction which is supported by recent advances in knowledge, according to which gambling is embraced as one of the common forms of addiction. Indeed, in some ways gambling can be seen as the purest form of addiction, not just peripheral to modern understanding of addiction, but central to it.

4

Modern Addiction Theory
Applied to Gambling

How can we explain the large numbers of people whose gambling becomes, to one degree or another, out of control – perhaps in the region of quarter to a third of a million adults in Britain at the present time, plus further tens of thousands of adolescents? How do we explain the strange phenomenon of gambling self-exclusion or the popularity of Gamblers Anonymous? It seems that some people have a strong need to curtail their gambling but at the same time such an attachment to it that they need outside help of some kind in order to manage it. The explanation is simple. Gambling is addictive. Or, to put it more precisely, gambling, like alcohol and a number of other drugs and behaviours, carries the potential for addiction. It is dangerous. Not everyone who gambles succumbs to the danger, but many do. In this chapter I want to try to explain what addiction is and how gambling fits that description. This is an important task because our thoughts about addiction have been so dominated by the idea of 'drug' or 'substance' addiction that it still seems strange to many people to think of something like gambling as being equally addictive. Even some addiction experts still only pay lip-service to the idea or believe that gambling, by comparison with drugs of addiction, is only mildly dependence-producing. In fact, that position rests on a now outdated view of addiction. According to modern understanding drugs constitute only one sub-class of the addictions and gambling is increasingly being seen – as I and others like me have been arguing for some time[1] – as one of the core addictions. This is far from being an academic debate. For those, like the present writer, who are alarmed by the spread of opportunities for gambling, the idea that gambling products are in and of themselves dangerous is central to the debate about how society should deal with gambling. Those who argue for minimal restraint on access to gambling are likely to dismiss such a view, arguing that any problems

An Unsafe Bet? The Dangerous Rise of Gambling and the Debate We Should be Having   By Jim Orford
© 2011 John Wiley & Sons, Ltd

associated with gambling are due, not to the inherent characteristics of the product itself, but rather to the irresponsibility or special vulnerability of a very small proportion of individual gamblers. They will wish to challenge the idea that gambling is addictive.

In this chapter I shall attempt to summarise modern addiction theory using as little technical language as possible. There are a number of strands to the total picture and each is necessary to fully understand why gambling can be so addictive. Let us begin with a definition of addiction. There are many such definitions and most to my way of thinking are unnecessarily complicated. Broken down to essentials, addiction is:

> An attachment to a particular object of consumption, so strong that the person finds it very difficult to curtail consumption despite the considerable harm that it is causing.[2]

Addiction is, then, a state of strong attachment which cannot easily be given up. There are a number of common indications that someone has developed such a strong or excessive appetite for a particular object of consumption (see the accompanying Figure 4.1 for a summary). Some of the indications come in the form of behaviour – engaging in consumption very frequently or in large quantity for example. Gambling several times a week, or with more than a modest amount of money, for example, are found in surveys such as the 2006/07 British prevalence survey to be associated with other indications of problem gambling.[3] Other signs of strong attachment are mental – a preoccupation with thinking about the activity, and often strong 'craving' for it, is a core component. We shall see later how cognitive elements are particularly salient in the case of a strong addictive attachment to gambling. The third facet is emotional: a particular form of consumption has come to play such an important role in

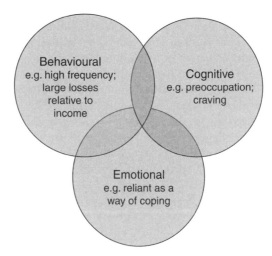

Figure 4.1 Signs of a strong addictive attachment to gambling

a person's life that he or she has become emotionally dependent on it. It may seem fanciful to put it this way, but the relationship of an addicted person to his or her object of addiction has sometimes be likened to a 'marriage' – or perhaps it would be more apt to refer to it as an illicit relationship since its effects are so destructive of positive aspects of life, including family life.[4]

How we acquire strong habits that are difficult to break

This state of strong behavioural-cognitive-emotional attachment is as characteristic of excessive gambling as it is of excessive alcohol consumption, drug addiction or binge eating disorder (bulimia). But how is that so? Why should gambling, which might otherwise be thought quite innocuous, carry the danger of the development of such a state? The simplest answer, and it is one that accords well with modern views of the origins of addictions more generally, lies in the way people acquire and maintain habits. William James,[5] considered by many to be the father of modern psychology, was adamant that the acquisition of positive habits, and the avoidance of developing negative ones, was at the heart of healthy human development. So important are habits thought to be that some would go so far as to characterise the human being as essentially a 'habit machine'.

The basic principle behind the theory of how habits are acquired is one with which every first year psychology student becomes thoroughly familiar. It is the idea that people become 'conditioned' as a consequence of the rewards – more technically referred to as 'reinforcement' – that follow from an action. We 'learn' to repeat those actions that are followed by rewarding consequences. This is generally known as *operant learning* or Skinnerian conditioning, after B. F. Skinner's and others' work with animals such as pigeons learning to peck at coloured panels or monkeys learning to press levers to obtain rewards in the form of food. Virtually all theories of addiction would put that basic mechanism somewhere near the centre of their thinking on the subject. In essence, addiction develops because consumption of the potentially addictive product is so rewarding. Gambling fits this idea particularly well. In fact it may be easier to see how gambling might become addictive on that basis than to appreciate the potentially addictive nature of many of the drugs of addiction. Gambling, after all, is motivated in the first instance by reward in the form of money. The latter has been described by behavioural psychologists as probably the most 'generalised reinforcer' of all, since it can be used in exchange for any one or more of a myriad of other things that are rewarding in themselves. Can anyone doubt the power of money to shape people's behaviour? Money is obviously central to gambling. There have been many clever psychological theories of problem gambling which minimise the role of winning money. One of the better known, of little more than historical interest now, was the psychoanalytic theory that compulsive gamblers actually had a neurotic 'wish to lose' in order to punish themselves. In fact, one of the commonest reasons that gamblers give for gambling, particularly in the early stages, is the wish to *win* money.[6] It is often said, but more difficult to prove, that a big win early on in a person's history of gambling is a risk factor for later uncontrolled gambling.[7] Even in the later stages of addictive gambling, when early sources of motivation have become overlaid with a whole complex of other motives consequent upon the problems that gambling has brought in its wake, gamblers will often still say that gambling to win is a big factor.

But how, it might be asked, can a strong, difficult to break habit be built on the idea of gambling being financially rewarded when, as everyone knows, the gambling operator must make some money and the odds are always to some degree or another stacked against the gambler? Mostly gambles result in losses, not winnings. Shouldn't this result in developing the habit of avoiding gambling rather than repeating it? Herein, of course, lies the central paradox of all addictions. How can people go on repeating actions that appear to be counter-productive for them? We can go a long way to explaining that paradox by recourse to a number of features of operant learning theory which our first year psychology student quickly finds out about. One is usually referred to as the *gradient of reinforcement*. This refers to the greater power of immediate consequences of action to shape future behaviour, in comparison with more delayed consequences. In many forms of gambling, any winnings, and the associated euphoria, arrive almost immediately, whereas the negative consequences of losing may not be apparent for many hours or even later. Wins are likely to promote the habit more strongly than losses restrain it.

The second feature is the *probabilistic* nature of habit learning. It is not that one type of action becomes totally dominant to the exclusion of others, but rather that certain actions gradually become more probable and other incompatible behaviours less so. Operant learning therefore provides part of the explanation for why the development of strongly habitual behaviour such as problem gambling is usually slow and insidious.

One of the most important features of operant learning, and one of clear relevance for gambling, is the fact that the most effective pattern or 'schedule' of reinforcement is one that is *partial or inconsistent* rather than consistent and regular. Skinner and others found that, once established, the best way to maintain a behavioural habit was to put the experimental animal on a 'reinforcement schedule' of a kind that he termed variable-ratio (VR). Under such a regime, not only did the animal have to produce the response (such as pulling a lever) several times before it was rewarded (for example, with food if it was hungry), but the number of responses required to produce reward varied. Under such a reward schedule it is predictable that reward will arrive sooner or later, but exactly when is variable. The relevance to gambling is obvious. Indeed introductory psychology textbooks have frequently given gambling, especially machine gambling, as an illustration of the principles of operant learning. Skinner himself wrote, in his general work *Science and Human Behavior*, 'the efficacy of such schedules in generating high rates [of responding] has long been known to the proprietors of gambling establishments'.[8] In fact, gambling operates on a reinforcement schedule which, although similar to the VR schedule, is different from it in a rather important respect. In the VR schedule, the probability of reward increases with each successive response since the last reward was given. Although many gamblers believe that gambling operates in that way (hence the 'gambler's fallacy' of believing that the probability of heads becomes greater the longer the succession of tails), gambling on games of chance truly corresponds to a random ratio (RR) schedule under which the overall likelihood of a win remains constant. Hence financial reward is even less predictable: the more one plays the greater the chances of having a win, but there is no way of knowing when, and the chances of a win on the next play do not increase the greater the run of losses.

There is a great deal more to human habit learning than just operant conditioning, as we shall see, but by itself alone that basic type of learning provides a powerful process for entrapping the unwary in a habit that may become very difficult to break. Skinner and his colleagues were able to demonstrate how their reinforcement schedules could result in animals continuing to emit behavioural responses at a high and exhausting rate, often to the neglect of other behaviours such as eating or drinking, even though the rewards they received had become highly infrequent and irregular. One could be forgiven for thinking that that looks very like human addiction.

Gambling is one of the powerful mood modifiers

Operant conditioning, of basic importance though it is, is only the beginning of the account of the set of processes – summarised in Table 4.1 – that between them are powerful enough to create a behavioural addiction. One layer of complexity is added if we take note of the evidence that emotional rewards, in the form of pleasurable modifications of mood, may be just as important in the

Table 4.1   The set of processes which between them are powerful enough to create an addiction

Operant or reward learning
    powerful schedules of partial reinforcement (e.g. random ratio)
    financial, mood change, and social rewards

Classical Pavlovian or cue conditioning
    previously neutral stimuli acquire incentive meaning

Cognitions
    beliefs, expectancies, mental biases, capturing of attention and memory
    biased informational processing

Conflict, approach-avoidance, and its consequences
    secondary addictive processes
    harassed decision-making, chasing losses, acute distress

Brain effects
    release of dopamine in the mesolimbic brain area
    overwhelms neo-cortical reflective or executive control

case of gambling as they are for drug taking, and may be equally important as financial rewards from gambling.[9] There is common agreement that gambling is like a 'drug' in this respect. One of the comparatively early interview studies of compulsive gamblers concluded, '*All* compulsive gamblers . . . talk of the action aspect of gambling. It is described in terms of "getting my rocks off", "adrenaline flowing", and most often compared to sexual excitement . . .'.[10] Another research group found that the pattern of responses of problem gamblers to a scale of emotions previously used with groups of drug takers was most like that associated with the taking of stimulants such as amphetamines.[11] A number of studies have found substantial increases in heart rate when gamblers are monitored gambling in a casino, while playing gambling machines or during a horse race on which bets had been placed.[12] Some of this physiological arousal may be directly related to the uncertainty and risk involved in gambling, and hence may be directly linked to the financial aspect. But of course there are other aspects of gambling settings – race commentaries, spinning reels, all that goes to make up the atmosphere of the casino or race track – that are arousing in themselves, therefore of advantage to the gambling operator, and partial contributors to habit development.

One of the things that is often said about the power of alcohol – and although the details are different much the same has been said about tobacco smoking – is that the power of the substance lies in its versatility. It is a powerful mood modifier but it can produce different emotional effects for different people and for the same person on different occasions. The same may be true for gambling. It has been pointed out many times that gambling can be motivated, not only by 'action seeking' or positive 'mood enhancement' (e.g. because it is exciting; to get a high feeling) but also by 'escape seeking' or 'coping' (e.g. to forget your worries; because it helps when you are feeling nervous or depressed).[13] There is evidence that men's gambling is more motivated by enhancement and women's by coping.[14] It has been reported on a number of occasions that those motivated by coping or escape describe their gambling as an 'an anaesthetic', a 'hypnotic', being in a 'trance', feeling 'like a different person' or feeling 'outside [oneself] . . . as in a dream'.[15]

There is a yet further set of motives – which we may loosely refer to as 'social' – which are known to be of the utmost importance in the development of alcohol, tobacco and other drug-using habits, and this set of motives appears to be important for gamblers too[16] (e.g. because it's what most of your friends do when you get together; to be sociable). The social rewards provided by gambling at the horse racing track for people who occupy different positions in the multitude of social worlds associated with that most traditional of all forms of British gambling, can scarcely be doubted. But it has long been pointed out, more generally, that gambling in a variety of settings can offer individuals powerful rewards of a social psychological kind. They include the opportunity to demonstrate the exercise of control, composure and the making of apparently rational decisions, 'beating the system', being seen to engage in risk taking, exhibiting valued traits such as courage, gameness, integrity, the opportunity to appear knowledgeable, even to prove one's superiority.[17] Such observations come from settings as diverse as Nevada casinos[18] and East End London betting shops.[19] Others have observed more mundane social rewards of gambling. For example, in a casino in Edmonton, Canada, it was observed that players could watch television, eat, meet friends and drink alcohol as well as gamble, and would often remain after losing all their own money to watch others play, to give advice to friends or to borrow money to get back into the action.[20] An observational study of young gambling machine players in one British 'amusement arcade' showed how socially rewarding that kind of gambling could be for some young players, whom the research referred to as 'the Kings', who had developed a 'quasi-professional' role and reputation as highly regarded masters of fruit machine playing skills.[21]

The sights and sounds of gambling: the power of conditioning

Whatever the mix of primary rewards that gambling can provide – financial, mood alteration, coping and social – the account of how habits are acquired and can grow into addictions needs to incorporate the way in which the numerous 'stimuli' associated with the addictive activity become conditioned and themselves take on rewarding properties. This is what is known as Pavlovian or *classical conditioning* and it constitutes a powerful mechanism whereby we build up a whole network of associations that contribute to the development and maintenance of a strongly habitual attachment. The important point is that the stimuli or 'cues' which we are talking about here carried no special or intrinsic value until they were repeatedly experienced in association with the rewarding object. By repeatedly associating the ringing of a bell with the presentation of food to a hungry dog, Pavlov was able to show that the bell, previously of no special interest to the dog, became so significant that the dog salivated when it rang, much as it would do when food actually arrived. Later experiments showed that animals had a preference for the particular place where an injection of a reinforcing drug had been administered: the place itself then had the capacity to attract the animal even in the absence of further drug injections. These formerly neutral cues, such as places and sounds, now themselves have the capacity to motivate behaviour. This is what is sometimes termed 'incentive conditioning'.[22]

There is nothing intrinsically interesting about a rolled up piece of paper with flaked tobacco inside it, but for someone who has developed an addiction to smoking tobacco cigarettes, the cigarette, along with the associated smell of tobacco smoke, plus people and places associated with smoking, have all long since ceased to be neutral and have taken on a special meaning for the smoker as part of the attachment that has developed towards cigarettes and everything associated with them. Injecting drug users have often spoken of their attraction to needles and the rest of the paraphernalia associated with their drug taking[23] and there have now been a large number of so-called cue-reactivity studies in which people addicted to heroin, cocaine, alcohol or tobacco reported increased craving for their preferred substance, and increases in heart rate and sweating and a decrease in skin temperature – all physiological signs of increased arousal – in the presence solely of cues associated with their particular object of addiction.[24]

Dostoevsky's autobiographical novel *The Gambler* provides a perfect example: 'Even while approaching the gambling hall, two rooms away, as soon as I begin to hear the clinking of money being poured out, I almost go into convulsions'.[25] A young British fruit machine addict described the same phenomenon:

> Although winning money was the first thing that attracted me to playing fruit machines, this was gradually converted to lights, sounds and excitement. I always received a great thrill from new machines with new ideas and new lights and sounds.[26]

An Australian study was one of the first to show this experimentally. Problem machine gamblers (playing Australian 'poker machines' or pokies), compared to purely social gamblers, showed significantly more physiological arousal when watching a video of poker machine playing taking place, and also when being instructed to imagine that they were winning at poker machine playing. The same was not true when engaged in a neutral task or even when watching a video of a non-preferred form of gambling (horse racing in this case).[27]

The important part played by cognition: thinking, attending, remembering

Up to this point most of what has been said about the development of a strong habitual attachment has rested on behavioural ideas that have been known and understood for quite some time. The principles were first demonstrated in animal experiments. It is now time to turn to a part of the whole picture of addiction which is more uniquely human and which has come much more to the fore in recent years. Modern theories of addiction give as much prominence to cognitive processes – thought, attention and memory processes – as they do to Skinnerian or Pavlovian conditioning. How people think about the objects of their addictions, how they attend to them and to the cues associated with them, and how they store relevant memories, are all now considered to be of the essence when it comes to understanding how certain activities can become the objects of addiction. This part of the picture is probably of particular importance for gambling.

Unlike other animals, humans have enormous capacity to dwell mentally on their behaviour including the objects of their habitual attachments. Once thoughts or memories of such an object are elicited, rumination about the object and its pleasures becomes possible. This process of 'cognitive elaboration', as it has been called, has the capacity to further bolster the addictive habit.[28] Some of this elaboration may be thought of as a kind of 'self-talk'. As an activity becomes more habitual, and associations with cues of different kinds become stronger and more diverse, so are thoughts likely to become more frequent which support the activity. Such self-statements take a variety of forms, but can include any of the following: 'Doing X is the only way I get to feel . . .', 'All men like me do X', 'If he's going to be like that then I'm entitled to X', 'If I didn't do X, then I'd probably do Y', 'X is one of the best things in life'. Habitual activities may become 'over-valued' in the process. Such thoughts may reside at any level of consciousness: they may be publicly stated to others, kept private, may only be semi-conscious, or scarcely be within a person's consciousness at all.

A related and now much studied aspect of addiction has been the 'expectancies' that people develop about the effects that consumption or activity will have for them. It has consistently been shown that those who are heavy and/or problematic consumers of drugs of various kinds are more likely than other people to hold positive expectancies about the effects of their drugs (once problems develop they are also more likely than other people to hold negative expectancies, but that is another matter).[29] They are also more likely to hold a specific expectancy that use of their preferred drug will have a positive mood altering effect even when the evidence of such an effect in reality is lacking.[30] One research group in the USA asked a group of medium security prisoners (a group containing a relatively high proportion of problem gamblers) about their gambling expectancies using a Gambling Expectancy Effects Questionnaire. The problem gamblers had significantly more positive expectations of gambling (e.g. gambling for money makes me: 'important', 'expert', 'in control') than was the case for non-problem gamblers or non-gamblers; and also significantly more expectancies of mood change of an arousing kind (e.g. gambling for money makes me: 'excited').[31]

Much of this mental support for a strong habit may have its beginnings prior to a person having any direct experience to go on. Social learning theory has emphasised how habits are acquired, not solely through direct experience of reinforcement and cue conditioning, but also via modelling one's behaviour on that of others, particularly on the behaviour of people who are well known, loved or admired. Cognitive social learning theory added the idea of picking up from other people perceptions and expectations.[32] For example, it has been shown that children have already acquired definite expectations about the effects of alcohol long before their teenage years.[33] This seems to be true for gambling as well. The results of both the 1999/2000 and the 2006/07 British national surveys showed regular parental gambling to be one of the factors most strongly associated with the likelihood of the person having become a problem gambler.[34] Even more relevant to the present discussion, the second of those surveys found regular parental gambling to be one of the factors most strongly associated with a person holding more positive attitudes towards gambling generally[35] (attitudes towards gambling were not asked about in the first survey). Even clearer evidence that perceptions and expectancies are already in formation early in life comes from an in-depth interview study of problem gamblers.[36] When talking about their earlier experiences with gambling, nearly all emphasised the key role played by other people, particularly family members and close friends, and most particularly parents. Although, exceptionally, motivation to try gambling was said to have been a reaction to parental disapproval of gambling, it was much more often the case that families had set a norm for gambling, creating an impression that it was acceptable and a natural activity, often demonstrating and coaching youngsters about how to gamble, conveying a positive image of it, taking a keen interest in it and making it appear as an attractive activity. For example:

> I remember my dad coming in on the odd time saying he'd won a £100 jackpot [on the fruit machines] . . . I remember thinking ooh how great I wish I could play those (Female, 35 years).
>   To me [accompanying my father to the bookie's] was just an everyday thing . . . like with the shop[ping], or go[ing] up the cash and carry with him – it's just one of them things that's gotta be done. It was a part of our life like . . . You know, see him taking money off people . . . [I] just thought that's the way life goes on like (Male, 39 years).

That is fertile cognitive ground on which to start building a strong attachment. For some, early experiences of winning quickly bolstered their developing thoughts about gambling. One person, for example, recalled being positively surprised at 'How easy it was to make money at gambling', and another commented, 'If you win something like that, then you tend to think there's more to come and you can keep winning'.[37]

Mental biases and gambling

As a result of experience, then, starting even before an individual's first personal engagement in the activity, a whole set of propositions develop about the activity, its rightness or wrongness, how exciting it is, its role in life, and how powerful it is to bring rewards or make one happy. Because modern cognitive science has been so influenced by models of the brain and of computers, such an interconnected pattern of cognitions has been termed by some a 'propositional neural network'.[38] Part of the modern theory of what constitutes addiction is therefore the idea of 'biased propositional networks'.[39] Part of the reason why addictive habits are so hard to break is because the behaviour is supported by a whole set of beliefs and expectations which are, at the very least, biased in a positive direction. This is thought to be true of all addictive habits but it is especially relevant in the case of gambling where the cognitive element has been particularly prominent, in the form of evidence of widespread cognitive biases held by problem gamblers. A variety of forms of bias have been described, some of which are shown in Table 4.2. They fall into two groups. One consists of biases based on a misunderstanding of chance and randomness. Most people have a less than perfect understanding of probability and tend to underestimate high frequency events and overestimate low frequency ones, often falling back on one or more of a variety of 'heuristics', or cognitive rules of thumb, that help them

Table 4.2   Some of the cognitive biases common amongst problem gamblers[42]

Biases based on a misunderstanding of chance and randomness
Overestimate of the probability of events that come easily to mind (e.g. a well-publicised jackpot win)
Assumption that a short run of events should have the appearance of randomness (e.g. the 'gambler's fallacy')
Belief in luck: as a personal trait, a temporary state, or associated with certain numbers or incidental actions (superstitious thinking)
The illusion of control
Belief that skill plays a greater role than it really does
Confidence in one's ability to master a game
Assumption that a 'near miss' means that one has nearly won and will do so soon

come to a decision.[40] One is the 'availability heuristic' whereby the probability of an event is overestimated if the event comes relatively easily to mind; for example, because it is distinctive, arousing or well-publicised – a lottery jackpot is a good example. Another is the 'representativeness heuristic', whereby people assume that a short run of events should look like a long run. For example, sets of lottery numbers that have the appearance of being quite non-random (e.g. 112233 or 123456) are less popular than others. The well-known 'gambler's fallacy' is of the same kind – numbers are thought to be 'due' in roulette because they have not recently come up or numbers that have been drawn in one week's lottery are thought unlikely to come up the next week. This can lead to one form of 'entrapment'; for example, many lottery players feeling trapped into repeatedly betting on the same numbers which have not yet come up. Belief in 'luck' – either as a trait which the gambler believes himself or herself to possess, or as a temporary state – as in a 'run of good luck' – is a common kind of cognitive bias.[41] Bergler, who wrote one of the first books on *The Psychology of Gambling*, and who is better known for his theory of the 'wish to lose', observed over 50 years ago that compulsive gamblers often showed an almost fanatical belief in the possibility of winning and that their recollections of past gambling were often highly selective in favour of recalling successes and forgetting losses.

That takes us on to the second group of cognitive gambling biases, namely the 'illusion of control'.[43] This is in effect a form of biased expectancy, in this case the expectancy of success, which is higher than in reality is the case. Studies of young problem gambling machine players in Britain and in Australia have found that they have a greater belief than others in the role of skill in machine gambling and overestimate the amount they are likely to win.[44] The Australian researchers commented about some of the young men in their study that they seemed to be 'quite naive about gambling in the sense of having over-inflated views about their chances of winning and their role in making winning occur'.[45] Canadian researchers asked machine gamblers to think aloud as they played, finding many examples of apparently irrational statements, such as, 'I won on three rows, I'm going to bet on those rows again, this is a good game', 'I'm getting good at this game. I think I've mastered it', and, 'I'm lucky today, I should buy a lotto ticket'.[46] It has been shown, also, that casino gamblers bet more if they are allowed to be more active in the play (for example, rolling the dice themselves) and that gamblers often develop confidence as they play even when the game they are playing is one of pure chance.[47] There is of course an element of skill, or of bringing knowledge to bear, in some forms of gambling, but an exaggerated belief in one's ability to predict the outcome will be as much a part of the biased propositional network associated with habitual gambling of that kind as it is of games of pure chance. Gambling machines occupy that part of the gambling spectrum where manufacturers and operators have the best opportunity to convey to the punter the idea that a form of gambling which in reality is a matter of chance, might be thought to be a matter of skill. It is no accident that as the technology of gambling machines has developed the available manipulanda have increased, thereby giving the impression that the outcome can be influenced by the player's skill and control.[48] Other features of gambling appear designed to encourage biased thinking. The 'near miss' – it should more correctly be called the 'near win' – is a good example. Some commercial gambling activities, gambling machines and scratchcards for example, are designed to ensure a higher than chance frequency of near misses (e.g. missing only one symbol on the payout line, the missing symbol appearing just above or below).[49] Even the otherwise apparently innocuous National Lottery draw has a prize structure that ensures that many players have the experience of winning small amounts, even if those wins are minute in comparison with the much publicised jackpot which figures prominently in most players' fantasies.[50]

The addict as biased information processor

Much of what we have been discussing occurs at a conscious level, but some of it is undoubtedly operating without the person's full awareness or even in a way about which the person is completely unconscious. Some of the biased propositions we have about the objects of our addictions are explicit but others are implicit. This moves us on to an area that is close to the core of modern addiction theory: biased information processing.[51] There has been a particular interest in something called *attentional bias*. This refers to the way in which cues associated with the object of an addiction (either intrinsic parts of the object itself or cues that have become conditioned by association with it) acquire the capacity to grab a person's attention.[52] Because this exaggerated capacity of addiction-related cues to catch and hold the addicted person's attention is not something of which he or she may be fully or at all aware, experimental psychologists have needed to be inventive in order to demonstrate attentional bias. The main experimental methods that have been used are listed in Table 4.3. There is now a mass of evidence that those who are addicted to a drug – tobacco, alcohol and cocaine have been the most studied – show this kind of

Table 4.3 Experimental methods that have been used to demonstrate attentional bias[57]

The Stroop task

Uses the finding that it takes longer for people to name the colour of the ink that a word is written in when the semantic content of the word is particularly salient to them (e.g. cocaine-dependent patients were slower to colour-name cocaine-related words, compared to other people)

The dual-task procedure

Uses the principle that people will be slower to respond to a new stimulus while engaged in doing something else which is particularly salient for them (e.g. problem drinkers were slower to respond to auditory cues while they were holding an alcoholic beverage than while holding a non-alcohol one)

The visual probe task

Uses the principle that people will attend more to part of the visual field where a particularly salient stimulus is placed, and that they will then be quicker to respond to a new stimulus that appears in that part of the visual field (e.g. heroin addicts were quicker to respond to a probe stimulus in that part of the visual field where a heroin-related picture had just been shown)

Eye movement monitoring

Uses the same experimental set-up as for the visual probe task, but in this case what is measured is the relative length of time in which eyes are fixated on the salient visual image compared to an image that is non-salient (e.g. smokers directed a higher proportion of their initial eye fixations towards smoking compared with control pictures)

---

attentional bias to cues associated with their preferred drug.[53] There has yet been comparatively little work of this kind on gambling but what work there has been supports the hypothesis that problem gamblers show significant interference on the Stroop test when stimuli were gambling-related.[54] A closely related area is that of memory bias and the same group of researchers have shown such bias in the case of gambling. For example, dependent drinkers are better than others at memorising alcohol-related words out of a list of words they have just been shown and are more likely to spontaneously interpret ambiguous words, such as 'bar', 'pint', 'spirits', 'shot', in alcohol-related terms when they are given a brief period of time to incorporate each word into a sentence.[55] Problem gamblers have been found to show memory bias towards gambling-related words in the same way.[56]

These mental processes are now thought to be central to addiction, which goes a long way towards explaining why an activity such as gambling can be as addictive as a powerful substance. Under the right circumstances gambling is every bit as capable as an addictive drug of capturing attention and memory processes in order to build a strong mental attachment, or what others have called a strong *incentive-motivational state*.[58] Others have referred to it as a 'schema' of memories about the appetitive object, where and how it is to be found, the cues, events and people associated with it and its consumption, and how one feels and expects to feel before and during consumption.[59] This whole complex memory schema can be evoked by a reminder of any part of it – feeling tense, fantasising about it, walking past a place where the object has been consumed in the past, meeting someone who reminds one of it, are all examples. Cognitive scientists have stressed the way in which much of this process is automatic, reflex-like, and at least partly outside conscious awareness.[60] They point out that automatic mental processes have a number of features that help explain why addictive behaviour is difficult to break. For one thing, automatised actions speed up with practice and become more fixed and less variable; they become more easily triggered by a relevant stimulus and therefore more 'stimulus bound'; once triggered they tend to initiate a whole chain reaction or automatic sequence of behaviour without time for explicit thought; and because they require little thought they are mentally without effort. These processes are, in short, 'autonomous and without intention, difficult to control, effortless and involving little conscious awareness'.[61]

The human psychobiological system is well adapted for the development of such automatic cognitive-behavioural habits. The process of developing such a schema is not unlike that of developing a valued skill. Driving a car is the example of developing automaticity that is often given, but of course there are countless others. A related idea is that of 'working memory': we all develop complex sets of memories consisting of stored information, not just an arbitrary or random collection, but one that helps us get around a familiar world and do the everyday things that we have to do. One way of thinking of addiction is as a kind of 'infiltration' of working memory, a kind of distortion of what would otherwise be an adaptive and functional set of memory and attention schemata.[62] The highly developed human capacity for acquiring complex sets of information and associated habits which are semi-automatic and quickly put into operation without the need for much thought, is of obvious evolutionary advantage. Addiction, whether to substances or activities, is an unfortunate side effect of that otherwise invaluable potential. As one leading cognitive psychologist in this field has put it:

> The normal evolutionary advantages conferred by automaticity of appetitive responses, however, turns against the individual who crosses some threshold of appetitive behaviour rendering it an automatic addictive cycle of self-destructive proportions.[63]

Conflict deepens addiction further

Lying at the very heart of the experience of an addiction, once it has got a hold, is a conflict of motives.[64] The development of a strong attachment brings conflict in its wake, and the deeper the attachment the more intense the conflict. The relatively immediate anticipated rewards of engaging in the addictive activity are then pitted against equally strong motives to use time and money for more essential purposes, to behave responsibly in the eyes of family, friends and work colleagues, and to behave in a way consistent with one's own standards and positive self-image. It is the existence of this motivational conflict which can be witnessed in the apparently paradoxical behaviour of someone who is in the grip of an addiction: for example, taking an anti-alcohol medication because the person likes alcohol so much, or asking to be excluded from a gambling venue because one is so attracted to gambling!

There are a number of theories which help us understand how the immediate pull of the addictive activity might win out against the opposition. One is based on the idea of a gradient of reinforcement (described earlier) whereby immediate rewards are more powerful in the shaping of future behaviour than are delayed punishments.[65] Another rests on the fact that cues reminding one of bills that need to be paid and family and other social obligations that need to be honoured may be less present in consciousness in circumstances where temptation is strongest, whilst all the cues that bring the addictive schema to mind increase in intensity as the prospect of the addictive activity nears (remember the gambler's increasingly excited state on entering the casino in Dostoevsky's novel *The Gambler*). Both of those perspectives adds to the picture of an approach-avoidance motivational conflict and each helps explain why a person who is addicted is always in danger of losing control.

Delay discounting

A third theory which does the same thing is that of *temporal discounting*, or 'delay discounting'. It comes from behavioural economics, an area of behavioural science that has grown rapidly in popularity in recent years. The model is based on the rather obvious fact that people judge a reward, such as a particular amount of money, as worth less to them the more delayed its arrival is going to be. For example, an average, non-addicted person would prefer to take 100 euros now rather than in a week's time but might wait a week if the choice was between 100 now or 120 delayed by a week. In fact it has been shown that the value put on a delayed reward falls off quickly with increasing small delays, with the fall-off in value slowing with further increases in delay (according to a hyperbolic curve).[66] The relevance for addiction lies in the finding that addiction is associated with a greater degree of delay discounting for the addictive object and for monetary reward.[67] As shown in Figure 4.2, people addicted to opiates discount delayed rewards – money and particularly heroin – to a greater extent than other people. It is easy to see how the development of an addiction would be associated with a progressively stronger preference for engaging with the object of one's addiction immediately, rather than having to wait for it, and an increasing preference for having sooner rather than later any resource which can be exchanged for the addictive object – money being the obvious example.

The 'cost' of a punishing or aversive event, such as a monetary fine, is also increasingly discounted with increasing delay, in a similar fashion.[69] Consider, then, the situation of a person with a gambling addiction faced with the imme-diate possibility of gambling (he or she is already somewhere where a gambling

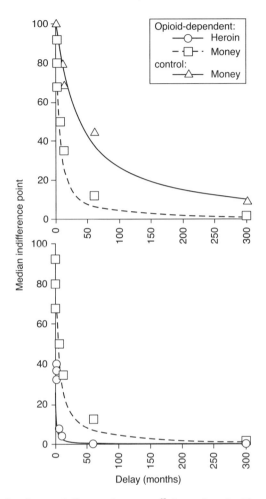

Figure 4.2   Delayed reward discounting curves[68] (reproduced with permission from Bickel et al, 2007)

Showing how, with increasing delay in the promise of a reward its subjective value, relative to immediate reward, falls off according to a hyperbolic curve. These data, first produced by Madden et al, 1997, and reproduced by Bickel et al, 2007, show how the subjective value of a delayed monetary reward falls off more quickly with time for opiate-dependent people compared to controls (the upper part of the figure); and how, for opiate-dependent people, the subjective value of a delayed heroin reward falls off even more rapidly than the subjective value of delayed monetary reward (lower part of the figure).

machine is immediately available, let us say) but with the thought also in mind of the likely punishing consequences of playing (for example, lack of money tomorrow for paying an outstanding bill or shame and embarrassment at the weekend when family members will find out). But because the latter are de-layed, their subjective cost value is reduced (and the longer the delay the greater the reduction in subjective cost) and their ability to counteract the immediate subjective value of gambling – now enhanced because the attachment formed to gambling has resulted in a stronger than normal preference for gambling-related reward – is correspondingly reduced.[70] Whatever was the person's earlier preference for immediate reward – and, as we shall see in the next chapter, some believe that a degree of impulsive preference for immediate reward is a factor predisposing to gambling addiction – the compulsion towards immediate satisfaction of a gambling urge or acquisition of money to gamble is now significantly increased.

Secondary addiction processes

What has been described so far is the state of strong attachment – behavioural, cognitive and emotional – which can develop towards a substance or an activity which has the dangerous property of being potentially addictive. That is the basic picture and gambling fits it well. But it is not the end of the story. Unfortunately things can get a lot worse. That is because of what I call *secondary addictive processes* which get added on to the primary processes.[71] In fact, it is these secondary processes that are the most dramatically obvious to other people and which make it more apparent that something is seriously wrong. Some of these secondary factors are listed, with brief descriptions, in Table 4.4. These are all in their different ways consequences of the conflict that arises when a strong attachment comes into opposition with other life interests, obligations and views of self. Faced with opposing motives of such strength caused by the rising 'costs' of a strong appetitive attachment, the addicted person becomes an even more biased information processor, a 'harassed decision-maker',[72] in trouble with family and friends, increasingly tense, guilty, confused, desperate and even suicidal. Trying to hide one's behaviour from others, finding devious and perhaps illegal ways of obtaining money, using transparent justifications, and tending to blame others or circumstances, do not endear the addicted person in others' eyes and social relationships are affected.[73] These are all natural human reactions to intense conflict. To put it another way they are all the consequences of *cognitive dissonance*. The latter refers to the unpleasant state that arises when one is aware that one's behaviour is out of line with one's attitudes, beliefs or moral precepts. Most of the items shown in the table can be seen as psychological attempts to reduce that uncomfortable state of dissonance. Understandable though this collection of secondary processes is from a psychological point of view, it is worrying and troublesome to other people and can easily be misconstrued as signs of character defect. In fact, it is not just lay people who are inclined to make that mistake. In the past, addictions have sometimes been medically classified as 'personality disorders' and academics and clinicians are still inclined to misconstrue these signs of addiction as personal antecedents – as causes of addiction rather than as part of the process of the development of an addiction.

One thing is certain: almost all the items shown in the table serve only to intensify the addictive attachment. Whatever the earlier motivation was – for

Table 4.4   Secondary addiction processes: the consequences of conflict[74]

Ambivalence and non-objective thinking about consumption
  Consumption behaviour becomes indecisive and inconsistent; attitudes towards
  one's consumption become defensive; rationalisations and justifications for
  consumptions are employed; the reality of one's consumption becomes distorted,
  with unfavourable consequences minimised and favourable ones exaggerated

Controlling consumption becomes a struggle
  Attempts are made to restrain consumption; relapses occur and consumption
  becomes more compulsive; consumption becomes less disciplined and greater risks
  are taken

Dissocialisation
  Attempts are made to hide consumption from others; there is a tendency to blame
  others; the people one mixes with changes so that greater company is kept with
  others whose consumption is also excessive

Demoralisation
  Guilt, shame, remorse and self-criticism are felt; mental health declines as tension,
  confusion, depression, panic increase

Pressure to change is felt
  An increased recognition that consumption is difficult to manage and that one may
  be addicted; change is contemplated and resolutions made; attempts at confession
  and reparation are made; actions to change are formulated

example, whether to win money or to change mood in the case of gambling –
the addictive conflict and its consequences add new sources of motivation.
Whether it was a motivation before or not, consumption is now sought as a
reliever of tension, a distraction from guilt feelings, and a filler in of time that is
left after losing a job or friendships. The addicted person is caught in a vicious
circle. Indeed those who have written about the psychology of conflict, quite
independently of an interest in addiction, have pointed out that recourse to
alcohol or drugs is one of the ways – not a constructive way – of responding
to intense decisional conflict. So one of the ways of dealing with the conflict
caused by a growing alcohol or drug addiction is to drink more or consume
more drugs! The vicious circle is clear. The affected person has been trapped
in a particularly nasty snare which could not easily have been foreseen and
which is not of the person's own making. This is the state of entrapment that
we call addiction. The paradox is that this state of affairs shows the glimmer of
a silver lining: it is out of this accumulated cost and associated conflict and its
consequences that contemplation of change is born. But that is another story.

Most of the items in Table 4.4 are common to all forms of addiction including
gambling. Two features are worth pausing over: 'chasing losses' because it is so
characteristic of gambling addiction; and 'acute gambling distress' because
there has been confusion about its centrality for addiction and its relevance to
gambling.

Chasing losses

Starting with some of the early modern descriptions of compulsive gambling – for example, in Lesieur's *The Chase* and Custer and Milt's *When Luck Runs Out* – chasing losses has been given a central place in descriptions of the process of deepening attachment to gambling. The following quotation makes clear two important points about secondary addictive processes such as chasing: it has its origins in the conflict caused by the previous gambling; *and* it changes and increases the motivation for gambling in the process:

> . . . a new and catastrophic element now dominates his betting style. Before all this happened – before the losing streak began – he was gambling to win. Now he is gambling to recoup. He is doing what gamblers call 'chasing' – the frenetic pursuit of lost money. The pursuit is fired by many fuels. There is the loss of the money itself and what that money could have bought for him. There is the loss of what the money symbolizes – importance, prestige, acceptance, recognition, friendship, power. There is the loss of self-esteem and of the feeling of invincibility . . . There is also the loss of face with the other gamblers . . . And there is just the plain sharp pain and chagrin of loss, the kind anyone feels when he loses or is robbed of something substantial. His obsessive gambling – his addiction – has now been in force for a number of years, but the motivating force has changed. Before, it was propelled by the euphoria of winning and the devouring desire to perpetuate it. Now it is propelled by the depression and anguish of losing and the overwhelming need to quell these feelings.[75]

One of the most thorough studies of gamblers chasing their losses is to be found in an Australian PhD thesis. The most important behavioural signs of chasing appeared to be increasing the size of bets or stakes after a loss (or after a win), plus continuing to bet instead of stopping after a loss. There were also important cognitive-emotional aspects to chasing, such as the anticipation of relief at the prospect of winning – especially important for people with little to lose and much to win, for example following the experience of heavy losses or the existence of debts. Central to the experience of chasing appeared to be the use of inferior betting selections, or less sensible play, under the pressure created by losing or badly needing to win. 'Near misses' were thought to be particularly important in encouraging chasing.[76]

Acute gambling distress

What I am calling here 'acute gambling distress', and which others have called – mistakenly in my view – 'withdrawal symptoms', is controversial in the field of problem gambling studies, and has been controversial in the addiction field generally. There was a time when withdrawal symptoms were thought to be one of the two central hallmarks of substance addiction (the other being increased tolerance as consumption continued, so that increased doses of a drug were required in order to get the same effect). Early ideas about drug addiction were strongly influenced by the withdrawal syndrome associated with heroin and withdrawal symptoms such as delirium tremens and morning-after withdrawal symptoms such as nausea and the shakes associated with alcohol dependence. Withdrawal symptoms lost their central place when it was realised that other drugs, such as cocaine and more recently cannabis (and non-substance activities such as gambling), could cause dependence despite withdrawal being less clear in those cases, and when the cognitive science ideas described earlier (and neuropsychological ideas about addiction to be discussed shortly) came more to the fore.

This remains an area of some controversy, however, and attempts to show that problem gamblers experience withdrawal symptoms when they stop gambling have continued.[77] These studies certainly concur in the finding that problem gamblers very frequently experience irritability, agitation, restlessness and depression when not gambling, and often psychosomatic symptoms such as headaches, insomnia, racing heart and even shakes. In one study colleagues and I compared what problem gamblers said about their symptoms when they stopped gambling, with what people with alcohol problems said about their symptoms when they stopped drinking. We found that although the more psychological symptoms were similar, the psychosomatic symptoms, such as shakes, nausea and muscle pains, were much more prevalent amongst the problem drinkers. We concluded that the symptoms gamblers described rarely corresponded to the classic drug withdrawal symptoms that come on a few hours after a sharp drop in alcohol or heroin concentration in the central nervous system. The symptoms which gamblers experienced appeared to be not so much related to the very recent cessation of gambling, but instead to the gamblers' recent experiences of loss, feelings of indecision about continuing gambling, worry and preoccupation about debts and other costs of gambling. This is consistent with the restlessness, irritability, paranoia, hypersensitivity, desperation, depression and heightened anxiety about whether to gamble again or whether to resist, which has been described by others.[78]

Gambling and the brain

While all this is happening at a psychological level, what is going on in the brain? The last few years have seen a veritable explosion of brain studies in the field of addiction, although not many specifically in the field of gambling addiction. This active field of research is still at a relatively early stage and it is full of loose ends and competing theories. But one thing it has done for addiction studies is to help move the field away from specific or 'provincial' ideas about particular drugs or specific kinds of addiction, and towards more general or 'cosmopolitan' notions based on the features and processes that are common to all addictions.[79] The following is just a brief summary, as the present author – who is not a brain scientist – understands it, of a rapidly developing, complicated and difficult to summarise area.

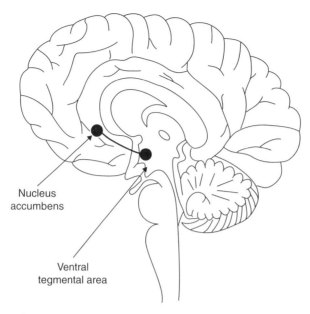

Nucleus
accumbens

Ventral
tegmental area

Figure 4.3 The principal brain dopamine pathway thought to be involved in addiction[80] (reproduced with permission from West, 2006, Fig 5.1)

A lot of the relevant work has focused upon one of the neurotransmitter brain chemicals, dopamine, and there is general agreement about its importance for addiction.[81] The crucial brain pathway runs from a site in the brain known as the ventral tegmental area, to another termed the nucleus accumbens (see Figure 4.3), and it is the accumulation of dopamine in the latter area, so it has been suggested, that is related to addiction. A number of potentially addictive drugs, including amphetamine, cocaine, nicotine, morphine and alcohol, have been shown to increase the concentration of dopamine in that part of the brain, and other drugs of addiction may do the same indirectly by stimulating or inhibiting other brain chemicals which affect dopamine. The importance of this lies in what is thought to be the significance of dopamine transmission in this part of the brain. The area involved is located quite deeply within the central, or limbic, area of the brain. This is an 'old' area in evolutionary terms, and there is much evidence to suggest that it plays a crucial role in such basic functions as motivation and emotion. Not only is the mesolimbic dopamine system affected by several types of drug that can become addictive, but it has also been found to play a role in eating and in sexual behaviour. Experiments have even shown that animals find electrical stimulation of that region to be particularly rewarding. So, is that the real secret of addiction? Is there a basic brain system which mediates pleasure and reward and which is activated by certain activities, including the taking of some drugs, and which therefore sets in train the development of a habit? Are some activities potentially addictive because of their capacity to hit the key brain 'pleasure centre'?

Although that simple idea continues to be part of the neuroscientists' understanding of addiction, the true picture is thought to be rather more complicated. For one thing other neurotransmitter systems may be just as important, including those involving the brain chemicals serotonin, noradrenalin, endorphins, gama-aminobutyric acid (GABA) and yet others.[82] It is really not surprising that the effects in the brain of substances and activities that become addictive should be rather complicated when it is borne in mind how rich and varied are their rewarding properties. The rewards that people can obtain from gambling are multiple and the same is true for tobacco smoking[83] and most other drugs of addiction.[84] Furthermore, neuropsychological understanding of the functions of these deep brain structures has been developing alongside neurochemistry. The idea of a brain 'reward centre' is now thought to be misleading. It turns out that all manner of stimuli are associated with increased dopamine in the mesolimbic system, including some that are aversive rather than rewarding. It is now thought that this brain system has more to do with signalling the importance or salience of particular stimuli, thereby helping to assign particular incentive value to them. The object with which those stimuli are associated may then become specially attractive or 'wanted', which is not necessarily the same thing as 'liking' or pleasure.[85] This fits with work on attention bias in addiction, described earlier, and is part of the more recent incentive motivation theory of addiction.

However we understand the part played in addiction by activation of this mesolimbic system, there is then the question of whether repeated activation with repeated use or consumption causes changes in the brain which consolidate the habit and make giving it up even more difficult. The older theory of addiction, based particularly on heroin and alcohol dependence, was that repeated use led to a form of neuroadaptation such that withdrawal of the drug led to a withdrawal syndrome which could be relieved by taking a further dose of the same drug. Although that process is still a factor to be reckoned with in the case of certain addictive drugs, as explained earlier it was only ever of central relevance for certain aspects of addiction and is no longer considered to be the key to addiction generally.[86] Of more general applicability now are theories that can apply equally to all addictions, including the idea that the key dopamine system becomes hyposensitive or 'down-regulated', so that over time it needs to be activated more strongly in order to produce the same effect – a variation of the older idea of increased tolerance to the substance or activity[87] – or the idea that repeated use or consumption results in increasing sensitisation of the dopamine system to the addictive object and stimuli associated with it. The latter is the *incentive sensitisation* theory that has been popular in recent years,[88] sometimes referred to as 'reverse tolerance' because, unlike classic tolerance theory, it suggests a process of increasing hypersensitivity rather than hyposensitivity.

Competing neural systems

Much of the research on dopamine and the mesolimbic system and addiction has been carried out with animals. More recent thinking about human addiction has shifted from an exclusive focus on the older, sub-cortical, areas of the brain, towards theories that include consideration of what is going on in the upper parts of the brain – the neo-cortex, well developed only in humans and higher mammals. An attractive idea here is the *competing neural systems* hypothesis.[89] One of the competing systems is the sub-cortical, mesolimbic one which we have been discussing, although it is thought to involve a variety of sub-cortical structures including the amygdala which may be important in emotional regulation generally and may have a special role in signalling the valence – positive or negative – of anticipated action.[90] Proponents of the competing systems theory see those parts of the brain as constituting a kind of 'impulsive' system, responsible for attractions and aversions and corresponding actions that occur without thought or reflection. The competing brain system, referred to by some as 'reflective' and by others as 'executive', is controlled, so the theory goes, by structures in the prefrontal cortex which are generally thought to be activated when working towards a goal, predicting non-immediate outcomes, determining future consequences, and social control and decision-making generally. In the context of addiction the prefrontal cortex may be responsible for considering the delayed consequences of consumption. The theory's recent proponents can point to some evidence that addiction is associated with dysfunction in prefrontal cortical areas such as the ventro-medial prefrontal cortex and the anterior cingulate cortex.[91] If this theory is right, then it follows that the secret of addiction, at the level of the brain, is not to be found just in one area but rather in the relationship or balance between two areas, one more impulsive, the other more controlling. Under the influence of a powerful substance or activity, and with repeated use or consumption, the sub-cortical impulse system may overwhelm the neo-cortical executive system. Alternatively, or in addition, the executive system – which also involves dopamine in a big way and may in itself become down-regulated as appetitive consumption goes on – may function less well and be less capable of holding the impulsive system in check. As an aside here, it might be noted that this theory, which calls on evidence of a neuroscientific kind, has obvious parallels in the many psychological and sociological theories of addiction which posit a balance or conflict between opposing motives, between promoting and restraining factors, or even psychoanalytic or religious ideas about the opposition between two sides of human nature, corresponding to appetite and control, *id* and *super-ego*, flesh and spirit, evil and good.[92]

When it comes to gambling addiction, work on neuroscience remains preliminary and small in quantity[93] but it is a growing area and the early findings are considered by reviewers to be showing consistency with the general neuroscience theories of addiction outlined above.[94] A number of studies have shown that winning money on a gambling game produces activation in the same deep 'reward areas' of the brain discussed above.[95] There is now evidence, also, that experiencing a 'near miss' during a simulated machine gambling game – especially when the player sees what would be a winning symbol pass through the payline and come to rest immediately beyond it – activates the same areas.[96] Coupled with other evidence that uncertainty about the receipt of a reward itself activates dopamine brain pathways,[97] these results are beginning to build up a picture of how the experience of gambling, with its panoply of wins and losses, sights, sounds and other conditioned cues, uncertainties and near misses, can activate the brain in ways very similar to the activation associated with other forms of consumption which are known to be dangerous because of their potentially addicting properties.

Another promising area of research on gambling and neuropsychology has been studies of a certain kind of decision-making, requiring 'response inhibition', which it has been shown is under the control of part of the prefrontal cortex. The experimental task used to explore this requires the person to make a decision to switch game-playing strategy on the basis of feedback that an earlier strategy was not working. Success on the task is achieved if the participant switches from choosing cards from a pack which have been associated with early experiences of success to those from packs that become more productive as the game goes on. Interestingly enough, the task, used in a number of different studies by different research groups, went under the name of the 'gambling task' (the Iowa Gambling Task, to give it the name by which it is usually known) before it was ever used with participants with addiction problems. Subsequently those with substance and gambling addictions were found to have difficulties succeeding on that task.[98] This is therefore another line of work that is helping to make the connection between neurocognitive findings in gambling and those modern general theories of addiction which are beginning to see a role for both mesolimbic motivational-emotional systems and neo-cortical decision-making or self-control systems.[99] In fact, the competing systems theory has been used to try to explain why problem gambling is so much more prevalent amongst adolescents than adults. It has been suggested that adolescence is a time of life when the sub-cortical 'impulsive' system is already well developed, indeed may be working in a particularly robust way, while the neo-cortical 'executive' or inhibitory system still has some way to go before it is fully mature.[100]

Chapter summary

This chapter has offered an account of what addiction is and the processes thought to account for its development. That *modern account of addiction embraces gambling, not merely as a marginal member of the class but as a central exemplar.* That is important because it has not always been appreciated that gambling, like alcohol and some other drugs, is potentially addictive.

The basic processes responsible for addiction are those of habit development. They include: *operant conditioning*, whereby behaviour is reinforced by obtaining rewards (usually some combination of mood modification, social and material rewards), usually delivered according to a powerful 'schedule of reinforcement'; and *cue conditioning*, whereby the many sights, sounds and other stimuli associated with the rewarded activity cease to be neutral and themselves take on the capacity to motivate behaviour. These personal learning processes are assisted by social learning from family, friends and others. Gambling offers monetary reward – delivered on a potent random ratio schedule – as well as reinforcement in the form of mood modification and social rewards. The provision of gambling makes deliberate use of conditioned associations by emphasising distinctive stimuli surrounding the gambling product.

In addition, the cognitive element is important in all addictions. Processes of thinking, attending and remembering are 'captured' in such a way that information processing becomes 'biased' in support of the developing addiction. This plays an important part in contributing to an altered incentive-motivational state and the increasingly automatic and unreflective nature of the addictive behaviour. *The cognitive element is particularly important in the case of gambling* which is encouraged by a number of mental biases, including misunderstanding of chance and randomness and the 'illusion of control', both of which are deliberately used in the promotion of gambling.

As addiction develops, and behaviour comes into opposition with other life demands and responsibilities, approach-avoidance conflict arises. *As conflict deepens, new sources of motivation are added* into the mix (e.g. to assuage guilt or to fill time after losing a job), which further strengthens the addictive process. Amongst these 'secondary addictive processes', starting to 'chase losses' plays a particular role in the case of gambling.

Addictive substances have been shown to affect the flow of neuro-chemicals in the brain, particularly the release of dopamine in a deep, mid-brain, or mesolimbic, area which is considered to be important for processing reward and directing attention. Although still preliminary, *research has started to show that gambling has an effect on the brain which is similar to that of addictive substances.* One theory is that of competition between the 'impulsive' demands of activity in the mid-brain and the more 'reflective' operation of parts of the evolutionary newer frontal brain cortex.

It is this combination of brain effects, conditioning, cognitive elements and the consequences of conflict that, according to modern theory, accounts for the phenomenon of a difficult to break addiction such as can develop in the case of gambling.

Does the Fault Lie in the Person or in the Product?

The previous chapter addressed the question of what addiction is and presented the case for seeing it as a general class of phenomena into which gambling addiction falls fairly and squarely as one of the chief species. The question the present chapter considers is a different one: What factors account for the fact that some people develop an addiction such as gambling whilst others do not? The first of those questions – What is (gambling) addiction? – is about the general nature of addiction – What are the features of it? How does it develop? The second question that we turn to now – Why do some people get it and others not? – is one about individual differences. What makes some people more vulnerable than others? If, as is being argued here, gambling is such a powerful, potentially dangerous, activity, then – it may reasonably be asked – why don't we all succumb to gambling addiction?

It is important to keep separate the two big questions – one about general processes, the other about individual differences – because otherwise it leads to confusion and misunderstanding. Take, for example, the research on delay discounting suggesting that problem gamblers may show more than the usual preference for immediate rewards, or the studies showing that problem gamblers are unusually poor at a decision-making task that is thought to depend on the functioning of parts of the brain cortex that inhibit impulsive behaviour. When describing those areas of research in the previous chapter I included them as part of the answer to the first question – about the nature of addiction itself. I was arguing that they were part of what happens when somebody becomes addicted. Part of the phenomenon of addiction is that the addicted person becomes focused on immediate rewards that are relevant to the addiction, including money. Another part of the addiction picture is that inhibitory and control systems fall into relative disuse and disrepair. But when cognitive scientists

An Unsafe Bet? The Dangerous Rise of Gambling and the Debate We Should be Having   By Jim Orford
© 2011 John Wiley & Sons, Ltd

report that kind of work they often fail to make it clear which of the two big questions they think they are answering. Sometimes they imply, without actually saying so, that they think they are answering a question about individual differences in vulnerability. As is so often the case in science, this is an example of being unclear about cause and effect.

Three important general points to bear in mind

1. The causes of addiction are multiple

Figure 5.1 attempts to depict some of the factors that between them may go some of the way towards us answering the individual differences question. There are three general points about this that need to be made at the outset. Each is relevant to addiction generally and to gambling addiction specifically. The first point is the rather obvious one that many factors of different kinds are involved. Gambling addiction is a *multi-factorial disorder*. Factors to do with the person

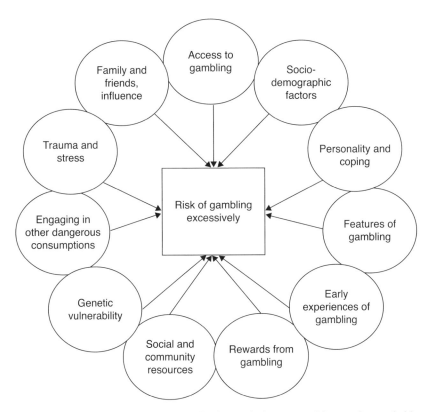

Figure 5.1 Gambling addiction is multi-factorial: the range of factors that probably explain individual differences in vulnerability to problem gambling

him or herself, the immediate environment, exposure to gambling opportunities, circumstances and life events and the wider macro-social environment, are all relevant. Nature and nurture, genes and environment, are both involved. The industry 'supply' side is important but so too is the personal 'demand' side of the equation. Although this may appear obvious it is surprising how often the principle of multi-factoriality is contravened in an expert's enthusiasm for his or her favourite theory. The implication of taking a multi-factorial view is that no uni-factor theory of gambling addiction is to be trusted. Why one person develops a gambling addiction and another does not is never that simple.

2. The development of addiction is a process involving several stages

The second general principle is that the development of an addiction progresses through *multiple stages* and that different factors may be important at different stages. Take the example of drug addiction. One British study broke down the development of youthful illicit drug-taking into three stages: 1) developing an interest in taking drugs, 2) experimenting, and 3) becoming a repeated user. Vulnerability and protective factors were different at the three stages: for example, being in trouble with parents and teachers was a vulnerability factor at the first stage; time spent on activities with family and attending church were protective factors at the next stage; and having a greater proportion of friends who also used illicit substances was a vulnerability factor at the third stage.[1] Similar work on gambling remains to be done but there is little doubt that the principle of addiction developing in a number of stages, with variation in the factors that are relevant at different stages, would hold true.

Genetics is a good case in point here. Lay ideas about genetics are often quite simple, based on the idea of disorders, usually relatively rare ones, that are caused by a single gene or the co-occurrence of a very small number of genes. There is evidence suggesting that genetic inheritance plays a role in explaining individual differences in the expression of addiction[2] and in the case of gambling addiction specifically[3] as it does for most human behaviour. It is not yet clear, however, whether genetic vulnerability is specific to a particular type of addiction (or even within gambling for a particular type of gambling activity) or whether, as seems more likely, we are talking about vulnerability for addiction whatever particular form it takes.[4] Nor is it clear whether the extent and type of genetic vulnerability is the same for men and women.[5] But in the case of addiction, genetic vulnerability is likely to be much more complex than the simple lay perception of genetics would lead one to expect. For one thing it is clear that many genes rather than just one are involved (it is polygenetic), and that different sets of genes may contribute to vulnerability or protection at different stages of the process – it is unlikely that genetic vulnerability to experimenting with gambling is the same as that for becoming a regular gambler, and neither may be the same as that for starting to chase losses or committing crimes to fund gambling.[6] Furthermore, modern understanding of genetics recognises that, in the expression of a behavioural condition such as an addiction, genes interact with, and may be correlated with, environmental factors; for example, adolescents may be exposed to environments that are not independent of their inherited genes; other people may respond differently to people with different genotypes; or individuals themselves may actively seek out environments that suit their genotypes.[7]

3. Controls and constraints are as important as factors that promote addiction

The third general principle about individual differences is particularly important for the argument I am putting forward in this book. It lies, I believe, at the heart of the answer to the question, Why are we not all addicted? It constitutes one of the main reasons why gambling should not be so encouraged that most of the constraints that formerly existed on the availability of gambling have been removed and gambling has become normalised in society. The principle to which I am referring is the following: the development of an addictive habit, across the various stages in its development, is under the control of individual difference factors of both protective and vulnerability kinds. It is not just a question of the 'pull' of the activity for people who are vulnerable because of their personal make-up, circumstances or exposure to gambling. It is as much to do with factors that protect other people because of *their* personal make-up, *their* circumstances or *their* lack of exposure to gambling. To put it another way, the course of a person's gambling (or non-gambling) career is influenced both by factors that promote gambling or greater involvement in gambling *and* factors that restrain a person from trying gambling or from getting more involved in gambling. Many theories of addiction focus on a person's vulnerability or the factors that promote the development of the habit. The protective or restraining factors, which are equally, and possibly more, important, are relatively neglected. Of the two expressions, 'protective factors' and 'restraining factors,' I prefer the latter term. I think it better conveys the active process of being restrained rather than the more passive tone of being protected. It also better captures, I think, the kinds of everyday restraints that I have in mind. It also fits more clearly with the idea of deterrence or control which has a long history in criminology[8] and was used by Derek Cornish[9] in his comprehensive and insightful review of gambling and problem gambling carried out for the British Home Office in the 1970s. It also fits with the idea of conformity to rules and norms which may go a long way towards explaining the very skewed curves that crop up repeatedly when the distribution of degree of engagement in potentially addictive behaviours is plotted for the population as a whole (see Chapter 3 and Figure 3.1).[10] The basic idea is that most people's behaviour most of the time is under quite tight control – some combination of the control we personally exercise ourselves and externally imposed control. When there are rules or laws, most of us keep to them more or less. When there are norms of moderation, or even abstinence, our behaviour mostly conforms to the norm, or near to it. It may be tempting to commit crimes, particularly of minor sorts, but most us are remarkably law-abiding most of the time. It is very tempting to jump a red traffic light, for example, but most people are conformist and do not do so to any more than a minor degree.

When it comes to gambling – and much the same can be said of other addictions – the restraints are many. Among the factors associated with non-gambling which Cornish cited in his Home Office review were: frequent church attendance, partner role-sharing, involvement in work-centred leisure activities such as studying at home, and involvement in political or community activities. These exercised inhibitory control over gambling not only because of the attitudes and social bonds antithetical to gambling which they implied, but also because they restricted 'freedom' to gamble on account of '. . . activities, interests and social roles making prior calls upon a person's attention, time and income'.[11] It was a question of using time and money in ways incompatible with gambling. This is the simple but appealing idea that vulnerability to taking up and becoming more involved in dangerous appetitive behaviour has much to do with what else there is of a rewarding nature to occupy our time.[12] Other constraining or regulatory factors are inherent in the activity rather than the person or his or her lifestyle. In the case of gambling, Cornish argued, controls were exercised over frequency of participation in certain forms of gambling because access was limited (e.g. on-course betting), membership was required (e.g. casinos), play was supervised (e.g. bingo) or participation was necessarily spaced out in time and not continuous (e.g. pools betting). These obstacles in the way of greater participation might be there because of national or local statute but they operate at the individual level by entering into the attraction-restraint equation which determines the behaviour of each individual.[13] From the perspective of deterrence or conformity theory, and appreciating the importance of restraints as well as those factors that promote an addictive habit, it becomes just as relevant to ask, Why are most of us not addicted? as it is to ask the more familiar question, Why do some people become addicted?

Bearing those three general principles in mind, the rest of this chapter will be devoted to considering two of the types of factor that have been considered when trying to answer the individual differences question in the context of gambling addiction – Why do some people develop gambling addiction and others don't? One concerns the personal make-up of individual people, the other the availability and characteristics of gambling itself. The reason for choosing to concentrate on those two domains is because they have been so much discussed and debated. They are often pitted against one another as explanations and the debate about their relative importance is of the utmost importance for questions of national and international gambling policy to which the later chapters of this book will be turning. When it comes to addiction, there have always been those who believe, as one early eighteenth-century medical observer of opium addiction commented, that, 'The mischief is not really in the drug but in people'.[14] There are others who believe, on the contrary, that the problem lies in the exposure of people to a dangerous commodity.[15] In the case of gambling there is, similarly, one view that gambling itself is addictive (some forms of gambling more so than others) and is therefore dangerous, and another which puts emphasis upon the special vulnerability of a minority of people on account of their personal makeup. The former view, towards which the present author leans, suggests that gambling should not be too much liberalised and that its spread should be controlled and its normalisation in society should be resisted. The latter view, on the other hand, suggests that more should be learned about what makes certain people particularly vulnerable, that constraints on the availability of gambling are beside the point, and that 'responsible gambling' should be encouraged and actively promoted.

The many other kinds of factor that may help account for individual differences, shown in Figure 5.1, are not being put to one side because they are unimportant. Far from it. Micro-social factors are probably extremely important, including the modelling and coaching in gambling that is often provided by family members and friends, as discussed in the previous chapter when considering the way in which the habit of gambling may be learned in the early stages. Similarly, life events and circumstances such as changes in financial circumstances, changes in accommodation, work or relationships, and stressful events at home or work, are all likely to be extremely important although they have been remarkably little studied in the context of gambling.[16] Wider, macro-social factors are also likely to be of great importance although once again they have been little studied. A hint of their importance comes from the finding – in the UK and the USA – that there is a significantly greater prevalence of problem gambling amongst people living in areas of greater social deprivation.[17]

Does the fault lie in the person?

When the term 'vulnerability' is used there is a tendency to assume that what is being referred to is some characteristic of certain individuals that makes them more susceptible than others to a certain disease or form of social harm.[18] This has certainly been true in my discipline, psychology, but it is a very prevalent general bias. The assumption is that the fault lies in certain individual consumers, who are personally vulnerable in some way that others are not. That has always been a popular idea. The question that I am asked more than any other, by the media or by friends who know that addiction is a special interest of mine, is 'Is there an addictive personality?' I long assumed that I was being asked a technical, psychological question about the evidence for there being a particular type of personality prone to addiction: I would embark on a lengthy explanation about the scientific search for personality correlates of addictions. I eventually came to the conclusion that really I was being asked a much more general question, along the lines of, 'Is it not the case that the cause of addiction lies in the person? You and I are safe, surely, because we would not succumb. Unlike some people, we are strong enough to resist temptation'.

In fact there has been a long, and mostly fruitless, search for a personality type associated with problem gambling, and the same is true for alcohol and drug addiction. That history includes psychoanalytic ideas about the neurotic and unconscious wish to lose or latent rebellion against the virtues that parents had tried to instil.[19] It includes later, and still current, psychiatric attempts to link addictive gambling to forms of personality disorder such as 'antisocial personality disorder' or 'narcissistic personality disorder', despite the questionable validity and usefulness of those 'diagnoses'.[20] The history also includes studies that have tested hypotheses relating problem gambling to one or more of a whole series of personality traits. One trait that was popular for a time was 'locus of control'. There seemed to be logical grounds for expecting that people with relatively *external* beliefs about where control lies – believing that rewards were largely the result of luck, chance, fate or powerful others, or were simply unpredictable – would be more attracted to gambling than those with *internal* control beliefs who believed their rewards to be largely contingent upon their own actions. Despite the logic of that, results were inconsistent and the popularity of locus of control waned in the gambling field. 'Sensation seeking' has suffered a similar fate despite the intuitive appeal of the idea that high sensation seekers – who seek out varied, novel and complex sensory experiences despite risks that might be involved in doing so – would be more attracted to gambling.[21]

Impulsivity

The focus now is upon the trait of impulsivity. Although the history of work in this field might suggest that impulsivity will before long go the way of its predecessors, there are some signs to suggest that it might be here to stay. Compared to personality ideas in the past, impulsivity is a much more broadly based idea, linking several different domains of scientific interest. For a start it has immediate appeal in psychiatry because pathological gambling has for some time been categorised in the Diagnostic and Statistical Manual (DSM) of the American Psychiatric Association as an 'impulse control disorder'. Where exactly gambling sits in that manual – always somewhat controversial – probably matters little. Of greater importance is the repeated finding that gambling, alcohol consumption and drug taking are positively correlated and that gambling and other forms of addiction co-occur in the same people to a significantly greater degree than would be expected by chance. These are consistent findings and come from studies of both adolescents and adults, from general community surveys and from studies of clinical populations of people in treatment either for gambling problems or for other forms of addiction.[22] This well-established finding encourages the suspicion that there might be a common factor conferring vulnerability to any one of this spectrum of addictions, which involve difficulty in controlling the impulse to engage in a rewarding but harmful activity. A further, influential reason for taking impulsivity very seriously is the fact that some neuroscientists are seeing it as a way of linking the real world phenomenon of out-of-control gambling (and drinking and drug taking) with the burgeoning field of work, described in the previous chapter, on neuropsychological tests of delay discounting and response inhibition and the areas of the brain – notably parts of the prefrontal cortex – which are thought to be involved.

Studies showing a link between gambling or problem gambling and the trait of impulsivity, assessed by one or other of a number of available questionnaire measures, had begun to be reported in the mid to late 1990s but the field remained a small one and at that time largely consisted of a number of very varied and unrelated studies.[23] More recently there have been additions to the questionnaire studies but they have now been joined by a rash of newer studies correlating gambling or problem gambling with impulsivity as assessed by behavioural measures. The latter include tests of delay discounting – where impulsivity is indicated by relative preference for small immediate rewards rather than larger delayed ones – and measures of cognitive impulsivity or difficulty in inhibiting responses such as the Iowa Gambling Task – both described in the previous chapter.[24] All these studies, which now constitute an impressive collection, appear to establish correlation. But that of course does not equal causation. Neuroscientists are now inclined to believe, however, that the results are in line with a pre-existing vulnerability. They have several reasons for leaning in that direction. One is evidence that impulsivity is found to be higher in groups of young people who are known to be at higher risk of later addiction problems, notably those with parents with problems of substance misuse.[25] A further piece of evidence, consistent with the impulsivity vulnerability hypothesis, lies in the results of a number of longitudinal studies, following people from birth or early childhood, in several countries, in the attempt to predict adulthood problem *drinking*. These and other studies of problem alcohol use agree that one of the childhood or adolescent predictors is *behavioural under-control* – not always assessed in precisely the same way from study to study but described in its various forms as 'externalising behavioural problems', 'aggressiveness', 'antisocial behaviour' or 'impulsivity'.[26] Although those were not studies of gambling, and there is as yet an absence of such longitudinal studies in the gambling field, those results are consistent with the picture, which some see as emerging, of a form of vulnerability for a range of addiction problems. There are follow-up studies beginning to be reported, with much shorter follow-up intervals, suggesting that measures of impulsivity during adolescence significantly predict problem gambling a few years later.[27] The very fact that gambling has been found to correlate with measures of impulsivity has itself been taken as a further reason for believing that what we are looking at is a pre-existing vulnerability since, it is argued, it is more difficult in the case of gambling, than in the case of alcohol or other drugs, to believe that those parts of the brain thought to be responsible for behavioural control have in some way been damaged or altered by gambling.[28]

Although a convincing case is beginning to be made for the impulsivity vulnerability theory, there are a number of holes in the argument. The first is the point that, despite some reasons for thinking otherwise, the greater impulsivity to be found amongst those who gamble more than others or who have definite gambling problems can largely be explained as being a *consequence* of the development of an attachment to gambling, not a cause. Take the preference for immediate over delayed reward – the phenomenon known as delay discounting. This was introduced in Chapter 4, not as an antecedent to the development of a gambling problem, but rather as a sign that a strong habit of gambling had developed: it would be hard not to believe that someone who had developed a gambling addiction would, as a consequence, be finding small immediate rewards increasingly tempting. If there is an element of vulnerability here, then surely part of the picture is the deepening of such a preference as a consequence of the development of an addictive habit. Even those who believe that impulsivity is controlled by what is going on in parts of the brain acknowledge that the development of problem gambling may not leave the brain unchanged and may alter responses to behavioural tests of impulsivity. Although gambling is itself not a drug,

> ... neural systems that process reinforcement and choice may nonetheless undergo neuroadaptive change as the PG [problem gambler] individual experiences a chronic regime of winning and losing, coupled with the changes in arousal that are induced by those events. Psychological experience can clearly affect brain function and even brain structure.[29]

The other reason for caution in accepting the impulsivity vulnerability theory uncritically is simply that it is looking too neat. There are many pieces of the argument that can be made to look as if they are consistent with each other. In reality the evidence consists of a large number of pieces which do not necessarily fit together tidily. One complication which has long bedevilled personality research is that traits which were thought to constitute cohesive types, on closer study have been found to consist of sets of only loosely interrelated elements. This may particularly be true in the case of impulsivity since the argument draws on the results of questionnaires and tests of very different kinds which themselves have not always been found to correlate highly with each other.[30] Impulsivity has certainly been defined in a number of different ways. One suggestion is that the general term 'impulsivity' embraces at least four separate constructs which are themselves only moderately related: '*Urgency* is the tendency to act rashly while experiencing distress; *sensation seeking* is the tendency to seek out novel and thrilling experiences; (*lack of*) *persistence* is the inability to remain focused on a task while distracted; and (*lack of*) *planning* is the tendency to act without thinking ahead'.[31]

A further complexity, acknowledged by most,[32] is that the development of an addiction, as was pointed out earlier, is a process occurring over time and one that is best thought of as occurring through a number of stages. Simple ideas of causation based on the idea that a vulnerability factor early in life is directly and strongly linked to the existence of a problem years later is just too blunt a theory to be uncritically entertained. Personality may be important, but the traits of most influence may be different at early, middle and late stages in the process. Furthermore, there are likely to be interactions with many other factors. Some traits may be more important for men than for women or vice versa, or might be more significant for some forms of gambling than for others. And whether a trait is important at all will depend on the presence of other factors, of which exposure to gambling opportunities constitutes one set.

Although impulsivity is now a leading candidate for describing personal vulnerability to gambling addiction, it is by no means the only one. An influential contribution has been the 'pathways model', proposed by a group of Australian psychiatrists, according to which there are three distinct, alternative pathways into problem gambling.[33] The model suggests that the general processes of habit development, described in Chapter 4, are relevant to all those who develop a gambling addiction, but that in the cases of two of the three pathways there exists, in addition, an important element of personal vulnerability. In both cases emotional vulnerability is thought to be important: indicated by disturbances in childhood and a personality characterised by risk taking and boredom proneness, poor coping and problem-solving, life stress, depression and anxiety. To that emotional vulnerability is added, in the case of the third pathway, impulsive traits, with a neuropsychological basis, indicated by attention deficit disorder, anti-social behaviour and substance misuse. That appealing model serves a useful purpose in drawing attention to the diversity which exists within any group of people who have problem gambling in common, and the likelihood that their histories and mix of vulnerability and protection factors will vary. However, the details of the model, and in particular the idea of three distinguishable types, remains untested. There is a history of typological proposals in the field of alcohol and drug addiction – one very influential early proposal was that there were five distinguishable types of 'alcoholism' and a later proposal was for two types – but they have not stood the test of time.[34] An alternative psychiatric angle on possible personal vulnerability comes from a number of large surveys of mental disorder from which it has been possible to calculate the prevalence of the co-occurrence of pathological gambling and each of a number of other psychiatric diagnoses. They include studies carried out in the USA, Canada and Britain.[35] The largest of those studies, carried out in the USA,[36] found a very significantly higher rate of each of nine psychiatric disorders amongst pathological gamblers than for non-gamblers, including not only alcohol and drug problem diagnoses, but also other common conditions such as depression, panic disorder and phobia. If these forms of psychiatric difficulty are true vulnerability factors, important on the pathway to gambling addiction, then this would demonstrate how very widespread in the general population vulnerability for gambling addiction is likely to be. The problem, of course, is that these cross-sectional studies can indicate the strength of association between problem gambling and other forms of mental distress, but cannot in themselves tell us how much of that association is a result of disorder and distress as a consequence of the development of a gambling problem.

Or does the fault lie in the product?

In the case of conditions such as gambling addiction the general bias in favour of personal vulnerability has been strongly underpinned by a psychobiological view that has dominated thinking about psychological problems generally. Advances in areas such as genetics and neuroscience have undoubtedly reinforced this tendency, as did broader late twentieth-century societal changes towards an emphasis on individualism, including an increasing emphasis on the responsibility of individuals for their own health.[37] It is almost as if recourse to personal explanation is the default position: unless stated otherwise, it is assumed that vulnerability refers to something about the individual person's genetic inheritance, personality traits, brain functioning or behavioural responsibility. Mostly this bias is taken for granted. Attention is not drawn to it and its influence is therefore unnoticed and pervasive. That it should remain unchallenged serves the interests of those who benefit from increased opportunities for gambling and who would stand to lose out if there was more emphasis on the role of the gambling product itself as something that is inherently dangerous and which puts people at risk, whoever they are. Vulnerability then becomes, not a characteristic of individuals, but something that is conferred on the whole population, or at least on those who are particularly exposed to the opportunity to gamble or who are collectively vulnerable because of the areas in which they live.

One who did notice that bias and called attention to it was Derek Cornish, the author of the 1970s British Home Office report which has already been referred to.[38] He pointed out that there had been, up to the time he was writing, an almost complete reliance upon person-centred types of explanation for problem gambling. Even then he was able to point to a number of studies that revealed the influence of the visibility and acceptability of gambling opportunities, however. He also noted commercial attempts that were being made at that time to increase such opportunities – examples were the free bussing of customers to Nevada casinos, the attempt to establish off-course betting facilities at sporting events including cricket and golf, and the situating of gambling machines in pubs. Nearly 30 years later it was still possible to say that '. . . processes within the person. . . [rather than] situational contexts exerting influence on the person. . . [have] tended to dominate research into gambler behaviour'.[39] Let us turn, then, to examine the evidence for the importance of 'the supply side' of the supply – demand nexus.

Opportunity and availability

Some of the clearest evidence for the importance of gambling 'supply' comes from studies that have correlated the availability of gambling and various indices of gambling behaviour across different geographical areas. Much of that research has been carried out in Australia and most of it concerns the availability of electronic gaming machines (EGMs). For example, as Figure 5.2 shows, the number of EGMs per thousand of the population is strongly related to the annual per capita expenditure on EGM playing across the eight Australian states and territories, and the same is true also across different areas within the cities of Sydney and Melbourne.[41] Although these correlations are striking, they only relate to expenditure, not problem gambling, and might partly be due to

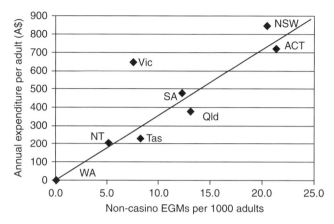

Figure 5.2   The relationship between numbers of EGMs per thousand adults and EGM expenditure per adult across Australian states and territories, 2000/01 (reproduced with permission from Marshall, 2005, Figure 3, p. 65)[40]

expenditure by people who do not live in the same area or even in the same state. Later research was able to go further, however, by linking data on the concentration of EGMs in different towns and suburban areas in one northern part of New South Wales with information on local residents' gambling, obtained by local house-to-house surveys. Not only was the concentration of EGMs correlated with the percentages of the samples who had recently used EGMs, but it was also correlated with the median expenditure on EGM playing and the average number of sessions a year of machine playing. Despite the fact that no respondents were without EGMs in their vicinities – the large majority were living within 2.5 kilometres of an EGM venue – the evidence was clear that the concentration of gambling machines made a difference to how much people gambled. The author of that report suggested that gambling was therefore 'producer driven' rather than 'consumer driven' – more influenced by supply than demand.[42] In passing it may also be noted that it was areas with less advantaged populations which tended to contain the higher concentrations of EGMs.[43] Of course gambling expenditure and frequency of gambling are not in themselves direct measures of gambling addiction, but we know from detailed analyses of survey findings from Australia, Canada and Britain that indices of extent of involvement in gambling, such as frequency of gambling and expenditure, are strongly associated with gambling problems.[44] National surveys in the USA have found the prevalence of gambling problems to be correlated with closeness of access to gambling venues. One found that having a casino within 50 miles of a person's home was associated with nearly double the prevalence, and another found that having a casino within 10 miles was one of a number of factors associated with having a gambling problem.[45] Also relevant here are studies from several countries which show there to be more Gamblers Anonymous groups in regions where there are more opportunities to gamble[46] and a study from the USA showing increased enrolment in Missouri's gambling self-exclusion programme following the opening of new gaming venues.[47]

Canada is another country where it has been possible to correlate the provision of gambling and the rate of problem gambling across different regions, in this case Canadian provinces. Data from 2002 show a significant positive association between provincial rates of problem gambling and the provision within a province, per head of the population, of each of several categories of gambling: casinos/racinos, EGMs, casino table games, and horse race venues.[48]

If the supply of gambling is what principally drives consumption and raises the prevalence of problems, then we should expect to see changes over periods of time during which supply goes up and, more specifically, changes in areas following the inauguration of new gambling facilities such as casinos. North American studies found a consistently higher prevalence of problem gambling as the twentieth century progressed,[49] and at the end of the century a review carried out by the National Research Council in the USA found that the results of six repeat surveys in different states in the late 1980s or 1990s were '. . . consistent with the view that increased opportunity to gamble results in more pathological and problem gambling'.[50] Although most of the findings of that review were in that direction, there were some exceptions, notably a reduction in the prevalence of pathological gambling (or what the review called level 3 gambling) in Connecticut between 1991 and 1996 despite the establishment of American Indian gambling during that time and the opening of a large casino (lower level risk gambling, 'level 2', had gone up however). Such studies are in any case often difficult to interpret because of such things as differences in sampling on the two occasions that are being compared, different survey response rates at the different times, or because of difficulties in establishing what changes in gambling opportunities had actually occurred during the time interval.

Two British gambling prevalence surveys have been conducted, the first in 1999/2000 and the second in 2006/07 (the latter already referred to in earlier chapters). The estimated prevalence of problem gambling was almost identical (0.6%) on the two occasions. Although sampling methods were unchanged and 10 of the same questions about problem gambling were asked in identical form on the two occasions (the DSM questions), the response rate had dropped (from 65% to 52%), which might have complicated the comparison of results from the two surveys. More difficult, however, is the question of characterising what had happened to gambling in Britain during those seven years. Although there had been substantial changes in national gambling policy, overwhelmingly in the direction of greater liberalisation, and new forms of gambling had come on the scene, such as fixed odds betting machines (FOBMs) and internet gambling, the new Gambling Act only became law in 2005 and was only due to come fully into operation in September 2007, several months after the second survey was completed. According to figures available to the new Gambling Commission, gross gambling yield (i.e. the amount retained by operators after the payment of winnings, but before the deduction of the cost of the operation) had increased from just over £7 billion in 1999/2000 to about £10 billion seven years later. Although that sounds like a considerable increase, once inflation is allowed for it was in fact very similar to the rate of growth in total expenditure across the economy as a whole. Although it was being said widely, prior to the second survey, that gambling had increased greatly, and scarcely anyone expected anything other than that the prevalence of problem gambling would show a rise (differences of opinion were only about the extent of the increase), the second survey appeared to show that neither gambling nor problem gambling had increased. The problem is one of interpretation. What seems most likely is that, at the time of the 2006/07 survey, some expanded opportunities for gambling were just beginning to happen and others would be waiting for the new Act to come into operation; engagement in gambling had, by and large, not yet had a chance to expand; and consequently problem gambling had not yet shown the anticipated increase in prevalence. In fact, the rate of participation in any form of gambling in the previous 12 months had dropped slightly, from 72% to 68%. That is less surprising when it is realised that the newer forms of gambling all had low participation rates ranging from 1% to 4%, and that three forms of gambling showed decreases, two of them substantial and predictable. Participation in the NL draw had fallen considerably from 65% to 57%, reflecting the well-known phenomenon of declining interest in a national or state lottery after an initial period of great popular enthusiasm. Also easily understandable was the very substantial decline, from 9% to 3%, in participation in football pools betting, a well-known loser from the rise of the NL (the third decrease was scratchcard gambling, which fell slightly). The British example is therefore not a straightforward test of the hypothesis that increased availability leads to increased engagement and thence to more problems, or at least not yet. The 2009/10 survey may throw more light on those questions but 2006/07 was too early to do so. One leading gambling survey researcher from the USA has noted that it takes several years after the introduction of new gambling opportunities for problem prevalence to rise.[51]

A similar interval of time separated two surveys carried out in Quebec province in Canada in 1989 and 1996 during which time the gambling industry had expanded greatly: the prevalence of problem gambling was estimated to have increased from 3.3% to 4.5%.[52] On the other hand, in New Zealand prevalence studies carried out in 1991 and 1999 did not find an increase in problem gambling prevalence despite an apparent significant increase in gambling availability and gambling expenditures during the 1990s.[53] In fact, it appeared that there might have been a decrease in the proportion of people gambling weekly or more often and a reduction in the current prevalence of problem gambling. However, there were some differences in the methods used in the two surveys which may or may not have been important.[54]

Canada has been the setting for a number of the studies that have considered the local effects of opening a new gambling facility. A particularly thorough study was conducted before and after the opening of a new casino in Niagara Falls in Ontario province. Ninety per cent of residents interviewed after the opening believed that the number of people who had become addicted to gambling had increased and there was other evidence that this was a real effect. The proportion of the local population gambling in a casino in the last year had gone up four-fold and the percentage reporting going to a casino two or more times a month had increased by almost as much. The proportion scoring above the threshold for problem gambling on a short screening questionnaire had increased (from 2.5% to 4.4%) as had the proportion experiencing problems with the gambling of other members of their families (5.0%–7.5%). None of these changes were observed to anything like the same extent in a control sample of Ontario residents outside the Niagara Falls area.[55] Other Canadian studies show similar effects, although in one case a later follow-up study showed that the prevalence of gambling problems had returned to the earlier level, or even lower, two and four years later.[56] A similar investigation was carried out before and after the opening of casinos in Malmö and another smaller town in Sweden. The conclusion was that gambling problems had not risen as a result of the casino opening in the smaller town but had done so in Malmö.[57]

The most convincing British study of the effects of increased availability used Family Expenditure Survey (FES) data in order to examine household expenditure for the last full year before the inauguration of the National Lottery (NL) and the first full year after its start, in the mid-1990s. In each household, adult members completed a two-week expenditure diary including recording outlay on several different forms of gambling separately. Before the NL, 40% of households were gambling, households were spending 0.5% of income on gambling on average and 0.4% were spending more than 10% of their income that way. After the NL started, 75% were gambling, average household expenditure on gambling had risen to 1.5% and the percentage now spending more than 10% of income on gambling had risen to 1.7. Although spending more than 10% of income on gambling is not itself a direct measure of problem gambling, it is likely to be a good indirect sign of it.[58]

Another Australian study illustrates some of the difficulties of interpreting the results of studies of change over time. This was a study of the impact of legislation in South Australia, passed in 2004, to remove a proportion of EGMs from for-profit gambling venues, in response to the evidence that people gambled close to home and that problem gambling was related to the propinquity of gambling venues – EGMs in not-for-profit venues remained, contrary to the recommendation of the Independent Gambling Authority in South Australia. Both data on revenue from EGMs and interviews with a sample of several hundred regular EGM players suggested that very little had changed: revenue had remained much as before and gamblers had not decreased their gambling. It seems that the numbers of EGMs removed was too little to have had much of an effect (the recommendation had been to remove 20% of all the state's EGMs) and many venues with previously under-utilised machines had been able to remove the least profitable ones and to continue replacing or upgrading existing stock with new and potentially more lucrative models.[59]

The total population consumption model

A leading theory in the public health field is the *single distribution theory*. It predicts that an increase in the whole population's participation in an activity that is risky for health will lead to an increased proportion of the population who engage in the activity at high volume or intensity, and thence to an increased prevalence of associated problems. In the case of health-related behaviours such as drinking or gambling it is sometimes known as the *total population consumption model*. That theory has generally met with support in the field of alcohol consumption and a very similar model has been found to hold true for a number of other health risk indicators such as body mass index, blood pressure and birth weight.[60] The single distribution theory is principally concerned with the relationship between the average for the whole population (for example, the average body mass index) and the proportion of the population who have a high value, indicating a risk to health (for example, a body mass index above a certain threshold). In the case of a health-related behaviour, the theory maintains that an index of the extent of engagement in a behaviour such as gambling (or drinking or eating fatty foods) is distributed in the population according to a continuous but strongly skewed distribution curve of the kind shown earlier (see Figure 3.1 in Chapter 3). The crucial point is that the curve acts like a single entity, rising or falling along its whole length in response to factors that influence the *whole population*. It follows that high frequency or high intensity gamblers – and questions about what has caused them to become such gamblers or what might be done to prevent other people becoming such gamblers – cannot be considered independently of questions about the whole population's gambling. It rejects notions that treat heavy or problem gamblers separately from the rest of us; for example, the idea that they are a distinct group whose gambling is quite independent from the gambling of ordinary or responsible gamblers.

A number of Norwegian studies have produced results supporting the single distribution theory in the case of gambling. One was a national adult survey of gambling conducted in 2002, and another was a national omnibus adult survey carried out in 2005. Both showed the frequency of gambling in the previous year to be distributed in the population, as expected by the theory, in a continuous and skewed fashion and, furthermore, showed a clear relationship between the average gambling frequency of the population of a county and the proportion of frequent gamblers in that county.[61] Two other Norwegian studies were studies of adolescents in a large number of schools throughout the country. Again, both found strong relationships between the average gambling frequency of pupils in a particular school and the percentage of high frequency gamblers in the school. One of those studies also used a brief measure of problem gambling and found a significant relationship between a school's average gambling frequency and the proportion of the school's pupils who obtained a positive response on at least one of the two problem gambling questions.[62]

The full model showing the link between availability and problem prevalence is shown in Figure 5.3. This proposes, not only that the prevalence of problem gambling in the population is related to the extent of gambling in the whole population, but also that the latter is affected by the extent to which opportunities to gamble are available to members of the population.

Figure 5.3   The full total population consumption model showing the relationship between availability, population consumption and problem prevalence[63]

Constraints on excessive gambling

But the question of availability and accessibility of gambling is a complex one, with many strands. Whether a casino opens within a few kilometres of a person's home, or how many gambling machines there are to be found in the area, does not begin to exhaust questions about how available gambling is, how accessible it is to citizens or to what degree they are exposed to opportunities to gamble. The whole question of accessibility was looked at comprehensively in the Australian Productivity Commission report on gambling.[64] Accessibility, they concluded, was not merely a question of the number of gambling outlets in an area. Also important were: the way in which those outlets were distributed spatially across an area, the number and diversity of opportunities to gamble at any one venue, opening hours, restrictions on entry or lack of them, the size of the outlay necessary to begin gambling and how inviting the venue was to different groups of people including women, young people and members of different ethnic groups. To those variables can be added the way in which the venue is advertised, whether incentives are offered to potential customers, the extent to which gambling at the venue is associated with further leisure and hospitality facilities, whether alcohol is served, the availability of facilities for cash withdrawal and many aspects of the environment created within the venue, including whether or not there are such things as clocks and windows to remind players of life outside the immediate gambling environment.[65] When he wrote his report for the British Home Office in the 1970s Derek Cornish had these kinds of situational characteristics in mind when he used the term 'ecologic opportunity' to refer to the whole collection of factors that contributed to availability.

In an important contribution to the discussion about this topic of accessibility – a subject that turns out to be so much more complicated than might at first have been thought – David Marshall of the Centre for Gambling Research at the Australian National University has used an approach that he calls 'time-geography'. This way of looking at things recognises that, whatever may be going on in the brains of individuals when they gamble and whatever are the influences of our personalities or our families and friends, the constraints imposed on all human behaviour by considerations of space and time cannot be escaped. Cornish anticipated this in his review of 30 years earlier, although he referred to the approach as 'control theory' (discussed earlier in this chapter).[66] Time geographers have written about three broad categories of space-time constraints which limit what people can do. One category consists of *capability constraints* which operate because of sheer physical limitations – for example, the lack of a casino within easy access, using one's normal form of transport, places a capability constraint on a person's casino gambling. The importance of capability constraints was recognised by a young woman who was interviewed as part of a study of problem gamblers:

> I wish it [machine gambling] wasn't so accessible, it wasn't right there in front of you. . . You know they ought to put it away somewhere else where it's not going to attract a load of young kids because you know you go down there and it's just there, you go to the beach and it's there and you can't help it so I mean I try not to go too near the beach because I know I would want to go in there. . . I think it should be down a road where people would have to go. . . If they want to do that they would have to go down that road, it's not a road you would normally go down unless you wanted to go there. . . .[67]

Coupling constraints constitute the second category. This refers to constraints due to the need to interact with other people, places and materials which themselves impose constraints. For example, if my preferred way of gambling is to bet on horse races, live at the race track, then I am severely constrained by the programme of horse race meetings.

The third category, *authority constraints*, are those imposed by a governing authority of some kind which lays down the rules and regulations under which the activity can take place. Not very long ago, for example, it was quite difficult in England to obtain alcoholic drinks during the daytime without entering a public house and even then the hours during which that could be done were limited. In some parts of Britain there were severe constraints on obtaining alcohol at all on a Sunday. These constraints, all imposed by law, no longer obtain. Much the same has taken place in the case of EGMs in some Australian states and territories. Marshall writes of the way in which the winding back of authority constraints on gambling, with a consequent reduction in both coupling and capability constraints, has led to a situation in which gambling in Australia has fewer space-time constraints on it than almost any other recreational pursuit – cinemas and live sporting events, for example, being much more restricted.

This is an important perspective because, mundane and obvious as time and space constraints may appear in comparison with such intriguing and scientifically dynamic fields as human personality, genetics and brain systems, they are basic to understanding the forces that constrain or promote the behaviour of individuals and whole populations. The presence of space-time restrictions probably constitutes the principal set of factors responsible for a more restrained level of a population's engagement in an activity. By the same argument, a relative absence of space-time constraints is probably the main source of pro-motion of increased population engagement in the activity.

The structural features of gambling

One whole branch of the ecology of gambling consists of features of the gam-bling activity itself. These are the characteristics of forms of gambling which Mark Griffiths, Professor of the Psychology of Gambling at Nottingham Trent University, has referred to as *structural characteristics* in distinction to the *sit-uational characteristics* which we have largely been considering up to now.[68] Some of the structural features of gambling which have been studied are listed in Table 5.1. Features of machine gambling are particularly well represented in that list. That is mainly because machine gambling has been the most studied, and perhaps partly because it is a form of gambling that is relatively easy to study in detail (either in live machine gambling venues or by setting up machine gambling studies in the laboratory) but also because it is machine gambling

Table 5.1 Some of the structural features of gambling which make one form of gambling very different from another[69]

Methods for paying and receiving winnings	e.g. the size of coins and notes that are accepted; whether credit cards or smart cards can be used; whether chips or tokens are used during play; whether winnings are displayed as credits or in money terms; whether winnings are returned in cash after each play or are accumulated; payout ratio
Speed of play	e.g. time elapsing between events; time elapsing before another bet can be placed; EGM reel spin speed; interval between staking and knowledge of result; interval between staking and receipt of winnings
Gambling features	e.g. maximum stake allowed; maximum prize available; range of stakes and odds offered; opportunity to bet simultaneously on multiple lines (EGMs), cards (bingo), options (roulette), in-game events (e.g. football, cricket), etc; special EGM features (e.g. stop and nudge buttons, trails, ladders, grids); frequency of occurrence of small wins and near misses
Ambience	e.g. use of stimulating light and colour effects; use of sound effects which call attention to winning; use of stimulating music; social stimulation (e.g. attractive croupiers, talking EGMs which encourage play); naming of EGMs which suggest winning; information and procedures which indicate potential dangerousness (e.g. warning signs, procedures for limiting time or money spent)

that has particularly been of concern in many countries, including Australia where much of the research has been done.

Gambling machines have come a long way since they were first invented in the USA at the very end of the nineteenth century. Their particular structural characteristics were recognised decades ago, for example by Britain's 1949–51 Royal Commission on Betting, Lotteries and Gaming whose recommendation regarding 'fruit machines' was as follows:

> The particular danger we see in this type of machine is that, since it does not require the intervention of an attendant in order to give the prize, it is capable of a rapidity of turnover which would render the element of gambling, even within the strict limits which we have set, no longer trivial. We, therefore, recommend the provision of machines of this type should be illegal.[70]

In the mid-1990s, Susan Fisher and Mark Griffiths, both pioneers of the study of young people and machine gambling, described the risky features of machine gambling as follows:

> Slot machines are fast, aurally and visually stimulating and rewarding, require a low initial stake, provide frequent wins, require no pre-knowledge to commence play, and may be played alone... structural characteristics of slot machines which are designed to induce the player to play and/or to continue playing are likely to play an important role. Such characteristics include frequent payout and event intervals, arousing near miss and symbol proportions, multiplier potential, bettor involvement and skill, exciting light and sound effects, and significant naming.[71]

Since then EGMs have evolved into even more sophisticated machines, building on many of the features shown in the table, and almost certainly making them more dangerous in the process. The lifetime of the average machine can be measured in months and machine designers are constantly aiming to produce 'better' machines.[72] All the enhanced features of modern machines are likely to have the effect of encouraging fast and continuous play. One group of Australian researchers has calculated that modern gambling machines allow people to play at a rate of 10 or more games a minute or several hundred an hour.[73] As they put it, this makes machine gambling unique as an 'entertainment' product, providing an automated activity at such speed.[74] By 2007, Griffiths and another of his colleagues were writing:

> ...the role of such factors has become even more significant within the past decade. Interactive feature plays, increased skill orientations and bettor involvement, and the manipulation of familiarity and sound effects are now combined to produce sophisticated and psychologically immersive EGMs.[75]

The view is widely held, in fact, that it is those structural features of gambling, permitting and encouraging repeated and often rapid cycles of staking, playing and receiving feedback about the outcome, that make some forms of gambling particularly dangerous.[76] That is one reason for concern about any

developments in gambling which either change a form of gambling that was previously constrained to be *dis*continuous (betting on separate horse racing events
at a betting office for example) into one where continuous playing is possible
(as in modern betting offices which allow betting on multiple events occurring
constantly in different parts of the world), or which add new, faster forms of
gambling at a venue where previously only slower forms of gambling operated.

There is evidence from many studies in different countries that different
forms of gambling are associated with very different rates of gambling problems.
Lotteries, for example, are regularly found to be associated with a much lower
rate of problems than playing the traditional table games to be found in a
casino.[77] In the 2006/07 British survey, fixed odds betting machines (FOBMs)
and online gambling – both modern forms of machine gambling which allow
continuous play – were associated with much higher rates of problem gambling
than betting on the National Lottery draw or playing scratchcards. For example,
of those who had played virtual gambling games online at all in the previous
12 months, 7% scored above the threshold for problem gambling but only
1% of those who had played the NL draw did so.[78] Interpretation of such
findings is not entirely straightforward, however, since nearly all of those who
had engaged in those forms of gambling that appear to be the most dangerous
had, in addition, engaged in other forms as well. Separating out the effects of
one form of gambling from another is not easy. Furthermore, risk appears to
depend crucially on how frequently a person engages in gambling.

Is population adaptation to gambling possible? A confused theory

One challenge to the theory that increased availability leads to greater population engagement, and thence to an increased prevalence of levels of gambling
that are problematic, comes from what has been termed 'adaptation theory'.
That theory looks at gambling as if it were a virus, the source of a contagious
disease. It follows that exposure to a novel virus, of which the population previously had little or no experience, leads to rapid spread of infection amongst
the most vulnerable. It also follows, and this is the novel suggestion as far as
gambling is concerned, that with continued exposure to the virus the population shows adaptation, partly because those not initially infected are naturally
more resistant and less vulnerable, but partly also because people may positively
adapt, learning ways of living with the presence of the virus without being so
harmed by it. In other words, people become more resilient; in a sense they
develop immunity. Although there have been no studies specifically designed
to test adaptation theory, proponents of this theory can point to a few studies
that at least seem to show some evidence consistent with it; for example, the
finding that rates of self-exclusion that escalated after the opening of the Missouri casino flattened out after a few years, or the finding that the prevalence of
problem gambling returned to a low level in the second and subsequent years
after the opening of a new casino in Canada.[79]

Those who support adaptation theory acknowledge that focusing too heavily on it could cause policy makers to underestimate the importance of increases in gambling problems that arise *before* populations have had a chance to show any adaptation and, furthermore, that because of constantly developing technology, populations are always having to face new risks. Nor is adaptation theory very clear about how adaptation might occur. One possibility is that the provision of specialist treatment for problem gambling might reduce overall prevalence by reducing the duration of problem gambling for those successfully treated. That is unlikely to be a big factor while the development of problem gambling treatment remains thin and patchy, as is currently the case in Britain. The alternative is that the whole population develops some kind of 'immunity' to the gambling virus. Proponents of the theory are not very explicit about what might be meant by this.[80] A greater awareness in the population at large about the dangers of problem gambling, acting as a protective factor, is one suggestion; but, again, that seems unlikely until such time as public awareness about problem gambling is raised significantly above its present level. Perhaps by 'immunity' is meant a waning of interest in gambling, or in certain forms of gambling, once the initial novelty has past. There is indeed some evidence for that in the case of national or state lotteries such as Britain's National Lottery. In terms of the public health theory summarised earlier (see Figure 5.3) this would imply that the amount of gambling in the population remained the same (or even decreased) in the face of gambling continuing to be available at the same level (or even becoming more available). It would *not* imply that the prevalence of problem gambling could be held steady (or even lowered) in the face of increasing gambling in the population as a whole. That has profound policy implications which will be considered further in the final section of this book. Apart from anything else, it would require of the gambling industry that it exercised restraint by refraining from developing new forms of gambling or making technological advances to existing forms, targeting its products in new markets or market sectors, or even expanding at all!

Notwithstanding the thinness of the evidence for the theory, those such as La Plante and Shaffer from Harvard Medical School who argue for the adaptation theory go on to develop the idea of adaptation by suggesting that the challenge is to identify those who can adapt and those who do not, and even to suggest that the temptation offered by an otherwise infectious and harmful agent such as gambling may be good for developing self-control and building character – an idea that has a long history in debates about gambling (see Chapter 6). One is struck when reading that by the thought that gambling promoters would surely draw great comfort from these suggestions emanating from such a prestigious source.

Recent supporters of adaptation theory have also argued that gambling problems tend to be 'transient'.[81] This represents a misunderstanding of the nature of addiction. They appear to be discovering what was discovered about alcohol and drug addiction several decades ago: addiction need not be a progressive, lifelong affliction, but can be overcome. Indeed it can often be overcome without formal treatment, particularly before it has developed to the fullest possible extent. It has been known for a long time that, over a period of some years, there is movement of people in and out of the group with problems. Addiction problems can be of brief duration and never return, but they are often cyclical in nature and sometimes chronic and never resolved.[82] In the case of gambling it is only relatively recently that the older idea of addiction, as something which inevitably persists without respite, has been challenged. But to conclude that gambling problems are mostly brief is thoroughly misleading. A review of the few longitudinal studies of problem gambling that have been carried out to date showed there to be 'substantial stability of individual differences in problem gambling... across 2 to 10 years'.[83] Even the 1998 follow-up of the 1991 New Zealand sample, which has been cited as evidence for the transient nature of gambling problems, showed considerable stability and problem persistence. Of those classified as current pathological gamblers in 1991, a third was still so classified seven years later, indicating problems of substantial chronicity, and just under a further third continued to have some problems of lesser severity. As would be expected from what is known about the course of addiction problems, many appeared to have successfully moved out of the problem category over that period of time. Over the same period others had moved into that category, particularly those who were regular gamblers in 1991 and/or who had experienced gambling problems earlier in life.[84] Other relevant studies include a four-year German follow-up of regular EGM players which found a high degree of continuity of problem gambling,[85] and a follow-up of US college students throughout the four years of college which found that the most extensive gamblers in the first year – who were much more likely than others to say that they had problems with their gambling – were highly likely still to be so in the fourth college year.[86] The general conclusion of the review of longitudinal studies was that:

> There is now consistent evidence emerging from longitudinal research suggesting that the course of problem gambling is variable – for some individuals the gambling problems are relatively transient, whereas for others the gambling problems are persisting and chronic.[87]

The general supposition that increased exposure to and availability of gambling leads to an increased level of gambling in the population, and thence to an increased incidence and prevalence of problem gambling, as is consistent with the leading public health model of addiction, and with repeated findings from around the world, has never seriously been questioned.[88] The evidence for that hypothesis has been considered carefully by official review bodies in Australia, the USA and the UK. Each concluded that an increased availability of opportunities to gamble was associated, not only with a greater volume of gambling, but also with an increase in the prevalence of gambling problems.[89] For example, the Gambling Review Body in the UK stated in its report:

> A central question for us has been whether increasing the availability of gambling will lead to an increase in the prevalence of problem gambling. The weight of evidence suggests that it will do so.[90]

That is particularly telling, coming as it did from a body that was always inclined to free British gambling from what government and the industry saw as constraints on gambling that were not consistent with the modern age, and which went on to recommend wholesale liberalisation of gambling in Britain. A slightly more nuanced conclusion was reached in a 2005 report prepared for the New Zealand Health Research Council, which reviewed the evidence from that country and internationally:

> ... it appears that the introduction and expansion of new gambling forms, especially continuous forms, has given rise to significantly increased rates of problem gambling. This has been found at the national level, across whole populations, as well as within sub-populations (for example, women), that previously had low levels of participation and problems.[91]

Chapter summary

After considering general processes of addiction development in Chapter 4, the present chapter turned to a different question. The question here was one about differences between people: not everyone becomes addicted to gambling, so why is it that some do, and not others? A number of general points about addiction need to be borne in mind when considering the question of why some people develop an addiction and not others. First, *addiction is multifactorial*: many factors are involved in its causation and no one causal theory is adequate. Second, *addiction develops through a number of stages*: vulnerability and protective factors are different at different stages. Third, *factors that restrain most people from developing an addiction to gambling are as important as the factors which positively promote excessive gambling for others*: it is just as relevant to ask why some people do *not* develop an addiction to gambling as it is to ask why others do.

The chapter went on to examine in more detail two particular ideas about causation. These were chosen because they are leading theories in the field and because they are representative of *two general positions that are currently being adopted* towards the question of responsibility for gambling problems. *According to one position, the fault lies with characteristics of individual people* who are vulnerable. *The second general position locates the fault with the gambling product*, the way it is designed and made available.

There has been a bias in the field of gambling studies towards looking for the cause of addictive gambling in the personality of the individual. There have been many attempts to identify the kind of personality that is prone to addictive gambling, as well as a more general search for the elusive 'addictive personality'. Most candidates have fallen by the wayside. One that remains is 'impulsivity'. *There is some evidence in support of impulsivity, but as a causal theory it has several shortcomings*: increased impulsivity may be as much a consequence of the development of addictive gambling as a cause; the theory takes little account of the development of addiction in stages; and impulsivity itself is probably not a single, coherent construct, but rather a loose collection of a number of separate traits.

In marked contrast is the theory which focuses, not on individual personality, but on *the degree to which opportunities to gamble are available to people*. This is consistent with the 'total population consumption model' – a leading public health model – which predicts that greater availability of an activity which is risky for health, leads to greater consumption throughout the population, and thence to higher problem prevalence. In the case of gambling and problem gambling *there is much evidence in its support*, including studies which compare different geographical areas with different concentrations of gambling outlets, and other studies which find increases in gambling and/or problem gambling after the inauguration of new gambling facilities such as a casino or a national lottery.

In addition to availability, there has been much research attention given to *the structural features of gambling*, or what has sometimes been called the 'ecology' of the gambling environment. That line of research has particularly focused on the more continuous forms of gambling – thought to be the more dangerous – especially the features of gambling machines and how they have changed with technological advance.

Some critics of availability theory have suggested that populations can show *'adaptation' to increased gambling availability*, similar to the immunity that may develop to a virus. There is some evidence that suggests this may occur, but *the theory is relatively new and untested, and it is unclear exactly what is meant by adaptation* and how it is thought to occur. We shall return to this in the final chapter.

Although the theories have been presented as if they were in opposition in order to bring out the contrast between them, it is *almost certainly the case that the causes of addictive gambling lie in both personality and availability*. Indeed it would be strange, and contrary to everything we know about human behaviour, if it were otherwise. It is important to be aware, however, that person and environment are likely, in the causation of gambling addiction as for any other form of addiction, to interact in complex ways over the period of time – often a lengthy one – during which an addiction develops. We should beware of simple ideas in this field. For one thing, by concentrating on two particular theories, this chapter has neglected many other causal factors.

Section III

Gambling is Controversial

6

Discourses of Gambling: Eleven Ways of Talking About the Subject

It is impossible to venture far into this field of gambling without recognising that there is a variety of ways of talking about the subject – what might now be referred to, following the rise of post modernism, and particularly the work of the French social theorist and writer Foucault, as different *discourses*. These gambling discourses go well beyond simply representing gambling as something that is either good or bad. They depict gambling in different lights, using – as we all do much of the time whatever it is we are talking about – metaphors and other tricks and devices for persuasively describing gambling in particular ways. Furthermore, and this is the really important point about discourses, they serve certain interests, often powerful ones, such as the interests of anti-gamblers in the nineteenth and early twentieth centuries, or the interests of an expansionist gambling industry in the late twentieth and early twenty-first centuries. In this chapter a number of different gambling discourses are outlined and illustrated. I have chosen to describe 11 discourses which seem to me to be reasonably distinct – although in practice different discourses are often found in combination, thereby rendering them even more powerful. Other people would no doubt produce a different list. My 11 discourses are summarised in Figure 6.1. They fall into two groups: those that are used to promote and defend restrictions on gambling; and those which serve to support gambling expansion.

An Unsafe Bet? The Dangerous Rise of Gambling and the Debate We Should be Having   By Jim Orford
© 2011 John Wiley & Sons, Ltd

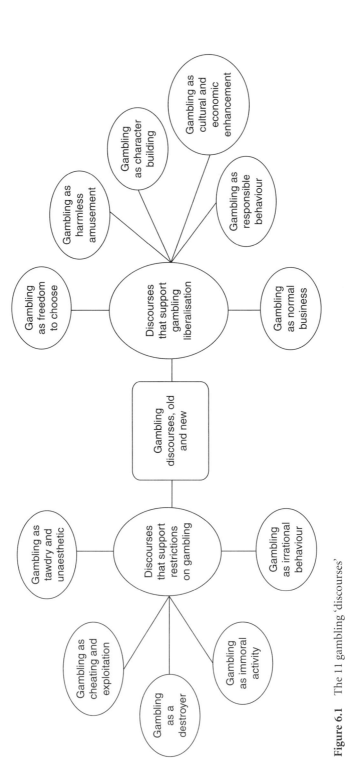

Figure 6.1 The 11 gambling 'discourses'

Discourses that support restrictions on gambling

Gambling as immoral activity

Historical accounts of gambling in Britain are full of quotations that illustrate a perspective on gambling that saw it as disreputable, appealing to baser instincts, wasteful, immoral, even satanic.[1] The nineteenth century is a fertile source of such quotations. For example, an anti-gambling tract of 1820, which like others deplored the bad example being set by upper-class gambling, was aimed at educating people '. . . to avoid this pernicious foreign vice and those who engage in it'.[2] The view of a Reverend from Cheltenham commenting on the approach of the town's annual races in 1827 was not untypical:

> Gambling is . . . a vice which appears to be growing in our land, though it be a vice which is more pre-eminently destructive both of body and soul, than any other which Satan ever devised for the ruin of mankind. Every vile passion of our corrupt nature is excited and inflamed by it; envy, malice, revenge, the lust of money, pride, contention, cruelty. . ..[3]

The National Anti-Gambling League (NAGL) was founded in 1890 with the stated aim of:

> Nothing less than the reformation of England as regards the particular vice against which our efforts are aimed . . . There is humiliation in the thought that the chosen Anglo Saxon race, foremost in the civilisation and government of the world, is first also in the great sin of Gambling.[4]

The late Victorian and Edwardian period was strong on anti-gambling senti- ment. The following, for example, appeared in *The Times* in July 1902:

> . . . if anything serious is to be done to correct a national evil, there must be a change in the education of the people to whom betting is now an absorbing passion – an enlargement of their interests and pleasure, an imparting of true education to these dupes; and not least, the substitution of a genuine interest in manly sports for one that is factious and mercenary.[5]

The idea that gambling has a pernicious effect on character was a common theme. In the first decade of the twentieth century, there was much debate about the rights and wrongs of prize competitions run by newspapers. Some newspapers eschewed such competitions on the grounds that the effects of gambling were demoralising, and that prize competitions, combining a short and childish amount of work with the prospect of a large prize, had a particularly marked negative effect on young people and the less educated. Gladstone agreed, writing about competitions and lotteries that they 'are sometimes harmless, they are rarely useful, they are frequently mischievous'.[6]

Seebohm Rowntree, the Quaker industrialist and social investigator, edited in 1905 a volume of essays entitled *Betting and Gambling: A National Evil*, and many prominent public figures were anti-gamblers. The NAGL took heart from the vibrancy of the Temperance Movement, contributed to the banning of street betting in 1906 and almost succeeded in having on-course betting on horse races made illegal. The fortunes of the NAGL declined from then on (it finally folded in the 1950s), as did gambling as immoral activity as a public discourse.

That discourse, however, took a long time to pass away. It was certainly alive in the 1920s when in 1927 the Lord Chief Justice stated that the slot machine 'was a pest and a most mischievous pest, because it operates on the minds of young persons and corrupts them in their youth';[7] and when Snowden, the Labour Chancellor who in 1929 abolished the betting duty introduced by Churchill in 1926, 'confessed to a feeling of dismay amounting to horror that the country should have come to such a pass that recourse should be had to legalizing and making respectable . . . the second greatest curse of the country'[8] – the first presumably being drink. In the 1930s, Perkins, of the NAGL, wrote a broad indictment of all gambling in *Gambling and Youth*, in response to the Royal Commission's recommendations to liberalise lotteries. He argued that gambling was particularly attractive to the young who were too immature to recognise its dangers, that it created, through the exercise of a belief in luck and chance rather than hard work, an unhealthy desire for excitement, encouraged meanness and generally undermined the Christian spirit.[9]

Successive twentieth-century British Government committees, commissions and review bodies, from the Select Committee set up in 1923 to 'consider the question of imposing a duty on betting and to report whether such a duty is desirable and practicable' (the Cautley Committee) to the Gambling Review Body set up in 1999 (the Budd Committee), have rejected the immorality discourse with growing confidence.[10] In March 2002 the Department for Culture, Media and Sport, newly responsible for the regulation of gambling in Britain, announced its proposals for regulatory change, based on the recommendations of the Budd Committee. Its dismissal of the immoral activity discourse was quite explicit:

> In the government's view the law should no longer incorporate or reflect any assumption that gambling is an activity which is objectionable and which people should have no encouragement to pursue.[11]

Discourses around appetitive behaviours rarely perish altogether, however, and, under provocation, the immorality discourse reappears in public to the present day. It reappeared in the debates on the National Lottery Bill. In the House of Lords debate in May 1993, for example, Lord Allen expressed his view that the National Lottery would contribute to 'the gambling culture of this country, to the dream of easy wealth and to the promotion of a chance ideology in opposition to the work ethic'; and the Bishop of St Albans stated, 'there is something implicitly deceitful about the state encouraging people to part with their money through the enticement of personal gain in order to spend the proceeds on matters which should be funded more properly from the public purse'.[12] In June 1998, a few years after the inauguration of Britain's National Lottery, Matthew Parris, an ex MP, referred in *The Times* to 'the perversion, by an agent of the State, of the language and imagery of hope and destiny, to sell a tawdry gambling scheme whose prize is money';[13] and in the same month, Melanie Phillips in the *Observer*, put her view in the following terms:

> [i]f there were one potent symbol of the way in which Britain vulgarised during the last two decades into a grasping, something-for-nothing society, it would surely be the National Lottery. [It] epitomises a society in which money is the dominant motif, greed is legitimised and private profit displaced public service'.[14]

In the week following the publication in July 2001 of the report of the Budd Committee, the subject was widely covered in the British press. Amongst articles appealing to an immorality discourse, a guest feature by the Deputy Editor of the *New Statesman*, which also appeared in the *Observer*, was notable. It raised the question whether, even at the beginning of the twenty-first century, gambling might be considered as an immoral activity:

> . . . a vote for gambling is also a vote for the collective abdication of responsibility. Gambling allows you to duck the consequences of your actions: you do not rely on your will or your moral compass to act as the agent of your fortune. Your fate is down to the roll of a dice rather than to you . . . Television is complicit in the creation of this grubby greed.[15]

It is hard not to agree with Peter Collins when he writes in his book *Gambling and the Public Interest* that ideas about the morality of gambling probably continue to play a substantial, if often unacknowledged, part in shaping views on the subject. He points to both religious and secular versions of the moral view – still alive today – that we have a responsibility to ourselves not to '. . . fritter it [life] away, for example, by wasting our time and money gambling'.[16] Nonetheless it has been increasingly difficult to use the immorality discourse without being shouted down. By the mid-twentieth century the Royal Commission on Betting, Lotteries and Gaming was already stating that, although gambling should be kept within reasonable bounds, 'this does not imply that there is anything inherently wrong in it'.[17] Anyone who attempts to revive the immorality discourse today is likely to be met with epithets such as 'anti-gambling lobby', 'moral entrepreneur', 'nanny', 'moral arbiter', 'wowser' or 'do-gooder',[18] and hence marginalised in the process. The submergence of the immorality discourse, historically inevitable though that may have been, can be seen as having unfortunate consequences. It will be argued later in this book that its loss has left us in something of a moral vacuum when it comes to discussing gambling and what society should do about it. We are left, it could be said, with a purely utilitarian basis for public debate. We discuss gambling in terms of costs and benefits, and rarely in terms of the personal, family and community values which may be affected – either encouraged or undermined – by the expansion of gambling.

Gambling as irrational behaviour

Closely linked to the immorality discourse is the idea that to gamble is to engage in an activity that is less than rational, sensible or educated. In the past an integral part of this discourse has often been the idea that gambling, being an irrational deviation from effective individual or collective action, is therefore inimical to the national interest or to the interest of a particular political party. For example, the House of Commons Select Committee on the laws relating to lotteries, in 1808, stated:

> ... [in] all the circumstances of a great manufacturing commercial nation ... it must be dangerous, in the highest degree ... to diffuse a spirit of speculation, whereby the mind is misled from those habits of continued industry which insure the acquisition of comfort and independence, to delusive dreams of sudden and enormous wealth, which must generally end in abject poverty and complete ruin.[19]

In a House of Commons debate on gambling, ten years later, Lyttleton spoke against legalised gambling whereby 'for a little filthy profit, this country should descend to imitate the scandalous practice of some continental nations...'.[20] Social historians who study the Victorian period have pointed to the advocacy of the respectable middle classes for 'rational' forms of recreation rather than irrational and morally debilitating forms such as racing, with its associations with gambling, and towards the end of that era working-class gambling was seen by anti-gamblers as both symptomatic and productive of Britain's economic decline relative to some of the other great powers.[21] Even in the mid-twentieth century, according to one social historian at least, national engagement in the Second World War was associated with a partial return to more hostile public opinion towards gambling, with its associations of misspent time and leisure.[22]

Along the same lines is the idea that gambling diverts attention and energy from facing social conditions that need to be challenged and changed. George Orwell, in *1984*, uses a state lottery as a metaphor for the emptiness of proletarian life.[23] The discourse of gambling as irrational and a barrier to progress can be seen in writings of early leaders of the British Labour Movement, many of whom saw gambling as an impediment to personal and political advance. Amongst the contributions to Rowntree's *Betting and Gambling* was Ramsay MacDonald, Secretary of the Labour Representation Committee and later Labour Prime Minister. In his article, entitled *Gambling and Citizenship*, he wrote:

> To hope ... that a Labour party can be built up in a population quivering from an indulgence in games of hazard is pure folly. Such a population cannot be organised for sustained political effort, cannot be depended upon for legal support to its political champions, cannot respond to appeals to its rational imagination.

Its hazards absorb so much of its leisure; they lead it away from thoughts of social righteousness; they destroy in it the sense of social service; they create in it a state of mind which believes in fate, luck, the irrational, the erratic; they dazzle its eyes with flashy hopes; they make it absolutely incapable of taking an interest in the methods and the aims of reforming politicians . . . Every Labour leader I know recognises the gambling spirit as a menace to any form of Labour party.[24]

Many Labour leaders of that period were anti-gamblers. Radical non-conformity was strong in the early British Labour Party, and the view was widely held that gambling, like drinking, held back the progress of the working class. For example, in a Clarion Pamphlet, Burns's 'tip to the workers' was, 'Spend on books what is often given to beer; to mental improvement what is given to gambling'.[25] Keir Hardie, giving evidence to the House of Lords Select Committee on betting, which preceded the 1906 Act, stated, 'Gambling as a rule is the outcome of an idol purposeless life'.[26] As late as the 1930s anti-gambling discourses were still painting punters in terms such as 'ignorant dupes', 'feckless', 'reckless', 'thriftless', 'wasteful', 'weak-willed' and 'selfish'.[27]

One variety of the irrationality discourse, well articulated by Goodman in his book *The Luck Business*, sees the expansion of gambling as part of modern, chance-oriented society, characterised by reduced opportunities for stable employment and much increased access to speculation through stocks and shares and investment in property – previously confined to the wealthy and powerful but now part of ordinary people's lives:

The rapid proliferation of government-promoted gambling in the 1980s and early 1990s was part of a much broader economic change taking place in America. As long-term investment in productive enterprises declined and the possibility of making a secure income sharply diminished, they were replaced by a host of ventures that stressed quick profits through enterprises of chance. People in all walks of life were offered new opportunities for financial risk taking. Gambling was just one of a myriad of techniques for making money through luck rather than work, which included new strategies for speculating in real estate, the stock market, and collectibles.[28]

The irrationality discourse is also to be seen in the modern writings of those who take a cognitive view of problem gambling and its treatment (see Chapter 4). In that arena, biases and distortions, such as the 'gambler's fallacy', the 'illusion of control' and superstitious thinking, figure large. In most such presentations the irrational side to gambling is attached to the minority with special problems and not to the activity itself. On occasions, however, irrationality is attributed more widely. For example, in a study of older adolescents and young adults recruited from secondary schools and universities in Melbourne, Australia, evidence was found for a '. . . complex of irrational beliefs that are related to gambling. . .'.[29] The view that the majority of those who bet are 'mug punters'[30] is probably still very prevalent.

Gambling as cheating and exploitation

Another closely related discourse speaks of gambling as exploitative. When most gambling was conducted between private individuals, it was mostly gamblers themselves who cheated one another. The very term 'gambler' has often been used as a pejorative one in the past; gambling promoters therefore sometimes preferring the term 'gaming' with its connotations of fun and playfulness.[31] Dr Johnson stated in his *Dictionary of the English Language* in 1755 that 'gambler' was a 'cant word' for gamester, a 'knave whose practice it is to invite the unwary to gain and cheat them'.[32] The verbs 'to bet' and 'to wager' meant the same thing and were less disreputable than the newer verb 'to gamble' which was associated in England with the lower class and with cheating and indulgence. As gambling became more commercialised, it was increasingly the operators who were thought to exploit the punters. In his account of the history of British bookmaking, Chinn[33] writes of the long battle that bookmakers fought to overcome their bad reputation for cheating their customers. Much of the concern about gambling that peaked at the end of the nineteenth and early in the twentieth centuries was about the dangers of working-class gambling, which was often phrased in terms of protecting the working classes from exploitation. A letter from the Metropolitan Police Commissioner to the Home Office in 1911 contained the following:

> The man who can afford to lose . . . need not be the object of our concern; contrary to the recognized principle, what is now required is one law for the rich and another for the poor. The poor have no grievance as to this. It would be for their protection against themselves. . . .[34]

In the second half of the twentieth century, with the decline of the immorality discourse, the exploitation discourse continued to exert a strong influence on public policy through the principle of 'unstimulated demand'. The principle that commercial exploitation should be tightly controlled was embodied in such regulations as: the invisibility of the insides of public betting offices; casinos only allowed in 'permitted areas'; and the banning of any advertising of gambling facilities.[35] Although such controls are now a thing of the past, the exploitation discourse lingers on in the form of references to the bad old days and the need to remain vigilant. Speaking in the House of Commons in February 1964 the Under Secretary of State at the Home Office stated that the Betting, Gaming and Lotteries Bill, then before parliament, was directed against the 'almost limitless ingenuity of the people who exploit gambling for their own profit'.[36] Although lead responsibility within the British Government has now passed from the Home Office to the Department for Culture, Media and Sport, statements from the latter department continue to recognise the potential danger of criminal involvement in gambling; which was one of the motives behind setting up the Gambling Commission with a broader remit and greater regulatory powers than the former Gaming Board.

The gambling as exploitation discourse, however, was not confined to activities that broke the law. The argument that gambling by its very nature exploits the punter is not often heard now, but it was, for example, in evidence in the US House of Representatives and Senate and in the US media at the time when gambling policy was being debated in that country in the 1990s. One senator expressed the view that, 'Many of the insidious tactics used by the gambling industry to bilk people out of their money must be considered by the Commission in order to understand fully the modern business of gambling'.[37] It was also to be seen in an article written by Roy Hattersley, former Deputy Leader of the British Labour Party, which had given such strong support to the anti-gambling movement nearly 100 years previously. The starting point for his article was his maternal grandfather's gambling problem (see Chapter 3), but he went on to argue that the libertarian philosophy on which the 2001 Gambling Review Body's report appeared to be based needed to be questioned:

> It seems possible that Britain . . . will become the gambling capital of Europe . . . The problem now is . . . a gradual and corrosive destruction of the values on which our society is based. Nobody can be sure the casinos will not become easy territory for drug pushers, but we can be certain that, once the international gamblers move in, they will be fertile ground for men who want to take money from people who cannot afford it . . . We have to ask, is it worth it?[38]

The idea that gambling is exploitative may be a greater survivor than either the immorality or irrationality discourses. In its advice to the licensing justices the Gaming Board in 2003 suggested that justices should seek 'to protect the public and prospective players from the improper attentions of competitive commercial operators anxious to drum up business'.[39] In his book *Gambling, Freedom and Democracy*, published in 2008, Peter Adams asked who was behind the push for expanded gambling opportunities. The gambling industry itself, with governments in league with it, was the answer he gave, suggesting that a large proportion of gambling revenue is extracted from people who are experiencing problems controlling their gambling, and hence that gambling is 'preying on the weak and vulnerable'.[40]

Gambling as something tawdry and unaesthetic

One variety of negative discourse about gambling, although it may appear closely related to others that we have already considered, can usefully be distinguished because it may have the capacity to survive while others, such as the immorality discourse, have declined in potency. This is the discourse which depicts gambling as something that is distasteful, sordid, tawdry. It was much in evidence when greyhound racing stadia were appearing in British cities in the 1920s. In 1927 Churchill wrote to the Home Secretary saying that, '. . . the spectacle of these animated roulette boards, where the attraction is betting pure and simple, is one which will arouse the moral and anti-gambling forces in the country',[41] and a magistrate at the time commented that there was 'no more loathsome spectacle of English women than to be observed at the greyhound races'.[42]

Amusement arcades were later spoken about in similar terms. Rowntree, for example, observed in 1951 that '[amusement] arcades are tawdry and sordid, and even apart from the actual gambling, their atmosphere is by no means that to which a prudent nation would desire a substantial proportion of its young people to be exposed'.[43] Even Professor Miers in his comprehensive and objective view of the regulation of commercial gambling, old and new, in Britain, could not resist voicing his own opinion that:

> Anyone who . . . has stood in the middle of a large urban amusement arcade when all machines are in use would be hard pressed to describe the experience as aesthetically uplifting.[44]

The aesthetic discourse has been used in relation to most forms of gambling at one time or another. To Harold Wilson is attributed the description of premium bonds as a 'squalid little raffle' when they were finally introduced in 1956,[45] and the demeaning nature of '16-year olds scratching lottery cards' was cited in the House of Lords debate as grounds for objecting to the introduction of the National Lottery in the 1990s.[46]

In his book, Collins recognises this discourse as one that is very real but perhaps more difficult to articulate than some others:

> . . .the real reason we don't want gambling machines to be located everywhere that there might be a market for them is that, for some rather undefined reason, we just don't. We don't think it desirable or appropriate that people should be confronted with gambling machines in . . . profusion . . . We don't want gambling machines everywhere, and we probably also want only a limited number of urban casinos and other gambling operations in our city . . . we [may] have aesthetic objections to having gambling houses on every corner. These considerations are not as strong as thinking that all gambling is immoral or dangerous, so the less of it we have the better. They do not support prohibition but rather a view that says, 'Let us have legal gambling in moderation'.[47]

Expansion of gambling is likely to provoke increased expression of the tawdry and unaesthetic discourse. The London borough of Hackney, one of the most deprived in the city, provides a good example. Several hundred local residents signed a petition complaining that the Old Town Hall – once the borough's administrative centre, later a bank, and now a site of an application for a gambling premises licence – would be detrimental to the character and feel of the area if the gambling licence were to be awarded.[48]

Gambling as a destroyer

Gambling has long been written about as a destructive force, something that robs people of their self-control and takes over people's lives. In 1674, Cotton described gaming as '. . . an enchanting witchery . . . an itching disease. . .', and in his early eighteenth-century three-volume *Traité du Jeu*, Jean Barbeyrac said of gambling:

> I do not know if there is any other passion which allows less of repose and which one has so much difficulty in reducing . . . the passion of gambling gives no time for breathing; it is an enemy which gives neither quarter nor truce; it is a persecutor, furious and indefatigable. The more one plays the more one wishes to play; . . . it seems that gambling had acquired the right to occupy all [the gambler's] thoughts. . . .[49]

The preamble to the Gaming Act of 1744 referred to:

> . . . divers young and unwary persons and others are drawn in to lose the greatest part and sometimes all their substance; and it frequently happens that they are thereby reduced to the utmost necessities and betake themselves to the most wicked courses, which end in their ruin.[50]

Depictions of gambling as thoroughly destructive are to be found in a number of Victorian novels including Dickens' *The Old Curiosity Shop* which depicts Nell's grandfather's mania for gambling and its consequences for the lives of him and Nell; and many of the writings of Thackeray, who himself had a problem with excessive gambling as a student. The novel in which gambling is most prominently and consistently depicted as destructive is *Esther Waters* by George Moore, who had an extensive knowledge of horse racing. Published in 1894, the novel never shows gambling as recreational but rather as something that destroys the lives of several characters, notably Esther's husband, William.[51]

In the mid-1930s a Methodist MP, R. J. Russell, conducted a campaign, in the end unsuccessful, to prohibit football pools – 'one of the gravest perils of our times', representing a danger to the family and a temptation to the wife, 'the guardian of the family exchequer'.[52] In their evidence to the 1949–51 Royal Commission on Betting, Lotteries, and Gaming, the Churches' Council on Gambling were in no doubt that gambling machines encouraged 'gambling fever among the young'.[53]

As we saw in Chapter 3, early twentieth-century psychiatrists recognised gambling as one of the 'manias'[54] and in the second half of the twentieth century clinicians and researchers started to quote directly from their patients and participants.[55] One of the earliest studies of what came to be commonly referred to as 'compulsive gambling' wrote of it as something that '. . . spreads out and affects every person with whom the compulsive gambler is closed involved. . .'.[56] One young, 'self-confessed addicted fruit machine gambler' who took part in research is quoted as saying that machines were 'deadly'.[57] Participants in another research project said of their problematic gambling: 'It's like a drug isn't it – it's like smoking really, it gets you, doesn't it, [it] catches you' (a man in his 30s); and 'it's like a need, it eats away inside you it really does. It's there gnawing at you and you get depressed, you get moody and you know get very,

very snappy and very argumentative [when you can't gamble]' (a woman in her 20s).[58]

Bergler's 1958 classic *The Psychology of Gambling* has been credited with marking a break with the past by viewing gambling problems within the powerful discourse of medicine and psychiatry. It was important that problem gambling should be construed as something that was not immoral or criminal but was rather non-rational or 'neurotic'.[59] The third edition of the American Psychiatric Association's Diagnostic and Statistical Manual (DSM) was the first version to include 'pathological gambling', conceived of as a disorder of 'impulse control'. Between 1980 when DSM-III was published and 1987 when the revised version (DSM-III-R) appeared, diagnostic criteria were modified and modelled more closely on those of alcohol and drug dependence.[60]

The discourse of gambling as destructive has therefore survived but in a highly modified form. The idea that gambling *per se* is life-destroying is no longer a dominant one. In its place is the more selective idea of gambling as pathological for some people but not for all, which opens up debate about whether the source of the destructiveness lies more in the gambling or in those persons whose lives it destroys (which was the subject of Chapter 5). An even more recent paradigm, in part an heir to the view of gambling as destructive, is the public health model. It takes a broader view, addressing not only the destructive potential of gambling for the gambler but more generally its potential for adversely affecting the quality of life for families and communities and for society as a whole. It 'embodies public health values that reflect concern for the impact of gambling expansion on vulnerable, marginalized and at risk population groups . . . [it] recognizes that there are both costs and benefits associated with gambling'.[61]

Some will see in the modern pathological and public health discourses an attempt by anti-gamblers to occupy ground lost with the passing of the immorality discourse. But the weight of research on gambling that has now accumulated, combined with modern addiction theory, lends support to the idea that the activity of gambling carries the seeds of destructiveness. It may be more accurate to describe that modern discourse as one that speaks of gambling as a *dangerous* form of consumption.[62] Much of Chapters 3, 4 and 5 were devoted to exploring that way of looking at gambling in some detail.

Discourses that support the expansion of gambling

Gambling as character building

Just as the immorality and irrationality discourses paint gambling as an activity that appeals to some of the worst sides of human nature, so there exists an opposite kind of discourse which depicts gambling as bringing out some of the best features of character. Amongst the positive features of human nature that have been said to be promoted by gambling are included playfulness, gameness, composure under stressful or risky circumstances, graciousness in adversity, courage, bravery and heroism, clear thinking and even improvement in the three R's.[63]

The character-building discourse has a long history. Commenting on the aristocratic 'gambling orgies' of the eighteenth century, Victorian historian Trevelyan commented that, 'The passion for gambling was not weakened or diverted by the rival attractions of female society; for the surest road into the graces of a fine lady was to be known as one who betted freely, and lost handsomely. . .'.[64] The nobles who frequented Crockford's gambling club in St James's in London in the 1830s were said to show 'gentlemanly bearing and calm and unmoved demeanour' whether winning or losing, rather as 'professional gamblers' are said to comport themselves to this day.[65] A later historian, McKibbin,[66] concluded that gambling which allowed the exercise of skill was seen, in the late nineteenth and early twentieth centuries, as less reprehensible than gambling that was purely chance, and, indeed, that the intellectual effort involved in studying racing form provided the working-class gambler with an opportunity for orderly thinking. During the time of controversy over newspaper competitions, the Newsagents Booksellers and Stationers National Union argued that such competitions offered young people an alternative to 'doing worse', and were constructive because to win it was necessary to show 'a sense of humour or a vein of originality'.[67]

The character-building discourse, or at least a manly version of it, is to be seen in Rudyard Kipling's poem *If*. It was published in 1910 and was still, at the end of the twentieth century, topping the poll as Britain's favourite poem. In that poem, the game of pitch and toss gets a glowing reference, keeping '. . . a cool head and staking all on a single throw' being associated with manliness. The poem was written at a time when anti-gambling sentiment and support for gambling prohibition was as strong in Britain as it had ever been. At a meeting in Manchester in October 1906, the year in which the Street Betting Act was passed which made street betting illegal in Britain for over 50 years, the maverick Liberal MP Horatio Bottomley proclaimed his intention to rouse Englishmen against 'the prevailing wave of puritanical and namby-pamby, goody-goody legislation [which] struck at those fundamental principles of self-reliance and robust manhood which made the English race what it was'.[68]

The character-building discourse is not often seen in pure form in the present day, but was much in evidence in the writings of social scientists in the 1960s and 70s, a number of whom declared their own gambling or got close to gambling and gamblers in the course of direct observational or participant observation studies. It was suggested amongst other things that gambling represented a milieu in which gamblers could appear to exercise control, show composure and make apparently rational decisions, uncover information (e.g. about horses) and 'beat the system'.[69] Irving Goffman, the most famous sociologist of them all, who worked as a blackjack dealer and croupier in the Nevada casinos, concluded that the gambler, by engaging in risk taking, could demonstrate character strength in a way unavailable to most people in ordinary life.[70] Observations of East End London betting shops by another social scientist also suggested that gambling provided an opportunity for exercising intelligent choice, the experience of control, and opportunities to discuss with others and to appear knowledgeable.[71]

Gambling as harmless amusement

Perhaps because of the history of anti-gambling sentiments and agitation, and because of the class prejudice that has attended investigations and legislation about gambling, late twentieth-century historians have mostly been at pains to defend working-class gambling (and by implication all gambling) against charges of irrationality, excess, the creation of poverty through losing and the inducing of idleness through winning. To do so they have employed a discourse of gambling as harmless amusement. For example, according to one:

> Gambling can be seen as a moderate, economistic and expressive form of recreation... In an unequal society, most people had a good idea of the odds facing them, and of how the dice were loaded, and they spent their time and money as best they could. Their regular and moderate betting was part of a continually evolving culture in which leisure and economy were and are fundamental to people's lives.[72]

The Birmingham local historian Carl Chinn also concluded, on the basis of the historical evidence available plus personal accounts of earlier twentieth-century betting that he collected, that working-class betting was largely for very small stakes (the 'penny punter' and the 'threepenny flutter', for example) and was rationally and carefully controlled. Much working-class betting was 'fairly regular, prudent, usually considered'.[73] It could not lift people out of poverty – the life-changing long-odds win on the pools or jackpot lottery win may have changed that – but it could offer the prospect of being able to afford a good night out, a luxury item or a present for the family. It was 'the only possibility of making a decision, of a choice between alternatives, in a life otherwise prescribed in every detail by poverty and necessity, and always the object of other people's decisions'.[74] Some picked horses with a pin, but others took great care in making selections. Chinn supported the suggestion that gambling, as a result of all the studying, calculating, note-taking and communicating that was involved, encouraged literacy as well as arithmetical ability amongst people who had had otherwise relatively little education.

The rise of football pools betting gave strength to that discourse. By the 1950s, 'doing the pools' was seen as an important and largely harmless feature of national life. As the Memorandum of the Roman Catholic Church to the Royal Commission on Betting, Lotteries and Gaming of 1949–51 put it, pools had become 'a national pastime [and were] beneficial, since in many homes happy evenings are spent by the family remaining together and filling up their coupons'.[75] By the time of the 1949–51 Royal Commission, urban on-course betting on dog racing had also become popular, changing the law on off-course betting was widely thought to be long overdue, and the Second World War had hastened changes in national attitudes on all manner of subjects. The much more relaxed view taken by the Commission about the dangers of gambling, compared to its predecessor of the early 1930s, is well summed up by one gambling historian:

> . . . it was discounted as a significant source of crime, serious social problems, or harm to individual character. Gambling was regarded as an unremarkable feature of everyday life which was much less distinct from other leisure activities and about which gamblers were much less naïve than anti-gamblers suggested . . . The problem of gambling was identified as being, not everyday participation, but rather the excessive, abnormal behaviour of certain individuals.[76]

There are a number of discernible strands to the harmless amusement discourse. A central theme is that most gambling is small-scale, modest, moderate. The 1978 Royal Commission on Gambling, for example, observed of casinos in provincial towns that, compared to some notorious London casinos catering to the rich end of the market, the reality was 'rather more prosaic', catering for local people 'who play for comparatively modest stakes in comparatively modest surroundings'.[77] The modesty strand to the harmless amusement discourse is closely bound to the theme of gambling as 'harmless' fun and pleasure. Gambling as just a bit of fun, a form of harmless entertainment like any other, is how the gambling industry prefers to see it. As the Chairman of the Gaming Board put it in 2001, the gambling sector was now part of the 'mainstream leisure industry'.[78] That was the year in which, following a general election, lead British Government responsibility for gambling was transferred from the Home Office to the Department for Culture, Media and Sport. The latter department's predecessor was the Department for National Heritage, created, amongst other things, to promote the National Lottery, and dubbed by its first Secretary of State as the 'Ministry of Fun'.[79] The argument of gambling promoters, and those – including a number of prominent academics in the field – who support them, is that gambling for most people is a harm-free form of pleasure, corresponding to the dictum of moderation in all things. One academic writes of gambling as an 'adult pleasure', suggesting that those who '. . . enjoy the occasional game of chance have lives that are not only more enviable but also more admirable than those who eschew all such pleasures and all play'.[80]

A minor strand to the harmless amusement discourse – but an important one because it runs counter to the tawdry, unaesthetic discourse described earlier – is that gambling, in the words of the Amusement Caterers' Association, giving evidence to the Royal Commission on Betting, Lotteries, and Gaming 1949–51, is an 'inexpensive and wholesome entertainment that is perfectly innocuous',[81] or, in the language of the initial regulator of Britain's National Lottery, OFLOT, referring to the Lottery, should be seen as being of 'high quality, tasteful and beyond reproach'.[82]

The final strand to this discourse is the idea of modernity – turning one's back on old-fashioned ideas and customs. Changing attitudes and habits following the First World War led many – the Chairman of the Commons

Select Committee on Betting Duty was one[83]– to conclude that gambling legislation was by then out of line with contemporary social life. The Government Cabinet Committee that received the final report of the Royal Commission on Lotteries and Betting 1932–33 concluded that, 'The law relating to lotteries, betting and gaming is out of harmony with modern conditions and requires amendment'.[84] As the liberalising Betting and Gaming Bill of 1960 was being debated in Parliament, one Conservative MP stated that, 'we are sweeping Victoriana from the Statute Book'.[85] The modernity argument was much in evidence again in the lead-up to the 2005 Gambling Act.

In the present day the harmless amusement discourse is well represented in debate on the controversial topic of the regulation of gambling machines. The lowest category of such machines have often been said not to constitute 'gaming' at all, and to have much closer affinity with end-of-the-pier amusements which offer no chance of financial return. Hence the popular term 'amusements' for such machines. Since the last decades of the twentieth century they are to be found in 'amusement arcades', particularly at the seaside. The government's Gambling Review Body in its report in 2001 preferred to call such premises 'family entertainment centres' and such machines 'low stake/low prize' machines. In its evidence to the Review Body, the British Amusement Catering Trades Association (BACTA) had argued that such machines were trivial and not to be regarded as gambling at all.

The harmless amusement discourse has now become one of the most powerful in underpinning support for the liberalisation and expansion of gambling. It is one of the main ways of thinking that gambling operators would like the public to accept when they think about gambling. It runs directly counter to the view of gambling as inherently dangerous or destructive.

Gambling as cultural and economic enhancement

A very modern discourse speaks of gambling as something that is enhancing of communities or for the whole nation, certainly economically and also in terms of leisure opportunities and cultural life generally. Not that such a discourse is only a recent invention. Economic enhancement has probably long been amongst the claimed benefits of gambling. For example, Carl Chinn tells us that the Reverend from Cheltenham, who was so alarmed about the approach of the town's annual races in 1827 (see the immorality discourse, above), was accused of 'ultra-piety' by a Tory correspondent in *The Gentleman's Magazine*. The latter pointed out that horse racing had brought prosperity to the town by giving employment and increased trade, and that suppression of the races would cause unemployment, greater rather than lesser crime, and local economic decline.[86]

That argument has changed little since then. The outcome of the British Government's Gambling Review Body, published in July 2001, was reported in the British press the following week as having been warmly welcomed by

the gambling industry for reasons that included economic and cultural enhancement.[87] Both *The Times* and *The Independent* reported *Ladbroke's* plans
to create 1,000 new jobs, and economic benefits were especially foreseen for
towns like Blackpool which could be revitalised by becoming gaming resorts.
Blackpool, then front runner to be Britain's first casino resort, was said to be
'poised', 'all set to go', with development plans by *Leisure Parcs* already on the
table. *The Sunday Express* for 22 July referred to the GRB report as being the
'first milestone in the project . . . to kick-start Blackpool'. Casino operators in
Britain had been complaining for some time about the restrictions placed on
their operations, including the fact that live entertainment was forbidden in
British casinos, unlike, for example, in France where casinos '. . . are expected to
provide entertainment of a quality that adds to the attractiveness of or culturally
enhances the area'.[88]

When controversy broke loose over the granting of a licence for a casino in
Hamilton, a small provincial city on the North Island of New Zealand, one of the
prominent arguments in favour was the cultural and economic enhancement
one. The following appeared in *The Waikato Times* in September 1997:

> Tourism Waikato has already had an enthusiastic response to the casino from
> international tour operators: They say 'finally Hamilton will be a real city'. And
> the casino may also tip the balance in the conference market. 'I've had nothing
> but positive reaction. The casino will lead the change in nightlife in Hamilton. I
> know it will make a difference'.[89]

Shortly after the casino opened, a columnist in the same paper opined, 'Hamilton is no longer a boring provincial city. It's a go-ahead place, a metropolitan
city which offers its populace a choice in what they can do'.[90] In general the
gambling industry in New Zealand, as elsewhere, has depicted gambling as
modern, sophisticated, enhancing 'our' way of life, being good for the economy
and, with contributions to charity, good for communities as well.[91]

In Britain, as elsewhere, public acceptance of the National Lottery has been
promoted by emphasising the contributions that playing makes to the National
Lottery distribution fund and hence to national 'good causes'. As the 1978 Royal
Commission on Gambling stated in its report, 'The case against a national
lottery for good causes is feeble – under modern conditions'. Well managed, it
would 'improve, indirectly, if not directly, the quality of British life'.[92] Within
the year of Britain's National Lottery being launched, the Director General of
OFLOT felt able to say that the NL was already becoming an 'important and
permanent part of our national life'.[93]

A related component of the enhancement discourse is the idea that gambling
is 'neighbourly'. In Britain this is best illustrated by reference to bingo which,
from the 1960s onwards, came to be thought of as providing a safe and congenial place to socialise, particularly for working-class women. The Gaming
Act of 1968 concluded that it was appropriate to take '. . . a benevolent view of
bingo provided it remained a neighbourly form of gaming played for modest
stakes. . .'.[94]

The claimed economic benefits that casinos in particular might bring to the communities where they are situated have figured large in gambling industry lobbying of national and state governments, but they have certainly not gone unchallenged.[95] They also form a large part of attempts by economists to put figures on the benefits of gambling to society, as we shall see in Chapter 8.

Gambling as freedom to choose without interference

The discourse that says that gambling is something that people should be free to choose to do without unnecessary interference is one that seems always to have been with us. In 1844 a House of Commons Select Committee on gaming stated, 'nobody now disputes the opinion of Adam Smith, that governments ought not to pretend to watch over the economy of private people'.[96] Half a century later, during the time of controversy about the legality of betting at horse race meetings, the Secretary of the Anti-Puritan League wrote to the Home Secretary complaining of the 'grandmotherly interference of self-righteous faddists . . . [and the] meddlesome attempts . . . to interfere with the national sports and pastimes of the people'.[97] Another half-century on, the 1949–51 Royal Commission on Betting, Lotteries and Gaming concluded that the object of gambling legislation 'should be to interfere as little as possible with individual liberty to take part in the various forms of gambling but to impose such restrictions as are desirable and practicable to discourage or prevent excess'.[98] When the National Lottery was being debated more than 40 years later, the government made use of the right to choose discourse:

> The government's policy on gambling is based on the principle that the state should interfere as little as possible in the individual's liberty to take part in various forms of gambling but that controls are necessary to prevent crime, to ensure that punters are aware what they are letting themselves in for and to protect the vulnerable, in particular young people.[99]

Writing from New Zealand, Peter Adams cites many examples of the use of this discourse to defend the right to set up new gambling facilities.[100] For example: a local Wellington politician wrote to the Editor of *The Wellington Evening Post*, 'In an age when how to spend increased leisure time is a significant social issue who are we to say that others should not be able to visit a casino in Wellington if that's their preference, especially when they can visit one in Christchurch and Auckland?'; the Chair of the charity Gaming Association declared in the press, 'Gambling is part and parcel of life in New Zealand and Australia. Our people are industrious, self-reliant and able to make their own decisions about their lives'; and a spokesman for the Hospitality Association was of the opinion:

> On legislative issues, we are faced by a Parliament obsessed with protecting the minority through controlling the majority. It seems that in today's environment, self-responsibility has been replaced with collective mediocrity.

Adams writes of the way in which those who have opposed the expansion of gambling are thereby cast in the role of 'radical puritans' who are motivated by a desire to restrict other people's pleasures. This device is much on display in Peter Collins book *Gambling and the Public Interest*, a book that is largely an exposition of the right-to-choose gambling discourse. Drawing on J. S. Mill's *On Liberty*, Collins' clearly stated view is that it is 'morally wrong for the state to interfere with the essentially private choices of individuals', that 'interfering with people's freedom of choice to protect them from harming themselves goes against and goes beyond the legitimate role of government in a free society', that 'government has no business interfering with the exchanges of goods and services between willing buyers and willing sellers', that 'not to accord to adults the maximum possible freedom to decide for themselves how to live their own lives is to violate their dignity as autonomous moral agents' and that there has always been 'officious interfering with the pleasures and liberties of the young'.[101] His clearest statement of this discourse is the following:

> ...I do not want to live in a society that is highly puritanical in that it frowns on pleasure generally and on many largely harmless pleasures in particular. Nor do I want to live in a society that is highly authoritarian in that it arrogates to itself the right to prescribe what pleasures people may and may not indulge in. I also do not want to live in a society that makes it difficult to be adventurous in the pursuit of pleasure or one that inhibits economic creativity by restricting the forms of entertainment that people may provide on a commercial basis. Above all, I want to live in a society in which I can think for myself and make up my own mind about how I wish to spend my time, money, talents, and energy without being bossed around and frustrated in my designs by the agents of impersonal government.[102]

Along with the harmless amusement and cultural and economic enhancement discourses, the addition of the freedom to choose discourse creates a formidable argument in support of unimpeded gambling expansion.

Gambling as normal unrestricted business

By the time of the 1976–78 Royal Commission on Gambling (the Rothschild Commission), the last of the twentieth century, legalised gambling in various forms was well entrenched in Britain, its regulation was considered largely satisfactory, gambling as immoral activity or irrational behaviour were discourses less and less heard, and the discourse of gambling as perilous and destructive was not yet strong enough to much influence the Commission. Altogether, commercialised gambling was considered primarily, not as a social problem, but rather as a business which provided entertainment for which people paid, and which was no different from other types of leisure and recreation. Everyday gambling was 'normalised'. It was treated as an acceptable part of everyday life, rather than as a marginally deviant activity.[103] According to one historian of gambling, the Rothschild Commission's recommendations for some relaxation of restrictions on betting offices '... accorded well with the neo-conservative enthusiasm for deregulating and encouraging business'.[104]

In his thorough review of the regulation of gambling in Britain, historically and more recently, David Miers pointed to the rapid appearance of the gambling-as-business discourse between the Gaming Act of 1968, which placed strict controls on casinos and established the Gaming Board, and the mid-1990s. At the former time, in his view, gambling was '... most emphatically not regarded as performing any desirable or any productive economic function'.[105] The controlling regime led by the Home Office was increasingly seen as anti-market and was increasingly frustrating to commercial operators and modern free marketers.[106]

One aspect that was causing uncertainty and consternation at the turn of the century, in Britain as elsewhere, was the impact of rapid technological change, and especially the likely future of internet gambling (both placing bets via the internet and, more particularly, playing 'virtual' games operated solely on the internet). The Gaming Board in 1999 conducted its own assessment of opinions about how internet gambling should be regulated, and, in preparing its own report, appeared to have been most persuaded by marketplace arguments:

> If the market develops and matures without British involvement, it will be too late to recover and make an impact. Inevitably, British companies will look for overseas opportunities themselves (... this is starting to happen) and once established abroad they will not return later.[107]

Not surprisingly, the general view of the gambling industry, well represented in a report carried out by KPMG for Business in Sport and Leisure (BISL) in 2000, was that the industry was subject to far too much unnecessary 'interference', and that aside from matters to do with the law, supplying opportunities for gambling in response to consumer demand '... is best left to market forces'.[108] Amongst the recommendations in that report was the particularly radical suggestion that the existing demarcation between different forms of gambling should be dismantled. Apart from the siting of gaming machines in such locations as casinos and bingo clubs, by and large it was still the case that gambling venues were specialised. The KPMG report cited Robin Oakley, a well-known BBC commentator and columnist, as saying that restrictions on the retail of betting products, was 'akin to having a law which said that Marks and Spencer can open their shops, but only if they restrict themselves to selling socks'.[109] KPMG themselves said: 'It could be argued that mature consumers should be allowed to exercise choice over where and when, and with what basket of other products, they consume gambling products'.[110]

The same changes in the way gambling was being talked about were taking place elsewhere in the world. In New Zealand, for example, the language surrounding gambling was now about 'freedom to trade', 'legitimate business', 'open markets', 'growth', 'sound commercial decisions', 'shareholder interests' and 'profits'.[111] In Australia, the Australian Gaming Machine Manufacturers

Association, making submissions to the New South Wales and Australian governments regarding what they saw as unnecessary restrictions on gambling machines, argued that legislation should facilitate 'an open technology environment' in which 'entertainment diversity' is encouraged. The industry needed to be allowed to develop, unhampered by restrictions, with 'the freedom and flexibility to expend major research and development resources, to innovate, to develop new products and in turn to make them available [elsewhere]'.[112]

In Europe, those representing gambling operators were challenging European Union law in order to oppose member states protecting their countries' existing, often state-run, gambling industries. It was argued that a fully free market in gambling products within the EU, and the privatisation of surviving state monopolies, would have a number of customer benefits. Better odds would be offered and lower commissions and/or high payouts; and customers would be encouraged to have a closer look at the products on offer and to be able to choose between them.[113]

In Britain, the change in the way gambling was to be seen was enshrined in the report of the Gambling Review Body at the turn of the century. At the time of setting up the GRB in December 1999, the Home Office Minister responsible for gambling policy said:

> Much of our current gambling legislation is over 30 years old. Social attitudes have changed and the law is fast being overtaken by technological developments. The government wants to get rid of unnecessary burdens on business, while maintaining protections necessary in the public interest.[114]

The very favourable response of the gambling industry to the GRB report was picked up by most of the papers in the week following the release of the report.[115] *The Mirror* named four betting companies which were said to be, 'thrilled at the proposals, which means they will be able to compete with National Lottery's massive prizes'. The share price of *The Hilton Group* (the owners of *Ladbroke's*) and of firms manufacturing gambling machines had risen. A report in *The Independent* the same day picked out the report's emphasis on the need to provide gambling customers with a 'better level of service'. The government also welcomed the report. The normal, unrestricted business discourse predominated in subsequent DCMS proposals in 2002. For example, it was proposed to remove 'unnecessary barriers to customer access to gambling'; 'gambling products [would be] more visible and accessible'; gambling debts would for the first time be enforceable by law, 'like other consumer contracts'; casino operators would be freed from the existing controls which 'unnecessarily discourage innovation and restrict customer choice'; there was an aspiration that Britain would be 'world leader' in online gambling. In summary, gambling was to be seen as '. . . an important industry in its own right, meeting the legitimate desires of many millions of people and providing many thousands of jobs',[116] 'creat[ing] a more open and competitive gambling sector . . . [giving] better choice for consumers and enhanced opportunities for business both in the UK and abroad'.[117]

Gambling as responsible behaviour

The normal, unrestricted business discourse – referred to by Goodwin in *The Luck Business* as the 'business-as-usual' discourse – adds a further late twentieth-century weight to the already forceful pro-gambling argument. The weakness that remains in that argument is the difficulty of dealing with the lingering presence of the gambling as destroyer discourse, now transmuted into its individual pathology and danger to public health forms. This is where the eleventh of the 11 discourses comes in. It is the discourse that speaks of 'responsible gambling'. It sits well with notions of gambling as business, amusement and free choice.

In the language of business, gamblers are cast as consumers. As consumers they are said to have responsibilities, to consume in a way that is responsible, towards others – their families, for example – and towards their own health. The successful operation of the market relies on consumers, or at least a large bulk of them, being responsible consumers – responsible gamblers in this case.[118] That was clear in the statement of the Chief Executive of the Christchurch casino in New Zealand, responding to media criticism for allowing one customer to lose several million dollars in the casino:

> We run a business. He used the business and the responsibility must stop with him. We can't be everybody's nanny and minder. It's extremely unfortunate. It does not help the image of casinos and does not help the business and allows all sorts of people to attack us without knowing the conditions we operate under.[119]

Since it is now generally accepted that gambling poses a serious problem, at least for some people, an essential element of the harmless entertainment discourse now consists of the minimising and marginalising of the numbers who are thought to be at risk. As one commentator from New Zealand points out, this part of the argument involves 'narrowing the responsibility down to a small group of people that cause the problems and arguing that their indiscretions cannot justify restricting the freedom to gamble for the public as a whole'.[120] He quotes from the Board Chair of a casino company, as follows:

> We agree that attention must be paid to people in the community who are not able to manage their gaming activity, but we stress that, like all things, an appropriate balance must be maintained between protection mechanisms for at risk persons and freedom of choice for the wider community.[121]

According to Peter Collins, a utilitarian morality, supporting the promotion of the greatest happiness for the greatest number of citizens, favours a liberal approach to gambling regulation, since the harm caused by a small minority is minimal compared to the pleasure that gambling brings to the majority:

> Addictive gamblers are a small minority even of regular gamblers . . . I consider the incidence of dangerously excessive gambling to be fairly small as a proportion of gamblers and the harm caused by excessive gambling to be relatively small compared to the damage caused by inter alia alcohol, drugs, and overeating.[122]

This also sits well with the freedom to choose discourse. In the words of the American Gaming Association (AGA) in a submission to the Australian Senate regarding a Bill which, if enacted, would bring in a number of restrictions on the operation of gambling machines designed to minimise their harmfulness, the proposed restrictions would 'reduce the enjoyment of the other 99 per cent of people who play the gambling machines for recreation'.[123] The AGA was clear in its submission who this small minority of people were who would be responsible for spoiling the enjoyment of the majority. They were 'troubled people . . . [with] alarming levels . . . [of] comorbidity . . . [suggesting] a disturbing picture of the individuals who are unable to control their gambling'.[124] Although AGA's *Code of Conduct for Responsible Gaming*[125] outlines principles to be followed, not only by gambling patrons, but also by gambling companies and their employees, their submission to the Australian Senate, faced with the possibility of some restrictions being placed on company activities, reinforces the suspicion that the responsible gambling discourse implies, principally, the responsibility of individual gamblers. Since, according to the other discourses with which a responsible gambling discourse is closely allied, gambling products are not inherently dangerous, it follows that responsible gamblers are in the overwhelming majority and that irresponsible gambling is confined to a tiny, deviant minority.

Chapter summary

Gambling is controversial and there are a number of very different ways of talking and writing about the subject. In this chapter, *11 separate gambling discourses have been identified. Five of them present gambling in negative terms. They view gambling, respectively, as immoral, irrational, exploitative, distasteful and destructive.* The immorality discourse was at its height in the late nineteenth and early twentieth centuries and gradually faded since then although it periodically reasserts itself, depicting gambling as motivated by greed. Those who support the expansion of gambling, including governments, have attempted to suppress the immorality gambling discourse and to marginalise those who continue to use it in any form. The irrational, exploitative and distasteful discourses have adapted and survived rather better into the modern era. *It is the gambling as destructive discourse, in its modern forms, which views gambling as pathological for individuals and as detrimental to public health, which now represents the strongest opposition to gambling expansion.*

The remaining six discourses view gambling in a positive light. The first, which viewed gambling as character building – for example, promoting playfulness, ability to calmly accept loss, clear-thinking and even the three R's – was important as a counterweight to the immorality argument when the latter was dominant, but is not often seen now. *It is a combination of the remaining five discourses which, between them, provide powerful support for gambling expansion. They depict gambling as, respectively, a harmless form of amusement, something that enhances cultural and economic life, something that citizens should be free to choose without interference, which is a matter of normal unrestricted business, and as an activity which consumers can engage in responsibly.* The last of these – the 'responsible gambling' discourse – is of special importance because it is a way of speaking about gambling that is increasingly being used by those who promote gambling as a way of minimising the challenge posed by modern forms of the gambling-as-destructive discourse. The whole set of five pro-gambling discourses is used to portray gambling liberalisation as something that is particularly modern and to attempt to marginalise those who put forward counter-arguments. It serves the interests of those who stand to profit financially from gambling expansion. Much of the rest of this book, and particularly the chapters that make up Section IV, may be seen as an effort to critique those discourses and to mount a challenge to their combined weight.

In the following chapter a start is made on that critique by considering where the public now stands in terms of its attitudes towards gambling. Part of the modern pro-gambling argument has been that the way people think about gambling has been transformed: it is said that the old anti-gambling discourses are dead or dying and have been usurped by modern pro-business, pro-leisure choice and harmless, responsible amusement discourses. The truth about public attitudes appears to be somewhat different, as we shall see.

7

Public Attitudes Towards Gambling Are Negative

In support of their liberalising legislation, governments such as that in the UK have argued that public attitudes towards gambling have changed utterly since the middle of the twentieth century. In those days, they tell us, at a time when the foundations for the tighter gambling regulatory regime of the second half of the century were being laid down, negative attitudes towards gambling were still much in evidence. The clutch of ways of thinking and speaking about gambling, identified in the last chapter, which between them supported a deeply suspicious and hostile attitude towards gambling, were by the end of the twentieth century a matter of history – or so we were told. No longer, it was argued, is gambling seen as something that is inherently immoral, irrational, exploitative, a menace to national life, unsavoury and disreputable or in itself dangerous to health and well-being. It is taken for granted that those negative ways of viewing gambling have now been replaced by a cluster of discourses of a more modern kind which between them support a positive attitude towards gambling: gambling should be seen as a perfectly wholesome, unremarkable source of fun and amusement which people have a right to freely engage in so long as they are properly informed about the leisure product they are consuming and so long as gambling activities are properly regulated. We are to see gambling as adding something positive to society because of its role in the entrepreneurial culture and through the part it plays in community and cultural life as a result of direct contributions to good causes and regeneration and indirectly via taxation. It is acknowledged that gambling can carry some perils but only for that very small minority of people who use gambling products irresponsibly or who are individually very vulnerable.

So in league are governments with gambling operators, and, as time passes, so dependent have governments become on the finances they gain from gambling, that it is hard for them to face the possibility that public attitudes might not actually be in line with those assumptions. There are two reasons why we might retain some scepticism about the picture of changed public attitudes towards gambling which governments have been promoting. The first is, simply, that discourses are always used to support certain actions rather than others. One of the functions of the analysis of discourse is to explain how the use of dominant forms of discourse may assist in maintaining power relations.[1] Discourses promoted by those in power are often used to maintain the interests and positions of the relatively powerful.

What interests, then, are best served by the current dominance of discourses of gambling as economic enhancement, harmless amusement and normal business, the minimising of the gambling as destroyer and exploiter discourses, and the virtual outlawing of discourses of gambling as immoral and irrational? The gambling industry seems the obvious main beneficiary, with the government as revenue collector not far behind. It is difficult to imagine an alliance more powerful than that of western governments and the colossal, now international, gambling industry. The promotion of the gambling-positive discourses discussed in the previous chapter is very much in their interests; any questioning of the validity of those assumptions about public attitudes would be a threat to those interests. Some representatives of some communities which expect to benefit economically might be added to the list. So might some individual gamblers whose opportunities to gamble may be enhanced, but their voice is entirely missing from present public talk on the matter. They are a silent constituency whose views are inferred and used in the service of the harmless amusement and normal business discourses.

Are any groups disempowered by the present dominance of certain ways of talking about gambling? One such, whose voice is occasionally heard in the media, consists of small hoteliers, operators of small gambling facilities and other members of communities who fear that the economic or cultural impact of new and improved forms of gambling on their communities will be the opposite of enhancing. Other potentially disempowered groups are, as ever, divided and largely unheard: children, those with gambling problems and their families.[2]

There are obvious grounds, therefore, for questioning the view of public attitudes towards gambling as portrayed by governments and representatives of the gambling industry. One observer of the gambling scene in the USA, who has questioned the industry-government portrayal, put it pithily:

> The morality argument is dead. It is no longer considered acceptable to oppose gambling on the ground it is immoral . . . Government no longer enforces morals . . . with no one to say what is right or wrong, everything has become a cost/benefit analysis . . . The corporate and government executives and accountants who run the games have convinced themselves that everyone has accepted gambling as merely another form of entertainment. They forget that for hundreds of years gambling was viewed as a vice, or worse, as a sin. You cannot erase a life-time of learning through even the best television ads . . . No one realizes that people will eventually rebel against the image of the state as bookie. . . .[3]

Perhaps, then, public attitudes may not have changed as much as we have been led to believe. In fact, very little attempt has been made to assess public attitudes to gambling in the modern era of gambling liberalisation – which is the second reason why we should question the official view of public attitudes. In view of the importance that is often given to public attitudes on all manner of topics, this may seem surprising. On the other hand, given the powerful vested interests involved, the avoidance of putting assumptions about public attitudes to the test may be considered less than surprising. Until the second British Gambling Prevalence Survey carried out in 2006/07, there had been no large-scale study of public attitudes towards gambling based on a representative sample of the adult population. There had been some studies of the attitudes of adolescents and of students,[4] studies of attitudes towards specific forms of gambling such as gambling in casinos, betting on horse races or playing a lottery[5] and studies of the attitudes held by people towards their own gambling.[6] There had also been in-depth interview studies of such aspects as what activities people define as gambling – for example, not everyone considers bingo, spread betting or premium bonds to be 'really gambling' – how people view gamblers or gambling locations – for example, some people think a day at the races is fun but that entering a high street bookmakers is not personally acceptable – and attitudes towards illegal practices in gambling such as match fixing, doping, fixing of fruit machines and the role of organised crime.[7] But there had been no systematic test of the public's attitudes towards gambling in general, anywhere, prior to the 2006/07 British survey.

Even before then there had been some indications that public attitudes were more negative than we had been told they were. The Gambling Review Body – the very committee set up by the UK Government to consider how to eliminate unnecessary restrictions on the promotion of gambling, whilst maintaining necessary protections in the public interest – had itself commissioned the Office for National Statistics to carry out a limited study. They were surprised by the results. Of those surveyed, the large majority said their attitudes to gambling had remained unchanged in the last 10 years, and those who said their attitudes had become more negative (15%) were more numerous than those reporting that their attitudes had become more positive (6%).[8] A survey carried out by National Opinion Poll, of nearly 1,000 18-plus-year-olds in 2003, provided a strong hint that British public opinion was against further liberalisation: for example, 93% said yes to the question *Do you think there are enough opportunities for people to gamble in Britain at the moment?*; 56% said no to the question *Would you be happy for a casino to open near to where you live?*; and 82% said no to the question *Do you think that children under 18 should be allowed to play fruit machines?* A few months later an ICM opinion poll, carried out for *The Guardian* newspaper (just over 1,000 18-plus-year-olds polled in three English regions), found that a larger percentage said they disapproved (53%) than approved (34%) (12% didn't know) ... *of the government's proposal to allow more casinos to be built in Britain.*

Even in Australia, generally thought to be liberal in its public attitudes towards risky leisure activities such as gambling, opinions appear to have remained much more negative than might have been expected. In the national survey carried out for the Australian Productivity Commission's[9] investigation of the impact of gambling on Australian society, two general gambling attitude statements were included. To the statement *Gambling does more good than harm*, only 15% indicated that they agreed (only 4% *strongly*) and 71% disagreed (47% *strongly*). To the statement *Gambling has provided more opportunities for recreational enjoyment*, 32% agreed (7% *strongly*) and 55% disagreed (34% *strongly*). A later survey confined to the Australian state of Victoria found the large majority of both gamblers (75%) and non-gamblers (85%) disagreeing that overall gambling does more good for the Victorian community than harm.[10]

In Canada also, according to the results of a national, random telephone survey of over 2,000 people, carried out in 1999, attitudes appeared to tend towards the negative. A strong majority (60%) thought that gambling-related problems in their province had increased in the last three years (only 12% disagreeing). Asked to agree or disagree with the statement *Gambling has improved the quality of life in . . . [the province]*, 68% disagreed (39% strongly) and only 14% agreed (3% strongly). Although most people thought gambling had had no overall impact on their own communities or upon themselves personally, those who thought there had been a negative effect on their own communities outnumbered those who thought there had been a positive effect (24% versus 9%), and the same was true for any personal impact of gambling (7% a negative effect versus 4% a positive effect).[11] Gallup surveys in the USA also suggested that public attitudes had not changed greatly in that country between 1975 and the end of the century, despite the dramatic changes in gambling provision and participation during that time.[12]

The attitudes towards gambling of British adults at the beginning of the twenty-first century

The large national gambling prevalence survey, described in Chapter 2, carried out in Britain in 2006-07 by the National Centre for Social Research (NatCen) for the Gambling Commission, provided the first opportunity to properly assess public attitudes in Britain, or indeed as far as I know anywhere in the world. Along with Mark Griffiths of Nottingham Trent University, I was an advisor to NatCen on the conduct of the survey. I was particularly interested in testing public attitudes and I took a lead on developing the questions about attitudes that we used in the survey. The process of setting up that part of the survey was an interesting one. My perception – and it is only my view – was that I had to work hard to overcome considerable resistance to asking about public attitudes on this particularly sensitive topic. The resistance came, unsurprisingly, principally from government and the gambling industry. Officials at the lead government department – the Department for Culture, Media and Sport – were concerned about adverse publicity. They were sensitive about criticism of their liberal policy towards gambling; for example, one of Britain's main daily newspapers had been running a concerted campaign against the expansion of casinos. The gambling industry, which was represented on the survey stakeholder group, was particularly suspicious about asking questions about attitudes. I felt I had to attend all the relevant meetings in the run-up to the survey, in order to defend the inclusion of attitude questions at all, and, later on, to defend and explain the particular method we were using.

This is not the place to go into a lot of detail about how the attitude questions were developed. Those details can be found in the full report of the survey[13] or in a report on the attitude results which was subsequently published in one of the two leading academic journals on gambling – *International Gambling Studies*.[14] Suffice it to say here that the conventional procedures for developing a set of questions to assess attitudes towards a topic were followed. That involves: starting with a much larger set of questions than the number finally chosen to be included; covering the whole domain of attitudes as far as is possible – in this case making sure that some questions were included that asked for people's attitudes towards the benefits and harms of gambling for individuals and others relating to benefits and harms to society more generally; having a panel of people inspect all the items and weed out any that are ambiguous or unclear; submitting a long list of items to inspection by a small sample of the general public to see if there are any problems in understanding or responding to the questions; and finally using a shortlist of questions in a pilot study with members of the public, leading to a final choice of the questions – in the present case a shortlist of 25 gambling attitude questions was reduced to a final set of 14 for the main survey.

The way in which the attitude questions were phrased follows a method which is probably the one most often used in formulating attitude questions related to almost any topic. Nevertheless it gave rise to a lot of debate and discussion. The method is very simple. Each question takes the form of a statement expressing an attitude towards the topic which might well be expressed by a member of the public: in fact, the best questions are usually exactly those that have been expressed by members of the public. In this case we were able to draw on an interview study of public attitudes towards gambling commissioned by the Department for Culture, Media and Sport and carried out with the specific purpose of contributing to the measurement of attitudes in the 2006/07 survey.[15] In their final form each attitude statement is followed by five reply options: *strongly agree; agree; neither agree nor disagree; disagree; strongly disagree.* If, as was the case here, the intention is to assess the degree to which attitudes are positive or negative on the topic, then the best set of statements will include a range from those that imply a very positive attitude to those indicating a very negative attitude. Coupled with the option to agree or disagree in each case, and to agree or disagree strongly if one so wishes, this method provides a set of questions which offer the maximum possible discrimination. At one end of the scale will be those people who strongly agree with statements that are positive towards gambling and strongly disagree with those that are negative; at the other end of the scale will be those who respond in the opposite way.

In between will be ranged all those who take a less extreme view, including those with a tendency towards a positive view of gambling, those who are fairly neutral, and those tending towards a negative attitude. This was exactly what we aimed for in the national survey. The final set of statements to which people were invited to respond therefore including gambling-positive statements such as *Most people who gamble do so sensibly* and *Gambling livens up life*, as well as gambling-negative statements such as *Gambling is a fool's game* and *Gambling is like a drug*.

Objections were raised, both about this general style of assessing attitudes which involved presenting people with some quite strongly worded statements, including a number that were quite negative towards gambling, and over the wording of some of the individual items. A number of representatives of the gambling industry reacted negatively to the inclusion of the gambling-negative statements. They seemed to find it difficult to accept that presenting people with a quite strongly worded negative statement on a topic is a good way of getting people to express a positive sentiment on the subject: the more extremely phrased the statement, the more likely are people to disagree with it. It is the inclusion of a balanced set of statements, some positive and some negative, which enables a more rounded assessment of attitudes to be made. Once the method was accepted, it came down to haggling over the question of whether that balance had been achieved and whether some of the more negatively worded statements should be excluded. The stakeholder committee raised the question of whether there was a bias in the selection of statements towards an over-inclusion of those that would encourage the expression of negative attitudes towards gambling. To meet that objection we dropped a small number of statements which in the pilot study had elicited the most negative attitudes towards gambling. For example, the statement *Nearly everyone loses at gambling in the end* was one that showed a strong trend towards agreement, so an alternative was substituted for it. There was one particularly controversial item to which both government and industry representatives took exception and which was in the end, with some reluctance, removed. The item in question was *Gambling is a curse on society*. The objectors wanted it removed because it implied such a negative attitude towards gambling, and government representatives were worried that we were in effect gifting the oppositional press a perfect headline. Paradoxically, the results of the pilot study suggested that, had it been included in the main survey, it would have elicited, on average, a more positive expression of attitudes towards gambling than most other statements that were included – a good illustration of the principle that a strongly worded item can have the effect of provoking disagreement.

So, after much perseverance in search of the public's attitudes towards gambling, what were the results of what was believed to be the first systematic attempt to answer this question with the help of a large, representative general population survey? The reader may recall, from Chapter 2, that the survey involved just over 9,000 adults – aged 16 years and over – living in England, Scotland and Wales. As is quite normal with population surveys, some weighting of the data was necessary in order to compensate for the fact that some demographic groups were less likely to complete the survey (particularly young men) and others more likely (older people, for example). Once corrected in that way this was a good, strong representative sample of the general British population. The main conclusion to be drawn was that British public attitudes towards gambling were, overall, more negative than positive. This was true of the set of attitude statements as a whole and of answers to most of the individual questions. Most people believed that gambling was more harmful than beneficial both for individuals and their families and for society as a whole. The distribution of people's scores on the set of 14 statements taken as a whole tended to lie to the negative side of the neutral midpoint. Three-quarters of the sample had scores lying to the negative side of the neutral point, while only just less than 1 in 5 obtained scores to the positive side.

The wording of the individual statements, in the same order in which they were included in the survey questionnaire, are shown in Table 7.1 along with the percentages who agreed or disagreed with each statement. Figures 7.1 to 7.4 provide a more detailed breakdown of the replies to four of the statements which cover a range from the statement that elicited the strongest expression of negative attitudes towards gambling – *There are too many opportunities for gambling nowadays*, with which 69% agreed and only 6% disagreed – to one that elicited positive attitudes towards gambling – *It would be better if gambling was banned altogether*, with which 21% agreed but 42% disagreed. In fact, the latter was one of only two statements that elicited positive attitudes on average.

Table 7.1   Attitude items included in the 2006/07 British Gambling Prevalence Survey: percent agreement and disagreement[16]

Item		*Agree or strongly agree %*	*Disagree or strongly disagree %*
1	There are too many opportunities for gambling nowadays	69	6
2	People should have the right to gamble whenever they want	53	17
3	Gambling should be discouraged	48	16
4	Most people who gamble do so sensibly	27	38
5	Gambling is a fool's game	64	11
6	Gambling is dangerous for family life	65	8
7	Gambling is an important part of cultural life	12	56
8	Gambling is a harmless form of entertainment	16	49
9	Gambling is a waste of time	52	16
10	On balance gambling is good for society	8	55
11	Gambling livens up life	19	45
12	It would be better if gambling was banned altogether	21	42
13	Gambling is like a drug	65	10
14	Gambling is good for communities	7	57

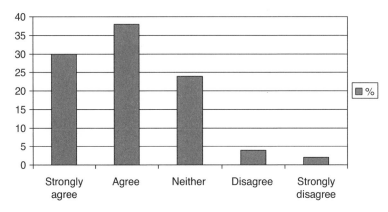

Figure 7.1 British Gambling Prevalence Survey 2006/07, responses to the statement... 'There are too many opportunities for gambling nowadays'

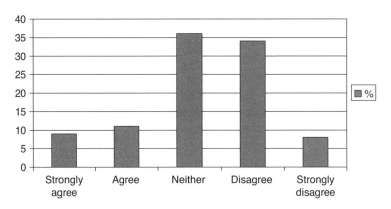

Figure 7.2 British Gambling Prevalence Survey 2006/07, responses to the statement... It would be better if gambling was banned altogether

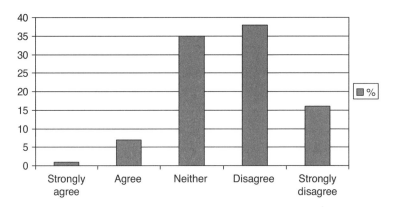

Figure 7.3 British Gambling Prevalence Survey 2006/07, responses to the statement... 'On balance gambling is good for society'

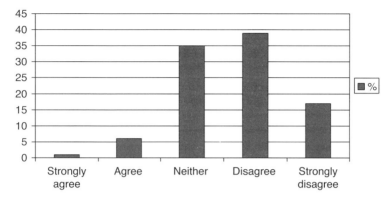

Figure 7.4 British Gambling Prevalence Survey 2006/07, responses to the statement . . . 'Gambling is good for communities'

The other was the statement *People should have the right to gamble whenever they want*, a statement with which three times as many agreed as disagreed. It seems that the average person was inclined towards believing that people have a right to gamble and towards rejecting a total prohibition on gambling. Otherwise, average answers were negative, and strongly so in the case of most of the questions. The indications from the small amount of previous research on gambling attitudes in Britain might have led us to expect that attitudes would not be as favourable as the government – industry alliance had suggested they were, but the strength of negative opinion in response to most of the statements was surprising. Those who agreed that gambling was dangerous for family life and those who disagreed that gambling was good for communities or society, outnumbered those who thought the opposite by six or more to one. The ideas that gambling livened up life, was a harmless form of entertainment or an important part of cultural life, or even that most people who gamble do so sensibly, were rejected by many more than those who accepted these views. Overwhelmingly people agreed that gambling was like a drug. Perhaps most surprising were the findings that those agreeing that gambling should be discouraged outnumbered those who disagreed by three to one; and that those who thought there were too many opportunities for gambling nowadays outnumbered those who disagreed by more than ten to one.

These really are impressive findings. It is quite unusual to find the general public expressing views that tend so strongly in one direction. This is the first time that this exercise has been carried out and perhaps we should be cautious. For one thing all the statements that were used refer to 'gambling' in general. The results cannot tell us anything about attitudes towards specific forms of gambling, like online gambling, sports betting or playing casino table games. The decision to go for attitudes towards gambling in general was a deliberate one: we wanted to obtain people's attitudes towards the topic as a whole and to develop a set of questions that could be used in Britain in later years and in other places where the mix of gambling opportunities would not be identical.

The key piece of modern legislation is, after all, termed 'The Gambling Act', and it is perfectly clear from the results of the survey and from other research that the general concept of 'gambling' is understandable to people and is something about which the general public are able to state opinions.[17] At the same time it must be acknowledged that some people do not think of some activities as gambling although they are within the scope of the Gambling Act – bingo is an example. If many people were confining their understanding of the term 'gambling' to the more dangerous forms, excluding from consideration those that may be less dangerous, then a survey of attitudes might obtain a spuriously negative impression of the public's view of the subject. Other people may have been thinking of forms of activity, not within the scope of the Act, which they viewed as gambling and viewed negatively – playing the stock market might be an example here. Although these are questions which should be addressed by future research, it seems unlikely that variations in definition could be responsible for the very clear results that were obtained.

Another caveat concerns the balance of statements that made up the set used in the survey – the question of balance which so exercised the survey stakeholder group. It is undeniable that a more favourable impression of public attitudes towards gambling could be obtained by focusing attitude statements on those that refer to the liberty of individuals to do as they choose with regard to gambling (the Canadian research also found the majority agreeing that it was their 'right to gamble regardless of the consequences').[18] On the other hand, every effort was made to use a set of questions that covered the topic broadly. A choice of statements that focused even more strongly on the potential harms of gambling would almost certainly produce an even less favourable picture than the one produced by the survey. My view is that the careful process that was undertaken in order to choose a diverse set of statements resulted in a fair assessment of the general position of the British public towards gambling. Indeed, we deliberately responded to the potential criticism of bias by excluding some items that produced the most negative attitudes in the pilot study. The conclusion that current British attitudes are more negative than positive towards gambling is probably, therefore, a sound one.

Not all groups within British society have the same attitudes towards gambling, needless to say. It was possible to look at this in the survey results. Men had more positive attitudes towards gambling than did women. Those aged under 35 had more positive attitudes than others, and those aged 55 or more had the most negative attitudes (previous Canadian and US studies have found a similar association between younger age and more positive attitudes about gambling).[19] Those who described themselves as Asian or Asian British had particularly negative attitudes. Those with higher household incomes had more positive attitudes than those with low incomes. Smokers and heavier drinkers had more positive attitudes than others. The biggest differences – no surprises here – were related to greater or lesser engagement with gambling. Those whose parents gambled, who started to gamble as teenagers, who were currently engaging in gambling relatively frequently, or in several different kinds of gambling, winning or losing more than a few pounds in a week, and those who answered questions suggesting that they might have a gambling problem, were all likely to express relatively positive attitudes to gambling compared to others. Those who indicated having a parent who had had a gambling problem, and those indicating that a close relative had been experiencing a gambling problem recently, expressed relatively more negative attitudes towards gambling than others. Despite those differences in attitude between the sub-groups of the general population, what was very noticeable is that, with only one single exception, all sub-groups expressed, on average, attitudes that placed them to the negative side of the neutral midpoint of the scale. Even young men, or those who gambled weekly, for example, although they had relatively less negative attitudes than others, were on average negative towards gambling according to the statements used in the survey. The single exception was the minority of people who had engaged in five or more of the 16 forms of gambling activity in the seven days prior to the survey. It was that group alone whose average attitudes tipped over slightly to the positive side – expressing on average agreement with gambling-positive statements and disagreement with gambling-negative ones.

It is hard in the light of these findings to maintain that negative attitudes are a thing of the past or that the public is behind the policy of making opportunities to gamble more available. In Britain, prevailing attitudes appear to be consistent, not with the position on gambling expressed by the Gambling Review Body report[20] or enshrined in the 2005 Gambling Act, but rather with the philosophy behind the earlier legislation of the 1960s. The Canadian report, a few years earlier, came to a very similar conclusion: the debate about gambling in Canada had not been informed by a knowledge of public opinion, and when the latter was tested it was found to run counter to provincial gambling policies in a number of important respects.[21]

Chapter summary

Promoting the idea that the pro-gambling discourses described in the previous chapter are now subscribed to by the majority of the population, and that public attitudes have changed and are now generally positive towards gambling, serves the interests of those who stand to benefit from gambling expansion. There have been hints in Australia, Canada, the USA and Britain, from surveys that incorporated some attitude questions, that the truth might be otherwise. *The 2006/07 British Gambling Prevalence Survey made a systematic study of general population attitudes towards gambling for the first time.* The results were clear-cut. Although most people were not in favour of prohibition of gambling, *the weight of public opinion was on the side of believing that gambling is foolish and dangerous, that on balance it is bad rather than good for families, communities and society as a whole, and that it should not be encouraged.* Although there were differences in attitudes between different groups of citizens – for example, men were more positive towards gambling than women, younger people were more positive than older, and frequent gamblers more positive than others – even the majority of gamblers were on balance negative in their attitudes and it was only the relatively small number of multiple-interest gamblers whose attitudes were on balance positive. Although, like all research results, these should not be interpreted uncritically, they do appear to represent a serious challenge to expansionist gambling policies. In the following chapter we look at the position of gambling in society from a different perspective; that of cost-benefit analysis favoured by economists.

8

The Costs and Benefits of Gambling for Society: a Hotly Contested Subject

One thing about gambling is certain – almost everything about it is a subject for lively debate. The lines are drawn between those who highlight the benefits that liberalisation of gambling brings to moderate, 'responsible' consumers of gambling[1] or the positive community regeneration effects of large casinos,[2] and, on the other side, those who express concern about the negative public health effects of problem gambling, the risks of associated crime and the dangers for children, or who are doubtful of the regeneration benefits.[3] Such conflict is hardly new, as the historian Gerda Reith points out:

> The relationship of most societies to gambling has always been ambivalent, vacillating between a climate of liberal promotion (usually based on economic grounds), and critical prohibition (usually based on ethical or moral or, more recently, medical grounds). The situation today is largely the result of centuries of tension between these opposing perspectives and the specific cultural, economic, and ideological assumptions that underlie them.[4]

Perhaps the conflict could be resolved if a scientific way could be found of calculating the benefits and harms that accrue to a particular town, or a whole nation, owing to its already existing or proposed gambling facilities. The problem is that such cost-benefit analyses are themselves highly controversial. The principal difficulty is a very basic one. Such analyses are economic analyses and they require that all costs and benefits be translated into monetary terms. Since many of the benefits and the costs of gambling are intangible and difficult to measure, it means that identifying and putting a figure on the pluses and minuses of gambling is extremely challenging.[5] Some of the potentially most important areas of social cost or benefit, such as effects on social capital and the

An Unsafe Bet? The Dangerous Rise of Gambling and the Debate We Should be Having   By Jim Orford
© 2011 John Wiley & Sons, Ltd

promotion or undermining of social and cultural values, have to be completely left out of the equation. Furthermore, when it comes to the detailed business of putting a figure on one of the costs or benefits which all are agreed should be included, it turns out that doubtful assumptions have to be made in order to arrive at the result. The room for disagreement is very large indeed. Some bodies – the US National Gambling Impact Study Commission (NGISC)[6] is an example – have baulked at the idea of trying to calculate the balance of costs and benefits associated with gambling.

Others have not been so reticent however. The first significant attempt was made by the Australian Productivity Commission in their report,[7] which remains the most comprehensive analysis of gambling and its benefits and harms for one nation and which is often quoted by others (an updated report, ten years on, was in preparation while the present book was being written). The other attempt at a gambling cost-benefit analysis which it is useful for us to look at was carried out by Yuliya Crane as part of her PhD in economics at the University of Salford, England.[8] Crane used the Australian analysis as a basis for her work although, as we shall see, she arrived at very different conclusions. Although these analyses are so controversial, some would say basically flawed, and produce inconsistent conclusions, it is useful to examine them in some detail. By looking at the assumptions that are made, and the factors that are included and excluded, it is possible to expose a number of the areas of conflict that underlie the opposing attitudes that exist towards gambling.

Estimating the costs

To take the costs first, Table 8.1 lists the different headings under which these fall. Note that some of these costs are directly related to gambling addiction: they therefore require an estimate of the number of people addicted to gambling and the average cost per person addicted. For example, one economist estimated the US prevalence of pathological gambling to be 1.4% and calculated that on average each pathological gambler created business and employment costs alone (lost productivity, lost employment time and other costs to firms) of almost $4,000 annually.[9] Other costs are more general, not linked to costs created by individual cases of gambling addiction. An example is an effect to which many economists and others point, namely the costs to a community as a result of other businesses being displaced by a large new gambling facility such as a casino complex.[10]

The effects of large casinos on the local economy is a controversial subject in itself. The positive regenerative effects on communities have often been lauded, especially by town and city mayors and other local government officials,[11] but a careful consideration of all the factors involved suggests that when the displacement effect on other businesses in a locality is taken into account, costs and benefits are likely to be much more evenly balanced. The effects of the new casino in Atlantic City, USA, is a case in point: a common complaint was

Table 8.1 Main costs associated with gambling[14]

---

1 Crime associated with problem gambling (police, court and prison costs)

2 Crime associated with gambling generally (e.g. corruption in sport, money laundering)

3 Employment costs associated with problem gambling (lost productivity, lost employment time, employer staff recruitment costs)

4 Business costs associated with new gambling facilities (displacement of other businesses)

5 Bankruptcy (legal and other costs)

6 Personal costs to those with gambling problems (psychological and physical illness, loss of earnings, etc.)

7 Costs borne by affected family members (emotional distress, psychological and physical illness, family abuse and neglect, other family impact)

8 'Abused dollars' (money or possessions acquired from family, friends or employers under false pretences)

9 Treatment and social service costs associated with problem gambling (unemployment and other social benefits, treatment costs, etc.)

10 Damage to the environment (e.g. traffic congestion, crowding and noise, change of the character of an area, loss of local control)

11 Costs associated with government regulation of gambling

---

that although the casino brought a lot of money into the city, most of it went into businesses located within the casino itself and not to restaurants and other businesses outside the casino.[12] Advocates of new casino facilities often refer to the amount of new employment that would be brought into the area, but the new business may be less labour intensive than other businesses it displaces in the area, or the new facility may employ more non-local than local residents.

A cost-benefit analysis that would satisfy most people slips further out of one's grasp if we want to include the less tangible, or less immediate – but arguably most important in the long run – effects on community life more generally. Some see the increasing commercialisation, standardisation and globalisation of gambling under the dominating influence of large, transnational businesses, and the crowding out of other, more local and traditional forms of entertainment, including local forms of gambling, as representing potential losses.[13] We shall return to these broader considerations in Section IV. For now we should just note that even the Australian Productivity Commission, which tried to put a figure on almost all the costs and benefits of gambling that they could think of, could not find a way to express such gains or losses in monetary terms.

Different cost analyses can come to very different conclusions, even when confining themselves to some of the much more basic considerations. Crane's analysis concludes that the costs of gambling in Australia should be considered as much more modest than the Australian report concluded. She then used the reduced cost figures from Australia to calculate the likely cost of gambling in Britain – on the grounds that Australian and British cultures were rather similar and gambling in Britain would be moving more towards the Australian pattern once the 16 new casinos allowed under the 2005 Act came on stream plus additional smaller casinos that were allowed to open under the 1968 Act in the last few years before the 2005 Act came into operation. The much more conservative estimate of the costs of gambling produced by the British analysis compared to the Australian was in large part due to taking a much stricter, and therefore narrower, view of what constitutes social costs. These were taken to be those costs imposed on society. It would therefore exclude things that economists call 'transfers', some of which the Australian analysis did include as costs. One of the largest items here was problem gamblers' debts – something that figures large in all accounts of gambling addiction. According to the strict economic theory espoused by Crane, these are not costs to society but simply transfers of money from one person or group of people to another: creditors lose out, debtors gain, and society is unaffected. Gambling-related theft is treated in the same way. The same goes for loss of work productivity, since this represents a transfer of utility from an employer, in terms of lost output, to the employee who gains leisure time, and it should not therefore be included in the cost estimate.

This really strains credulity. It may be classic economics but it is hardly sense. No allowance is made here for the disruption caused to creditors and debtors, the victims of crime, employers and employees, let alone to the less tangible but societally highly valued sense of trust that is at the heart of relationships in organisations and communities.[15] What it amounts to, of course, is that the kind of narrow economic calculation represented by the British analysis is really only an estimate of the financial costs to the public purse. It does not do justice to what I believe most citizens would think of as the potential 'costs' of an activity, in this case gambling. It was acknowledged, however, that there were some real costs of unemployment, for example an employer's cost of recruiting and training a new employee, and that bankruptcy – otherwise treated as a transfer – could bear a real social cost in the form of the cost of bankruptcy proceedings. In general the costs of crime were only included if they involved the police, the courts or prisons. Not all economists agree on these things however. Some would include theft itself as a cost, even if the theft is borne by a relative or friend and is never reported – all part of what one economist has called 'abused dollars', which then constitute one of the largest cost items associated with gambling addiction.[16]

The largest costs in the Australian analysis were personal and family costs. These are of course especially hard to put a price on. Quantifying the 'pain and suffering' experienced by addicted gamblers and their families was a particular challenge: the compilers of the report used the amounts of money that Australian courts had awarded in compensation for moderately disabling chronic psychological or psychiatric disorders. Crane was sceptical about including personal costs at all unless there was a cost of treatment borne by the state or insurance. She presented two scenarios, one including, and the other excluding, personal costs. But her preference, based on a reading of neo-classical economics, was for the latter. That preference was based on an argument that

I find particularly contorted, especially in the light of what is now thought to be the nature of addiction (as described in Chapter 4). The Australian analysis had assumed that personal costs associated with gambling addiction should be counted as real social costs attributable to gambling, on the grounds that once addicted, a gambler is not making a fully informed choice about whether to gamble or not or how much to gamble. He or she cannot therefore be considered to be behaving as a 'rational consumer'. If, on the other hand, it can be supposed that problem gamblers continue to act rationally – what Crane refers to as the *rational addiction model* – then personal costs should not be included as real social costs because it is assumed that the addicted person took them into account in making a rational consumer choice. Again what we seem to be up against here is the simplifying assumptions of these kinds of economic analyses. There is no simple answer to the question of whether an addicted person is behaving rationally or not. For example, it was established some years ago that people with serious alcohol problems modified the level of their drinking, to some extent, depending on the cost of the alcoholic beverage they were consuming.[17] The idea that drug addiction renders a person's behaviour totally out of control is no longer accepted. On the other hand, the very essence of addiction is the strong appetitive attachment to the object of the addiction which it entails and the diminished degree of control that the affected person can therefore exercise over its consumption (much of Chapter 4 amounted to an elaboration of that very point). It may make sense economically to make a decision whether to include certain costs or not on the basis of an assumption about rationality, but in the context of addiction it makes no psychological sense. Perhaps half the costs should be counted in on the grounds that rationality is partly diminished and partly retained, but that seems to be carrying the exercise in an absurdly contorted and pseudo-scientific direction. This vexed question of rationality comes up again when it is the benefits of gambling that are under consideration (see below).

Even if personal costs are included there is the further question of whether they can be wholly attributed to a person's gambling. Not all of addicted gamblers' depressions or divorces or separations are necessarily due to gambling; a proportion would presumably have occurred irrespective of the gambling. The Australian analysis estimated that at least 80% of these outcomes could be attributed to gambling. They therefore applied a 20% 'causality' discount to the estimate of the number of people affected.

Estimating the benefits

The theory of consumer surplus[18]

Estimating the benefits from providing an activity such as gambling is no less challenging. Once again the way economists do this seems to me and others to be tortuous and highly problematic.[19] The most obvious benefit is the pleasure and satisfaction enjoyed by those who partake happily in the activity. This might seem to be almost impossible to calculate but economists do it by way of finding out what consumers are prepared to pay for engaging in the activity. The key idea here is that of *consumer surplus*. This refers to the difference between the amount that consumers would be willing and able to pay for a product and what the providers of that activity are actually selling it for. This depends crucially on the *price elasticity of demand* which is a measure of how sensitive demand is to changes in price. If price elasticity is low, indicating that consumers would be willing to pay more, then consumer surplus is relatively high. Gambling promoters like to suggest that this is the case because it looks as if they are then responding to a 'need'. If, on the other hand, elasticity is relatively high, indicating that any increase in price would result in a relatively large reduction in demand, then the estimate of consumer surplus is lower.[20]

Freemarket thinking on the subject is that consumer surplus is maximised under conditions of market competition, so that prices are driven down, near to the point below which it would no longer be economic for the operators to continue to sell the product. Consumer surplus – or to put it another way, the amount a consumer is saving and can spend on other things (perhaps value for money is another way of expressing it) – is then at its maximum. As an aside here it should be noted that gambling is an unusual product because the price for it is only paid by those who lose. 'Price' in the case of gambling is generally taken as the 'take-out' or, in other words, the proportion of stakes which is not returned to consumers in the form of winnings. In many forms of commercial gambling the take-out is in the region of 5–15%.

The UK National Lottery is exceptional in the UK – its take-out is around 55%. That illustrates what economic theorists refer to as the opposite state of affairs to one in which open market competition drives down prices. This situation is one of a monopoly, but with a competitive element coming in every few years when alternative operators tender for the government franchise (*Camelot*, the existing provider, won a new 10-year licence to begin in 2009, having been identified early on as the preferred bidder, with only one other firm competing). Under these conditions the price to the consumer is relatively high and consumer surplus much less. One way of putting it is to say that what would otherwise have been consumer surplus has been 'captured' in the form of what economists call *economic rents*. In the case of the lottery these largely go the General Exchequer as tax and to 'good causes' through the National Lottery distribution fund (and now the Olympic Lottery Distribution Fund as well) – a total of £1.36 billion in 2007/08.[21] In this case, therefore, the surplus is enormous, but the public is foregoing it, perhaps partly because people are pleased to think they are contributing to good causes and partly because they are prepared to put up with such a relatively high 'price' for the product because it is so well marketed and because of the possibility – although in reality of course extremely unlikely – of a 'life-changing' large win.[22]

State-sponsored monopolies of that kind, common in other European countries also,[23] are not the only forms in which consumer surplus can be captured. An argument used by those who had favoured the legalising of forms of gambling that were formally illegal is that illicit, and often unscrupulous, suppliers could demand high prices, thus reducing the surplus value available to consumers. To that loss of consumer surplus could of course be added the public costs of fighting gambling-related crime and the private costs to consumers of engaging with criminals and a criminal activity. Legalisation enables governments to take out some of the potential consumer surplus in the form of taxation. This, needless to say, constitutes one of the great attractions of gambling for governments. Like alcohol and tobacco, gambling is seen as a very suitable target for taxation. It is a luxury rather than a necessity, so, although consumers may grumble loudly, relatively high taxation on such an activity is likely to be better accepted than taxation on other things. There is, however, a quite other motive for taxing such 'vices', namely the need to do something to try to keep the level of consumption within bounds because of the evidence of the health and social harms associated with the activity – what economists call the *negative externalities* caused by gambling. These two motives for government taxation create the familiar bind that governments find themselves in: a government says it is trying to constrain an activity by taxing it relatively highly whilst at the same time it is fiscally benefiting. The more of the activity there is, the more it benefits.

Industry profits constitute the other main way in which part of potential consumer surplus is captured. The greater the profit, the higher the price consumers have to pay above the minimum that the market might otherwise stand and the greater the erosion of what would otherwise be consumer surplus. It is in the interests of those in a legalised industry to argue that profits are no more than is required to maintain the business by reinvesting in new plant, research and development, and to pay sufficiently attractive emoluments for staff, and sufficient dividends to shareholders to maintain investment. Interestingly, in her estimate of the cost and benefits of gambling in the UK, Crane[24] estimated this 'producer surplus', in the case of new casinos, to be zero! Her justification was that large amounts need to be spent on lobbying to protect the operators' positions in the market, as well as the requirement to offer, in addition to gambling, non-gambling facilities, some of which might be non-profitable – the examples she gave were a conference centre or a new wing for a local hospital. A contrary view is that, with increasing commercialisation and globalisation, gambling of a certain type comes to be provided by a small number of very large companies, and that unless carefully regulated, such oligopolies will act as a cartel, keeping prices high and contributing to the erosion of consumer surplus.[25]

Gambling operators are likely to argue for lower rates of government taxation of their products. Not only, they would argue, do high taxes constrain demand – to the extent that demand is price elastic – thus diminishing industry profits, but if prices are then increased, consumer surplus also diminishes. Promoters are likely to emphasise the loss of consumer surplus rather than diminished producer surplus. Arguments continue about the appropriate level at which gambling should be taxed. At the time of writing Britain was maintaining a rate of taxation on casino gambling that was relatively high compared to some other countries. At the same time the British government had reduced the rate of taxation on betting in the face of overseas competition.[26] At the height of speculation about how many super regional casinos there might be in Britain, and then where the first one might be located, there were media reports that international casino companies were putting pressure on the British Government to offer a low casino tax regime.

The foregoing economic discussion is only valid if it can be assumed that gamblers are rational consumers, behaving as they do in the possession of sound information about the price of the product and the benefits to be had from its consumption, and in a way designed to maximise utility or value for money – the rationality issue again. If, on the other hand, gambling is a compulsive or pathological activity, then the logic of consumer surplus benefit no longer applies. Demand would then have been artificially created by the addictive nature of the product itself. Demand would be highly inelastic – people would be prepared to pay high prices – not because gambling is an activity which gives great satisfaction but because an addiction has been created. Producer profits, government taxes and any contributions to good causes would be taken out at the expense of players who had been rendered addicted. Anything left over, corresponding to consumer surplus in the rational consumer model, would not be consumer surplus at all but rather a measure of the extent to which people were addicted. It would not be an index of joyful satisfaction at all, but rather an indicator of the degree to which people are trapped in a joyless activity which they would give up if they could. That of course is an extreme picture and no more true as a complete description of gambling than the pure rational consumer model. Note, however, that it may not be far from a realistic portrait of the provision and consumption of tobacco products. A lot of evidence suggests that tobacco addiction develops, usually in adolescence, within only a small number of years of starting to consume, and that most smokers are 'dissonant' about their smoking – in other words, given a free choice they would rather not be smoking or at least would rather they were able to choose to smoke only occasionally. The question of which picture best fits the case of gambling can therefore be seen as a question of whether gambling is more like smoking – most smokers are more or less addicted and the rational consumer model has only limited applicability – or whether they are more like consumers of a non-addictive activity such as eating meals in restaurants.

The answer for gambling is that the truth lies somewhere in between the two models. One assumption, favoured by those who emphasise the benefits of gambling to society and minimise the harms,[27] is that the rational consumer model is the correct one for estimating the cost-benefit balance of gambling, either because the number of addicted gamblers is so small that they can be ignored, or, to use an intriguing recent argument, but one that is specious, that even addicts are rational – a contradiction in terms as pointed out earlier in this chapter when discussing the costs associated with gambling. The Australian Productivity Commission tried their best to find a middle way, arguing on the basis of their best evidence that as much as 33% of money spent on gambling in Australia at that time was spent by problem gamblers (a figure that went up to 42% of money spent on gaming machines).[28] They also built into their calculations an attempt to adjust for the possibility that problem gamblers' gambling was rational up to a certain point and irrational thereafter, and also that problem gamblers could be divided into those who had moderate problems and those whose problems were severe. Although that reasoning may seem contrived, it was at least a serious attempt to grapple with the realities of normal and addicted gambling. Economists may prefer to make simpler assumptions. For example, at the end of her detailed analysis of the costs and benefits of the introduction of new casinos in Britain under the 2005 Gambling Act, Crane's preference was to assume that all gamblers, including problem gamblers, were acting rationally. Her estimate of consumer surplus then lay between a minimum of £4.55 billion per annum (if demand elasticity was relatively high, at -1.3) and a maximum of £7.38 billion (if demand elasticity was low, at -0.8). The assumptions being made about the rationality or irrationality of problem gamblers' gambling made a lot of difference. If it was assumed, instead, that problem gamblers were not gambling rationally above a certain 'normal' level of consumption, then consumer surplus was calculated to range between £1.57 and £2.94 billion, and estimates dropped still further, to between £0.97 and £2.03 billion, if it was assumed that problem gamblers' gambling was not rational at all. These various assumptions, combined with different estimates of likely demand elasticity, and different positions about what should legitimately be counted as social costs of gambling, led to widely differing estimates of the net benefit of this kind of gambling to society – varying from a low of just under £2 billion to just under £10 billion.[29]

Estimates of gambling costs and benefits are complicated still further by whether they are being calculated for a local area, a region or a nation as a whole. In some instances, for example a casino tourist resort, it could be argued that while many of the benefits accrue to the local or 'host' area, some of the principal costs, to problem gamblers and their families, are 'exported', in the sense that gamblers take them back with them when they go home. In other cases, perhaps for example in the case of an urban casino operated by a foreign multinational company, there is a stronger argument that harms are most likely to accrue to local residents whilst many of the benefits may be exported. The balance is going to be difficult to determine and is going to vary case by case.[30]

Are taxes on gambling regressive?

One of the controversial things about taxing gambling – quite apart from misgivings that governments have certainly had in the past, and may in some cases continue to have in the present day, about the ethics of benefiting fiscally from an activity of questionable morality[31] – is the concern that in all probability it is likely to be a *regressive tax* rather than a progressive one. Many who have wrestled with issues of social policy and gambling have voiced their concern that instead of tax having the overall effect, as is usually intended, of redistributing

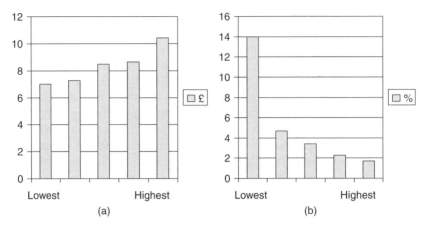

Figure 8.1   British Gambling Prevalence Survey 2006/07, the relationship between personal income and a) absolute weekly gambling losses (left), and b) losses as a percentage of income[33]

wealth from the relatively well off to the relatively poor, in the case of gambling it might be failing to do so, or might even tend to have the opposite effect of redistributing wealth from the poor to the rich.[32]

Some of the results from the 2006/07 British prevalence study, shown in the accompanying graphs, are relevant here. Although personal income was positively associated with the amount that those gambling were losing weekly on gambling (the left-hand graph) the relationship looks very different when amounts lost are expressed as percentages of median income. When that is done (the right-hand graph), then it becomes clear that it is the relatively less well off who are spending relatively more on gambling and therefore contributing more of their fair share in gambling tax. In several other European countries, too, concern has been expressed that gambling is disproportionately affecting the poor, for example the rural poor in Poland and those in the poorer southern parts of Italy.[34]

The other side of the equation is how the economic rents associated with gambling, probably taken disproportionately from the poor, are then used and to whose advantage. In his book *Gambling and the Public Interest*, Peter Collins, Director of the Centre for the Study of Gambling at Salford University in the UK, argued that although there may be fairer ways of collecting tax, whether economic rents from gambling are fair depends on how they are used. If national and local taxes are used to support regeneration in relatively deprived areas, as he suggests has been the case in countries such as the USA, Canada, France and South Africa, then the overall effect may be more progressive. Answering this question is likely to be fraught with difficulties, as our earlier discussion about estimating the costs and benefits of gambling should already have made clear. In the context of the British National Lottery for example, there has been endless debate about whether activities such as opera, favoured by the better off, have gained more than schemes that contribute to the alleviation of poverty (another bone of contention has been the charge that urban areas have benefited more than rural from the good causes supported by lottery funds).[35] Earlier objections to the idea of a British National Lottery, for example by the 1933 Royal Commission, were often on the grounds that it would appeal most to those who could least afford it. As Miers put it:[36]

> Like all long-odds gambling, while the Lottery objectively offers a poor return to the player, it has a very high subjective utility for precisely those individuals who have no or little discretionary income for this kind of expenditure.

To some this may sound like paternalism. There is no doubt that historically British gambling has been characterised by an enormous class divide and a large measure of hypocrisy on the part of the better off and those of higher social standing, who believed that lower- or working-class gambling was the problem that needed to be legislated against, whilst their own preferred forms of gambling should be left unrestrained.[37]

Chapter summary

In this chapter I have posed the question whether it is possible to arrive at some resolution over the controversy surrounding gambling's impact on society by attempting to cost the benefits and harms which it brings. Two serious attempts to do that were used as illustrations. One was the exemplary work of the Australian Productivity Commission (APC), the other being a British economics PhD which used some of the APC figures, examined them critically, and translated them for use in the UK. When these studies are looked at in detail it becomes clear that *the scope for including or excluding different categories of gambling-related benefit and harm, the ways the different criteria are measured, and the difficult and doubtful assumptions that have to be made, render the analyses inconclusive* and leave the question of net cost-benefit 'unresolved and hotly contested'.[38]

In the process of trying to understand these, often convoluted analyses, a number of issues and sources of bias are exposed. One is the bias of some economists towards confining an estimate of the costs of gambling to those that are directly borne by the public purse, ignoring the more personal costs borne by individuals on the grounds that they should be thought of only as 'transfers' from one individual or group of individuals to another, or because they are simply too intangible to calculate. Not all economists agree about these things. *Some of the most intangible, but in the long run possibly most important, costs for communities have to be completely left out of consideration* – effects on the character of an area or the risks to young people, for example. However, there is general agreement that the costs associated with problem gambling are high; estimated in the USA to be in the region of $4–10,000 per pathological gambler per year and approximately $4bn a year in total.[39]

The attempt to calculate the benefits of gambling in financial terms is even more difficult. Economists attempt to put a figure on the pleasure and satisfaction enjoyed by gamblers using the theory of consumer surplus, the calculation of which is problematic in the case of an unusual commodity such as gambling. One of several problems is the assumption of rational consumer choice. *Only if it can be assumed that gamblers are wholly, or at least largely, making their gambling choices rationally, can the theory of consumer surplus be used as a guide.* Some very contorted assumptions need to be made in order to arrive at a figure for consumer benefit.

These analyses throw up a further question: If there are benefits from gambling, who sees them, and if there are costs, who bears them? It has been suggested, with some evidence to back it up, that *gambling has an overall regressive effect, with costs bearing most heavily on the poorer sectors of society* – for example, those on lower incomes spending a higher proportion of income on gambling – and that poorer families and communities do not benefit in proportion.

Section IV

Gambling Expansion is Not Being Challenged

Governments are Complicit in Supporting the Interests of the Gambling Industry

Support for gambling expansion means role conflict for government

'Dramatic' has been the term used by a number of commentators to describe the shift in policy on gambling that has been seen in many countries. The nature of that change has been described as one that has taken us from containment to market-led expansion.[1] This change in gambling policy, which has transformed the regulatory environment in only a few years, has of course been just part of a broader shift in political and economic thinking, away from government management, towards favouring free markets as little constrained as possible by regulation. When the Gambling Review Body was set up by the British Home Secretary in 1999 it was explicitly asked to consider how the commercial gambling market could be strengthened in the interests of the British economy.[2] This itself represented a fundamental change. Equally profound were the regulatory changes brought in by the subsequent Gambling Act of 2005. Amongst its many derestricting provisions was one that particularly encapsulated the new pro-market and anti-regulation philosophy. That was the dropping of the 'demand test' requirement for the setting up of new gambling facilities (see Chapter 2). That requirement, which had been central to the previous regulatory regime, meant that a new gambling outlet would only be licensed by the Justices of the Peace if it could be demonstrated that there existed a demand for gambling which was not already being met. Commercial gambling was only permitted if it was responding to 'unstimulated demand'. It was not to be artificially stimulated by providing any more gambling than was absolutely necessary. That principle had '. . . worked as a rough and ready rule of thumb for the legalization of

An Unsafe Bet? The Dangerous Rise of Gambling and the Debate We Should be Having   By Jim Orford
© 2011 John Wiley & Sons, Ltd

popular gambling and the control of its commercialisation in the 1960s and 1970s'.[3] Now, in the new century, the demand test was a thing of the past and free commercial competition was the order of the day. No longer were the local authority licensing committees – who were to take over the licensing functions from the Justices of the Peace – allowed, when considering a licence, to take into account the area in which the facility was to be set up or the existing level of provision of gambling in the locality.[4]

Once the provision of gambling is seen as just like any other business activity in the entertainment domain, it follows that innovation and expansion are to be welcomed. As law professor Roy Light has put it, the 2005 Act '. . . allows operators to generate increased customer numbers and retention . . . Competition for customers in such an environment will intensify design, marketing and operational practices aimed at increasing custom and thus stimulating demand'.[5] It is only to be expected that the industry will expand; indeed it would represent a failure in business terms if it did not. For example, there is a clear expectation that the number of casinos will increase and that there will be new casino-goers who would not previously have taken part in casino gambling.[6] Indeed a British Government report prior to the passing of the 2005 Act stated, 'while the figures vary all predict that the gambling industry will increase significantly as a result of the government's proposals, with ensuing benefits to the Exchequer'.[7] As Mike Atherton puts it:

> Gambling will continue to take advantage of technological advances because it has been embraced by governments and encouraged to become part of a legitimate and mass-market leisure industry, and because that industry is run by conglomerates out to offer entertainment and maximise their profits. . . .[8]

As overall policy moves from partial prohibition to containment to market encouragement, so the interests of government become ever more entangled with those of commercial suppliers. As with any dangerous form of consumption, when attitudes towards it are strongly negative and government policy one that supports prohibition, or at least partial prohibition, there is a widespread mood of reluctance about moving in the direction of further decriminalising and officially regulating the activity. That has always been true of prostitution, is true in the present day for many classes of drugs, and was true of gambling in the first half of the twentieth century. Legalising and regulating the activity would be taken as implying a condoning of it. Following the 1960 Betting and Gaming Act, in Britain, the role of government shifted. It was no longer seen as being the function of government to prevent people gambling, but neither was it seen as an appropriate function of government to do any more than facilitate people to do so. Gambling was not seen as a productive economic activity. If the market expanded at all, it should only do so to the extent that was necessary to stifle unregulated supply.[9] A key moment, consolidating the transition to a new era, in which government viewed gambling as part of the mainstream leisure industry, was the passing of responsibility for British gambling from the Home Office to the Department for Culture, Media and Sport (DCMS) in 2001. Hence responsibility had shifted from a department charged with reducing the harms, particularly crime-related ones, associated with an activity that was tolerated but hardly thought of in glowing terms, to one that was responsible for promoting and encouraging the activity in the interests of a growing, successful and tax-contributing industry, and helping modern citizens to have fun. As Mike Atherton saw it, 'Gambling had been moved from a department that regulates, to a department that exploits'.[10] DCMS was said not to have been amused when, in January 2006, the then Chairman of the Gambling Commission described the Commission's role as that of a 'laissez-faire' regulator. The department's annoyance can be well understood. The government's modern liberal stance on gambling had to be dressed up, to disarm its many critics, as one that was principally that of tough regulation, designed to protect the young and the vulnerable and to keep crime out of gambling, whereas in fact from the very outset its main thrust had been one of liberalisation. The Commission Chairman's remarks were probably very apt, but they were out of line with how government wished to present its new era policies.

Government can get itself in a mess when it comes to dealing with dangerous forms of consumption like gambling. The conflicts involved, and the serious issues of public ethics that have to be faced in the process, have been examined by a number of writers on the subject. A popular option for modern governments is to try to combine the regulation of gambling, in order to minimise associated addiction and crime, with capturing gambling consumer surplus in the form of taxation (see Chapter 8).[11] There is great attraction for governments in using gambling to raise money, particularly in difficult times such as following an expensive war or during an economic slowdown.[12] In his book *Gambling, Freedom and Democracy*, Peter Adams, of the School of Population Health at the University of Auckland in New Zealand, has pointed out how, in an era of gambling liberalisation and normalisation, a government tries to combine a number of not easily compatible roles, including most or all of those shown in Table 9.1. In those countries such as Britain that operate a National Lottery, and particularly in countries such as Canada and the Netherlands where the government is the main provider of most forms of gambling, one of those roles is that of gambling provider. As Adams puts it, 'The opportunities for role conflict [for government] are widespread and significant'.[14] In his review of the field for the Home Office in 1978, Derek Cornish questioned the rightness of government dependence on the proceeds of gambling; a dependence, in effect, on their citizens' gambling losses:

> there are ... powerful arguments against this method of raising funds, not the least of which is that the state (wearing its fiscal hat) has an interest in expanding and increasing participation in order to maintain its revenues, while at the same time (wearing its caring hat) it attempts to prevent excessive involvement.[15]

Once a government is dependent on the proceeds of a National Lottery, it then has an inevitable interest in keeping up the public's level of gambling spend. Since the lottery is not in itself a public good, as a public library is for

Table 9.1 Roles and functions that governments try to play in an era of gambling expansion (taken with permission from Adams, 2008a, Table 3.1)[13]

1	Law maker	Put in place the regulatory framework that determines the environment in which gambling occurs
2	Law enforcer	Enforce regulations
3	Gambling provider	Develop government associated industries, often lottery products, sometimes racing and casinos
4	Gambling promoter	Actively support positive public views on the benefits of increased gambling consumption
5	Revenue collector	Ensure government maximises its return from gambling
6	Policy maker	Develop overarching policy framework with clearly defined principles
7	Harm alleviator	Develop robust and integrated services, spanning public health to treatment
8	Honest broker	Provide an impartial base for decisions regarding sector development, regulation and knowledge

example, and since the state is thereby promoting a consumer good for the purpose of redistributing wealth, then '... questions of fiscal equity assume importance'.[16] Remember that the scale of government revenue from gambling, in many countries, is now colossal (see Chapter 1). In Britain, for example, gambling duty collected in 2004–05 amounted to £1.42 billion.[17]

Parallels with alcohol and drug policy

Many of the same questions about policy and a government's position arise in relation to the supply of other forms of consumption that are known to be highly dangerous. These issues have been even more widely debated publicly in relation to dangerous substances such as tobacco, alcohol and other dangerous drugs. Alcohol perhaps offers the closest parallel because its supply is legal and largely commercialised and, unlike tobacco, it can be consumed, and often is, in a fashion that is not generally considered to be harmful socially or to one's health. In Britain, as in much of the rest of the world, policies regarding the sale of alcohol are now liberal and drinking is normalised. But many feel that the balance has now been struck in the wrong place. In Britain, for example, the government has been taken to task for merely paying lip-service to the need to tackle rising levels of alcohol-related harm and for adopting legislative policies that are thought by many to be likely to increase levels of harm rather than to decrease them – such as repealing earlier legislation which restricted where alcoholic drinks could be bought and the hours of the day during which they could be served.[18] Although the British Government looks unlikely to modify its basic liberalisation approach to alcoholic drinks supply, there has been so much publicity given to such things as city centre public disorder associated with the 'night time economy' and rising levels of liver cirrhosis, that the government has been forced to consider restraining the exercise of the free market – for example, by making it illegal to sell alcohol at very low prices in supermarkets and in pubs and bars.[19] What is not on the agenda is prohibition. The latter has a bad reputation: the fact that it 'didn't work' in the USA in the 1930s is the charge frequently made against it. But even that is an over-simplification. Much less often remarked than the increased crime that occurred is the fact that alcohol consumption in the USA was down overall during prohibition as was the incidence of liver cirrhosis.[20]

Although 'dangerous drugs' may seem like an entirely different matter from gambling, in fact there are many parallels. One striking similarity is the way both the drug and gambling scenes are constantly shifting, partly because of the spread of fashions around the world, but most particularly because of inventiveness in producing new drugs and new games and because of technological advances which make for new ways of administering drugs or greater sophistication in gambling games. Most of these changes render the products more powerful and more dangerous. The invention of the hypodermic syringe and the gambling machine were highly significant events in the history of drug and gambling addiction, respectively, although the former of course also has its pro-health uses. The prohibition of a whole range of different drugs, including opiates, stimulants of various kinds, recreational drugs, hallucinogens, and so on – the fact that there is such a wide variety of drugs, as there is a great variety of ways to gamble, is another striking feature in common – is a policy that many believe is not working very well. The criminalisation of the supply and use of a number of classes of drug under the 1971 Misuse of Drugs Act in Britain is believed, as under alcohol prohibition in the USA, to have gifted the profits of drug supply to criminals, in the process filling prisons with people who are suffering from drug addiction, unnecessarily stigmatising and marginalising people who take such drugs, whether addicted to them or not, and creating problems for neighbourhoods – especially those already more deprived – through a combination of the involvement of some people in the illicit trade and the degradation of the environment for others.[21] Those who criticise the criminalisation/prohibition approach to drugs include a surprising variety of people, some senior police officers included. Although the current policy on gambling is so very different, there are nevertheless some striking parallels in very recent history. After the 1906 Street Betting Act, the police were for some time enthusiastic about enforcing the law, but as time went on they increasingly saw it, much as a few decades later some police viewed the pursuit of small-scale cannabis use, as a waste of precious time and something that did not endear them to sections of the population.[22]

So, is the legalisation and regulation of these classes of drug the answer? That would bring that area of policy into line with that on alcohol and gambling. Griffith Edwards, of the National Addiction Centre in London, speaks for many when he rehearses the arguments against drug legalisation. Much crime and its associated problems would decrease but, he argues, illicit supply would not cease, particularly if legal supply was not set at a very affordable price. Meanwhile,

> Legalization would mean increased access, increased access would result in increased use, and increased levels of use would result in increased harm, just as night follows day.[23]

Furthermore, he asks, how would legalisation affect the government's independence of judgement regarding drugs and their costs and benefits to society. Almost certainly, he suggests, '. . . tax imperatives would take precedence over health. . .'.[24] And, thinking of the difficulties being experienced with alcohol policy, does the commercialisation of drugs supply conjure up an attractive picture? Probably not:

> No one in these deregulatory days can safely expect that the profitable commodities which are drugs would be left for long to state monopolies and dreary brown packaging with the fun taken out. The multinationals would invent and market their alluring images and strive to conceal the nastier truths, and popular culture would be cajoled into supporting those images.[25]

The dilemmas are much the same for gambling. South Africa is often cited as an example of the benefits of legalisation and regulation: the legalising of casinos in 1996 is reported to have resulted in substantial reduction in a number of adverse consequences such as loan sharking, corruption of law enforcement officers and politicians, and links to other illegal vices; and government benefited through taxation.[26] At the same time, legalised gambling increased the general appeal to South Africans of gambling as entertainment, resulting in '. . . greater spending on gambling among the population at large and probably in an increased incidence of problem and pathological gambling'.[27] For Professor Light it is a question of achieving the right balance between the interests of government, the trade and those who fall casualty to gambling:

> As with the [alcohol] Licensing Act 2003, the government appears to be driven by a commercial imperative masquerading as a desire to allow greater freedom for the 'sensible majority'. No evidence has been produced of any pressure from the public for the liberalisation of gambling. The new regime is a compact between the government and the industry, each of which stands to benefit considerably from an expanded gambling market.[28]

His point about lack of public pressure for gambling liberalisation is one that several writers on the subject have made. In his book *The Luck Business*, Robert Goodman had the following to say:

> One of the most surprising findings of our research is that we didn't come across a single popularly based organisation that lobbies for more gambling. Many other government prohibitions – such as laws against the smoking of marijuana – have inspired popular legalization movements. But not gambling. In fact, when given a chance to make its views known, the public usually rejects gambling. . .

So if it's not the public, who is behind the push for more gambling opportunities? Two parties are almost entirely responsible: legislators in search of easy answers to tough economic problems, and the gambling industry itself.[29]

Writing about the inauguration of Britain's National Lottery and the de-regulatory government agenda underpinning it, David Miers wrote, '. . . that agenda was not driven by any perceived substantial change in the level of con-sumer demand, but by supply-side self-interest'.[30] In his book, Mike Atherton summarises what he sees as a deep unease about new era liberalisation of gambling:

> . . . for many, the government-inspired liberalisation of the industry, enshrined in the Gambling Act 2005, threatens to destabilise an area of life that has been regulated, crime-free and relatively controlled for four decades.
>
> Prohibition . . . will never work. Nor is it sensible for responsible governments, given the damage that gambling does to the vulnerable, to encourage people to gamble. An industry that is fairly taxed and carefully regulated, one that is allowed to operate legally but not given the ability to stimulate demand, is the commonsense approach.[31]

Responsible gambling, harm reduction and corporate social responsibility

A lot is now heard about what is being called 'responsible gambling'. In Chapter 6 it was identified as the most recent of the modern gambling discourses which underpin new era policies. It appears to be a concept that is widely signed up to by governments, gambling regulators, many parts of the gambling industry and even by some organisations whose main aims are the prevention and treatment of problem gambling.[32] It is being treated as if it is clearly understood and is uncontroversial. The truth is very different. For one thing, if an attempt were made to define it – mostly its meaning is taken for granted and no such attempt is made – it would certainly lead to much debate. For some it denotes simply the opposite of problem gambling: gambling responsibly means gambling within one's means regarding time and money, and gambling in a way that causes no harm to oneself or to others.[33] Perhaps, to draw a parallel with British Government policy on alcohol consumption, it might be thought of as gambling which is 'sensible'. Gambling within 'sensible limits' might mean never or rarely gambling too frequently, nor for too long at a time, nor spending too much, either in an absolute sense or as a percentage of one's income. Unlike in the alcohol case, the British Government has not set out any such sensible limits. But one suggestion from Canada is that the guidelines for responsible gambling might include not gambling more than three times a month, or for more than an hour at a time, and limiting gambling expenses to no more than $1,000 per year or 1% of one's income, whichever is the lower. Along with those numerical limits were other such suggestions as: not to borrow money to gamble; to pursue other leisure activities in addition; not to use cash machines at gambling venues in order to get more money for gambling; not to chase losses; to gamble for entertainment, not as a way to make money; and to limit exposure to continuous play games such as gambling machines which might carry a higher risk of addiction.[34]

The main problem with the idea of responsible gambling, and the reason why it should not be as uncritically accepted as it appears to have been throughout much of the gambling field, is that it begs the question about where responsibility for any harmful effects might rest. The present writer is not alone in believing that the implication people are meant to draw is that they, the gamblers or potential gamblers, are the ones who should be showing responsibility. As David Miers also points out, much of what has been written about responsible gambling '. . . emphasizes *players'* responsibility for their own gambling decisions'.[35] But, as he points out, both the suppliers and the consumers have responsibilities. In fact, in discussions about consumer protection policies generally, where the balance should be struck between suppliers' responsibilities and those of their consumers, has been a central debate.[36] But in practice the term responsible gambling, and its implied opposite, irresponsible gambling, are used, as the wording suggests, as descriptors of the ways in which individual people gamble, rather than of the ways the industry supplies its products. The clear implication is that problem gambling is largely the fault of the individual rather than being inherent in the product itself.

The crucial element in consumer protection is the provision of sufficient information for the consumer to be able to make an informed choice about whether to consume the product and if so in what quantity. In the age of liberalisation it is assumed that consumer protection is best served by having businesses compete in the marketplace for the custom of 'informed consumers'.[37] Even here there may be a balance to be struck, since consumers might also be said to have a responsibility to keep themselves informed. When it comes to gambling the question of information becomes even more problematic because it is by no means clear what information should be provided. There could be said to exist in the gambling case a state of 'information asymmetry', with the provider holding detailed information about how games operate – highly technical in the case of computer-controlled machine schedules, for example – and about the odds of winning and losing. Gambling has of course been notorious for providing those who lay the bets or deal the hands opportunities to cheat and exploit the punter. Very few jurisdictions require that operators publish the odds pertaining to the different games they offer or to the different machines available.[38] Gambling regulators are now asking whether all operators should be required to do so, like racing and other sports bookmakers, complicated though that might be. Should gambling machines carry warnings of their dangerousness, and if so in what terms, and how severe should the warnings be? Regulators struggle with even more mundane questions such as how large should the warnings be, should they only appear when a machine is in operation, and should they be confined to the machine itself or should they be displayed prominently elsewhere inside and outside the gambling venue? How is it to be judged whether enough information has been supplied to ensure that consumers are sufficiently informed to make a 'responsible' or 'sensible' choice?[39]

The whole matter of consumer protection gets murkier still when applied to gambling because of the increasing complexity and sophistication of gambling products and opportunities and the consequent growing possibilities for crime, including fraud and match fixing.[40] Canadian commentators have pointed out, for example, that insider winning and fraud can be a problem for lotteries, as it has been in Canada; that the schedules by which gambling machines pay out are not always as random as they should be; and that besides other potential crimes such as identity theft and theft of account details, beating the machine by hacking into it with the aid of a laptop computer and radio equipment is a risk. Whether perpetrated by operators, fellow players or others, all such crime ultimately works to the disadvantage of the majority of players, and the Canadian commentators argued that regulators should be much more vigilant than they are in detecting and exposing such crime.[41]

Much of the gambling industry has now moved from a position of denial about problem gambling to one of 'awareness' of its existence – albeit, as they see it, affecting only a very small number of people. Problem gambler 'awareness training' for gambling venue staff is now part what has come to be called *corporate social responsibility* (CSR). Much of CSR in the case of potentially dangerous forms of consumption such as gambling consists of minimising the harm – often referred to simply as harm minimisation or *harm reduction* (HR). But once again, applied to gambling, the concepts of CSR and HR are very far from being unproblematic. Let us take HR to start with. The term has found favour in the field of drug misuse where it embraces such programmes as those that provide clean and sterile syringes and needles so that those addicted to a drug such as heroin are less likely to contract and spread blood-borne diseases such as hepatitis C and HIV. Alcohol HR includes such things as the serving of beer in plastic rather than glass containers so that alcohol-related fights are less likely to result in serious injury; or the encouragement of drinking groups to nominate a non-drinking member who will be responsible for driving home.

There has been debate in the drug and alcohol fields about how broadly or narrowly HR should be defined[43] and the same matter has been taken up by two Canadian scholars in the *Journal of Gambling Studies*.[44] They are amongst those who argue for defining HR tightly to include only those measures that do not require a reduction in gambling *per se*. HR would therefore include the control of crime associated with gambling, intervention available on-site for gamblers who became distressed over losing or who suffered a heart attack, and measures aimed at helping the families of problem gamblers. These measures, and quite a range of others which are sometimes embraced by a broader definition of HR, are shown in Table 9.2. The argument is that all the other measures, if successful, should lead to a reduction in gambling. Some may be thought of as *supply reduction* measures since they aim to reduce harm by controlling or limiting the supply of gambling in some way. *Demand reduction* measures,

Table 9.2   Examples of gambling harm reduction (HR) measures[42]

Harm reduction (defined broadly)		Harm reduction (defined narrowly): does not require a reduction in gambling
Measures that aim to reduce gambling		
Demand reduction	*Supply reduction*	
Public education campaigns designed to reduce excess demand	Limit availability (e.g. by confining to certain areas, capping numbers of events, machines, etc.)	Legalising previously illegal forms of gambling to reduce criminality
Controls on advertising		Help for partners, children and other relatives
Reduced access to cash withdrawal and credit	Limit accessibility (e.g. by age, hours of service, membership)	On-site crisis intervention for gamblers who become distressed or ill
Measures that assist placing limits on one's gambling (e.g. pre-specifying money limit; reminder of time spent; self-exclusion option)	Modifications to gambling features (e.g. reduce maximum stake and jackpot sizes, reduce EGM reel speed or options on multiplying or re-staking winnings)	Counselling for those who win large National Lottery jackpots
Ban on alcohol use during gambling		

on the other hand, are intended to act directly on consumers so as to limit their demand for the product. The distinction between supply and demand reduction is admittedly difficult to maintain in some instances – self-exclusion programmes being an example (see Chapter 3). Whether the preference is for a narrower or broader definition of HR may seem a purely semantic consideration since all of the measures shown in the table are designed to reduce harm. The choice may be of the utmost importance, however, when it comes to matters of policy. HR programmes – in the narrow sense of the term – have often been highly controversial because they seem to 'send the wrong message', accepting the normalisation of the behaviour concerned, or even that they signal a likely future move in the direction of greater liberalisation.[45] In other words, they are addressed to the harm – the 'negative externalities' to use the economists' term – associated with the dangerous activity, but do not challenge the extent of the activity itself. The opposite side of the same coin is that all the other measures, shown in the table under the headings of demand reduction and supply reduction, although they may be termed HR by those who promote them, in fact go beyond the narrowly defined HR and do challenge the extent of the activity itself. If successful, drug use, or in this case gambling, will diminish rather than expand.

That is why the debate about definitions is more than semantic. Gambling promoters whose policies embrace HR as part of their CSR policies, and governments in favour of supporting the promotion of gambling, and even in many cases promoting it themselves, have not faced up to the implications of supporting HR in the broader sense. The distinction between narrowly defined and broadly defined HR has been blurred and as a result the objectives of many of the measures shown in the table have not been thought through and specified at all precisely. Government, charged with regulating a now liberalised industry, wants, of course, to have its cake and to eat it. It is an explicit element of policy to reduce gambling-related harm using a range of measures taken from all parts of the menu. On the question of whether, in the process, the extent of gambling in the population and the profits made from it, including government revenues, would thereby be limited, the government has been silent. Needless to say, it is not part of the industry's CSR policies that industry growth should be curtailed.

The question of whether the measures shown in the table work at all is a separate issue. Some of them may not do so. For example, there is some evidence that slowing down the reels of gambling machines (a form of supply reduction) may simply result in people playing longer (an increase in demand).[46] There is a parallel for tobacco smoking: reducing the nicotine content of cigarettes may result in smokers simply smoking a larger number of cigarettes.[47]

There is therefore a potential paradox in an industry, and its government supporters, aiming to innovate and expand whilst at the same time supporting some broad definition HR measures which, if successful, would limit expansion. Indeed there are those who believe that such a contradiction is inherent in the very notion of CSR. Critics of CSR, which has in the past included mainstream economic papers such as *The Financial Times* and magazines such as *The Economist*,[48] are fond of quoting Milton Friedman, guru of free market economics, who is reputed to have said such things as, 'the primary purpose of corporations is to make a profit . . . [CSR is] a means to symbolically cloak their real motivation to increase profits by building greater community goodwill to obtain more customers',[49] and, 'Few trends could so thoroughly undermine the very foundations of our free society as the acceptance by corporate officials of a social responsibility other than to make as much money for their stockholders as possible'.[50] Those who have studied the CSR policies of alcohol and tobacco companies have generally been sceptical. They point out the inherent contradiction between the basic motive to increase profits and returns to shareholders, and the motive, which is bound to be secondary, to reduce harmful impacts. They see the advantages of CSR to companies who wish to position themselves as socially responsible, with policies in line with those of government, whilst giving the impression that they are well able to regulate themselves, hence forestalling calls for tighter regulation. Companies are keen to 'build partnerships' and to be seen to engage in dialogue with government and non-government agencies involved in education, health and the environment. The conflicts of interest involved are evident in the lengths to which alcohol and tobacco companies will go to resist measures which might seriously challenge demand, such as significant price increases, advertising restrictions, or restrictions on easy access sales such as small packs of cigarettes, happy hours or incentives for women drinkers.[51] Critics point to what they see as the industry's preference for preventive measures which are least effective, such as education, and which are unlikely to seriously reduce demand or supply, but which at the same time help create an image of an industry that is fully in support of harm reduction. For example, an analysis of tobacco industry-sponsored Youth Smoking Prevention (YSP) programmes, first initiated in the USA in the 1980s and then promoted more widely, concluded that:

> ... the intent of the industry was not to reduce youth smoking but to forestall tobacco control legislation, marginalise health advocates, preserve industry access to youth, create allies within regulatory bodies, bolster industry credibility and preserve its influence with policymakers. The expansion of such programs in the last decade, often with governmental support, has occurred in the absence of evidence that YSP actually deters youth smoking.[52]

The most sceptical conclusion is that CSR activities, as practised by those companies whose products are dangerous, is really a cover-up exercise. It would follow from that conclusion that the conflicts and contradictions CSR embodies should be better recognised and brought out into the open. Part of the business of examining CSR more objectively should, according to some, be the establishment of a register of the institutions and agencies receiving financial support from such companies.[53] Some go further and argue that if an industry whose main motive is the making of profit out of the supply of a dangerous form of consumption is permitted to be very influential in setting the agenda for regulation, then an important aspect of democratic society itself is in danger. One critic of CSR quotes from Klein's *No Logo*: 'looking to corporations to draft our collective labour and human rights codes [means] we have already lost the most basic principle of citizenship: that people should govern themselves. . .'.[54]

It may be argued that it is unfair to compare the gambling industry with the tobacco industry. But the case of alcohol is an apt comparison to make and there has been much criticism of alcohol industry CSR. It is worth noting Miers' remarks about the change of attitude on the part of the gambling industry in Britain during the 1990s, a change that he believes was:

> ... undoubtedly due to enlightened self-interest: an acceptance that the promotion of responsible gambling is a better public position than one that merely seeks to exploit the consumer . . . The operators' acceptance of responsibility for its product became, in effect, part of the price of the government's promotion of the changes. . ..[55]

Gambling industry arguments for minimising restrictions

Not surprisingly, the push for dismantling controls on gambling has mainly come from spokespeople for the gambling industry. Let us take a few examples. One is Martin Arendts, founder of a leading German law firm specialising in gaming and betting law, whose clients include many private gambling operators licensed in the UK, Austria, Malta and Gibraltar. In a chapter in a book on European and national perspectives on the regulation of gambling, he bemoaned the continued presence of the state gambling monopolies – controlling at least certain sectors of gambling provision – which exist in a number of European countries (see Chapter 1). These he saw as constituting impediments to the creation of a fully free market in gambling products within the European Union. He accused some EU Member States of using their laws to bar foreign private gambling operators from advertising products in their countries. For example both *Ladbroke's* and *William Hill* had been forced to close down their German language internet sites following a legal judgement in favour of the North Rhine-Westphalia state gambling operator. Bank accounts of Austrian bookmakers had been frozen in Germany on the grounds that offering cross-border sports betting constituted illegal gambling. Private operators were fighting back, however, by appealing to the European Court of Justice and submitting complaints to the European Commission which had started investigations on the matter in a number of Member States. A number of Europe-wide associations of gambling operators had been founded, including the European Betting Association and the Remote Gambling Association.

Arendts used a number of familiar arguments which form part of the gambling as normal business discourse (see Chapter 6). One interesting argument was that, by themselves promoting gambling, governments had allowed themselves to get far too involved in seeking higher gambling turnover and profits from gambling, which was the appropriate domain of the private sector. It accused state gambling promoters of failing to fulfil their correct role, that of fighting gambling addiction. That argument had been the basis, for example, of a ruling in 2005 by the Administrative Court of Breda in the Netherlands that *Holland Casino* was in breach of an article of the EC Treaty, and that competition should be permitted. The position of the European Court of Justice on gambling, as on other matters, is that trade restrictions are only permitted if they are justified by being in the general interest, and in any case should not go beyond what is necessary. Because there continues to be controversy about whether complete liberalisation is in the general interest, there is currently no pan-European Union law which instructs Member States how gambling should be regulated.[56]

As a second example let us look at the arguments made by the Australasian Gaming Machine Manufacturers Association (AGMMA) in submissions that they made to the New South Wales and Australian governments.[57] Their 2007 submission regarding the Gaming Machines Act 2001 is a fascinating document and in many ways encapsulates gambling industry thinking world-wide. The document's basic point is that a more balanced approach to regulation should be enshrined in law than was the case with the 2001 Act. Table 9.3 shows the two primary objectives of the latter Act alongside three which AGMMA submitted should be the objectives. The two sets of objectives could hardly be more different. A main argument was that NSW was losing its pre-eminent position in the gambling machine manufacturing business and was now becoming an 'emerging backwater'. The Act was inhibiting '. . . the development of world

Table 9.3   The New South Wales, Australia, Gaming Machines Act 2001: actual objects of the Act and those suggested by the Australasian Gaming Machine Manufacturers Association (AGMMA)[58]

The stated primary objects of the Act	What the primary objects should be according to AGMMA
• Gambling harm minimisation; that is, the minimisation of harm associated with the misuse and abuse of gambling activities • The fostering of responsible conduct in relation to gambling	• The social, healthy and pleasurable entertainment of players • The economic stability and growth of the industry • Taxation revenue growth that parallels economic growth

class gaming entertainment for NSW venues and their stakeholders'. Between 2002–03 and 2006–07 business had declined by a third: just under 10,000 new machines were installed in clubs and hotels in 2006–07 compared to just under 15,000 four years previously. Nevertheless, AGMMA members were said to be collectively planning research and development expenditure of just under AU$1 billion over the following five years. Their members' international activity had increased markedly as casino-style gaming had been '. . . progressively legalised in some of the world's most scrupulous nations (such as Singapore)'. Indeed AGMMA declared that its members were being hampered in their efforts to supply in NSW itself the very products that they were designing and supplying for the international market. It submitted it was most important that regulations should not prevent the industry taking advantage of current and future technological advances in machine design.

In line with those general arguments, AGMMA had a number of specific recommendations. One was that capping the overall number of gambling machines in an area – as had been the policy in NSW – was counter-productive. Another was that the restrictions on multi-terminal gaming machines (MTGMs) should be eased, no longer limiting them to larger clubs and allowing larger numbers in hotels. The definition of an MTGM should be made more flexible, it suggested, 'to accommodate undetermined future games and configurations'. The NSW Game Design Harm Minimisation Register, which outlines 'responsible game design practices', in their view served no useful purpose and should be abandoned. Nor should new games necessarily be limited by current bet and prize limits. Over the next five years AGMMA was expecting its members to release, internationally, new products, including: new generation gaming machine terminals; new generation gaming platforms; client-server gaming systems; gaming venue management systems; and new generation games. In short, the NSW industry needed to be allowed to develop, unhampered by unnecessary restrictions – a familiar call.

AGMMA's 2008 submission to the Australian Senate Community Affairs Committee commented on two Bills brought to the Australian parliament by one senator – the Poker Machine Harm Reduction Tax Bill, which, according to

AGMMA, sought to gradually force gambling machines out of certain venues through the imposition of a tax, with revenue generated being paid into a fund that would compensate clubs and other organisations that had become dependent on gambling revenue; and the Poker Machine Harm Minimisation Bill, which sought to make mandatory a number of restrictions on the operations of machines.[59] This submission is interesting because it illustrates the use of two persuasive arguments. One is that the industry can be trusted to cooperate with government and other interested parties in order to do all it can to minimise harm – an argument which, of course, carries with it a recognition that gambling products are potentially harmful. AGMMA argued that gambling machine manufacturers had worked collaboratively and proactively to put harm minimisation policies in place. These had included the inclusion of on-screen clocks and credit meters on all new machines, proposing player information screens which had since become mandatory in some Australian states, and the provision of education and information, including the distribution of a Responsible Gaming Machine Play leaflet.

The second argument was that AGMMA, unlike the senator who had proposed new legislation, was up-to-date with relevant research. First, it claimed that the harm minimisation policies which AGMMA had supported, as well as other policies such as restricting machine numbers – the submission fails to point out that the latter is actually opposed by AGMMA – had been responsible for a significant decline in the prevalence of problem gambling in Australia since the time of the 1999 Australian Productivity Commission report. As an example of data that they considered now to be out of date was the senator's figure of 53% as the estimate of the percentage of money spent on poker machines in hotels and clubs in Victoria which could be accounted for by problem or at-risk gamblers – although this figure is cited as being based on quite recent, 2005–06, data. When it came to some of the specific recommendations made in the new harm minimisation Bill, the AGMMA submission leans strongly on a report from the University of Sydney which was prepared for the Gaming Industry Operators Group. That report, they say, found no evidence supporting the harm minimisation effects of limiting to $20 the size of notes that a machine would accept and to $100 the total amount of accumulated credit allowed, nor for slowing the rate of reel spin allowed. Other recommendations, such as incentives for players to use 'smart cards' rather than cash or credit or debit cards, AGMMA said lacked any support from objective research.

Very much the same arguments were used by the American Gaming Association – whom we met briefly in Chapter 6 – in their submission to the Australian Senate regarding the Poker Machine Harm Minimisation Bill.[60] In this case, however, the argument was developed further and in a cruder, less sophisticated way. They also used the argument that a number of controls on gambling machines which had been proposed, some of which were included in the Bill, were unlikely to have harm reduction effects according to the evidence. They included limiting the maximum bet permitted, restricting the length of each gambling session and requiring clocks (supported by AGMMA) and anti-gambling messages to be displayed on screens. Again the University of Sydney report is cited several times, along with a report of the Atlantic Lottery Corporation on research in Nova Scotia, a review in the *Journal of Gambling Studies*[61] and two other unpublished reports. Also used is the poorly supported argument that the prevalence of problem gambling remains remarkably stable, even in some instances declining, at around 1–2% of the adult population, irrespective of whether or not harm minimisation restrictions on the provision of machine gambling are in place (see Chapter 5 for a detailed consideration of the association between gambling provision and problem gambling).

This takes the AGA submission into the area of its main argument which is that there is no mileage in supply restriction, or what they call 'technology-based harm minimisation'. The emphasis should be placed, they say, not surprisingly, on harm minimisation of the demand reduction type. On the wider debate about where the emphasis of harm reduction should fall, the AGA takes a very one-sided position. Not only, they argue, is the prevalence of 'pathological gambling' stable, but at 1–2% it is 'by no means the public health crisis depicted in the comments of [the] Senator. . .'. Furthermore problem gamblers are 'troubled people' and their gambling would not respond to restrictions on game technology. Not surprisingly the AGA recommends policies that focus on the gambler, which they state are now favoured by the large majority of gambling jurisdictions in the USA. Such policies focus on: intensive public education; making information about treatment available to gamblers; promoting research on pathological gambling; adopting programmes that include informing customers of odds and educating employees; and establishing self-exclusion programmes 'that help individuals to take control of their gambling'. Put bluntly, '. . . the central problem is not in the machine. It is in the individual':

> When an activity is performed safely by 98 to 99 percent of the population, measures to protect the few who may be at risk must be proportionate, and should not unnecessarily disrupt the interests of the vast majority. In that respect, legalized gambling is no different from other ordinary forms of human activity – eating, consuming alcoholic beverages, driving a vehicle, or surfing on the Internet – that can cause injury if done to extremes or in an unsafe manner.

The argument is a familiar one – drawing on a number of pro-gambling expansion discourses discussed in Chapter 6. The implication is that problem or pathological gambling is largely the fault of the individual, someone who cannot control his or her gambling, whose gambling is not responsible. The fault does not lie in the product itself and attempts to restrict the product do not help prevent problem gambling, but instead restrict proper business innovation. The activity itself is depicted as essentially harmless, a source of fun and entertainment for all but a small, deviant minority. As explained in Chapter 5, that is a very one-sided and misleading view of the causes of gambling addiction – or of any addiction – and it represents a convenient fiction for the promoters of gambling expansion.

Encouraging the loyal big spenders

It is well known that gambling operators invest highly in the acquisition and retention of good customers.[62] The practice of casinos offering various incentives to their biggest players is well known. Complimentary offerings – known as 'comps' in the USA or, when offered *en masse*, as 'junkets' – include food and beverages and, in London casinos catering for richer gamblers or in remote locations such as Las Vegas, such things as a chauffeured car or hotel accommodation.[63] They may include ingenious schemes such as 'dead chip' programmes in which non-negotiable gaming chips can be purchased at a discounted rate, thus giving players more of an edge, in return for a commitment to a certain level of play.[64] A good example of a loyalty rewards programme in the gambling field is *Harrah's* Total Rewards Program which allows members access to special events, complimentary privileges such as free meals and hotels stays, and cash-back programmes, the benefits varying depending on a consumer's level of spending.[65]

Naturally enough, incentives are most likely to be targeted at players who are the most profitable for the operator; those who, in the US casino world, according to Mike Atherton, are referred to as high-rolling 'whales', as opposed to the 'minnows' or other varieties of small fish. Marine analogies seem to be popular in the gambling world: in the casino poker scene there are 'sharks' who easily devour eager 'plankton'.[66] Since some gamblers spend very much more on gambling than others, and since the distribution of total gambling spend in the population is likely to be highly skewed, with the majority spending relatively little and a 'tail' to the curve wherein is to be found an ever-decreasing proportion of people spending an ever-increasing amount (see Chapter 3, Figure 3.1), then it follows that a minority of the very heaviest gamblers will be contributing to operator profits to an extent out of all proportion to their numbers. Estimates of the proportion of gambling expenditure that is contributed by problem gamblers vary greatly from around 10% to more than 50%. One of the most often cited figures is the estimate – approximately 33% – produced as a result of the very careful calculation made by the Australian Productivity Commission in 1999. In the case of casinos the proportion may be even higher.

It is bound to be to an operator's advantage to cultivate the big spenders. A number of papers that have appeared in the academic journal *International Gambling Studies* have made that quite clear. One, written by two authors from Bond University in Queensland, Australia, used data from the Australian National Gaming Survey conducted in April 1999 by the Australian Productivity Commission[68], in order to draw conclusions that might be helpful to the casino gaming industry in their 'customer relationship and management' (CRM). They used the concept of 'customer lifetime value' (LTV), which is the estimated profitability of the customer over the whole course of his or her relationship with a company. One area, they state, where casinos have excelled in applying CRM strategies is in the gambling machine market. Loyalty programme cards allow for sophisticated tracking of spending in order to analyse customers' LTV and to tailor individual future marketing efforts. Using the Australian data, the Bond University paper divided blackjack and baccarat players into the four casino customer segments shown in Table 9.4. This showed how much more valuable in the long run certain customer segments are to the firm than are other segments. In particular, because of their big spending and/or loyalty, prime customers (PCs) and mobile customers – especially PCs because they combine high spending and regular visits – have very high LTVs. In fact, contrary to the general marketing principle that 20% of a firm's customers produce 80% of a firm's revenue, these data suggested that a mere 3% of table games customers could generate about 90% of all revenue. The advice to casino operators was therefore to put resources into finding out if customers in other sectors 'can be upgraded to a more profitable customer segment'. Incidental customers were probably a lost cause although they had their value in helping to make the casino look busy and perhaps in spending on non-gambling services offered by the casino. Most productive of effort would be promoting 'valued customers of tomorrow' (VCT), mostly in the age group 18–24 years, into the PC segment: 'It is important to learn to recognise VCTs with high conversion potential and to groom them slowly over time to become future PCs'.

A similar paper in the same journal, but emanating from a different part of the world, was written by two authors, one from Bishop's University, Canada, the other from Michigan State University, USA.[70] It also focused on casino consumer loyalty and made recommendations about where a casino might concentrate its efforts, and how, in maximising the loyalty of its bigger spenders. In this case the data came from a questionnaire mailed to members of a players' club of a large Native American casino. They divided respondents into categories according to the amount players said they budgeted annually for casino gaming, the proportion of visits made to the respondent's primary casino, and the amount a respondent budgeted for gaming per casino visit. The resulting eight 'exploitable market segments' were reduced to the six shown in Table 9.5, the other two being very small in size. Again it can be seen how certain customer segments are disproportionately very profitable on account of the high frequency of visits to the casino and/or the high level of their spending once they are there.

The paper's recommendations are designed to fit the segments. It questions the benefits of directing market attention to the 'disloyal low spender' segment given the low number of visits and the small amount they spend. The same is true for the 'loyal low spenders' for whom it is suggested that marketing might focus on non-gaming activities such as free trips, and food festivals. There was thought to be potential to develop the 'infrequent big spenders' into 'loyal big spenders' by building their loyalty and increasing their awareness of gaming opportunities at casinos. 'Frequent loyal low spenders' were on average the oldest (averaging 66 years) and they often joined the players' club to receive complimentary privileges: promotions and rewards such as frequent buyer meal cards or offering bonus points during off-peak hours, were recommended for them. 'Loyal big spenders', it was concluded, would be open to new customer incentive plans. The recommendation for 'transient big spenders' was that 'any

Table 9.4 The customer lifetime value (LTV) of different casino client segments in Australia[67] (taken with permission from Watson and Kale, 2003)

	Prime customers	Mobile customers	Valued customers of tomorrow	Incidental customers
Average visits per year	104	2	24	2
Average hours of play per visit	3	48	3	1
Average bet per hand (AU$)	200	5,000	25	10
LTV per customer (AU$)	107,827	388,800	2,624	15
% of customer base	2.5	0.5	15	82
% of total revenue	53.4	38.5	7.8	0.3
Customer profitability	A casino's most desirable target customers	A small group but the highest volume customers	Have a serious interest in gaming although average bets are low; some could become prime customers over time	Not really interested in gaming

An Unsafe Bet?

Table 9.5 Maximising the loyalty of different categories of casino patrons in mid-west USA[69] (taken with permission from Palmer and Mahoney, 2005, Table 2)

	Disloyal low spenders	Loyal low spenders	Infrequent big spenders	Transient big spenders	Frequent loyal low spenders	Loyal big spenders
Average gaming US$ per year	314	318	278	5154	3842	8785
Average gaming US$ per trip	37	32	224	240	45	258
Average trips per year	8.8	13.1	1.3	21.5	88.5	38.7
Number of casinos visited per year	8.6	3.7	1.2	8.9	10.6	5.7

marketing strategy should focus on the excitement of gambling as opposed to the value derived from the membership in the players' club'.[71] Possible promotions include free trips to exotic gaming locations and gaming tournaments. That group is of interest because, using the figures cited in the paper, it would appear that members of this group were spending an average of between 9 and 10% of their estimated income on casino gambling. 'Frequent loyal low spenders', although they made more trips to casinos, spent much less per trip. 'Loyal big spenders' spent per year more than the 'transient big spenders' but had average incomes over twice as great. Even so, 'frequent loyal low spenders' and 'loyal big spenders' also appear to have been spending over 7% and over 6% of their incomes, respectively, on casino gambling. These are large percentages and inevitably raise the question of whether amongst their numbers would be found a relatively high proportion of those with gambling problems.

The challenge of gambling regulation

As the immorality and irrationality discourses have waned and the gambling as harmless entertainment and as normal business ones have risen to take their place, the continued recognition of the perils of gambling have been met with much talk of the need for proper regulation of gambling. In the face of continued controversy about the expansion of gambling, this is an aspect of policy on which government strongly relies and which it makes much of. Since the inauguration of the National Lottery in the 1990s meant, in effect, that the government was entering the gambling field as a promoter of gambling, the emphasis on regulation became even more important. The National Lottery Commission stated in 2002 its commitment to '. . . maintaining our leadership in the consumer protection field and to setting a high standard of consumer protection as new lottery products develop . . . [and] ensuring that vulnerable members of our society are not put at risk by the activities of the National Lottery'.[72] As the Gambling Review Report[73] said, it was essential that 'the punter should be fully informed about the odds that he is facing and the proportion of stakes retained by the operator'. Statements of government policy made it clear, however, that speaking of regulation was at the same time to speak of the right of operators to ply their business, hampered by as little regulation as possible, and the right of consumers to choose to gamble: 'regulation will be confined to what is necessary to keep crime out, protect the vulnerable, and ensure that gambling products are fair to the consumer'.[74]

The power of the big gambling operators is undeniable. Writing about the growth of gambling in the USA in the early 1990s Goodman spoke of the way in which new gambling ventures '. . . create powerful new political constituencies that will fight to keep gambling legal and expanding',[75] pressing for reduced taxation and relief of restrictions, and wielding immense power because of the jobs they control and revenues they provide to the public sector. He gave the example of the Clinton proposal to impose a 4% federal tax on gross gambling revenues: no less than 31 state governors wrote to the President complaining of the damage that would do to their gambling-dependent budgets. A number of powerful collective organisations represented the interests of gambling companies; for example, the Nevada Resorts Association, the Casino Association of New Jersey and the American Gaming Association. The big operators command resources – for example, in order to employ expensive legal help – far in excess of those available to small operators or to public health campaign groups. The UK gambling regulator, in the wake of the 2005 Gambling Act, is already finding that standing up to the gambling industry can be a challenge.[76] The power of those who purvey dangerous forms of consumption is wielded on an international scale. The alcoholic drinks industry is a good example. It is an immensely powerful supporter of world and regional free trade agreements which threaten to undermine policies of individual countries which impose some restrictions in the interests of public health.[77] As we saw earlier, large gambling companies are attempting to use European Union free trade laws to oppose the policies of individual countries in much the same way.

Because the rapidity of technological change is allowing gambling games and the ways in which they are delivered to change and develop so rapidly, and because of the ever-increasing diversity of gambling, those charged with gambling regulation are faced with an enormous problem of getting on top of the complexity of the field. In the face of a highly 'ingenious' and 'challenging' industry,[78] regulators struggle in trying to close loopholes, and generally attempting to make regulation 'future proof'. Operators are likely to want the regulatory environment to be future proof in a different sense: they would like regulation to be sufficiently light so that technological innovation is not hampered. As already described in Chapter 2, new gambling products have come on the market in just the last few years which have totally transformed the gambling scene. They include playing virtual games via the internet, spread betting, betting exchanges and machines offering casino-style games (the fixed odds betting machines or FOBMs, in Britain, now under the 2005 Gambling Act categorised as B2 gambling machines).

Meanwhile there have been innovations in the design of gambling machines that almost certainly make them more dangerous.[79] Like lottery games, they tend to have a 'rapid product life cycle'.[80] There was a time, not long ago, when gaming machine wins were determined solely by the order in which symbols came to rest on those parts of the reels showing in the 'window'. Modern machines include a number of 'features' that have made play considerably more complicated (see Chapter 5 on structural characteristics of EGMs, and Table 5.1). One would expect an innovating industry to try to circumvent 'petty and outdated restrictions', but the effects of these developments in machine design are likely to make them more potentially addictive. That is not only because modern, more sophisticated, machines are likely to be more attractive generally, but more specifically because they encourage a player's 'illusion of control' and create multiple new experiences of the 'near miss', both of which are known to be factors that promote excessive gambling. EGMs have been identified in a number of European countries as constituting the form of gambling associated with the greatest problems.[81] Some Australian commentators have gone so far as to say:

> The EGM system provides an excellent example of those systems and technologies controlled by the powerful for the purpose of extracting wealth from consumers, in particular via the exploitation of some of the most vulnerable of citizens . . . As long as the discourse of business as usual is able to focus attention on individuals as the authors of their own misfortune, the continuation of the EGM techno-commercial system is assured.[82]

A gambling regulator, such as the Gambling Commission in Britain, is going to have to respond to repeated industry requests to put on the market new gambling products, or variations to existing ones, that are thought to make the product more attractive. Those very innovations and changes may often, in themselves, be ones that may make gambling that bit more dangerous. Very often, for example, they will be ones that encourage more continuous or more repetitive play. How are regulators to get the balance right? Will they, in the absence of any conclusive evidence that an innovation or change is itself dangerous, err on the side of the operator and take a risk on behalf of consumers and potential consumers? In Britain, the Department for Culture, Media and Sport has encouraged the Gambling Commission to take that risk in a number of cases – notably supporting the continued legality of children and young people playing Category D gambling machines – on the grounds of 'lack of evidence' of harm. Will regulators, on the other hand, use the 'precautionary principle', erring on the side of protecting the public from possible harm, thereby pleasing those who are concerned about the dangers to public health but displeasing the industry? When it comes to the fine detail of the regulations regarding different forms of gambling, old and new, the matters that need to be covered are legion. Just some of the matters that have arisen in the process of

Table 9.6 Just a few of the regulatory issues following the 2005 Gambling Act in Britain

---

How easy should it be to change the nature of gambling premises licences once they are awarded?

Are the 'grandfather' rights too liberal for those premises licensed prior to the Act?

How easy should it be for premises not otherwise licensed for gambling to obtain temporary use notices, e.g. hotels for gaming tournaments?

Should cash withdrawal machines be permitted within or close to gambling venues?

How liberal should the regulations be about children being present in locations where adults can play bingo, EGMs, etc.?

Should private member clubs be given special rights to allow gambling, including regulations regarding invited guests and under 18 year olds?

What gambling should be permitted in what areas in public houses licensed for the sale of alcohol?

What controls should there be on the advertising of different forms of gambling, including the question of sports sponsorship?

When should maximum stakes and prizes be allowed to increase as time goes on?

If challenged, how does the regulator define a 'gambling machine', or one set of 'premises', to give just two examples?

---

formulating regulations arising from the 2005 Gambling Act in Britain are listed in Table 9.6.

Chapter summary

This chapter has provided a critique of the position taken by government in the modern era of gambling expansion. It has been argued that *government, by acquiescing in the liberalisation of gambling, has become complicit in supporting the interests of gambling promotion.* At the heart of the matter is a paradox which government has not fully acknowledged and cannot easily resolve. By accepting the gambling discourses which speak of it as a leisure activity, intrinsically harmless and a productive part of a modern nation's business sector, government finds itself in a dilemma. If gambling is to be viewed as a commodity like any other, governed by market principles and contributing to the national economy, then growth must be expected and welcomed. Forced to recognise that gambling carries dangers for its citizens, governments experience 'role conflict', trying to combine diverse roles. The latter include those of regulator, protector of the public health, supporter of business, tax collector and very often in addition the role of providing gambling in the form of a state lottery and perhaps other gambling products besides. There are parallels to be drawn between the policy dilemmas surrounding gambling and those that pertain in the cases of other dangerous forms of consumption. The closest parallel is with alcohol: in that case also governments find themselves wearing many hats. Although the illegality of trading in and possessing dangerous drugs makes that case appear rather different, in fact the issues are much the same: there is a widespread view that prohibition is not working but at the same time there is recognition that drug legalisation and commercialisation would bring with them the same kinds of dilemma which governments are now experiencing in relation to the expansion of gambling.

The government – industry consensus on gambling liberalisation is bolstered by a set of ideas which suggests that gambling expansion and protection of the public are compatible. They include *the notions of 'responsible gambling' (RG), 'harm reduction' (HR) and 'corporate social responsibility' (CSR). These are problematic ideas and serve the interests of an expanding gambling providing industry.* RG, as well as suggesting that the source of the danger lies in the way in which consumers use the product, is ill-defined. No 'sensible limits' have been set, as they are in the case of alcohol consumption. Nor is it clear what should be the messages contained in information campaigns designed to prevent problem gambling. Should the message be that the safest thing is not to gamble at all? – presumably not since that would be tantamount to giving support to an industry and then advising the public not to use its products. Since many Britons play the National Lottery at least once a year but do not engage in any other form of gambling, should the advice be to confine gambling to NL products? HR is equally difficult to define. According to some definitions it is neutral on the question of the total volume of gambling in the population as a whole. According to other definitions it includes stronger forms of harm minimisation which involve a reduction in supply and/or demand, hence reducing overall gambling volume or at least limiting future expansion. It is that issue – whether gambling harm can be reduced without reducing overall consumption – that governments, complicit with an expanding industry, have not faced up to.

The gambling industry argues for reducing existing restrictions on its operations and for resisting new ones. To support its arguments it uses all the pro-gambling expansion discourses which were outlined in Chapter 6. As part of CSR, those ways of attempting to prevent problem gambling which are generally considered to be the weakest – notably public education – and the limited form of HR which does not threaten overall level of consumption, are favoured. In many quarters, CSR, in the context of the provision of dangerous products including alcohol and tobacco, has been met with considerable scepticism. There seems to be a conflict of interest involved in trying to maximise profits and at the same time attempting to reduce harm. CSR is seen by some as a form of industry promotion, a way of disarming criticism, maintaining alliance with government, in short a cover-up, a form of enlightened self-interest. It is difficult to reconcile a serious commitment to HR with evidence of the effort which operators devote – and must devote if their industry is to expand – to acquiring and retaining customers of various 'segments', especially big spenders who are often spending a relatively high proportion of their incomes on gambling and who are therefore particularly at risk of problem gambling.

Gambling is characterised by rapid technological change involving the enhancement of existing forms of gambling such as EGMs, and the development of new forms, particularly different ways of gambling remotely. *Many of the operators are large and powerful. Standing up to them represents a considerable challenge for government* in its role as regulator and defender of public health. It is hard for a government complicit in gambling expansion to fulfil those roles effectively.

Trapped: the Disempowering Effects of Failure to Challenge the Growth of Gambling

The consequences of complicity with gambling expansion

For government and its employees

As gambling moves further into the era of liberalisation, the independence of individuals and bodies which should remain objective and independent is in serious danger of being compromised. It is only too easy to become complicit in the liberalisation and expansion of gambling, and conflicts of interests can easily arise. The processes involved are many and subtle and often go unrecognised. Peter Adams, in his book *Gambling, Freedom and Democracy*, is one of the very few to have articulated these dangers at any length. He was writing from the experience of having witnessed liberalisation of gambling in New Zealand but his comments are highly pertinent to what I have found to be the case in Britain and I am sure the same applies elsewhere.

The first arena in which independence may be sacrificed is that of government. Adams points out that as liberalisation progresses the numbers of people and bodies concerned with gambling, either as part of government itself or very closely linked to it, increases greatly. There is an increasing number of relevant ministerial offices, other official appointments, committees, working groups and boards. Gambling providers are keen to engage with government at as many points in this system as possible. Government and government-related bodies 'find themselves increasingly tied into negotiations and bartering with gambling provider stakeholder groups in order to implement policy objectives'.[1] What Adams calls a 'culture of permissiveness' regarding gambling gradually evolves and permeates throughout this government system. For some people who are well placed in the system there may be attractive inducements such as funded business trips and opportunities to meet some quite rich and powerful people, and for quite a number there may be opportunities to travel to attractive conference locations funded by the gambling industry. There is even the prospect of being 'scooped up' for future employment within the gambling industry.[2] But for the most part the culture of permissiveness develops in a much more hidden and insidious fashion. Certain positions on the topic in question – gambling in this case – will become the norm and be readily articulated in open discussion, whilst others will be avoided, marginalised or forgotten about altogether. Where people's jobs depend on remaining reasonably well within the limits that define what is normative and acceptable, employees 'will be alert to attitudes and behaviours that may jeopardize their prospects and will act carefully to avoid missing out'.[3] Adams describes how, in his dealings with a government agency involved in managing gambling in New Zealand, he experienced repeated disappointment at the bias he found there in favour of the interests of gambling expansion.

Part of my own experience has been that of someone who was asked to comment on a whole series of draft regulations that were necessary in order to put into operation the 2005 Gambling Act in Britain. I found myself repeatedly making the point that the draft proposals, in my view, were tilted in favour of the convenience of gambling operators and the expansion of gambling. For example, there were frequent references to the need to make the process of obtaining gambling premises licences as little burdensome as possible for proposed licensees: the application process should be streamlined and, as far as possible, should not disadvantage the industry. The balance seemed to me to be all in favour of helping the gambling promoters as much as possible rather than allowing time for public consultation and consideration. In general, proposed timescales for representations to be made about licence proposals were very short; hearings would be conducted as quickly as possible. Operator licence fees were to be kept to the minimum necessary to cover the costs of processing an application, thereby making no allowance for the possible cost to a local licensing authority of any 'pollution' caused by the licensed facility. When it came to gambling machine regulations, although concern was expressed from time to time about the danger of unregulated gambling, there were frequent explicit references in the proposals to the general desire to liberalise machine gambling, presumably on the premise that the activity was by and large harmless. As already discussed in Chapter 2, the continued legality of children and young people in Britain playing certain types of gambling machine (Category D) has been particularly controversial. I was surprised, therefore, that when it came to proposed regulations governing permits for gambling machines in 'family entertainment centres', a guiding principle for regulation was that it should be regulation with a 'light touch'. This was reiterated several times. It was proposed that permits would last for 10 years, which seemed to me completely out of line with what the government had been saying about the care with which this aspect of the Act would be monitored and their pledge to reconsider the whole issue of children and young people and machines if evidence suggested that was necessary. In general it appeared that the government and their gambling regulators were again bending over backwards to make life as easy as possible for gambling operators.

For the academic community

It is the academic research community that one hopes would be least likely to be drawn into a position in which independence was compromised. The independence of research is just too important for that to be allowed to happen. It is crucial to democracy itself, Adams argues, that universities remain sufficiently independent to be able to challenge received wisdom wherever that comes from. There is clear evidence that those representing powerful commercial interests, in the tobacco and alcohol industries for example, have attempted to co-opt researchers to support findings consistent with the promotion of their interests, and to distort and discredit researchers' findings which run counter to those interests.[4] It would be surprising if the same were not true in the case of powerful commercial gambling interests. A possible example is the theory, mentioned in Chapter 5, of population adaptation to the increased availability of gambling.[5] Notwithstanding the thinness of the evidence for it, that is a theory from which the gambling industry can surely draw great comfort, particularly if it comes from a prestigious academic source. It is not surprising therefore to learn that the work on which it was based was partly supported by the industry. To some this is just part of a worrying, more general movement towards commercial funding of university research and its exploitation.[6]

Peter Adams' view, when it comes to gambling, is that academic research in New Zealand, and probably in the UK and elsewhere, is not sufficiently independent at the present time. He describes his surprise on first attending an international conference on gambling. Quite unlike conferences he had attended in other areas such as psychology, mental health, and alcohol and drugs, the gambling conference was attended by not only the expected mix of academics and service providers and policy people; but in addition a good proportion of the delegates were industry representatives. Many of the presentations at the conference, he notes, either focused on the social and economic benefits of gambling or took a very medical perspective on problem gambling which gave the impression that it was a condition affecting very few people who would likely have developed another addictive or mental illness disorder, if not gambling. What seemed to be missing was 'a critical voice on the expansion of gambling'.[7] The conference dinner, he tells us, was a lavish affair held in a local casino. It has been his experience that gambling conferences are often underwritten by gambling industry funding; hence organisers are naturally careful to avoid embarrassing their donors.

I have had some similar experiences. Alerted to the nature of some of the big international gambling conferences, I have managed to avoid them. But like Adams, my previous experience, particularly of events attended by researchers and service providers in the alcohol problems field, had not prepared me for the very different state of affairs that pertains when it comes to gambling. For one thing gambling industry representatives are very often present in a significant proportion, something that in my experience has never been the case in the area of alcohol studies. Industry presentations usually figure alongside other kinds and, again unlike conferences in related fields, there are relatively few presentations which seriously challenge the expansion of gambling and a number which explicitly or implicitly support it. I have been surprised, also, by the willingness of event organisers to accept industry funding or hospitality without questioning whether that might compromise them or compromise the presenters and attenders in any way. On one occasion my refusal to speak at an event that was scheduled to take place in a casino was met with some surprise. On another occasion, when I submitted, for a presentation I had been asked to give, a title which clearly signalled that I would be challenging gambling expansion, I was telephoned by one of the organisers who persuaded me, against my better judgement, to tone down the title on the grounds that it might otherwise discourage industry representatives from attending.

Researchers are constantly chasing limited amounts of research funding, particularly in a small but growing field such as gambling. They are motivated to advance the lines that they have been working along, and if an opportunity arises to do just that by applying for funds offered by a commercial source, the result for many is a difficult dilemma. Nor is it just research grants that may be available, but also opportunities to travel to present research findings, consultancy fees, positions on advisory boards, and so on. An even more worrying trend, identified by Adams, is the direct employment of academics, out of industry funds, to review research areas for industry sponsors. The results of any academic work funded by an industry whose interests lie in showing that their products are essentially benign, are bound to be put in doubt because of the conflict of interests involved. There are those in the gambling field who disagree strongly with that view and see nothing wrong in accepting industry funding. They argue that industry funders do not interfere with the conduct or reporting of the academic work they fund and that provided research aims, methods, results and conclusions are presented openly and honestly, then to suggest that academics have been compromised and their findings put in doubt is quite uncalled for.[8]

A few years ago I had an experience that gave me some insight into one of the ways in which the industry might influence research. I was approached by the National Centre for Social Research (NatCen) asking if I would provide the 'academic link' for the first British Gambling Prevalence Survey (see Chapter 2) sponsored by GamCare, the leading non-government gambling organisation in the UK. In my enthusiasm I did not enquire too closely about funding, but quickly discovered that the gambling industry was heavily involved, and that its representatives were in a majority on the project steering committee. My experience of the steering committee left me in no doubt that industry representatives would in those circumstances argue for methods and procedures that served their interests. For example, because there was some disagreement internationally about where the threshold was to be drawn between problem gambling and non-problem gambling in terms of scores on screening instruments, there was lively discussion on that point and certain industry representatives argued for placing the threshold higher than I would have advised. I believe expert opinion prevailed in that case, but there was also lengthy discussion about how to define gambling 'expenditure' (a very tricky matter in the case of gambling), and I think we may have been unduly influenced in that case. The dilemma then was that, without some industry support, it is unlikely that such an important study would have taken place when it did. A few years later, during planning for the second national survey, I again experienced the force of the industry – government consensus over the inclusion of questions for testing public attitudes towards gambling (see Chapter 7).

A lively debate has occurred in relation to funding of research by the tobacco and alcohol industries. Many leading journals that publish research in those areas have taken a strong line against industry funding and at least require published papers to be accompanied by a statement about funding sources.[9] In the case of gambling, by comparison, Adams' conclusion, published in 2008, was that 'the infrastructure for independent gambling research has yet to evolve'.[10] In the UK there are signs that things may slowly be moving in the right direction in that regard. Following the report of the Gambling Review Body in 2001, problem gambling services and research have principally been funded by voluntary contributions from the gambling industry, distributed by a body termed the Responsibility in Gambling Trust (RIGT). Earlier named the Gambling Industry Charitable Trust, many of the RIGT trustees were senior executives of gambling trade organisations. The Gambling Commission published a review of these arrangements.[11] Although it has been recommended that the arrangement whereby problem gambling services and research are largely funded from gambling industry contributions should continue – quite wrongly in my view – there does seem to be recognition that the freedom of the academic community to set the research agenda, and the objectivity of research findings, are both compromised by such an obvious industry presence on the Trust board. Although RIGT's research panel had no industry representation on it, and despite many in the industry and those serving on RIGT's expert panels firmly rejecting the suggestion of lack of independence, the review concluded:

> . . . there is a perception that the work undertaken by the Trust cannot be completely without industry influence. There are specific research institutes which would not at present be prepared to accept research funding from the Trust as a result of the perceived level of industry involvement in the Trust's priority setting and distribution functions. The lack of a strategic framework and priorities determined independently of the industry and service providers leaves the research and treatment panels largely reactive and at risk of bias by omission. The voluntary nature of donations adds to the perception that, were the Trust to propose research or prevention work which was unpalatable to parts or all of the industry, funding would be withdrawn. The fact that little research has been undertaken in relation to specific gambling products or the operators' relationships with customers and problem gamblers . . . has exacerbated this perception.[12]

The report recommended that RIGT's two present functions, on the one hand fundraising from the industry and elsewhere and supporting the industry's interest in the promotion of responsible gambling, and on the other hand the distribution of funds raised, should be separated and fulfilled by two separate bodies. Since the gambling industry in Britain, which in any case has difficulty speaking with one voice because of its diversity, failed even to meet the modest target of £3 million a year in voluntary donations, the same report recommended that the government start planning for a mandatory levy of £5 million a year in the first instance (which would have been higher if it were not for the current adverse financial situation).

Industry influence is not confined to the direct funding of research. Influence is more often indirect and therefore more difficult to detect. Again, the alcohol and drug research community is further advanced in detecting this kind of influence. The last two decades have seen a steady increase in the number of 'social aspects' organisations, around the world, funded by the drinks industry. Examples are the International Center for Alcohol Policies (ICAP) and the Portman Group in the UK. Since it is unclear '... whether they are devoted primarily to benefitting the ... industry or the public good', some think they might more appropriately be termed 'social aspects/public relations organisations' or SAPROs.[13] Not only is their mission ambiguous, but their methods also are not always transparent. A good example is a book on preventing alcohol-related harm which appeared in 2007. It was an edited book, representing a collaboration between drinks industry representatives, including ICAP, and a number of leading academics in the field, although, unusually, individual chapters were not attributed to particular collaborating authors. The book, which was launched in London at the Houses of Parliament and had other launches in Nairobi and Tokyo, has been criticised for focusing attention on specific groups such as 'hardcore drunk drivers' and pregnant women and failing to promote less targeted public health measures which might harm the interests of the drinks industry by threatening a reduction in population per capita consumption.[14]

In the gambling arena the US Gambling Study of the early 1990s found that community leaders mostly relied on '... research that had been produced either by the gambling industry itself or by researchers who worked for it'.[15] Others have pointed out since then that researchers can inadvertently find themselves complicit with industry interests in ways that may not be immediately apparent. The present author is an example of one who has collaborated with the government regulator in using standard screening instruments such as the Canadian Problem Gambling Severity Index (PGSI) and one based on the American Psychiatric Association's Diagnostic and Statistical Manual (DSM)[16] – see Chapter 3, Table 3.2 – leading to the production of an estimate of the number of people in the population who can be defined as 'problem gamblers'. This activity, supported by government and the gambling industry, can be criticised for helping to perpetuate a gambling discourse which sees problems related to gambling as being attached to particular individuals rather than to the 'behaviour-shaping capacities of sophisticated technologies and practices' and the policies that support them, thus in the process reinforcing the notion that the product itself is basically safe.[17]

The two articles cited in Chapter 9, looking at how the casino industry can best encourage loyalty amongst certain segments of their customers, appeared in a respected academic journal, *International Gambling Studies*, but both failed to declare their sources of funding although both were clearly written from the perspective of casino operators who want to increase loyalty and the amounts of money that customers spend. This raises the question of what is appropriate in an academic journal. My own view is that if the academic gambling field wishes to establish itself as a serious one, then it should adopt the standards followed in other areas. In the drug addiction field, for example, papers *about* a promoter industry would be acceptable, but not papers written from within the gambling industry and/or with the clear purpose of contributing to industry profitability.

For service providers

Adams includes, amongst those whose independent thinking on gambling policy might be compromised, organisations that provide problem gambling services. It is not in the interests of the gambling industry, nor of a government that supports gambling expansion, that organisations providing services should step out of line and challenge the main line of policy on which government and the industry are agreed. Nor would that be in the interests of the management of service providing organisations themselves, always concerned as they are with thinking ahead to the next funding round. Challenging the policy of gambling liberalisation is likely to be particularly counterproductive for an organisation if it is funded wholly or in part by the gambling industry. Even if they are funded from other sources, it is not uncommon for agencies to get involved in such things as training gambling industry staff or advising operators on screening for problem gambling. Such activities are good for the organisation's income generation but they bind the organisation into industry collaboration, making opposition to liberalisation policy more difficult. This can create conflict between colleagues who hold different views. At the very least, employees will be aware that they are not in a position to speak out in a way that challenges the unspoken consensus of which their organisation may have become a part. On more than one occasion I have been encouraged to keep challenging that consensus by people who told me that they felt unable to do so themselves because of their positions in problem gambling-related organisations.

Gamblers Anonymous, like Alcoholics Anonymous and other 12-Step mutual help organisations, is very firm in its position that it has no position on gambling policy.[18] Such organisations are there to help individuals who have developed an addiction to gambling, and they consider that it would be a diversion to get involved in policy, and one that would probably undermine the good work they do in helping each other. In Britain, the one national organisation to which we should look for an independent view of gambling policy is GamCare, a non-statutory body which, amongst other activities, operates a national counselling and information service as well as a telephone helpline for people with gambling problems. It plays a vital role in an otherwise poorly resourced field. Its work is highly valued by all. But, as one of its senior staff told Mike Atherton when he was preparing his book, regarding national policy 'GamCare's position is gambling neutral'.[19] In fact, however, there is reason to argue that, far from being neutral, it is itself part of the gambling liberalisation consensus. It happens to be funded by the gambling industry and industry representatives are on its board and have been prominent in its publicity material and at its public events. I was surprised, naively perhaps, that it welcomed the 2005 Gambling Act. Consciousness of the dangers of complicity for service-providing organisations is not well developed in the gambling domain, or at least it is not something that is openly spoken about and challenged. There is far greater awareness in related areas; for example, in relation to the tobacco, alcohol and pharmaceutical industries. For example, in 2008 it was reported in the *British Medical Journal* that health care professionals in Spain had set up a group, called *No Gracias*, to promote relations between doctors and the pharmaceutical industry that would be based on transparency, independence, and proportion. It was reported to be an initiative of the Federation of Associations for the Defence of Public Health and is part of the international *No Free Lunch* movement, a network of non-profit organisations aiming to 'encourage health care providers to practise medicine on the basis of scientific evidence rather than on the basis of pharmaceutical promotion'.[20] Awareness has been slow to dawn among researchers, government officers and service-providing organisations that there is 'no free lunch' when it comes to collaborating with gambling promoters.

Adams is very clear about the importance of all this. If governments are too committed to gambling expansion, as they probably are in countries such as Britain and New Zealand, and if academic researchers and service providers have also largely been drawn into supporting gambling expansion and are compromised in their ability to challenge that position, then they find themselves in what he calls 'moral jeopardy'. Indeed, if there exists no site of independent challenge to the consensus, then there may be a collective failure to protect the public from dangers about which they cannot be expected to be expertly informed. The ability of society to have a full and informed debate about policy is foregone and to that extent democracy itself is eroded. In his view these matters should be much more openly discussed than they are. That would include a requirement on all individuals and organisations in the field to declare their sources of funding and to acknowledge any potential conflicts of interest to which they are exposed.

How should a community and its residents be involved in deciding on gambling expansion?

The transformation of gambling at the end of the twentieth century is as good an example as any of the effects of globalisation on an activity that was once of much more local significance. Whereas activities such as horse racing, card playing and bingo used to be the predominant forms of gambling, new international forms such as urban casinos and gambling machines have become more dominant. The overriding driver of profit, increasing dominance of transnational corporations, vigorous global competition and progressive standardisation of gambling products, have changed the nature of gambling. As one leading Australian scholar has put it:

> ... we are now less likely to play games instilled with local meanings and practices than were our parents and grandparents. Whereas gambling in the past was shaped by the cultural values of localized communities, contemporary gambling is increasingly commercialized, standardized, and global. It has become big business, central to the activities, values, and commercial imperatives of national and transnational organizations.[21]

Although it would be too simplistic to contrast the results of gambling globalisation with an idealised view of the past characterised by harmonious local communities – for example, the internet has potential for development of new patterns of sociability and citizen participation which might impact positively on gambling by enabling citizens to express their rights, to share information, voice concerns and propose alternatives – it has nevertheless become 'a crucial issue for policy makers . . . to assess the potential community benefit against the potential social costs'. There remains 'the unanswered moral question of who is responsible for addressing any social harm that might result'.[22]

How might a major new gambling facility in an area, such as a large urban casino, or the proliferation of betting shops along a high street, each offering numerous sports betting opportunities, affect an area's social capital? By analogy with other forms of capital that accompany development, such as human, business, natural, knowledge and public institutional capital, social capital has been widely seen as a previously missing element in the mix of resources that a community needs for health and development.[23] Social capital refers to the complex of constructive relationships that exist in any social group in order to give that group the strength and cohesiveness to collectively solve problems effectively. Since social capital has been identified as so important an ingredient for the functioning of natural human groups, it is highly relevant to pose the question whether the expansion of gambling generally, and more specifically the expansion of particular kinds of gambling, helps build social capital or serves to undermine it. For example, might betting shops, as one social geographer has suggested, contribute to general well-being through offering opportunities for social networking and social structure for a group of people who might otherwise be leading fairly chaotic lives?[24] Or might they discourage some groups of residents from using their local shopping area and hence damage the neighbourhood socially and financially?

Mike Atherton describes walking up Kilburn High Road in one of the more rundown parts of London, passing in a short stretch five bookmakers, three pawnbrokers and a bingo hall – 'a sure sign that gambling has infiltrated deep into this working-class community'.[25] He also describes part of Las Vegas which the tourists rarely see, what he calls its 'underbelly', an area of shabby motels, low-income housing and plenty of downmarket opportunities for gambling, few other community amenities, home to some of the poorly paid locals who service the upmarket casinos elsewhere in town. Because casino resorts offer their customers a whole range of gambling and non-gambling products and services, there is little need for them to spend much time or money outside the casino itself – Atlantic City is another well known example of this phenomenon. Atherton is left in no doubt that 'casino-resorts and urban generation do not go together'.[26]

Some secondary analyses of data from the 2006/07 British Gambling Prevalence Survey are relevant here. Figure 10.1 shows how the degree of deprivation of the area in which a survey respondent was living – divided into five roughly equal-sized groups from the fifth of respondents living in the least deprived areas to the fifth living in the most deprived – was related to a) the likelihood

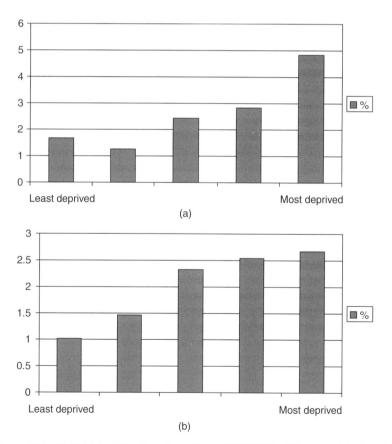

Figure 10.1 British Gambling Prevalence Survey 2006/07 (English data only), the relationship between area deprivation and a) having a close relative with a gambling problem and b) having a gambling problem oneself[27]

of respondents reporting in the survey that a close relative had had a gambling problem at some time in the previous 12 months, and b) the likelihood of respondents themselves answering the problem gambling screening questions in a way that suggested they had a gambling problem or were gambling in a way that put them at risk of having such a problem. The first of those relationships is particularly strong: those in the most deprived areas being nearly three times as likely to report having a close relative with a gambling problem compared to those living in the least deprived areas. This is not peculiar to Britain since some very similar findings have come from a national survey in the USA.[28] In that study, areas of residence were divided into ten groups and problem or pathological gambling was found to be 12 times as prevalent amongst those living in the most deprived areas compared to those living in the least deprived.

The question was raised in Chapter 8 of whether taxes on gambling are actually regressive rather than progressive, in effect robbing the poor to pay the rich rather than the other way round – a kind of Robin Hood effect in reverse.[29] If the poor spend proportionately more of their incomes on gambling than do the rich and are not compensated by receiving more public goods than the rich in return, then taxation on any form of gambling may indeed be regressive. But the charge of regressivity is particularly apt in the case of a national lottery if it is the case that the poor spend more of their money and see the proceeds going towards public works which seem to benefit the better-off. That was certainly a criticism in the early days of Britain's National Lottery, and economic studies of public lotteries in Canada and the USA have also concluded that the redistributive effect is regressive.[30] Whether a state lottery functions as a regressive form of tax, and the more general ethical question of whether it is right to raise money for good causes in this way, are important questions if it is considered that the state, by promoting the lottery, is playing a role in the chance-based redistribution of wealth in the course of its efforts to raise public money in this way.[31] There is also the question of whether, as some have argued, the relatively rich benefit most from a national lottery, not just as disproportionate beneficiaries of the funding of good causes, but also as the managers and shareholders of gambling companies.[32]

The relationship of gambling to poverty and social class in the modern era is worrying. Evidence is slowly accumulating that urban forms of convenience gambling, such as EGMs and high street betting shops, are to be found at higher density in the poorer areas of towns and cities;[33] that people of lower socioeconomic status, although they may spend no more on gambling than those of higher SES, have higher rates of problem gambling;[34] and that people on lower incomes spend a considerably higher percentage of their incomes on gambling than do people who are better off.[35] The way Goodman put it in *The Luck Business* was that, while it is literally true that no-one forces people to gamble, gambling is one of the few opportunities for investment and trans-forming lives – something that is often highlighted in gambling advertising – and hence the relationship between social class, poverty and gambling means that the willingness of the poor to gamble could be called the 'coercion of circumstance'.[36]

Community (dis)empowerment and gambling

The principle of community empowerment is an important one when it comes to the provision of gambling in a neighbourhood. People living in the area should have the right to participate in a democratic process of deciding what gambling should be provided locally. Particular consideration should be given to the views of minority ethnic groups who may not share the majority view on the ethics of gambling. From those principles it follows that there is a requirement on state and local governments to keep community members well informed and to consult fully with them about the levels and types of gambling that they think are appropriate for their localities.[37] In practice public opinion about gambling has not been sought; the business interests of the gambling industry and the revenue-raising interests of governments have prevailed. That statement has probably been less true in the USA since local referenda on the opening of new casinos started to be called in the early 1990s. The first US casinos of the modern era came in without such public consultation and voters were bypassed. But by the mid-1990s public debate had grown, the National Coalition Against Legalized Gambling and numerous state or local organisations, with names such as CASI*NO* and NO DICE and Citizens Against Gambling Expansion, had arisen; and 'right to vote' campaigns were being successful. By the mid-1990s new casino proposals were mostly subject to referenda and the large majority were failing.[38] Since then there have been moves towards greater public accountability in countries such as Canada, Australia, New Zealand and the Netherlands. There have been referenda on the opening of new gambling outlets in some Dutch towns[39] and Canadians have also had some experience of gambling referenda. In a national Canadian survey in 1999 as many as 84% agreed with the statement that 'governments should hold public consultations before introducing new forms of gambling', with only 11% disagreeing.[40] 'Gambling-watch' organisations have been formed in some countries in order to make sure that challenges to the reliance of governments and community organisations on gambling profits are represented in the media, and a number of community groups are challenging government complicity. Some organisations, including the Problem Gambling Foundation of New Zealand, are developing databases with details about the recipients of gambling profits.[41] To date there is very little sign of such public activity in Britain although there are increasing reports of local political and media interest in the granting of new gambling premises licences.[42]

A related development which is gathering momentum is the requirement for a detailed social and economic impact assessment to be made whenever a new gambling facility is proposed. This is a new field and there is as yet no consensus about how exactly such an assessment should be carried out. Most Australian states are reported to be moving in that direction and Queensland is said to be unusual in requiring a particularly detailed assessment from any operator who applies to set up a new gambling outlet, including an assessment of the risk of increased problem gambling. More applications are now being refused in that state than in others.[43]

In Britain the 2005 Gambling Act gives local authorities in England and Wales (licensing boards in Scotland) responsibility for the granting of gambling premises licences, permits for gambling machines in public houses and clubs, notices for temporary use of premises for gambling, and for registering small scale lotteries.[44] Professor Light has been critical of the lack of representation of local people in making decisions about an area's gambling facilities. For a start the licensing authority can no longer use the 'demand' argument to refuse a licence (under the previous legislation a committee of local magistrates – then responsible for gambling licences – could refuse a licence if they were not satisfied that there was a substantial unmet demand in the area). Relaxation of restrictions on advertising under the new Act now allows demand to be stimulated further. I am now meeting people who are surprised that new betting shops are sprouting up in their local high streets where several already existed. Local objections that there are already enough are over-ruled, as they are bound to be, since the argument that demand is already met is no longer valid under the new legislation. Nor is the objection allowable that new gambling facilities will have a negative effect on the character of the local area.[45]

The Gambling Review report which preceded the Act recommended that a local authority should have the power to ban gambling from all or part of its area, but that was rejected by the government (although they later conceded that local authorities should have that power specifically where casinos were concerned).[46] The government claims that the new system gives local people a say in the nature and extent of gambling in their area. Representations to the local authority concerning any application can be made by 'responsible authorities' and 'interested parties'. This is vague and unsatisfactory. How is an interested party defined? How will local residents obtain information, for example about whether gambling will be conducted in a fair and open way in the facility? How will the protection of children and the vulnerable – a major licensing objective – be assured? Could a local resident object about a proposed facility near to a school or because there are many disadvantaged people living in the area, Professor Light asks. Responsible authorities such as the police and the planning authority can make representations, but how will the danger of an increased prevalence of problem gambling be considered?[47]

I had the same concerns when asked to comment on the detailed draft regulations that were necessary in order to put the regulatory flesh on the legislative bones of the Act. I found myself repeatedly coming to the point about local representation, which also seemed to me to be generally quite insufficient and unsatisfactory. For example, I thought the ways in which it was suggested the public would be informed about a new premises licence application were nowhere near sufficient. The requirement to display one public notice and to publish one notice in a local paper, and for the representations to be made within 28 days, not only gives the proposed licensee a great deal of leeway over how prominently the proposal is advertised locally, but also gives individuals and representative groups of interested people a very short time indeed in which to 1) spot the public notice or notice in the paper, and 2) to consult with others locally, put the item on the agenda of the local residents' association meeting and to make any kind of representation. This falls very far short of any serious attempt to engage local people in any kind of meaningful discussion. It is obviously based on the idea that operators should have the right to go ahead with a licence application for a new gambling facility in the area, with the minimum of difficulty and delay, with the onus on unsuspecting ordinary members of the community to be alert to everything that is being proposed around them and to have the time and resources to act very quickly. More thought needs to be given to how the principle of giving local people a real say can be operationalised.

Local authorities do have the right to inspect gambling premises but no thought seems to have been given to the possibility that an inspection team might include ordinary members of the public as observers. If there were objections and there was to be a hearing, there is a list of people to whom the licensing authority would be required to give notice of the hearing, but that does not include the general public. Ten day's notice of a hearing seems a quite insufficient period of time to prepare and make necessary arrangements. Parents and others with responsibilities for children are likely to be particularly interested in the granting of permits for gambling machines in 'family entertainment centres'. The regulations regarding the different types of gambling machine are so complicated (see Chapter 2) that it is difficult for anyone who is not directly involved to understand them. It is very important that parents understand what is allowed and where. It was surprising, therefore, to see that the public is not mentioned in this set of regulations as a stakeholder group who might have a special interest.

A community's need to protect its young people

With such rapid development of new ways of gambling, plus the enhancement of old ways, whole groups of people may be at increased risk who previously were naturally protected by the barriers and restraints which were in place without anyone realising that they were there. Women, for example, were naturally protected from gambling in the past by the very nature of most gambling activities and the places where they happened. Betting shops and casinos were probably not attractive to most women, and certainly not to women visiting such premises on their own: Mike Atherton uses words such as 'menacing' and 'intimidating' to describe how they must have appeared to many women, and perhaps often still do. Internet gambling may have changed all that.[48]

But it is their young people about whom members of any community are most concerned. Whatever the controversies about gambling and society, one thing that all seem to be agreed on is the need to protect children and adolescents. Indeed this is one of the basic objectives of the gambling regulatory regime in Britain and therefore one of the principal aims of the Gambling Commission. As noted in Chapter 3, it is one of the most solidly established findings in the gambling problems field that young people are especially vulnerable.[49]

In the cases of alcohol, tobacco and drug use and misuse, the evidence is very clear that the earlier the use of a substance begins in childhood or adolescence, the more likely it is that a young person will use the same and other substances later on and the more likely is the later experience of heavy or problematic use.[50] It is for that reason that much of the effort devoted to trying to prevent substance misuse is directed at trying to delay the initiation into use of substances in adolescence. Because gambling has been much less researched there is less evidence available, but what evidence there is is in support of the long-held hypothesis that starting gambling early in childhood or adolescence puts young people at greater risk of subsequent gambling problems.[51] There is also evidence from a number of countries that having a parent with a gambling problem puts a young person at risk.[52] There is also a hypothesis, more difficult to test, that the experience of a big early win is very likely to start a young person off on a career that may lead to problem gambling. Interestingly enough, in his book Mike Atherton notes how common it was for the very big spending gamblers whom he interviewed – most of whom acknowledged being addicted at some stage – to have experienced a large early win and to have been very influenced at a young age by parents or grandparents who were strongly and positively engaged with gambling.[53]

The adult problem gamblers who took part in a British in-depth interview study helped explain the importance of those early experiences (see Chapter 4). They emphasised the key role played early on in their lives by other people, particularly parents, who set a norm for gambling, conveying a positive image of gambling, taking a keen interest in it and making it appear an attractive and acceptable activity, often demonstrating and coaching youngsters in how to gamble. Those findings and hypotheses fit well with psychological theories of development and habit formation generally.[54] The earlier a young person has positive experiences of an activity such as gambling, the more likely it is that the ground will be laid for the development of an attraction or attachment to the activity. Because adolescence can be an emotionally unsettling time of life for many, young people may be particularly susceptible to the attractions of gambling. Indeed the similarity of most forms of gambling to other forms of play may make gambling even more attractive to children and adolescents than might be the case for other potentially addictive activities.

I was therefore looking out specially for efforts to protect children and young people when asked to comment on detailed gambling regulations. One of the most difficult issues in the new liberalisation era, when forms of gambling are multiplying and there has been a strong move towards providing a number of different forms of gambling on the same premises – rather than, as formerly, keeping different types of gambling separate – is the question of how to prevent exposure of children and young people to the conditions that might put them at risk. For example, it was proposed that direct internal access should be allowed between 'family entertainment centres' (FECs) and private member clubs, and also between those types of premises and pubs. Since clubs are places where category B and C gambling machines are permitted, then easy access between FECs and clubs is not doing sufficient to protect children. The evidence suggests that anything that makes it easy for children to accompany adults on outings that involve witnessing their elders gambling, and at the same time makes it easy for children to gamble in a similar way on the same occasion, is running the risk of providing the very set of circumstances that puts children at risk. The proliferation of potentially dangerous forms of gambling in pubs and clubs makes the protection of children and young people all the more difficult. Although it is clear that they should not participate directly in the forms of gambling available, that does not prevent them being present when gambling is taking place and therefore 'participating' in most important respects – for example, learning about the games, strategies, sharing the excitement, sharing the pleasure of winning or the disappointment of losing.

Bingo clubs may constitute another set of premises where, because of liberalisation, the protection of children and young people has become more difficult. Again, these are premises where children and young people can be admitted but where they are not permitted to take part directly in gambling, except by playing Category D gambling machines that may be available. It was proposed that there be no limit to the hours during which machines could be played on bingo premises and that direct internal access between a bingo hall and an associated FEC and pub facility be permitted. That seems to me to make bingo halls a place where young people might readily be introduced to gambling, both by accompanying their elders and witnessing them gambling and by having easy access at any time to the controversial category D machines. Similar issues apply to the new generation of large and medium-sized urban casinos: children and young people can be admitted to parts of the premises but not to the adult gaming areas, which should not be visible from the areas to which children and young people have access. There are in addition all manner of other detailed regulations that bear on this question of protecting the young. Just one of these is the set of regulations regarding 'temporary use notices', required for example by a hotel that wishes to provide a gambling tournament. Because no ordinary premises licence would be required in such a case, and because it is very likely that families, including children, will be involved directly or indirectly, this seems to be another area where the protection of children is not being taken seriously enough.

Whether children's replica football and other sporting strips should carry the branding of gambling operators is yet another contentious area of the regulations. One proposal made by the Gambling Commission – citing with favour policies recommended in the alcoholic drinks sector by the Portman Group which represents the drinks industry – was that children's sports clothing should be available with and without gambling branding and that parents should be given the choice. That is of course exactly the kind of thing that one would expect an industry group to support. In the alcohol field the Portman Group has the reputation of being an organisation which only supports policies that are in the industry's interest, having consistently opposed those forms of prevention of alcohol problems, such as price increases, which have the greatest supportive evidence for them but which might run the risk of damaging the profits of the industry. Most parents would of course not be aware that they were supporting gambling by choosing one type of football shirt over another, and it would therefore amount to a subtle way of promoting gambling to young people whilst appearing to put the responsibility on parents who are likely to be unaware of the risks.

The public health perspective

There are now increasing calls for a proper public health approach to be taken towards gambling. If gambling and the dangers associated with it were treated as matters of public health importance, then the issues we have been discussing in this chapter would be much more questions for public debate than they are currently. It has been pointed out, repeatedly, that the model which has dominated theorising and research on the subject – with the approval of, and often direct or indirect funding by, the gambling industry and its government supporters – has been a psychological/medical one, placing emphasis on a minority of people who receive a gambling problem diagnosis and who might be specially vulnerable. This is seen by many as a very limited way of conceptualising the risks that the expansion of gambling poses for whole communities.[55] A broader, public health approach enables the impact of gambling for society as a whole to be viewed through 'other lenses' – social, political and economic.[56] A purely clinical approach, so the argument runs, fails to address the underlying causes of gambling problems. A public health approach would not just consider individual gamblers, but also questions of policy and regulation which change 'the consumption environment', changes to the nature of gambling products themselves, and changes in beliefs and norms that influence patterns of consumption.[57] The public health model presented by a group of Canadian researchers, with youth gambling problems particularly in mind, illustrates the breadth of such a public health model (Figure 10.2).

Most progress in adopting a public health model towards gambling has probably been made in New Zealand, with much encouragement from the 2003 Gambling Act which formally recognised gambling as a public health issue.[59] The New Zealand health model offers a picture rather different from one based solely on individual cases of problem gambling. It views gambling as producing harm that is much more pervasive, affecting families, communities and whole societies. Gambling is seen as being about 'our families, our communities, our problem'.[60] It requires a response which goes far beyond individual treatment.

> The driving concept . . . is that of resilience – the quality required by both individuals and communities to withstand the demands and pressures of life in a positive way to enable them to overcome difficulties, and to learn from this process to increase strength and capacity. The overwhelming pressures represented by the ubiquitous presence of gambling in so many forms represent such pressures, and hence resilience in the face of these and the ability to recover and come back strong is clearly relevant.

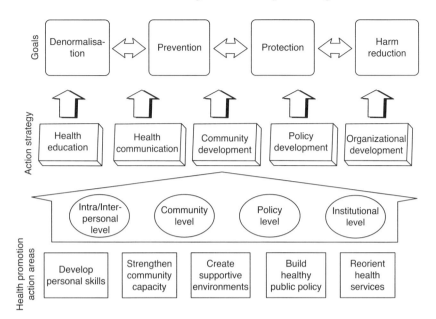

Figure 10.2   The Canadian public health policy framework for action (reproduced with permission from Messerlian et al, 2004, Fig 1)[58]

It is widely agreed that gambling has almost overnight become a major social issue in New Zealand, and is having a major impact on communities, with Maori, Pacific and Asian communities and young people especially affected. It is also clear that the overall 'social capital' of communities is being eroded by modern and increasingly technological styles of gambling. The increasingly prevalent poker machine is emerging as being the form of gambling with the most potential for damage. It is a huge industry, creating significant revenue not only for providers of gambling, but also for government.[61]

Recognising gambling, and the problems associated with it, as an issue for public health leads to a consideration of how gambling-related harms can best be prevented. The public health perspective, because it draws attention to the multiple causes of problems and to the diverse ways in which gambling can be harmful – to individuals, families, communities, and to society as a whole – emphasises the many different forms that preventive efforts can take. The great diversity of possibilities for prevention is illustrated in Table 10.1 – which has already been much condensed in order to fit it onto a single page. Note the very varied nature of these suggested preventive actions. Some are addressed to all members of a community, others to those thought to be at risk and yet others to those who are already experiencing problems – the latter corresponding to what is sometimes termed 'tertiary prevention', including forms of medical and psychological treatment for individual problem gamblers. Some methods are clearly aimed at increasing the knowledge or changing the attitudes or behaviour of individual people, whereas other methods are targeted at the situational and

Table 10.1	The wide range of options for the prevention of problem gambling[62]

Raising public awareness about the dangers of gambling
  e.g. public campaigns such as 'Think of what you're really gambling with' in
  Victoria, Australia; programmes aimed at young people such as 'Count me out' and
  'Hooked city' in Quebec, Canada; gambling awareness weeks or no-gambling days

Building general community resilience
  Measures designed to build the capacity of young people, parents, teachers, the
  media, etc. to resist the effects of potential dangers such as violence, delinquency,
  educational drop-out, alcohol and drug misuse, problem gambling

Restrictions on the availability and accessibility of gambling
  e.g. restricting the number of gambling venues and events; confining gambling to
  certain areas; raising the legal age for different forms of gambling; making illegal
  certain forms of gambling such as 'convenience gambling' in the form of EGMs
  outside casinos

Controlling the way in which gambling is provided
  e.g. reducing maximum stake and prize levels or frequency of lottery draws; banning
  or tightly controlling advertising of gambling; restricting EGM features to make
  them less addictive; restricting premises to the provision of one type of gambling
  only

Community control of gambling opportunities
  e.g. better public notice of changes to the provision of gambling; public
  representation in the licensing process; stimulation of public debate; social impact
  assessment to be mandatory for proposed new gambling facilities

Early intervention for risk or problem gambling
  e.g. warning notices about the dangers of gambling to be displayed; time and money
  limit setting; training about the identification of risk of problem gambling for
  premises staff; easy access to on-site information and self-exclusion; centralised
  systems for monitoring gambling to aid early detection of problems; well publicised
  help lines and access to counselling services

---

structural features of gambling products, and yet others at the type or amount of
gambling available to people. Some might be thought of as 'micro-level' forms
of prevention, targeted at individuals or families; others, on the other hand, are
more in the nature of 'macro-level' methods, aimed at altering prevailing laws
or norms. In any case, this wide view of the preventive options that are available
goes far beyond the more limited harm reduction measures discussed in the
previous chapter (see Table 9.2).

Public health experts are fond of using the analogy of a river where people
are repeatedly being rescued from drowning, until someone has the bright
idea of going upstream to see why people are repeatedly falling in – or are
they being pushed? Moving the emphasis away from one that is exclusively
on the treatment of those people who already have a health problem, towards
putting more resources into prevention, is often referred to as going upstream
or 'attending to upstream issues'. A general conclusion is that the prevention of
any kind of psychological problem requires sustained application of a package
consisting of a number of different forms of preventive effort of different kinds,
operating on different levels. In practice, however, there appears to have been

Table 10.2 Ethical principles for reasonable gambling (reproduced with permission from Black and Ramsay, 2003)[70]

Reasonable Gambling and the Industry
- Provide gambling activities that promote social interaction, recreation, dreaming and hoping.
- Provide gambling that does not aim to exploit people for whom gambling may create personal or financial problems.
- Publicise and engage in a community-wide dialogue about any major new gambling product, such as a new form of lottery.
- Engage in an open and creative dialogue with local communities about the provision of gambling facilities.
- Pay a fair burden of taxes.
- Provide support for charitable purposes.
- Display publicly as much information as a reasonable person would want or need to decide the extent of their participation in the gambling activity.
- Advertise and make available further sources of information about the activity to ensure that their operation is wholly transparent.
- Ensure that the presentation, promotion and conduct of the activity communicates the humanly enriching opportunities it offers.
- Ensure that the presentation, promotion and conduct of the activity does not exploit tendencies towards unreasonable gambling.
- Ensure that no communication is deceptive or misleading.
- Ensure that minors cannot be involved in the activity.
- Operate activities in a way that supports self-control.
- Produce and operate gambling activities in ways that support and develop self-control and reasonable choice.
- Operate gambling activities in a way that avoids taking advantage of people when their self-control is impaired.
- Ensure that adequate warnings are provided for people with gambling problems.
- Provide assistance to people whom a relevant qualified person would judge to be losing control.
- Seek to prevent from gambling people whom a relevant qualified person would judge to have a psychological disorder that would predispose them to problem gambling.
- Provide those who become distressed while involved in gambling activities with access, on-site or by immediate referral, to people who are professionally qualified to deal with their problems.
- Provide funds for those who care for and treat people with gambling problems and those affected by them.
- Support the efforts of all people struggling with problem gambling.
- Pay an additional tax to compensate the community for the diminution of the common good that results from problem gambling.
- Support the general development of recreation other than gambling in the community.

---

a movement in the field of mental health prevention, believed by some to have accelerated since the 1980s, away from forms of prevention that challenge social policies and structures, and towards those that are more person-centred.[63] In the case of gambling, the conclusion of one of the most comprehensive reviews of prevention was that 'the most commonly implemented measures tend to be among the less effective options'.[64] Those measures tend to be those that are person oriented – for example, gambling awareness and information campaigns – or which make minor changes to features of the gambling product or its availability. Very much the same thing has been going on in the closely related public health world of alcohol and alcohol problems: preventive methods favoured by the drinks industry and by their government backers are the very ones for which there is least evidence of effectiveness – educational campaigns in particular – and those methods which are most likely to be effective – substantial price increases, for example – are resisted by government.[65] The main reason for this is likely to be the same in both the alcohol and gambling cases. Governments, because of their complicit relationships with gambling industry expansion, have not faced up to the fact that really effective prevention is unlikely without a corresponding reduction in the supply of the addictive product and is likely to be incompatible with an expansion in product availability and product sales:

> There seems to be a desire to prevent problem gambling without reducing revenues, which is very difficult if not impossible to achieve, considering that problem gamblers account for a significant percentage of gambling revenue . . . Indeed, a good measure of overall success in preventing problem gambling will be an overall decrease in jurisdiction gambling revenue. *Jurisdictions need to accept this fact*. . .[66]

The common good: an ethical perspective

Part of a broad view of gambling, but one that is usually missing even from the broader public health perspective, should be the question of how gambling fits with the values that a society holds to, wishes to champion and defends and tries to pass on as part of its culture. It is the present author's contention that we, collectively as members of society, in Britain and elsewhere, are avoiding looking at gambling from a moral, ethical or values-based perspective. In part that may be because of a reaction against the high-minded moralising of the late nineteenth and earlier twentieth centuries, of which the temperance and anti-gambling movements of that time were part. It has also been encouraged by the gambling industry–government alliance, and the commercialisation and commodification of dangerous consumptions as part of free trade in leisure, hospitality and entertainment, all of which has strongly discouraged an examination of gambling from an ethical point of view. The discourse about gambling which saw it as immoral and corrosive of character (see Chapter 6) no longer has wide appeal. But we are left with a kind of government-supported 'commercial amoralism'.[67] It is refreshing, therefore, to find a published article on the very subject of the ethics of gambling written by two Australian authors describing themselves as consultant ethicists. As they put it, 'Despite our society's deep concern about and discussion of gambling, sustained ethical reflection on its contemporary practice is rare'.[68] They asked two philosophical questions. Is gambling rational? And if so, is it also reasonable? – questions explored by the philosophers Aristotle and Kant, respectively. The two are not the same. Theft may be rational, but is probably not reasonable. Gambling may be rational, these ethicists argued, on the grounds that it might promote: hoping and dreaming, making money, social interaction, recreation, and charity – the main motives for gambling according to the Australian Productivity Commission Report,[69] although of these the authors dismiss making money and charity. They might be rational reasons for gambling in a purely instrumental sense but they are probably unreasonable ones – making money because most gamblers will lose money rather than make it, and charity because if benefiting charities was a main end of gambling, then there would surely be more reasonable ways of achieving it.

The remainder of this interesting article is devoted to arguing for a number of principles which, if followed, would ensure that gambling was reasonable. The first three of these are addressed to the individual gambler, the remainder to the gambling industry. The principles addressed to the industry (shown in Table 10.2) are demanding and the authors clearly believe that current practice falls far short:

> An industry that benefits economically... while serious side-effects continue has an obligation to help reverse that injustice. Its contribution could be more imaginative and effective than it has been... The identified harms caused by contemporary problem gambling have demanded a swifter and more effective response than they have generally received.[71]

A number of the principles can be subsumed under the general heading of promoting the common good, a long cherished principle in western philosophy. The *common* good, however, is not the same as the overall good, according to these authors. The latter pertains when the community chooses against the good of some of its members, 'for the sake of the overall good'.[72] A commitment to the common good, on the other hand, means never choosing to act against the good of any of their members, a much more demanding principle. Why should the rights of one group to enjoy gambling be privileged over the rights of another to be protected from harm?[73] The general principle of promoting the common good is also used by these authors as grounds for directing gambling businesses to engage in full dialogue with local communities regarding the provision of gambling facilities. That would include, for example, holding a well-advertised public meeting to present a plan for any new gambling facility and to receive comments on it. They have interesting things to say about harm minimisation (see Chapter 9). In their view, to speak only of *minimising* harm on the grounds that it is impossible to eliminate it is a 'counsel of despair, and almost certainly self-fulfilling'.[74] Although difficult, the aim should be to eliminate harm. The elimination of gambling-related harm and the pursuit of the common good, in the real meaning of the term, are demanding but fine and worthwhile aims. Presently our sights are set much lower and as a consequence we are failing individuals, families and communities by putting the public's health at risk.

Chapter summary

This chapter has outlined the serious consequences which follow from a national policy which requires widespread complicity with the expansion of gambling. *A wide variety of actors – including those who work for governments, academics and service providers – are trapped in a consensus view about the benign nature of gambling expansion, which is then difficult to challenge.* Those who work for government, either directly as civil servants or as part of semi-independent bodies set up by government or as advisors or board members, are compromised in their ability to seriously challenge gambling expansion. The independence of the academic community is crucial but in the case of dangerous forms of consumption promoted by a powerful industry there is always the risk that it will be co-opted to serve industry interests – as has been very evident in the case of alcohol and tobacco. The pressures on researchers are often subtle, coming in the form of distortions of the research agenda which head off challenges to the consensus. The gambling research field is still a relatively new and under-developed one and as yet it lacks an independent critical voice. Those who provide services are often in a weak position because their organisations are either funded by or have chosen to work with gambling promoters. Open challenge to the consensus is not easy under those circumstances.

The strength of the consensus around gambling expansion, the subtle ways in which it operates, and the effectiveness of the industry in dictating how gambling is viewed, have resulted in a situation in which *the consequences have been very little recognised in the gambling field.* Those affected have been slow to realise that there is 'no free lunch' when it comes to collaborating with the gambling industry. It has been pointed out, however, that the effects are serious. Independence of thought on the subject is compromised, full debate stifled and criticism silenced. Democracy itself may suffer as a result.

With the commercialisation of gambling, now promoted as a commodity, often on an international scale, it has been argued that *local citizens have lost control of an activity that was once a stable part of local culture.* Evidence on the proliferation of betting and machine gambling in poorer urban areas, and the association of problem gambling with area deprivation, suggests that poorer people may be contributing disproportionately to gambling industry profits without benefiting proportionately. Communities are disempowered in the process. In Britain, under the 2005 Gambling Act, local people can no longer challenge a proposed new gambling facility on the grounds of lack of demand for it nor that it would be to the detriment of the character of the local area. Countries such as the USA and Australia have seen referenda on new casinos, 'gambling watch' and other anti-gambling expansion campaign groups, and the requirement for detailed social and economic impact assessments when new facilities are proposed. In Britain local people have little say about the gambling outlets in their areas.

An important element in the consensual discourse supporting gambling ex-pansion has been the assumption that gambling is generally benign, excepting for that of a small minority whose gambling is 'pathological' or not 'responsible'. *The call is now increasingly heard for a broader public health view of gambling in society which looks at its effects, not just on some individuals, but on whole families, communities and the population as a whole* – concern for the protection of children and young people being a particular consideration – and which considers a range of causes of problems, not solely at an individual level but including also social causes and both supply and demand aspects. Such a view – more strongly promoted in some countries, such as New Zealand, than in others such as the UK – sees prevention also in broad terms, embracing both person-centred efforts and those that are more 'upstream' in their focus. One unfortunate effect of the dominant consensual view, and the rather limited psychological/medical view of problem gambling which goes with it, has been a reluctance to consider gambling from a moral, ethical or values-based perspective. We have been left with what one commentator has called 'commercial amoralism' when it comes to gambling. One element of that amoralism is the opinion that the pleasure of the many should not be sacrificed because of the problems experienced by a few. That view can be challenged if a more demanding principle is adhered to – that a commitment to the common good means never choosing to act against the good of any of a society's members.

11

Conclusions and Recommendations: the Debate We Should be Having

Waking up to the addictive nature of gambling

Gambling is dangerous. Its danger lies in the fact that it has the potential to draw people into an addictive relationship which it may then be difficult to break away from. The evidence for this statement was provided in Chapter 3. Gambling can be fun but it can also be destructive because of its addictive qualities. Publics and their governments have been slow in the modern era to appreciate the dangers. That may have much to do with the way we have been conditioned to think that addiction is only relevant in the cases of substances such as tobacco, alcohol, heroin, cocaine and other dangerous drugs. But the signs that gambling was dangerous have always been there, for example in the form of historical accounts, biographies or the observations of social reformers. In the later twentieth century, as the partial prohibition of earlier decades was cast aside and technological advances added new forms of gambling to old, consciousness of the dangers was aroused. Clinicians were concerned on behalf of their patients, teachers on behalf of their pupils and parents on behalf of their children. Some of those who were experiencing the destructive potential of gambling directly themselves got together in Gamblers Anonymous. Psychiatrists recognised the dangers and called it 'pathological gambling'. Those who ran gambling establishments such as casinos and gambling halls, 'shops' and arcades of various kinds began to recognise that there were people who had become addicted to their products to the extent that they were asking for help to exclude themselves from the premises. This became formalised in 'self-exclusion contracts' which now exist in one form or another in many countries.

The strange phenomenon of self-exclusion is as good an indication as any that gambling is no ordinary commodity. It is, rather, one that can induce that agonising state of conflict which is the hallmark of addiction. Our under-standing of addiction has advanced considerably since the time when heroin addiction was the prototypical example and when an activity such as gambling was excluded or at best considered only as a marginal example. Partly due to a recognition of the wide variety of drugs that can be associated with addiction, and much assisted by developments in cognitive psychology and neuroscience, modern addiction theory – summarised in Chapter 4 – now embraces gambling as a fully legitimate member. Indeed it has even been suggested that gambling now occupies a central position in the addiction lexicon since it is an example of a 'pure' addiction uncomplicated by the side-effects of drugs.

This heightened consciousness of gambling addiction has led to a small explosion of research on the subject – small in comparison with the amount of research on alcohol, tobacco and other drugs but large in comparison to what went before. Epidemiological surveys, using standard sets of questions designed to screen for individuals with gambling problems have now been carried out in a number of countries (see Chapter 3). In Britain the best estimate is that approximately one third of a million people aged 16 years and above have, in the past 12 months, had difficulties with their gambling sufficient to be categorised as 'problem gamblers'. Many people, particularly those associated with the gambling providing industry, have sought to minimise the importance of such figures by pointing out that they represent only a small percentage (less than 1%) of the adult population. In absolute numbers, however, a third of a million represents a significant public health problem. In fact it is similar in extent to other health problems which cause great public and policy concern and which have led to demand for a substantial commitment to prevention and treatment provision. Drug dependence is one example; dementia is another. Expressing the size of the problem as a simple percentage of the whole adult population is in any case misleading since large sections of the population are not at risk because they gamble hardly or not at all, and risk is concentrated in certain sectors of the population. One group which research in several countries has shown to be at high risk consists of teenagers, including those too young to be included in adult surveys. The consistent finding is that the risk for young people is of the order of three to five times as great compared to those who are older. The changing face of gambling – more accessible, more diverse – may also be resulting in new groups being recruited to problem gambling who were previously at much lower risk. Women are one such group: an increasing 'feminisation' of gambling has been noted. Students may be at increased risk because of the rise of internet gambling.

Not all forms of gambling have the same addictive potential. By analogy with dangerous drugs, some forms of gambling are 'harder' than others and others comparatively 'soft'. The weight of research evidence and expert opinion suggests that speed and continuity are important factors: the harder forms of gambling are thought to be those which allow the outcome of a play to be known almost immediately and permit re-staking to take place without delay. Filling in a football pools coupon once a week and waiting for the result of the Saturday games – a form of gambling which has been on the decline in Britain – may have relatively low addiction potential. So may a national lottery whilst it retains its original features as a once a week draw. Casino table games have probably always been comparatively dangerous, which may be why almost all jurisdictions which have permitted casinos at all have surrounded them with restrictions which in one way or another have protected local citizens from the dangers. It is those forms of gambling which appear to have the features associated with relatively high addiction potential, and which have become widely and easily available, which are giving rise to some of the greatest concerns. Internet gambling is one. Electronic gambling machines (EGMs) is another: particularly worrying to many countries has been their proliferation in public spaces outside casinos – referred to sometimes as 'convenience gambling'.

Addiction theory is clear that the development of addiction is a complex process involving the interplay of multiple factors, often operating over a lengthy period of time during which a person's gambling may go through a variety of changes and stages – dealt with in Chapter 5. One of the perennial debates has been whether the fault lies in the person – his or her genes, upbringing, personality and/or later environment – or in the substance or activity to which he or she has become addicted. Put in those terms, the debate is probably as unhelpful as the well-known debate about nature versus nurture in the determination of human behaviour. Just as both nature and nurture play their parts, interacting in complex ways, so too are both the drug and the person who consumes it – not to mention the setting and circumstances in which it is consumed – important in the development of drug addiction. In the case of gambling both the product and the person are important. Obvious though that may be and fruitless though it may be to pit one type of explanation against another, the fact is that the question of where the fault lies becomes important politically if one side of the argument is used to support certain policies. In the gambling case the argument for liberalisation and expansion of gambling has been supported by the argument that the risk is small in percentage terms, that the small minority at risk are personally vulnerable due to some abnormality or deficiency – in other words, that the fault lies in the person – and that the product itself is safe. This line of argument also neglects the fact that gambling addiction, like all forms of addiction and like so many health-related behaviours and conditions, lies on a continuum. For every person who falls above a threshold used to define 'problem gambling', there is a larger number of people who fall below the threshold but whose gambling is 'risky'. Their risky gambling may be harmful to some degree and may, or may not, develop later into gambling that is more harmful still.

Gambling is being allowed to expand without public consultation and debate

Around the world the last decades of the twentieth century saw restraints on gambling removed (Chapter 1 gave a brief overview of gambling in three regions of the world). This can partly be seen as moving with some of the major currents of the times: with that facet of modernity which speaks of the freedom of citizens to act, within limits, as they choose; and the move towards globalisation and the increasing hegemony of freemarket thinking. Intense lobbying for derestriction, by gambling operators, was an important element. Lack of awareness of the dangerous, addictive nature of gambling products played a part. The expansion of gambling opportunities in only a few years was dramatic in many countries. Britain moved, in the half-century between the late 1950s and the coming into full operation of a new Gambling Act in 2007, from a gambling regime characterised by restricted availability and partial prohibition, via one in which gambling was accepted but not encouraged and was still limited in availability, to one in which a wide range of old and new forms of gambling is widely available with government approval (developments in British gambling were summarised in Chapter 2). Britain now has one of the most diverse gambling markets in the world, with fully legalised internet gambling, high street sports betting, convenience machine gambling in gambling arcades and a National Lottery, alongside ever more sophisticated technology and gambling industry inventiveness which threatens to increase the mix and dangerousness of gambling in traditional sites such as casinos, bingo halls, race tracks, clubs and pubs. Globally, and in numerous individual countries, the gambling market is now colossal – in the region of £10bn annually in Britain alone.

With a few exceptions – for example, sections of the British media became heated in opposition to the prospect of Britain having its first large, regional casino complex – a blind eye has been turned towards this dramatic expansion of gambling opportunities and the dangers it carries. Expansion has taken place without informed public debate. There have been a number of attempts, carried out by economists, to estimate the costs and benefits of gambling to society but, as was concluded in Chapter 8, these have been contested and are inconclusive. So many of the costs are intangible – for example, the costs of problem gambling for affected family members and for family health generally – that the results are almost meaningless. The same is true for the benefits. It is no easy matter to put a monetary figure on the pleasure that some people may get from gambling and too many questionable assumptions have to be made. In the domain of economic benefit to a community in which a new gambling facility such as a casino is planned it might be thought that it should be possible to carry out a reasonably objective cost-benefit analysis. Even in that case, however, there is little agreement. Those in favour – usually potential gambling providers plus local mayors and other officials – point to regeneration benefits, increased employment and local government revenue, but others reject that analysis, being able to point to communities where such benefits were not delivered. There is evidence of different kinds – for example, there being a higher density of gambling opportunities and/or a higher prevalence of gambling problems in areas of higher deprivation – that gambling may have a regressive effect on communities, with poorer areas disproportionately bearing the costs of gambling. At the same time local communities may be losing control over gambling in their midst as gambling becomes more commercialised and global and as free trade agreements and more liberal country and state laws further remove local powers to object to gambling expansion (see Chapter 10).

The government and gambling industry consensus and the arguments they use to support gambling expansion

Statements that gambling enhances communities, both economically and also culturally in terms of increased leisure, restaurant and other facilities that may come with it, is one of the 'gambling discourses' that have been much heard during the era of rapid gambling expansion (Chapter 6 identified 11 separate ways of speaking about gambling). Others which support gambling liberalisation include statements that gambling provision offers people freedom of choice, that gambling is to be seen simply as a harmless amusement like other benign forms of entertainment, and that the provision of gambling is just like other forms of business and should therefore be encouraged, supported and as little restricted as possible. An important additional discourse, increasingly witnessed more recently as consciousness of the dangers of gambling has grown, is the 'responsible gambling' discourse. The latter points to people's behaviour as the key to preventing problem gambling. It is an important member of that group of discourses which support the expansion of gambling. Between them they represent a powerful force in opposition to those ways of viewing gambling which support restrictions on gambling and oppose expansion. Some of those anti-gambling-expansion discourses – such as the one which says that gambling is an immoral activity – have been important historically and are now dismissed altogether by the pro-gambling lobby. Others, such as gambling as exploitation or as irrational behaviour, have survived better into the modern era, as perhaps has the discourse that speaks of gambling as something that is unaesthetic and unsavoury and therefore to be kept at a distance. The most powerful opposition continues to come from the idea that gambling can be dangerous, addictive, destructive.

The real power of discourse analysis lies in its ability to expose the arguments that are marshalled in support of different policies and the interests that they serve. The interests that are most directly served by gambling expansion, and the arguments which support it, are those of organisations which profit financially from gambling, principally those who provide commercial forms of gambling and governments which benefit from taxing commercial gambling operations or which themselves directly provide lottery or other forms of gambling from which they obtain revenue. In fact it is the alliance between providers and governments which has driven gambling expansion. These powerful allies have formed a consensus in favour of gambling expansion using the same pro-gambling – expansion discourses (the argument of Chapter 9).

Government and industry have developed a consensus around the trinity of RG, HM and CSR – responsible gambling, harm minimisation and corporate social responsibility. RG is ill-defined; there are yet no approved 'sensible limits' to gambling as there are for alcohol consumption. HM is also difficult to define and highly controversial. In some of its weaker forms it is neutral on the question of whether the total supply or consumption of a dangerous product – gambling in this case – matters or not. In its stronger forms HM requires that supply and/or demand be reduced. Although it is never overtly stated, it has to be assumed that it is the former, weaker, type of HM which is favoured by the government – provider alliance. Education about RG is particularly favoured as a preventive method by the gambling industry and its allies. It is favoured, understandably, because it represents a weak form of HM, offering the least challenge to the continued promotion and expansion of gambling. In fact, research in related fields has shown it to be one of the least effective methods of prevention. CSR appears to offer the promise that the providers of the dangerous product admit their responsibility and take appropriate action. But many remain sceptical, believing that, as with other industries that market dangerous products, CSR represents a cover-up, a way of ensuring government support, of disarming criticism and promoting self-interest. It is difficult to reconcile with estimates that a good proportion of gambling industry profits – perhaps as much as a third – is derived from the playing of people who have gambling problems, and with the little hidden efforts of gambling promoters to acquire and retain customers who are likely to be big spenders.

How government, and most of the rest of us, have become complicit in gambling expansion

The role of commercial gambling providers in the consensus that has formed around gambling expansion is hardly surprising. They are naturally delighted. Innovation is welcome. Their products can be widely advertised as never before. There are apparently endless new markets to penetrate. They are on a roll. It is the position of governments which is questionable. They have become complicit in the expansion of a set of dangerous products. They find themselves hopelessly caught up in a conflict of roles. They are charged with providing a business environment in which this ordinary business activity can flourish. But at the same time they are responsible for promoting public health and protecting citizens from danger. They are responsible for regulating gambling; but at the same time benefit greatly, financially, from gambling operations. They even operate gambling themselves – a National Lottery in Britain and other countries, and in some other countries other forms of gambling besides. There are of course parallels here with questions about how other potentially addictive products should be provided and regulated, including the question of whether their provision and consumption should be legal at all – alcohol and other dangerous drugs are obvious examples. But there are few forms of dangerous consumption where change has been so rapid and where the roles for government are so many and so conflictual.

One of the most dispiriting things about the consensus that has formed around gambling expansion and the ways of talking about the subject which support it, is that the consensus has extended, entrapping others, such as academic researchers and organisations providing information and services for addicted gamblers and those concerned about problem gambling (see Chapter 10). Instead of operating as an independent constituency on the subject, acting as sites for critical appraisal and challenge to the government – industry consensus, they have themselves become complicit. They have either taken a neutral position on the question of expansion, thereby in effect condoning expansion, or they have more actively embraced the RG, HM, CSR position, working with government or the industry, thence knowingly or inadvertently supporting expansionary interests. The professional and academic gambling world is a small one and, unlike the situations that pertain in the parallel tobacco and alcohol worlds, there is little evidence of serious challenge to the now prevailing consensus. Unlike in other fields, there seems to be little awareness that, when it comes to working with the industry or those that support it, there is 'no such thing as a free lunch'.

At the heart of the debate that we should be having is a question that governments and their supporters are not facing up to. That question is whether the prevention of gambling addiction – making sure that prevalence does not rise further and if possible reducing prevalence – is possible whilst the supply and consumption of gambling continue to rise. Those whose business is the provision of gambling are bound to be in favour of expanding their part of the business and, collectively, gambling providers are bound to be hoping for an increase in total consumption. They must be innovative and must be seeking new, ripe markets. They would hardly be doing their jobs properly if it were otherwise. Governments support them as examples of flourishing good business practice. Governments must therefore surely be on the side of increased consumption also. Or are they? They probably won't admit it. Meanwhile they pay lip-service to the notion that HM – the weaker form which leaves supply and demand unchallenged – will prevent gambling problems, even in the face of increased supply and rising consumption. This seems to amount to a bad case of wanting to have your cake and eat it. The general view in public health circles is that as the availability of a form of consumption dangerous to health rises, overall population consumption goes up, and in turn the prevalence of the condition associated with that form of consumption rises also. Government and all those who support the expansionary consensus are complacent in the face of that logic.

Signs of complacency in the face of gambling expansion

Although spokespeople for the British Government are fond of saying 'we must not be complacent', statements by the government, their gambling industry allies and others in the field who are failing to challenge the prevailing consensus, are in fact replete with statements that indicate just that – complacency. Some of these complacency statements – or what others have called elements of the 'comfortable orthodoxy'[1] – are listed in Table 11.1. Alongside each such statement I have tried to summarise why I believe the statement indicates undue

Table 11.1   Gambling complacency statements

The statement	*Why it is complacent*
The prevalence of problem gambling in our country is very low	In absolute numbers it is a significant public health problem and prevalence is unacceptably high
Gambling problems can largely be attributed to the vulnerability of a minority of individuals; gambling products are intrinsically safe	Gambling products are intrinsically dangerous and addiction is the result of a complex interaction of person, product and environment
Our country has a well-regulated and problem-free gambling industry	Up to a third of gambling industry profits come from problem gamblers; the gambling industry is looking to expand and innovate
Gambling is universal and we are a nation that loves gambling	Gambling is not universal and most people in our country gamble very little or not at all
Negative attitudes towards gambling are a thing of the past	Most people continue to think that gambling is on balance bad for individuals, families and communities
Gambling problems are mostly transient	Like other addictive problems, people can move in and out of gambling addiction but many problems become chronic
Populations successfully adapt to a higher level of gambling availability	It is more likely that there exists a high level of population resistance to the dangers of gambling, which is in danger of being eroded over time
Our country has no choice but to accept gambling liberalisation and expansion	Different jurisdictions regulate gambling in very different ways, and resistance is possible

complacency. Some of the complacency statements have been around for some time and are quite familiar. For example, the twin claims that the prevalence of problem gambling is very low, confined to a small number of otherwise deviant individuals, and that it is therefore irreducible – and by implication, acceptable – are hardy perennials. Such a view is contrary to everything we know about the complex mix of factors that influence the rate of almost any kind of health or social problem related to human behaviour, and the way prevalence rates vary historically and geographically dependent upon, amongst other things, exposure of the population to risks and opportunities. Applied to the gambling case, this point has been made several times in the present book but most particularly in Chapter 5. The idea that the problems experienced by a minority is a price worth paying for the freedom of the majority is also contrary to a humane understanding of what is meant by 'the common good' (see Chapter 10) and is perhaps indicative of the kind of greedy, individualistic society which many fear and regret we have become.

Others amongst the popular complacency statements have appeared only latterly. These are potentially dangerous statements, not just because they encourage complacency, but because they appear to come from reputable scientific sources. We know from exposures of the activities of the tobacco and alcohol industries that finding scientists with strong personal reputations and/or good addresses, and whose theories seem to support industry arguments about the safety of their products, represents a particularly valued coup for the industry (see Chapter 10). Some of the recent complacency statements about gambling problems are highly palatable to those who favour expansion. Two of them are worth considering in a little more detail.

The first is the more easily dealt with of the two. This is the statement that gambling problems are often, even usually, transient – and therefore, by implication, unimportant. The idea that any health problems are unimportant simply because they last only for a matter of months or a few years at most, is itself of course unsustainable. But to imply that most gambling problems are short-term in nature is itself highly misleading. Those who make such a statement usually refer back to a single follow-up survey carried out in New Zealand, which, as explained in Chapter 5, actually showed that some problems did not recur after a period of seven years whilst others did. Other more careful reviews of all the evidence show, as would be expected, that the picture is a mixed one. Some people who develop a degree of gambling addiction recover from it within a small number of years; others do not and for some people problems become very chronic indeed. The more serious problems become, the more difficult it is to overcome them. None of that is at all surprising. That mixed picture is exactly what occurs in the case of other addictions. This is not the place to go into the factors which influence recovery from addiction, but suffice it to say that there is an equally complex mix of factors at work as there is in becoming addicted in the first place. What is surprising is that anyone with an interest in gambling problems would have thought that it was otherwise. That misunderstanding probably goes back to an over-simplified idea about the 'disease' of addiction which assumed that it was inevitably chronic. The more nuanced view of addiction as something to be viewed as lying on a continuum, subject to the interplay of multiple factors, and with movement into and out of different levels of addiction over the lifespan, has been accepted for some time by those who study alcohol and drug addiction. It is often said that the study of gambling addiction is 20 or 30 years behind the times. Hence the apparent 'discovery' that not all gambling problems persist even if they are not treated. But to conclude from that that most gambling problems are merely transient is a gross error.

The second complacency statement that deserves close attention is the new theory that populations 'adapt' to an increased level of availability of a dangerous commodity such as gambling, much as populations may develop immunity to a virus. Although those who are in favour of gambling expansion may not find the virus analogy attractive, they can draw great comfort from adaptation theory.

Although, as was pointed out in Chapter 5, there is yet very little direct evidence for it,[2] and it appears contrary to the much longer established public health view which predicts rising consumption and thence increased problem prevalence as a response to increased availability, it has certain attractions. The relationships between availability, consumption and problems, although generally positive, are not simple or straightforward. Minority immigrant groups, and colonised indigenous groups, tend to have higher rates of addiction problems, including gambling, compared to others living in the same country. Adaptation to an increased level of availability of a dangerous form of consumption may be more difficult for such groups. Some sectors of country populations show patterns of consumption that are more unhealthy even though the total volume of their consumption may be no greater than for other sectors: binge drinking as opposed to more frequent but lighter drinking, for example. The rapid expansion of availability, in an uncontrolled way, in a population not previously acquainted with the dangerous activity – new forms of illicit drug or new forms of gambling for example – may be much more dangerous than controlled and regulated supply to a population that has long familiarity with the potentially dangerous commodity in question.

But that is very different from saying that the continued expansion of gambling can safely be encouraged because, once we have got over the initial shock associated with the dramatic expansion of gambling just before and after the turn of the twenty-first century, we shall show mature adaptation and a stable, perhaps even falling, low level of associated problems. That qualifies as one of the biggest complacency statements of all. There are three related reasons for saying that. The first – pointed out several times in the present book but particularly in Chapter 3 and earlier in the present chapter – is simply that the present level of gambling problems is hardly well conveyed by the term 'adaptation' – in Britain alone a third of a million adults plus several tens of thousands of teenagers plus those close family members whose quality of life is affected. The second point has also been made earlier (see Chapters 1 and 2): the gambling scene is by no means static. Governments that have liberalised the gambling laws may be surprised at what they have unleashed and may not wish to see a great deal more expansion and provision. But the laws they have created encourage further innovation and expansion and that is certainly what the gambling industry intends to provide. Even in a country with a comprehensive set of gambling regulations, the population has been required to adapt to the rapid introduction and expansion of new and old forms of gambling in modern times and its ability to adapt will continue to be tested in the future.

Natural resistance to gambling and the danger of its erosion

It is the third part of this argument against the complacent reading of adaptation theory that I believe has escaped notice. It is this. In Britain, and much the same may be true elsewhere, the population as a whole currently shows a high level of *resistance* to gambling. Although the cases of gambling and alcohol are very similar in many ways, the level of population resistance is completely different. According to the British Gambling Prevalence Surveys of 1999/2000 and 2006/07 a very large minority of Britons – nearly one in three – adapt to the presence of gambling in society by avoiding it altogether. In other words they are total gambling abstainers. The comparable figure for alcohol is about 1 in 10. Another substantial minority – about one in four – gamble but confine their gambling to playing the National Lottery. Less than half the population have engaged in any other form of gambling even once in the last 12 months; and there is no other form of gambling in which more than a very small minority (never more than 5% and usually lower still) engage on a weekly basis. By analogy with alcohol, it is as if a large majority of the population were either teetotallers, strictly confined themselves to low alcohol beer or, if they ever indulged in drinking wine or spirits, made sure that they did so only infrequently.

A nation's attitudes are an important part of resistance to a dangerous form of consumption. Evidence from the second British Gambling Prevalence Survey showed how negative are the attitudes of British people towards gambling. That was the subject of Chapter 7. In summary, although most people are not in favour of total prohibition on gambling, they do believe that on balance gambling is not good for individuals, families and communities and they believe it should not be encouraged. These negative attitudes are shared by all groups in society – young and old, men and women, ethnic majority and minorities (although older people, women and ethnic minorities tend to be more negative). That puts a very different complexion on the public face of gambling compared to the one which the liberalising government convinced itself it was seeing. It further shows what a high level of resistance to gambling exists in the population as a whole. What evidence exists on attitudes in other countries suggests that attitudes on the whole are negative elsewhere as well. Whoever it is who has been arguing for gambling expansion, it is not the mass of the general public.

In my view, therefore, it is inaccurate and a misunderstanding to suggest that the population of a country like Britain – which is in the forefront of gambling liberalisation and therefore may be able to offer lessons to other countries – is in the process of successfully adapting to increased gambling opportunities. It is not so much a matter of adaptation developing but rather one of pre-existing resistance being maintained and being in danger of being undermined.

It then becomes a relevant question to ask why people are so comparatively abstemious when it comes to gambling and why they seem to be so resistant to it. Perhaps those ways of thinking and talking about gambling – the gambling discourses – which are in opposition to liberalisation and expansion have survived better into the modern era than some people had supposed. Perhaps awareness that gambling is potentially destructive is lodged in most people's minds despite efforts of late to normalise it. Many people have examples of gambling's destructive potential in their family histories or in their current family lives, have witnessed it in others, or have felt the addictive potential of gambling themselves. Maybe the ideas that gambling is distasteful, foolish and irrational, involves exploitation of one group of people by another, or even that it is fundamentally immoral, are sufficiently deeply engrained that, for the moment at least, they are proving strong enough to resist the opposition. But for how long? The opposition consists of a mighty gambling industry – huge in scale, global in reach, diverse, powerful, technologically sophisticated and innovative, and which is surely bent on expansion – plus governments which have formed a consensus with the industry but which find themselves wearing too many hats and are confused about whether they want to see the expansion of gambling or not, others who are passive and complicit, and an uninformed general public which has not been consulted. The danger is that our inbuilt resistance to the spread of gambling will be eroded as time goes on. Unless we are careful, constraints on gambling will be further wound back, gambling will become more normalised, attitudes will gradually become less negative, and more people will gamble more often in more varied ways. As resistance is eroded more people will be at risk because they are gambling more often with larger proportions of their income. None of those changes would be sudden or dramatic; change will take time and it may take a decade or more to become apparent, by which time it may be more difficult to reverse the trends. Some will dismiss this as a gloom-and-doom scenario. They might be right and I may be quite wrong. But resistance theory is just as plausible as adaptation theory.

We do have choices about gambling in society but in order to exercise choice we need to have an informed and critical debate

Perhaps the most dangerous complacency statement of all is the one that tells us that the direction of change is out of our hands, part of global trends over which we have no control and hence that we have no choice. It was that kind of argument that the British Government relied on when deciding to legalise both the provision and playing of internet gambling. It is the same argument that has been used in many jurisdictions when failing to hold the line against the diffusion of gambling across country or state boundaries. It turns out, however, that much more choice is possible than governments claim. The brief overview of gambling in different countries that was offered in Chapter 1 makes that very clear. Internet gambling is a good case in point. Not all governments have rushed into full legalisation as Britain did. EGMs, in their 'convenience' form in very public settings outside casinos – recognised by many countries to be one of the most problematic forms of gambling – is another good example. Some countries ban this dangerous form of gambling altogether and others have moved towards capping the numbers of EGMs or putting restrictions on their structural characteristics in order to make them less attractive and less addictive. Many countries have moved in the direction of tighter restrictions, for example in terms of a minimum age for players, and Britain is now virtually alone in permitting low stake/low prize EGM playing by children and young people. Not all countries have allowed the provision of gambling to be almost entirely commercialised as Britain has. There are countries where almost all gambling is not-for-profit, with proceeds going to charity, sport or government revenue. There are a number of countries where all or most gambling is in the hands of a government monopoly. This is true for a number of countries in the European Union which contains a very diverse range of legal gambling regimes.[3] There are also signs that public resistance may be growing. In some

Table 11.2   What to do about gambling: recommendations for debate

1	All forms of gambling should be given a dangerousness rating, as is the case for dangerous drugs; and all proposed new forms of gambling, or modifications to existing forms, should be assessed for dangerousness by an expert panel, and a recommendation made on their legality.
2	A minimum age of 18 years should immediately be imposed for all EGMs whatever their stake and prize size.
3	All proposed new gambling premises or changes to facilities provided on existing premises should be subject to a full social and economic impact assessment.
4	Gambling should be more a matter for local option, with local citizens given more opportunity to be informed and to voice opinions, and local authorities given much more discretion.
5	All EGMs outside casinos should be phased out over a period of a few years, starting with EGMs in pubs and bars.
6	UK-based gambling internet sites should be made illegal.
7	Advertising of any form of gambling should immediately be restricted to information-only; and all gambling advertising should be phased out over a period of a few years.
8	A percentage of commercial gambling profits (perhaps 10%) should be directed towards problem gambling prevention, treatment and research and compensation for harm caused by gambling addiction.
9	All players in public gambling facilities should be required to register and playing records should be kept, and linked between venues, so that risky patterns of gambling can be detected and appropriate advice given.
10	The Health Ministry should play a lead role in gambling policy. It should advise on frequency and quantity 'safe limits', above which it is thought gambling is risky, as for the consumption of alcohol.
11	A properly financed national programme should be undertaken to make sure that health services in all areas include facilities for the treatment of those with gambling problems and their families; with a programme of awareness-raising amongst health and social service professionals to enable them to detect, manage and refer cases of problem gambling appropriately.
12	The significance of the dangers of gambling for public health should be recognised. A national body – 'observatory' or national institute – should be set up, with full independence from government, to keep watch on gambling and problem gambling nationally.
13	A national campaign should be mounted to oppose the further expansion of gambling.
14	Consideration should be given to phasing out all commercial gambling over a period of a few years with all gambling run under government franchise like the National Lottery, and all profits going to good causes.

countries the public has demanded referenda on gambling expansion issues and 'gambling watch' and anti-gambling groups and campaigns have sprung up. In some areas there have been 'no gambling' days to call attention to the opposition to gambling expansion. In other countries there has been a call for detailed social and economic impact assessments whenever new gambling facilities are proposed.

Many countries – Britain is one – have gone down the path of gambling liberalisation, or are in the process of doing so. I have set out in general terms what I believe might be the consequences and why I think expansion is dangerous. It is taking a risk with the public health and in my opinion it is far from being a safe bet. My prescription for staying safe, and for maintaining our natural defensive resistance to addictive gambling, is very different. Some of my ideas are listed in Table 11.2. None of those ideas is new: some are things which already occur in certain jurisdictions and others are actions which are under discussion at least somewhere in the world. They are offered as ideas for debate. It is that which I believe we need but which we have not been having – a well-informed and critical debate about the place of gambling in our societies.

Sources

(for the full references, see References list)

Chapter 1: The extraordinary international growth of gambling

1. Fisher & Griffiths, 1995, p. 239
2. Reith, 2003, p. 9
3. Tasmanian Gaming Commission, 2004, cited by Marshall, 2005
4. Markland, 2007
5. Zhonglu & Dongmei, 2007
6. Reith, introduction; Eadington, Ch 1, both in Reith, 2003
7. McMullan & Perrier, 2007
8. Meyer & Hayer, Ch 6 in Meyer et al, 2009
9. Croce et al, Ch 10 in Meyer et al, 2009
10. Australian Productivity Commission (APC) 1999, p. xv
11. Livingstone, 2005, p. 524
12. Monaghan, 2000, cited by Eadington, in Reith, 2003, p. 38
13. Marshall, 2005, p. 63
14. Banks, 2003, cited by Dickerson & O'Connor, 2006, p. 6
15. Eadington, 2008, in Coryn et al, p. 79
16. Tasmanian Gaming Commission, 2002, cited by Marshall, 2005, p. 65
17. Dickerson & O'Connor, 2006, pp. 124–125
18. Livingstone, 2005, pp. 523–24
19. Dickerson & O'Connor, 2006, Ch 7

An Unsafe Bet? The Dangerous Rise of Gambling and the Debate We Should be Having   By Jim Orford
© 2011 John Wiley & Sons, Ltd

20. Dickerson & O'Connor, 2006, p. 125
21. Abbott, 2006
22. Tanasornnarong et al, 2004; Oei et al, 2008; Oei & Raylu, 2008
23. Breen, 2008
24. McMillen, 2003
25. Wood & Williams, p. 497, in Smith et al, 2007
26. Abbott, 2006
27. Markland, 2007
28. Wood & Williams, p. 497, Ch 9 in Smith et al, 2007
29. Tse et al, 2004; Clarke et al, 2007
30. Dyall & Hand, 2003
31. Zhonglu & Dongmei, 2007
32. Collins, 2003; Eadington, Ch 1 in Reith, 2003
33. Collins, 2003, p. 102; Eadington, in Coryn et al, 2008, pp. 88–9; Vong, 2007
34. Tanasornnarong et al, 2004; Ariyabuddhiphongs, 2006
35. Guardian Weekly, 14 March 2008
36. Eadington, Ch 1 in Reith, 2003
37. Fisher & Griffiths, 1995
38. Brooks et al, 2008
39. Brooks et al, 2008
40. Eadington, in Coryn et al, 2008, p. 90
41. Rose, Ch 6 in Reith, 2003
42. Shaffer et al, 1994; Frey, 1998; Eadington, Ch 1, in Reith, 2003; Stitt et al, Ch 5, in Reith, 2003
43. Eadington, in Coryn et al 2008, p. 78; Pierce & Miller, Ch 23 in Smith et al, 2007
44. Eadington, Ch 1 in Reith, 2003
45. Eadington, Ch 1 in Reith, 2003
46. Eadington in Coryn et al, 2008, p. 78
47. Goodman, 1995
48. Eadington, Ch 1 in Reith, 2003
49. Eadington, Ch1 in Reith, 2003
50. Koo et al, 2007
51. Goodman, 1995
52. Pierce & Miller, Ch 23 in Smith et al., 2007
53. Wood & Williams, Smith et al, 2007, p. 498
54. Atherton, 2007, pp. 309–10
55. Belanger, 2006, reviewed in International Gambling Studies, 2007, vol. 7 pp. 384–6
56. Eadington, Ch1 in Reith, 2003
57. Korn, D. & Reynolds, J., *Commercial gambling advertising: exploring the youth connection,* presentation at the conference, Gambling and Social Responsibility Forum, Manchester, Sept 2008
58. Eadington, Ch1 in Reith, 2003

59. Canadian Partnership for Responsible Gambling, 2004, cited by Korn & Reynolds, presentation at the conference Gambling and Social Responsibility Forum, Manchester, Sept, 2008

60. Stevens & Beristain, 2004, cited by Mohsin & Lockyer, 2008

61. Wood & Williams, in Smith et al, 2007, p. 497–8

62. Cited by Eadington, in Coryn et al, 2008, pp. 71–90

63. Eadington, Ch 1 in Reith, 2003; Häfeli, Ch 21 in Meyer et al, 2009

64. Eadington, in Coryn et al, 2008, pp. 84, 96

65. Eadington, in Coryn et al, 2008, p. 97

66. Kingma, 2004; Fijnaut, in Coryn et al, pp. 1–12, 2008 ; Goudriaan et al, Ch 12 in Meyer et al, 2009

67. Huls, in Littler & Fijnaut 2007, pp. 69–79; Goudriaan et al, Ch 12 in Meyer et al, 2009

68. Eadington, in Coryn et al, 2008, p. 76

69. Verbiest, in Littler & Fijnaut, 2007, pp. 127–59

70. Munro, G., *Gambling Legislative and Policy Frameworks and the Transition to Market Economies: The View from Central and Eastern Europe*, presentation at the conference Gambling and Social Responsibility Forum, Manchester, Sept 2008; Kassinove et al, 1998

71. Eadington, p. 76 in Coryn et al, 2008; Munro, presentation at the conference Gambling and Social Responsibility Forum, Manchester, Sept 2008; Demetrovics, Ch 8 in Meyer et al, 2009

72. Meyer et al, 2009

73. Becoña et al, 1995; Becoña, Ch 19 in Meyer et al, 2009

74. Häfeli, Ch 21 in Meyer et al, 2009

75. Lund, 2006; Linnet, Ch 2, Jaakkola, Ch 4, Götestam & Johansson, Ch 13, Jonsson & Rönnberg, Ch 20, all in Meyer et al, 2009

76. Fijnaut, p. 9, Eadington, p. 81, in Coryn et al, 2008

77. Eadinton, pp. 97–8, in Coryn et al, 2008

78. Binde, 2005; Mohsin & Lockyer, 2008

79. Eadington, Ch1 in Reith, 2003

80. Binde, 2005

Chapter 2: The rise of gambling in Britain

1. Light, 2007, p. 626

2. Miers, 2004, pp. 371–2

3. Dixon, 1991, pp. 341, 351–5; Miers, 2004, pp. 324–5

4. Miers, 2004, pp. 324–5

5. Miers, 2004, p. 451

6. OFLOT, 1993, cited by Miers, 2004, p. 414

7. Miers, 2004, pp. 451–2

8. Miers, 2004, pp. 416–19

9. Miers, 1996; Creigh-Tyte, 1997

10. Miers, 1996, pp. 364, 368
11. Miers, 2004, pp. 489–90
12. Miers, 2004, p. 386
13. Gaming Board, 2000; Miers, 2004, p. 499
14. KPMG, 2000
15. Gaming Board, 2000
16. Gaming Board, 2000
17. Miers, 2004, p. 504
18. Forrest, 1999
19. Dixon, 1991
20. cited by Miers, 2004, p. 472
21. Gaming Board, 2000
22. Miers, 2004, p. 474
23. Gambling Review Body (GRB) report, 2001
24. Miers, 2004, p. 325
25. Dixon, 1991; Atherton, 2007, p. 267
26. Light, 2007, pp. 630, 650
27. Light, 2007, p. 650
28. Collins, 2003, p. 96
29. Light, 2007, p. 635
30. Light, 2007, p. 647
31. Collins, 2003, p. 191
32. Gambling Commission website, August 2009, www.gambling commission.gov.uk
33. GRB report, 2001, paras 23.21 and 23.23
34. Miers, 2004, p. 490
35. Miers, 2004, pp. 490–1
36. Department for Culture, Media and Sport (DCMS), Gambling Act: Regulatory Impact Assessment, 2004, para 2.18, cited by Light, 2007, p. 641
37. Atherton, 2007, p. 109
38. Light, 2007, p. 641
39. Light, 2007, p. 641
40. Light, 2007, p. 637
41. Gambling Commission website, August 2009, www. gamblingcommission.gov.uk
42. Collins, 2003, Ch 5
43. Collins, 2003, Ch 5
44. Royal Commission 1978, 18.3, cited by Miers, 2004, p. 376
45. Light, 2007, p. 637
46. Light, 2007, pp. 638–9
47. Light, 2007, p. 637
48. DCMS, 2002, para 72, cited by Light, 2007, p. 639
49. Light, 2007, p. 639
50. Atherton, 2007, p. 162
51. Atherton, 2007, p. 159
52. Miers, 2004, p. 494

53. Atherton, 2007, pp. 156–7
54. Miers, 2004, p. 495
55. Atherton, 2007, p. 161
56. Miers, 2004, p. 505; Light, 2007, p. 642
57. Dixey, 1996
58. Gaming Board report, 1969, cited by Dixey, 1996, p. 138
59. Miers, 2004, p. 505; Light, 2007, p. 642
60. Collins, 2003, p. 160
61. Collins, 2003, p. 159
62. Gaming Board, 2000, p. 111
63. Gambling Review Body, 2001, para 30.13
64. Miers, 2004, p. 502
65. Collins, 2003, pp. 160–61; Light, 2007, pp. 644–5
66. Light, 2007, p. 645
67. Gambling Commission, Gambling Industry Statistics 2007–2008, p. 12
68. Atherton, 2007, pp. 254, 257, 311; Griffiths, in Meyer et al, 2009, Ch 7; Wood & Williams, in Smith et al, Ch 19
69. Griffiths, M.D., *Social Responsibility in Internet Gambling: Behavioural Tracking to Help Spot Internet Gamblers*, presentation at the conference Gambling and Social Responsibility Forum, Manchester, Sept 2008
70. Wood & Williams, in Smith et al, 2007, Ch19
71. Smeaton & Griffiths, 2004, cited by Wood & Williams, in Smith et al, 2007, Ch 19
72. National Children's Home, 2004, cited by Wood & Williams, in Smith et al, 2007, Ch 19
73. Griffiths & Wood, 2007, cited in Griffiths et al, 2009
74. Griffiths, M.D., 2008, *Social Responsibility in Internet Gambling: Behavioural Tracking to Help Spot Internet Gamblers*, presentation at the conference Gambling and Social Responsibility Forum, Manchester, Sept 2008; Wood & Williams, in Smith et al, 2007, Ch 19
75. BBC Radio 4, January 2009
76. Miers, 2004, p. 356
77. Atherton, 2007, pp. 171–2
78. Atherton, 2007, p. 172
79. Atherton, 2007, p. 278
80. Atherton, 2007, p. 172
81. Miers, 2004, p. 356
82. Miers, 2004, p. 93
83. Miers, 2004, p. 95
84. Miers, 2004, p. 498; Light, 2007, pp. 642–3
85. Gambling Commission annual report, 2007/08
86. Miers, 2004, p. 497
87. Light, 2007, pp. 642–3
88. Miers, 2004, p. 473
89. Collins, 2003, p. 80

90. Miers, 2004, p. 414
91. Light, 2007, p. 630
92. Miers, 2004, pp. 88, 225
93. Miers, 2004, pp. 486–7; Light, 2007, p. 630
94. KPMG, 2000, summarised in Orford et al, 2003, Table 2.1, p. 24
95. Gambling Commission annual report 2007/08, Gambling Industry Statistics
96. Gambling Commission annual report 2008/09, Gambling Industry Statistics
97. Wardle et al, 2007, Ch 2
98. Meyer et al, 2009

Chapter 3: Gambling addiction

1. Lewin, 1924, cited by Jaffe, 1977, p. 207
2. cited by Jaffe, 1977
3. Rolleston, 1926, quoted by Jaffe, 1977, pp. 207–8
4. Van Lancker, 1977
5. Gambling Review Body, 2001
6. White et al, 2001; Kerr et al, 2009
7. Barker & Miller, 1968, pp. 288–9
8. Blaszczynski & Farrell, 1998, p. 98
9. White et al, 2001, cited by Orford, et al, 2003, pp. 205–6
10. Chinn, 1991, p. 175
11. Clapson, 1992
12. Dement, 1999
13. Squires, 1937, p. 372
14. France, 1902
15. Atherton, 2007, pp. 26–27; Brenner & Brenner, 1990, p. 139
16. Lesieur, 1990
17. Bellringer, 1999
18. Lesieur, 1990
19. Lorenz & Yaffee, 1984; Ladouceur et al, 1994
20. Orford, 1985, p. 39
21. Orford, 1985, p. 39
22. Potenza, 2006; Petry, 2006
23. Nower & Blaszczynski, 2006; Blaszczynski et al, 2007
24. Gambling Commission annual report 2008/09, Gambling Industry Statistics
25. Ladouceur et al, 2000; O'Neil et al, 2003, both cited by Blaszczynski et al, 2007
26. Nower & Blaszczynski, 2006
27. Nower & Blaszczynski, 2006
28. Blaszczynski et al, 2007

29. National Lottery Commission delegate, Gambling Commission round-table meeting, 12 May 2006
30. Atherton, 2007, pp. 287, 291, 293
31. Orford et al, 2005
32. Castellani, 2000, p. 177
33. Kalischuk et al, cited by Patford, 2007
34. Lesieur, 1984
35. Australian Productivity Commission report, 1999
36. Orford et al, 2010a
37. Custer & Milt, 1985, pp. 122–3
38. Lesieur, 1984
39. Kalischuk et al, cited by Patford, 2007
40. Barker & Miller, 1968, pp. 287–8
41. White et al, 2001, cited in Orford et al, 2003, p. 206
42. Giacopassi et al, 1999
43. *The Daily Mail*, 18 July 2001
44. Horvath & Pierce, pp. 389–409 in Marotta et al, 2002
45. Lorenz & Yaffee, 1988
46. Lorenz & Shuttleworth, 1983; Heinman, 1987, both cited by Patford, 2007
47. Orford et al, 2005
48. Krishnan & Orford, 2002
49. Horvath & Pierce, pp. 389–409 in Marotta et al, 2002
50. Jacobs, 1989; Jacobs et al, 1989, both cited by Horvath & Pierce, pp. 389–409 in Marotta et al, 2002
51. Velleman & Orford, 1999
52. cited by Clapson, 1992
53. Moran, 1987, p. 12
54. Griffiths, 1990, p. 123
55. Griffiths, 1993a, pp. 35, 36, 41
56. Jacobs, 1989; Shaffer & Hall, 1996; Meyer & Hayer, Ch 6; Croce et al, Ch 10; Skokauskas, Ch 11; Lupu, Ch 15; Becoña, Ch 19; Jonsson & Rönnberg, Ch 20, all in Meyer et al, 2009
57. Jacobs, 1989
58. Shaffer & Hall, 1996
59. Fisher, 1999
60. Hallebone in Marotta et al 2002, pp. 375–87
61. Volberg in Reith, 2003, pp. 221–38 – the quote is from p. 223
62. Trevorrow & Moore, 1998
63. Hallebone in Marotta et al, 2002, pp. 375–87
64. Hallebone in Marotta et al, 2002, pp. 375–87
65. Wardle et al, 2007, Ch 2
66. Trevorrow & Moore, 1998
67. Lesieur et al, 1991, cited by Hallebone, in Marotta, 2002, pp. 375–87
68. Horvath & Pierce in Marotta et al, 2002, pp. 389–409
69. National Research Council, 1999
70. Lesieur, 1993, p. 1, cited by Horvath & Pierce, in Marotta, 2002, p. 396

71. Griffiths, 1993a
72. Corney, R. *Female internet gamblers: a qualitative study of their gambling, its impact on their lives and mental health*, presentation at the conference Gambling and Social Responsibility Forum, Manchester, Sept 2008
73. McNeilly & Burke, in Reith, 2003, Ch 15; Clarke, 2008; Southwell et al, 2008; Zaranek & Lichtenberg, 2008
74. Southwell et al, 2008
75. Lund, 2007
76. Lund, 2008; Wardle et al, 2007, Ch 2
77. Wardle et al, 2007, Ch 4
78. Wardle et al, 2007, Ch 4
79. Information available on the internet
80. Wardle et al, 2007, Ch 5
81. Fisher, 1996, 2000
82. Australian Productivity Commission 1999; Livingstone & Woolley, 2007
83. Jaakkola, in Meyer et al, 2009, Ch 4
84. Wardle et al, 2007, Ch 4; Meyer et al, 2009
85. Fisher, 1999
86. Shaffer & Hall, 1996; Wardle et al, 2007, p. 85; Druine, Ch 1; Linnet, Ch 2; Jaakkola, Ch 4; Meyer & Hayer, Ch 6; Goudriaan et al, Ch 12; Götestam & Johansson, Ch 13; Becoña, Ch 19; Rönnberg, Ch 20, all in Meyer et al, 2009
87. Scholes et al. 2008
88. May-Chahal, C., *Measuring social harm and benefits from an international perspective*, presentation at the conference Preventing UK Gambling Harm, London, Oct 2007; and *Implications of gambling impacts for public and third sector community-based agencies: criminal justice, health, education and social care*, presentation at the conference International Transformations: the Gambling Evidence Base for Local Authorities, London, Feb 2009

Chapter 4: Modern addiction theory applied to gambling

1. Orford, 1985, 2001a; Griffiths, 1996; Shaffer, 1996; Shaffer et al, 2004
2. Orford, 2001b
3. Currie et al, 2006
4. Adams, 2008
5. James, 1891
6. Hodgins, D, *Natural recovery in gambling*, presentation at the annual symposium of the Society for the Study of Addiction, York, Nov 2008
7. Moran, 1970; Dickerson, 1974; Cornish, 1978; Custer & Milt, 1985
8. Skinner, 1953, p. 104, cited by Knapp, 1997, p. 131
9. Lesieur, 1984; Griffiths, 1995a
10. Lesieur, 1984, p. 44

11. Hickey et al, 1986
12. Leary & Dickerson, 1985; Coulombe et al, 1992; Carroll & Huxley, 1994; Griffiths, 1995b; Coventry & Hudson, 2001
13. Lesieur & Rosenthal, 1991; Stewart & Zack, 2008
14. Lesieur & Rosenthal, 1991; Stewart & Zack, 2008
15. Lesieur & Rosenthal, 1991; Jacobs, 1993; Reith, 1999; Diskin & Hodgins, 1999
16. Stewart & Zack, 2008
17. Rosecrance, 1988; Newman, 1972; Griffiths, 1995a; Chinn, 1991
18. Goffman, 1967
19. Newman, 1972
20. Ocean & Smith, 1993
21. Fisher, 1993
22. Wise, 1994; White, 1996
23. O'Brien et al, 1992
24. Carter & Tiffany, 1999
25. cited by Minihan, 1967, p. 319
26. cited by Griffiths, 1993b, p. 393
27. Sharpe et al, 1995
28. Field, 2006, in Munafò & Albery, Ch 3
29. Cooper et al, 1992; Albery et al, 2006, in Munafò & Albery, Ch 1
30. Young et al, 2006, in Munafò & Albery, Ch 7
31. Walters & Contri, 1998
32. McCusker, 2006 in Munafò & Albery, Ch 5
33. Jahoda & Cramond, 1972; Sher, 1991
34. Sproston et al, 2000 Ch; Wardle et al, 2007, Ch 5
35. Wardle et al, 2007, Ch 6; Orford et al, 2009a
36. White et al, 2001 ; Orford et al, 2003, Ch 6
37. White et al, 2001, cited in Orford et al, 2003, p. 185
38. Niaura et al, 1991
39. McCusker, 2006 in Munafò & Albery, Ch 5
40. Tversky & Kahneman 1982; Wagenaar, 1988, both cited by Rogers, 1998
41. Ladouceur & Walker, 1996; Rogers, 1998
42. based on Ladouceur & Walker, 1996; Rogers, 1998
43. Langer, 1975
44. Carroll & Huxley, 1994; Griffiths, 1995a
45. Moore & Ohtsuka, 1999, p. 345
46. Gaboury & Ladouceur, 1989
47. Langer, 1975; Ladouceur et al, 1986
48. Parke & Griffiths, in Smith et al, 2007, Ch 9
49. Reid, 1986; Parke & Griffiths, in Smith et al, 2007, Ch 9
50. Miers, 1996
51. Albery et al, in Munafò & Albery, 2006, Ch 1
52. Field, 2006 in Munafò & Albery, Ch 3
53. Albery et al, Ch 1; Field, Ch 3; McCusker, Ch 5, all in Munafò & Albery, 2006

54. McCusker & Gettings, 1997; Albery et al, Ch 1; Field, Ch 3, McCusker, Ch 5, all in Munafò & Albery, 2006
55. McCusker et al, 1995; Glautier & Spencer, 1999
56. McCusker, in Munafò & Albery, 2006, Ch 5
57. Field, in Munafò & Albery, 2006, Ch 3
58. Field, in Munafò & Albery, 2006, Ch 3
59. Leventhal & Cleary, 1980; Niaura et al, 1991; White, 1996
60. Tiffany, 1990; Albery et al, in Munafo & Albery, 2006, Ch 1
61. McCusker, in Munafò & Albery, 2006, p. 127
62. Ryan, F. *The hidden agenda: cognitive processes as vulnerability factors in addiction*, presentation at the British Psychological Society clinical division annual conference, London, Dec 2007
63. McCusker, 2006 in Munafò & Albery, p. 138
64. Orford, 2001a
65. Heilizer, 1964; Astin, 1962
66. Ainslie, 2005 cited by Madden et al, 2007
67. Bickel et al, 2007
68. Madden et al, 1997, reproduced by Bickel et al, 2007
69. Madden et al, 2007
70. see Madden et al's, 2007 example, p. 77
71. Orford, 2001a, Ch 12
72. Janis & Mann, 1977, p. 17
73. Orford, 2001a, Ch 12
74. based on Orford, 2001a, Fig 12.4, p. 269
75. Custer & Milt, 1985, p. 106
76. O'Connor, 2000
77. Wray & Dickerson, 1981; Rosenthal & Lesieur, 1992; Orford et al, 1996; Blaszczynski et al, 2008
78. Elster, 1999; Rachman & Teasdale, 1969
79. Shaffer, 1996; Shaffer et al, 2004
80. West, 2006, Fig 5.1, p. 96
81. Wise, 1994; Joseph et al, 1996; Petry, 2006; Goodman, 2008
82. Potenza, 2006; Goodman, 2008
83. Ashton & Golding, 1989; Pomerleau & Pomerleau, 1989
84. Orford, 2001a
85. Robinson & Berridge, 1993, 2003 cited by Albery et al, Ch 1, in Munafò & Albery 2006; Legg, pp. 1–10; Toates, pp. 305–27, both in Legg & Booth, 1994
86. Orford, 2001a; Jaffe, 1992; Goodman, 2008
87. Lingford-Hughes, A., *Pleasure, pain and the brain*, presentation at the conference Brain, Behaviour and Addiction, Bristol, Nov 2007
88. Robinson & Berridge, 1993, 2003 cited by Albery et al, in Munafò & Albery, 2006, Ch 1
89. Bickel et al, 2007; Bechara, 2003, 2005 cited by Bickel et al, 2007
90. Shaffer et al, 2004; Bickel et al, 2007
91. Garavan & Stout, 2005; Bickel et al, 2007

92. James, 1891; Myerson, 1940; Orford, 2001a
93. Ibáñez et al, 2003; Goudriaan et al, 2004
94. Goudriaan et al, 2004; Potenza, 2006; Petry, 2006; Goodman, 2008
95. Clark, 2008; Breiter et al, 2001; Knutson et al, 2003, both cited by Clark et al, 2009
96. Clark, 2008; Clark et al, 2009
97. Fiorillo et al, 2003, cited by Da Silva Lobo et al, 2007
98. Petry, 2001; Cavedini et al, 2002; Bechara, 2003
99. Lubman et al, 2004
100. Chambers & Potenza, 2003

Chapter 5: Does the fault lie in the person or in the product?

1. McCusker et al, 1995
2. Buckland, 2008
3. Eisen et al, 1998; Winters & Rich, 1998; Lobo & Kennedy, 2009
4. Lobo & Kennedy, 2009
5. Winters & Rich, 1998; Lobo & Kennedy, 2009
6. Lobo & Kennedy, 2009
7. Plomin et al, 1977; Searles, 1988
8. Hirschi, 1969
9. Cornish, 1978
10. Allport, 1934; Hyman, 1979; Orford et al, 2001a, b
11. Cornish, 1978, p. 158
12. Johanson et al, 1996
13. Orford, 2001a, Ch 10
14. cited by Kurland, 1978, pp. 1–2
15. Babor et al, 2003
16. for one of the few gambling studies to focus on them see White et al, 2001; Orford et al, 2003, Ch 6
17. Orford et al, 2003, 2010a; Welte et al, 2004
18. Orford, 2008, Ch 1
19. Bergler, 1958; Rosenthal, 1987
20. Blaszczynski & Steel, 1998; Cunningham-Williams et al, 1998
21. Walker, 1992; Coventry & Norman, 1998
22. Fisher, 1999; Gupta & Derevensky, 1998; Weinstock in Smith et al, 2007, Ch 12
23. Castellani & Rugle, 1995; Vitaro et al, 1998
24. Verdejo-García et al, 2008
25. Verdejo-García et al, 2008
26. Zucker, 2008
27. Vitaro et al, 1999; Slutske et al, 2005, cited by Verdejo-García et al, 2008
28. Verdejo-García et al, 2008
29. Verdejo-García et al, 2008, p. 794

30. Verdejo-García et al, 2008
31. Fischer & Smith, 2008, p. 790
32. Orford et al, 2003, Ch 4; Zucker, 2008; Verdejo-García et al, 2008
33. Blaszczynski & Nower, 2002
34. Jellinek, 1960
35. Weinstock, in Smith et al, 2007, Ch 12; Wardle et al, 2009
36. Petry et al, 2005, cited by Weinstock, in Smith et al, 2007, Ch 12
37. Orford, 2008, Ch 1
38. Cornish, 1978
39. Marshall, 2005, p. 66
40. from Marshall, 2005, Fig 3, p. 65
41. Marshall, 2005
42. Marshall, 2005
43. Marshall, 2005
44. Australian Productivity Commission, 1999; Currie et al, 2006; Wardle et al, 2007, Ch 5
45. Gerstein et al, 1999; Welte, 2004, both cited by La Plante & Shaffer, 2007, p. 618
46. Lester, 1994; Australian Productivity Commission, 1999
47. LaBrie et al, 2007, cited by La Plante & Shaffer, 2007, p. 618
48. Williams et al, in Smith et al, 2007, Ch 16
49. Shaffer et al, 1999, cited in La Plante & Shaffer, 2007, p. 618
50. National Research Council, 1999, p. 84
51. Volberg, 1997, cited by Ladouceur et al, 1999b
52. Ladouceur et al, 1999
53. Abbott, 2006, cited by Hansen & Rossow, 2008, p. 136; Abbott, 2006
54. Abbott, 2006
55. Room et al, 1999
56. Govoni et al, 1998; Jacques & Ladouceur, 2006, both cited by La Plante & Shaffer, 2007
57. Westfelt, 2004, cited by Jonsson & Rönnberg, in Meyer et al, 2009, Ch 20
58. Grun & McKeigue, 2000
59. Delfabbro, 2008
60. Rose & Day, 1990; Rose, 2001, both cited by Lund, 2008
61. Lund, 2008
62. Hansen & Rossow, 2008; Lund, 2008
63. Lund, 2008, p. 254
64. Australian Productivity Commission, 1999
65. Dowling et al, 2005
66. Cornish, 1978
67. White et al, 2001; Orford et al, 2003, p. 208
68. Griffiths, 1993, 1999a, cited by Dowling et al, 2005
69. based on Park & Griffiths, Ch 9 in Smith et al, 2007; Dowling et al, 2005; Livingstone, 2005; Ladouceur et al, 2005; Blaszczynski et al, 2005
70. cited by Moran, 1987, p. 12
71. Fisher & Griffiths, 1995, pp. 240–1

72. Parke & Griffiths, 2004; Dowling et al, 2005
73. Haw, 2000, cited by Dickerson & O'Connor, 2006, p. 118
74. Dickerson & O'Connor, 2006, p. 118
75. Parke & Griffiths, in Smith et al, 2007, p. 245
76. Dickerson, 1979; Griffiths, 1995b
77. Sproston et al, 2000; Wardle et al, 2007; Welte et al, 2007; Dickerson & O'Connor, 2006
78. Wardle, 2007, Ch 5
79. Shaffer et al., 2004; La Plante & Shaffer, 2007; Storer et al, 2009
80. Abbott, 2006; Tse et al, 2005
81. Abbott, 2006
82. Orford, 2001a; Scott & Dennis, 2009
83. Slutske, 2007, Chapter 6 in Smith et al, p. 143
84. Abbott, 2006
85. Sonntag, 2005, cited by Meyer & Hayer, in Meyer et al, 2009, Ch 6
86. Goudriaan et al, 2009
87. Slutske, in Smith et al, 2007, p. 145
88. Wildman 1997, cited by Marshall, 2005, p. 65; Becoña Ch 19 and Häfel, Ch 21 in Meyer et al, 2009
89. Australian Productivity Commission, 1999; National Research Council, 1999; Gambling Review Body, 2001
90. Gambling Review Body, 2001, para 17.7
91. Tse et al, 2005, p. 24

Chapter 6: Discourse of gambling: eleven ways of talking about the subject

1. Reith, 1999
2. Harcourt, 1920, cited by Miers, 2004, p. 47
3. cited by Chinn, 1991, pp. 60-1
4. Bulletin of the National Anti-Gambling League, 1893, vol 1, no.7, p. 1, cited by Reith, 1999, p. 85
5. cited by Miers, 2004, p. 262
6. cited by Miers, 2004, pp. 181–2
7. cited by Clapson, 1992, p. 88
8. cited by Dixon, 1991, p. 189
9. Miers, 2004, p. 116
10. Dixon, 1991
11. Department for Culture, Media and Sport, response to the Gambling Review Body recommendations, Section 7.1
12. cited by Miers, 2004, pp. 440–1
13. cited by Miers, 2004, footnote p. 441
14. cited by Miers, 2004, p. 441
15. The Observer, 22 July 2001

16. Collins, 2003, p. 172
17. cited by Miers, 2004, p. 296
18. Collins, 2003, p. 163; Miers, 2004, pp. 87, 482; Adams, 2008a, pp. 60, 65; Etches, M. *The politics of gambling: a UK retrospective*, presentation at the Conference Gambling and Social Responsibility Forum, Manchester, Sept 2008
19. Miers, 2004, p. 145
20. Miers, 2004, p. 265
21. Miers, pp. 8, 242
22. Smithies, 1982, cited by Miers, 2004, p. 114
23. Miers, 2004, p. 458
24. MacDonald, 1905, pp. 127–128, cited by Chinn, 1991, p. 179 and Dixon, 1991, p. 73
25. 1902, pp. 9–10, cited by Dixon, 1991, p. 74
26. cited by Laybourn, 2008, p. 204
27. Huggins, 2007, p. 285
28. Goodman, 1995, p. 146
29. Moore & Ohtsuka, 1999, p. 345
30. Atherton, 2007, p. 154
31. Clapson, 1992; Collins, 2003
32. cited by Clapson, 1992, p. 1
33. Chinn, 1991
34. cited by Dixon, 1991, p. 132
35. Dixon, 1991
36. cited by Miers, 2004, p. 123
37. Whyte, 1999, p. 317
38. The Daily Mail, 18 July, 2001
39. cited by Miers, 2004, p. 377
40. Adams, 2008a, p. 45
41. cited by Miers, 2004, p. 307
42. cited by Miers, 2004, p. 308
43. cited by Miers, 2004, p. 118
44. Miers, 2004, p. 346
45. cited by Miers, 2004, p. 185
46. cited by Miers, 2004, p. 346
47. Collins, 2003, pp. 76–7
48. Hawes, presentation at the conference The Gambling Evidence Base for Local Authorities, London, Feb 2009, Mathieson on The World Tonight, BBC Radio 4, 10 April, 2009
49. both cited by France, 1902
50. cited by Miers, 2004, p. 31
51. Flavin, 2003
52. cited by Miers, 2004, p. 319
53. cited by Miers, 2004, p. 118
54. Stekel, 1924
55. Barker & Miller, 1968

56. Custer & Milt, 1985, p. 122
57. Griffiths, 1990, p. 123
58. White et al, 2001; Orford et al, 2003, Ch 6
59. Castellani, 2000
60. Orford et al, 2001a, Ch 3
61. Korn et al, 2003
62. Adams, 2005
63. Chinn, 1991; Dixon, 1991; Clapson, 1992; Reith, 1999; Collins, 2003, p. 177; Miers, 2004, p. 28
64. Trevelyan, 1881, pp. 88–9, cited by Miers, 2004, p. 36
65. Atherton, 2007, pp. 39–40, 83
66. McKibbin, 1979, cited by Miers, 2004, p. 65
67. April 1913, cited by Miers, 2004, p. 182
68. cited by Clapson, 1992, p. 32
69. Zola, 1963; Herman, 1976; Scott, 1968
70. Goffman, 1967
71. Newman, 1972
72. Clapson, 1992, p. 210
73. McKibbin, 1971, p. 163, cited by Chinn, 1991, p. 178
74. Pilgrim Trust, 1938/1985, p. 99, cited by Chinn, 1991, p. 178
75. cited by Clapson, 1992, p. 174
76. Dixon, 1991, p. 331
77. cited by Miers, 2004, p. 376
78. cited by Miers, 2004, p. 325
79. Miers, 2004, p. 325
80. Collins, 2003, p. 176
81. cited by Miers, 2004, p. 118
82. OFLOT, 1993, cited by Miers, 2004, p. 414
83. Miers, 2004, pp. 284–5
84. Cabinet 16 January 1934, cited by Laybourn, 2008, p. 212
85. House of Commons, 17 November 1960, cited by Laybourn, 2008, p. 221
86. Chinn, 1991
87. Orford et al, 2003, Ch 8
88. KPMG, 2000, p. 10
89. cited by Adams, 2008a, p. 65
90. July 20, 2002, cited by Adams, 2008a, p. 66
91. Adams, 2008a, p. 137
92. cited by Miers, 2004, p. 211
93. OFLOT, 1995, cited by Miers, 2004, p. 436
94. Gaming Board report, 1969, cited by Dixey, 1996, p. 138
95. Goodman, 1995
96. cited by Miers, 2004, p. 59
97. cited by Miers, 2004, p. 257
98. cited by Miers, 2004, p. 83
99. House of Lords debates, 22 May, 1993, cited by Miers, 2004, p. 216
100. Adams, 2008a, pp. 69, 75, 76

101. Collins, 2003, pp. 31, 33, 40, 49, 70
102. Collins, 2003, p. 49
103. Dixon, 1991, p. 341
104. Dixon, 1991, p. 351
105. Miers, 2004, p. 395
106. Miers, 2004, p. 395
107. Gaming Board, 1999, p. 111
108. KPMG, 2000 p. 80
109. The Spectator, 15 April 2000, cited by KPMG, 2000, p. 83
110. KPMG, 2000, p. 83
111. Adams, 2008a, pp. 72–74
112. Australasian Gaming Machine Manufacturers Association, 2007, pp. 9, 11
113. Littler & Fijnaut, 2007
114. cited by the Gaming Board, 1999, p. 3
115. Orford et al, 2003, Ch 8
116. Department for Culture, Media and Sport, 2002, paras, 4.2, 4.4, 4.7, 4.23, 4.52
117. Department for Culture, Media and Sport, draft Gambling Bill: Regulatory Impact Assessment, 2003, cited by Miers, 2004, p. 482
118. Miers, 2004, p. 485
119. Christchurch Press, February 28, 2003, cited by Adams, 2008a pp. 72–73
120. Adams, 2008a p. 70
121. New Zealand Press Association, October 28, 2005, cited by Adams 2008a, p. 74
122. Collins, 2003, pp. 36, 50
123. American Gaming Association, August 2008, p. 1
124. American Gaming Association, 2008, pp. 2, 4, 5
125. American Gaming Association, 2003, cited by Dickson-Gillespie et al, 2008, p. 44

Chapter 7: Public attitudes towards gambling are negative

1. Willig, 2001
2. Orford et al, 2003, Ch 8
3. Rose, 1991, pp. 67–83
4. Furnham, 1985; Kassinove, 1998; Kassinove, et al, 1998; Moore & Ohtsuka, 1999; Peltzer & Thole, 2000; Strong, et al, 2004a, 2005b; Wood & Griffiths, 2004
5. Ellison & Nybroten, 1999; Kassinove, 1998; Kassinove et al, 1998
6. Sproston et al, 2000 ; Strong et al, 2004a, b
7. White et al, 2001; Corr Willbourn, 2006
8. Gambling Review Body, 2001
9. Australian Productivity Report, 1999

10. Centre for Gambling Research, 2004
11. Azmier, 2000
12. Volberg in Reith, 2003, p. 226
13. Wardle et al, 2007, Ch 6
14. Orford et al, 2009
15. Corr Willbourn, 2006
16. Wardle et al, 2007, Ch 6; Orford et al, 2009
17. Kassinove, 1998; Strong et al, 2004b; Centre for Gambling Research, 2005; Corr Willbourn, 2006
18. Azmier, 2000
19. Azmier, 2000; Volberg, in Reith, 2003, Ch 13
20. Gambling Review Body, 2001
21. Azmier, 2000

Chapter 8: The costs and benefits of gambling for society: a hotly contested subject

1. Forrest, 2008, in Coryn et al, pp. 103–17
2. Leers, 2008, in Coryn et al, pp. 179–84
3. BBC Radio 4 Any Questions, 19 Jan 2007; TV Channel 4, Dispatches 22 Jan 2007
4. Reith, 2003, p. 15
5. Eadington, 2003, in Reith, pp. 31–48
6. National Gambling Impact Study Commission, 1999, cited by Reith, 2003, p. 10
7. Australian Productivity Commission, 1999
8. Crane, 2008, in Coryn et al, pp. 119–78
9. Grinols, 2003, in Reith, p. 82
10. Creigh-Tyte, 1997; Room et al, 1999; Collins, 2003
11. Giacopassi et al, 1999; Leers, in Coryn et al, pp. 179–84, 2008
12. Collins, 2003, p. 117; Goodman, 1995, Ch 2
13. Australian Productivity Commission, 1999; McMillen, 2003, in Reith, pp. 49–64
14. Crane, 2008, in Coryn et al, pp. 119–178; Grinols, 2003, in Reith, Ch 3; Turner et al, 1999; Room et al, 1999
15. Adams, 2008b
16. Grinols, 2007, in Smith et al, Ch 20
17. Heather & Robertson, 1983
18. Eadington, 2003, in Reith, pp. 31–48; Collins, 2003, pp. 88–91; Forrest, 2008, in Coryn et al, pp. 101–17
19. Orford et al, 2003, Ch 2; O'Neill, M, *Community impact lessons from Australia: regional and local benefit of gambling?*, presentation at the conference the Gambling Evidence Base for Local Authorities, London, Feb 2009

20. Forrest, 2008, in Coryn et al, pp. 103–17
21. National Lottery Commission, annual report and accounts, 2007/2008
22. Casey, 2007
23. Arendts, 2007, in Littler & Fijnaut, pp. 41–52
24. Crane, 2008, in Coryn et al, pp. 157–8
25. Reith, 2003, p. 19; Collins, 2003, p. 88
26. Forrest, 2008, in Coryn et al, pp. 101–17
27. Forrest, 2008, in Coryn et al, pp. 101–17
28. Australian Productivity Commission, 1999, cited by Crane, p. 163, 2008, in Coryn et al; Grinols, 2003, in Reith, p. 69
29. Crane, 2008 in Coryn et al, pp. 171–2
30. Eadington, 2003, in Reith pp. 43–44; Collins, 2003, pp. 122–3
31. Orford et al, 2003, Ch 1
32. Miers, 2004, Ch 15
33. Secondary analysis of data from the 2006/07 British Gambling Prevalence Survey, Wardle et al, 2007
34. Croce et al, Ch 10, Dzik, Ch 14, in Meyer et al, 2009
35. Miers, 2004, Ch 15; Collins, 2003, Ch 5
36. Miers, 2004, p. 458
37. Chinn, 1991; Dixon, 1991; Clapson, 1992; Miers, 2004; Reith, 1999
38. Reith, 2007, in Smith et al, p. 16
39. Grinols, 2003, in Reith, p. 82; Grinols, 2007, in Smith et al, Ch 20; Gerstein et al, 1999, cited by Reith, 2007, in Smith et al, Ch 1

Chapter 9: Governments are complicit in supporting the interests of the gambling industry

1. Light, 2007, p. 626
2. Miers, 2004, p. 477
3. Dixon, 1991, p. 353
4. Miers, 2004, p. 481; Light, 2007, pp. 635–6
5. Light, 2007, pp. 635-6
6. Light, 2007, p. 639
7. Department for Culture, Media and Sport, 2004, cited by Light, 2007, p. 651
8. Atherton, 2007, p. 304
9. Miers, 2004, p. 341
10. Atherton, 2007, p. 269
11. Collins, 2003, pp. 8, 96
12. Miers, 2004, p. 287; Eadington, 2003, in Reith, pp. 36–7
13. based on Adams, 2008a, p. 30
14. Adams, 2008a, p. 35
15. Cornish, 1978, p. 44, cited by Miers, 2004, p. 443
16. Miers, 2004, p. 445

17. Department of Customs and Excise annual report 2005, cited by Light, 2007, pp. 626–7
18. Room, 2004
19. National Alcohol conference, discussion at the National Alcohol conference, Nottingham, 5 Nov 2008
20. Edwards, 2005, Ch 19
21. Edwards, 2005, Ch 19; Reuter, 2009
22. Dixon, 1991; Chinn, 1991; Clapson, 1992
23. Edwards 2005, p. 248
24. Edwards, 2005 p. 249
25. Edwards, 2005 p. 250
26. Collins, 2003, Ch 5; Eadington, 2003, in Reith, Ch 1
27. Eadington, 2003, in Reith, p. 42
28. Light, 2007, p. 653
29. Goodman, 1995, p. x
30. Miers, 2004, p. 474
31. Atherton, 2007, pp. xvii, 310
32. Miers, 2004, p. 426
33. Light, 2007, p. 652
34. Currie et al, 2006, 2008
35. Miers, 2004, p. 487, his emphasis
36. Miers, 2004, p. 487
37. Miers, 2004, p. 350
38. Collins, 2003, pp. 62–3
39. Department for Culture, Media and Sport/the Gambling Commission draft regulations following the 2005 Gambling Act
40. Atherton, 2007, Ch 8
41. McMullan & Perrier, 2007a, b
42. based on figure 1 and pp. 40, 44–8 in Cantinotti & Ladouceur, 2008, plus Dickson-Gillespie et al, 2008; Williams et al, 2007, in Smith et al; Dickerson & O'Connor, 2006
43. Weatherburn, 2009, and associated commentaries
44. Cantinotti & Ladouceur, 2008
45. Cantinotti & Ladouceur, 2008, p. 42
46. Blaszczynski et al, 2001, cited by Cantinotti & Ladouceur, 2008, p. 49
47. West, 2006
48. Macalister, Guardian Weekly, finance, 14 March, 2008
49. Givel, 2007, pp. 85-86, cited by Barraclough & Morrow, 2008, p. 1786
50. Caulkin, *Observer/Guardian Weekly,* 28 March 2003
51. Barraclough & Morrow, 2008; Hill, L, *The role of the alcoholic beverage industry in alcohol problems and public policy*, presentation at the Society for the Study of Addiction annual conference, York, Nov 2008
52. Barraclough & Morrow, 2008, p. 1792, citing the results of Landman et al, 2002
53. Barraclough & Morrow, 2008, p. 1793
54. Sadler, 2004, p. 867, cited by Barraclough & Morrow, 2008, p. 1793

55. Miers, 2004, p. 483
56. Arendts, 2007, in Littler & Fijnaut, pp. 41–52
57. Australasian Gaming Machine Manufacturers Association, 2007, quotes are from pp. 4, 7, 11
58. Australasian Gaming Machine Manufacturers Association, 2007, p. 5
59. Australasian Gaming Machine Manufacturers Association, 2008
60. American Gaming Association, 2008, quotes are from pp. 2, 6, 8, 9
61. Peller, et al, 2008
62. Atherton, 2007, p. 265
63. Miers, 2004, pp. 350, 376
64. Hannum & Kale, 2004
65. cited by Palmer & Mahoney, 2005, p. 272
66. Atherton, 2007, pp. 208–11, 265
67. from Watson & Kale, 2003, Figure 1, Table 1, p. 94, and from p. 93
68. Watson & Kale, 2003, quotes are from pp. 98–9
69. Palmer & Mahoney, 2005, Table 2, p. 280
70. Palmer & Mahoney, 2005
71. Palmer & Mahoney, 2005, p. 283
72. Miers, 2004, p. 420
73. Gambling Review Body, 2001, cited by Miers, 2004, p. 420
74. Miers, 2004, p. 481
75. Goodman, 1995, p. 9
76. Scantlebury, E, Local Authorities panel member; Hill, M, *Gambling regulation, policy and working with Local Authorities*, both presentations at the conference, the Gambling Evidence Base for Local Authorities, London, Feb 2009
77. Baumberg & Anderson, 2008; Zeigler, 2009
78. Scantlebury; Hill, both presentations at the conference the Gambling Evidence Base for Local Authorities, London, Feb 2009
79. Parke & Griffiths, 2004; Dowling et al, 2005
80. Goodman, 1995, p. 141
81. Griffiths et al, 2009, p. xxi
82. Livingstone & Woolley, 2007, p. 34

Chapter 10: Trapped: the disempowering effects of failure to challenge the growth of gambling

1. Adams, 2008a, p. 40
2. Goodman, 1995, p. 79
3. Adams, 2008a, p. 39
4. Adams, 2008a; Barraclough & Morrow, 2008
5. Shaffer et al, 2004; La Plante & Shaffer, 2007
6. Hutton, Observer/Guardian Weekly, 7 March 2008

7. Adams, 2008a, p. 102
8. Collins, 2003, pp. 4, 12
9. for example the International Society of Addiction Journal Editors (ISAJE)
10. Adams, 2008a, p. 103
11. review of Gambling Research, Education and Treatment, final report and recommendations, Gambling Commission, October 2008, available via the Gambling Commission website www.gamblingcommission.gov.uk
12. ibid, para 4.20, p. 13
13. Babor, 2009
14. Caetano, 2008
15. Goodman, 1995, p. 65
16. Sproston et al, 2000; Wardle et al, 2007; Orford et al, 2009a, 2010
17. Livingstone & Wooley, 2007, p. 364
18. Atherton, 2007, p. 293
19. Atherton, 2007, p. 283
20. British Medical Journal, 2008, p. a1579, cited in News and Notes, Addiction, 2009, pp. 63–4
21. McMillen, 2003, in Reith, pp. 49–50
22. McMillen, 2003, in Reith, pp. 55, 56
23. Sachs, 2005; Orford, 2008, Ch 6
24. Woolrych, R, *Betting shops and community hubs: a magnet for young men?*, presentation at the conference Gambling and Social Responsibility Forum, Sept 2008, Manchester
25. Atherton, 2007, p. 93
26. Atherton, 2007, p. 217
27. Orford et al, 2009b
28. Welte et al, 2004
29. Livingstone, 2005
30. Livernois, 1987; Clotfelther & Cook, 1989, both cited by Miers, 2004, p. 465
31. Miers, 2004, pp. 129, 444
32. Collins, 2003, p. 124
33. Livingstone, 2005; O'Neill, M, *Approaches of regulators and local authorities to local impact and regeneration*, presentation at the conference, the Gambling Evidence Base for Local Authorities, London, Feb 2009
34. Toneatto & Nguyen, 2007, in Smith et al, 2007, Ch 11
35. Goodman, 1995, pp. 40–2; Orford et al, 2003, p. 157
36. Goodman, 1995, p. 39
37. included in the Auckland international gambling charter, revised discussion draft, March 2006
38. Goodman, 1995
39. Huls, 2007, in Littler & Fijnaut, pp. 69–79
40. Azmier, 2000, p. 11

41. Adams et al, 2009
42. comments from the floor, at the conference the Gambling Evidence Base for Local Authorities, London, Feb 2009
43. O'Neill, M, *Approaches of regulators and Local Authorities to local impact and regeneration*, presentation at the conference Gambling Evidence Base for Local Authorities, London, Feb 2009
44. Light, 2007, p. 633
45. Hawes, A, Member of Local Authorities panel at the Gambling Evidence Base for Local Authorities, London, Feb 2009
46. Light, 2007, pp. 633–4
47. Light, 2007, pp. 650–1
48. Atherton, 2007, pp. 249–65, 284; Griffiths, M.G., *Social responsibility in Internet Gambling: behavioural tracking to help spot internet gamblers*, presentation at the conference Gambling and Social Responsibility Forum, Manchester, Sept 2008
49. Messerlian et al, 2004
50. Macleod et al, 2008
51. Griffiths, 1990; Fisher, 1996; National Research Council, 1999
52. Australian Productivity Commission, 1999
53. Atherton, 2007, pp. 32, 65, 108, 164, 192, 245
54. Orford, 2001a
55. Reith, Ch 1; McMillen, Ch 18; Borrell & Boulet, Ch 22, all in Smith et al 2007; Messerlian et al, 2004, Dickerson & O'Connor, 2006, pp. 107–8
56. Korn et al, 2003, cited by Dickerson & O'Connor, p. 107
57. Adams et al, 2009
58. Messerlian et al, 2004, Figure 1, p. 150
59. Adams et al, 2009
60. Ferguson, K, *Experiences from New Zealand*, presentation at the conference Preventing UK Gambling Harm, London, Oct 2007
61. Raeburn & Herd, 2003, pp. 42, 120
62. Williams et al, 2007, in Smith et al, Ch 16; Dickson-Gillespie et al, 2008 ; Orford, 1992, 2008
63. Orford, 2008, pp. 15–20
64. Williams et al, 2007, in Smith et al, p. 425
65. Babor et al, 2003
66. Williams et al, 2007, in Smith et al, p. 425, original emphasis
67. Slater, 1997, cited by Livingstone & Woolley, 2007
68. Black & Ramsay, 2003, p. 213
69. Australian Productivity Commission, 1999
70. Black & Ramsay, 2003, pp. 206–13
71. Black & Ramsay, pp. 212–14
72. Black & Ramsay, 2003, p. 207
73. Livingstone & Woolley, 2007, p. 370
74. Black & Ramsay, 2003, p. 212

Chapter 11: Conclusions and recommendations: the debate we should be having

1. Livingstone & Woolley, 2007, p. 362
2. Storer et al, 2009
3. Meyer et al, 2009

References

Abbott, M.W. (2006). Do EGMs and problem gambling go together like a horse and carriage?, *Gambling Research*, 18, 7–38.

Adams, P.J. (2005). Editorial. Identity talk on dangerous consumptions down-under, *Addiction Research and Theory*, 13, 515–521.

Adams, P.J. (2008a). *Gambling, Freedom and Democracy*, London: Routledge.

Adams, P.J. (2008b). *Fragmented Intimacy: Addiction in a Social World*, New York: Springer-Verlag.

Adams, P.J., Raeburn, J. and de Silva, K. (2009). A question of balance: prioritizing public health response to harm from gambling, *Addiction*, 104, 688–691.

Allport, F. (1934). The J-Curve hypothesis of conforming behaviour, *Journal of Social Psychology*, 5, 141–181.

American Gaming Association (2008). Submission to the Australian Senate regarding the poker harm minimisation and harm reduction tax bills.

Ariyabuddhiphongs, V. (2006). A test of the social cognitive model of lottery gambling in Thailand, *International Gambling Studies*, 6, 77–93.

Ashton, H. and Golding, J.F. (1989). Smoking: motivation and models, in T. Ney and A. Gale (eds.) *Smoking and Human Behaviour*, Chichester: Wiley.

Astin, A. (1962). 'Bad habits' and social deviation: a proposed revision in conflict theory, *Journal of Clinical Psychology*, 18, 227–231.

Atherton, M. (2007). *Gambling*, London: Hodder & Stoughton.

Australasian Gaming Machine Manufacturers Association (2007). Submission to the New South Wales Government regarding the Gaming Machines Act 2001.

Australasian Gaming Machine Manufacturers Association (2008). Submission to the Australian Senate regarding the poker harm minimisation and harm reduction tax bills.

Australian Productivity Commission (APC) (1999). *Australia's Gambling Industries*. Report No. 10, Canberra: Ausinfo.

Azmier, J. (2000). Canadian gambling behaviour and attitudes. Gambling in Canada Research Report No. 8, Calgary, Canada.

Babor, T.F. (2009). Alcohol research and the alcoholic beverage industry: issues, concerns and conflicts of interest, *Addiction*, 104, 34–47.

Babor, T., Caetano, R., Casswell, S., Edwards, G., Giesbrecht, N., Graham, K. et al (2003). *Alcohol: No Ordinary Commodity, Research and Public Policy*, Oxford, Oxford University Press.

Barker, J. and Miller, M. (1968). Aversion therapy for compulsive gambling, *Journal of Nervous and Mental Disease*, 146, 285–302.

Barraclough, S. and Morrow, M. (2008). A grim contradiction: the practice and consequences of corporate social responsibility by British American Tobacco in Malaysia, *Social Science and Medicine*, 66, 1784–1796.

Baumberg, B. and Anderson, P. (2008). Trade and health: how World Trade Organization (WTO) law affects alcohol and public health, *Addiction*, 103, 1952–1958.

Bechara, A. (2003). Risky business: emotion, decision-making, and addiction, *Journal of Gambling Studies*, 19, 23–51.

Becoña, E., Labrador, F., Echeburúa, E., Ochoa, E. and Vallejo, M.A. (1995). Slot machine gambling in Spain: an important and new social problem, *Journal of Gambling Studies*, 11, 265–286.

Belanger, Y.D. (2006). *Gambling With the Future: The Evolution of Aboriginal Gaming in Canada*. Canada: Purich Publishing.

Bellringer, P. (1999). *Understanding Problem Gamblers: A Practitioner's Guide to Effective Intervention*, London: Free Association Books.

Bergler, E. (1958). *The Psychology of Gambling*, London: Harrison.

Bickel, W.K., Miller, M.L., Yi, R., Kowal, B.P., Lindquist, D.M. and Pitcock, J.A. (2007). Behavioral and neuroeconomics of drug addiction: competing neural systems and temporal discounting processes, *Drug and Alcohol Dependence*, 90S, S85–S91.

Binde, P. (2005). Gambling across cultures: mapping worldwide occurrence and learning from ethnographic comparison, *International Gambling Studies*, 5, 1–27.

Black, R. and Ramsay, H. (2003). The ethics of gambling: guidelines for players and commercial providers, *International Gambling Studies*, 3, 199–215.

Blaszczynski, A. and Farrell, E. (1998). A case series of 44 completed gambling-related suicides, *Journal of Gambling Studies*, 14, 93–109.

Blaszczynski, A. and Nower, L. (2002). A pathways model of problem and pathological gambling, *Addiction*, 97, 487–499.

Blaszczynski, A. and Steel, Z. (1998). Personality disorders among pathological gamblers, *Journal of Gambling Studies*, 14, 51–71.

Blaszczynski, A., Ladouceur, R. and Nower, L. (2007). Self-exclusion: a proposed gateway to treatment model, *International Gambling Studies*, 7, 59–71.

Blaszczynski, A., Sharpe, L., Walker, M., Shannon, K. and Coughlan, M. (2005). Structural characteristics of electronic gaming machines and satisfaction of play among recreational and problem gamblers, *International Gambling Studies*, 5, 187–198.

Blaszczynski, A., Walker, M., Sharpe, L. and Nower, L. (2008). Withdrawal and tolerance phenomenon in problem gambling, *International Gambling Studies*, 8, 179–192.

Breen, H. (2008). Visitors to Northern Australia: debating the history of indigenous gambling, *International Gambling Studies*, 8, 137–150.

Brenner, R. and Brenner, G.A. (1990). *Gambling and Speculation: a Theory, a History, and a Future of Some Human Decisions*, Cambridge: Cambridge University Press.

Brooks, G., Ellis, T. and Lewis, C. (2008). Pachinko: a Japanese addiction?, *International Gambling Studies*, 8, 193–205.

Buckland, P.R. (2008). Will we ever find the genes for addiction?, *Addiction*, 103, 1768–1776.

Caetano, P. (2008). About smoke and mirrors: the alcohol industry and the promotion of science: why this editorial?, *Addiction*, 103, 175–178.

Cantinotti, M. and Ladouceur, R. (2008). Harm reduction and electronic gambling machines: does this pair make a happy couple or is divorce foreseen?, *Journal of Gambling Studies*, 24, 39–54.

Carroll, D. and Huxley, J.A.A. (1994). Cognitive, dispositional, and psychophysiological correlates of dependent slot machine gambling in young people, *Journal of Applied Social Psychology*, 24, 1070–1083.

Carter, B.L. and Tiffany, S.T. (1999). Meta-analysis of cue-reactivity in addiction research, *Addiction*, 94, 327–340.

Casey, E. (2007). Women and UK National Lottery play, report prepared for the National Lottery Commission.

Castellani, B. (2000). *Pathological Gambling: The Making of a Medical Problem*, New York: State University of New York Press.

Castellani, B. and Rugle, L. (1995). A comparison of pathological gamblers to alcoholics and cocaine misusers on impulsivity, sensation seeking, and craving, *The International Journal of the Addictions*, 30, 275–289.

Cavedini, P., Riboldi, G., Keller, R., D'Annucci, A. And Bellodi, L. (2002). Frontal lobe dysfunction in pathological gambling patients, *Biological Psychiatry*, 51, 334–341.

Centre for Gambling Research (2004). 2003 Victorian longitudinal community attitudes survey. Gambling Research Panel Report no. 6, Victoria.

Centre for Gambling Research (2005). Young men and gambling in the ACT: an exploratory study of attitudes, perceptions and engagement. *Commissioned by ACT Gambling and Racing Commission.*

Chambers, R.A. and Potenza, M.N. (2003). Neurodevelopment, impulsivity, and adolescent gambling, *Journal of Gambling Studies*, 19, 53–84.

Chinn, C. (1991). *Better Betting With A Decent Feller*, London: Harvester Wheatsheaf.

Clapson, M. (1992). *A Bit of a Flutter*, Manchester: Manchester University Press.

Clark, L. (2008). Gambling-related brain response in social and problem gamblers. Report to the Economic and Social Research Council.

Clark, L. (2009). Gambling near-misses enhance motivation to gamble and recruit win-related brain circuitry, *Neuron* (in press).

Clarke, D. (2008). Older adults' gambling motivation and problem gambling: a comparative study, *Journal of Gambling Studies*, 24, 175–192.

Clarke, D., Tse, S., Abbott, M.W., Townsend, S., Kingi, P. and Manaia, W. (2007). Reasons for starting and continuing gambling in a mixed ethnic community sample of pathological and non-problem gamblers, *International Gambling Studies*, 7, 299–313.

Collins, P. (2003). *Gambling and the Public Interest*, Westport: Praeger.

Cooper, M.L., Russell, M., Skinner, J.B., Frone, M.R. and Mudar, P. (1992). Stress and alcohol use: moderating effects of gender, coping, and alcohol expectancies, *Journal of Abnormal Psychology*, 101, 139–152.

Cornish, D. (1978). *Gambling: a Review of the Literature and its Implications for Policy and Research* (Home Office research study, 42), London: HMSO.

Coryn, T., Fijnaut, C. and Littler, A. (eds) (2008). *Economic Aspects of Gambling Regulation: EU and US Perspectives*, Leiden: Martinus Nijhoff (see Chapters by Eadington; Forrest; Crane; and Leers).

Corr Willbourn Research and Development (2006). Attitudes to gambling: a qualitative investigation for the Department for Culture, Media and Sport, Final Report, London.

Coulombe, A., Ladouceur, B., Desharnais, R. and Jobin, J. (1992). Erroneous perceptions and arousal among regular and occasional video poker players, *Journal of Gambling Studies*, 8, 235–244.

Coventry, K.R. and Hudson, J. (2001). Gender differences, physiological arousal and the role of winning in fruit machine gamblers, *Addiction*, 96, 871–879.

Coventry, K.R. and Norman, A.C. (1998). Arousal, erroneous verbalizations and the illusion of control during a computer-generated gambling task, *British Journal of Psychology*, 89, 629–645.

Creigh-Tyte, S. (1997). Building a National Lottery: reviewing British experience, *Journal of Gambling Studies*, 13, 321–341.

Cunningham-Williams, R.M., Cottler, L.B., Compton, W.M. and Spitznagel, E.L. (1998). Taking chances: problem gamblers and mental health disorders: results from the St Louis epidemiological catchment area study, *American Journal of Public Health*, 88, 1093–1096.

Currie, S.R., Hodgins, D.C., Wang, J., el-Guebaly, N., Wynne, H. and Chen, S. (2006). Risk of harm from gambling in the general population as a function of level of participation in gambling activities, *Addiction*, 101, 570–580.

Custer, R. and Milt, H. (1985). *When Luck Runs Out; Help for Compulsive Gamblers and their Families*, New York: Facts on File Publications.

Da Silva Lobo, D., Vallada, H.P., Knight, J., Martins, S.S., Tavares, H., Gentil, V. and Kennedy, J.L. (2007). Dopamine genes and pathological gambling in discordant sib-pairs, *Journal of Gambling Studies*, 23, 421–433.

Delfabbro, P. (2008). Evaluating the effectiveness of a limited reduction in electronic gaming machine availability on perceived gambling behaviour and objective expenditure, *International Gambling Studies*, 8, 151–165.

Dement, J.W. (1999). *Going for Broke: The Depiction of Compulsive Gambling in Film*, London: The Scarecrow Press.

Department for Culture, Media and Sport. (2002). *A Safe Bet for Success: Modernising Britain's Gambling Laws*. London: The Stationery Office.

Dickson-Gillespie, L., Rugle, L., Rosenthal, R. and Fong, T. (2008). Preventing the incidence and harm of gambling problems, *Journal of Primary Prevention*, 29, 37–55.

Dickerson, M. (1974). The effect of betting shop experience on gambling behaviour, PhD thesis, University of Birmingham.

Dickerson, M. (1979). FI schedules and persistence at gambling in the UK betting office, *Journal of Applied Behavioral Analysis*, 12, 315–323.

Dickerson, M. and O'Connor, J. (2006). *Gambling as an Addictive Behaviour: Impaired Control, Harm Minimisation, Treatment and Prevention*, Cambridge: Cambridge University Press.

Diskin, K.M. and Hodgins, D.C. (1999). Narrowing of attention and dissociation in pathological video lottery gamblers, *Journal of Gambling Studies*, 15, 17–28.

Dixey, R. (1996). Bingo in Britain: an analysis of gender and class, in J. McMillen (ed.) *Gambling Cultures*, London: Routledge, 136–151.

Dixon, D. (1991). *From Prohibition to Regulation: Bookmaking, Anti-Gambling, and the Law*, Oxford: Clarendon Press.

Dowling, N., Smith, D. and Thomas, T. (2005). Electronic gaming machines: are they the 'crack-cocaine' of gambling?, *Addiction*, 100, 33–45.

Dyall, L. and Hand, J. (2003). Maori and gambling: why a comprehensive Maori public-health response is required in New Zealand, University of Auckland, New Zealand, Published online September 15, 2003. www.problem-gambling.info.

Edwards, G. (2005). *Matters of Substance: Drugs, is Legalization the Right Answer – or the Wrong Question?*, London: Penguin.

Eisen, S.A., Lin, N., Lyons, M.J., Scherrer, J.F., Griffith, K., True, W.R., Goldberg, J. and Tsuang, M.T. (1998). Familial influences on gambling behavior: an analysis of 3359 twin pairs, *Addiction*, 93, 1375–1384.

Ellison, C.G. and Nybroten, K.A. (1999). Conservative Protestantism and opposition to state sponsored lotteries: evidence from the 1997 Texas poll, *Social Science Quarterly*, 80, 356–369.

Elster, J. (1999). Gambling and addiction, in J. Elster and O. Skog (eds.) *Getting Hooked: Rationality and Addiction*, Cambridge: Cambridge University Press.

Fischer, S. and Smith, G.T. (2008). Binge eating, problem drinking and pathological gambling: linking behaviour to shared traits and social learning, *Personality and Individual Differences*, 44, 789–800.

Fisher, S. (1993). The pull of the fruit machine: a sociological typology of young players, *Sociological Review*, 41, 447–474.

Fisher, S. (1996). Gambling and problem gambling among casino patrons, a report to a consortium of the British casino industry, University of Plymouth.

Fisher, S. (1999). A prevalence study of gambling and problem gambling in British adolescents, *Addiction Research*, 7, 509–538.

Fisher, S. (2000). Measuring the prevalence of sector specific problem gambling: a study of casino patrons, *Journal of Gambling Studies*, 16, 25–52.

Fisher, S. and Griffiths, M. (1995). Current trends in slot machine gambling: research and policy issues, *Journal of Gambling Studies*, 11, 239–247.

Flavin, M. (2003). *Gambling in the Nineteenth-Century English Novel, 'A Leprosy is o'er the Land'*, Brighton: Sussex Academic Press.

Forrest, D. (1999). The past and future of the British football pools, *Journal of Gambling Studies*, 15, 161–176.

France, C. (1902). The gambling impulsive, *American Journal of Psychology*, 13, 364–407.

Frey, J. (1998). Federal involvement in US gaming regulation, *The Annals of the American Academy of Political and Social Science*, 556, 138–152.

Furnham, A. (1985). Attitudes to, and habits of, gambling in Britain, *Personality and Individual Differences*, 6, 493–502.

Gaboury, A. and Ladouceur, R. (1989). Erroneous perceptions and gambling, *Journal of Social Behavior and Personality*, 4, 411–420.

Gambling Commission, annual report 2008–2009. Norwich: The Stationery Office.

Gambling Commission, Gambling Industry Statistics, 2007–2008. Norwich: The Stationery Office.

Gambling Review Body, Department for Culture, Media and Sport (2001). *Gambling Review Report*, Norwich: HMSO.

Gaming Board (2000). *Report of the Gaming Board for Great Britain 1999/2000*, London: HMSO.

Garavan, H. and Stout, J.C. (2005). Neurocognitive insights into substance abuse, *Trends in Cognitive Sciences*, 9, 195–201.

Giacopassi, D., Nichols, M. and Stitt, B.B. (1999). Attitudes of community leaders in new casino jurisdictions regarding casino gambling's effects on crime and quality of life, *Journal of Gambling Studies*, 15, 123–147.

Glautier, S. and Spencer, K. (1999). Activation of alcohol-related associative networks by recent alcohol consumption and alcohol-related cues, *Addiction*, 94, 1033–1042.

Goffman, E. (1967). *Interaction Ritual*, New Jersey: Doubleday.

Goodman, A. (2008). Neurobiology of addiction: an integrative review, *Biochemical Pharmacology*, 75, 266–322.

Goodman, R. (1995). *The Luck Business: The Devastating Consequences and Broken Promises of America's Gambling Explosion*, New York: The Free Press.

Goudriaan, A.E., Oosterlaan, J., de Beurs, E. and Van den Brink, W. (2004). Pathological gambling: a comprehensive review of biobehavioral findings, *Neuroscience and Biobehavioral Reviews*, 28, 123–141.

Goudriaan, A.E., Slutske, W.S., Krull, J.L. and Sher, K.J. (2009). Longitudinal patterns of gambling activities and associated risk factors in college students, *Addiction*, 104, 1219–1232.

Griffiths, M. (1990). Addiction to fruit machines: a preliminary study among young males, *Journal of Gambling Studies*, 6, 113–126.

Griffiths, M. (1993a). Factors in problem adolescent fruit machine gambling: results of a small postal survey, *Journal of Gambling Studies*, 9, 31–45.

Griffiths, M. (1993b). Fruit machine addiction in adolescents: a case study, *Journal of Gambling Studies*, 9, 387–399.

Griffiths, M. (1995a). *Adolescent Gambling*, London: Routledge.

Griffiths, M. (1995b). The role of subjective mood states in the maintenance of fruit machine gambling behaviour, *Journal of Gambling Studies*, 11, 123–135.

Griffiths, M. (1996). Behavioural addiction: an issue for everybody? *Employee Counselling Today: The Journal of Workplace Learning*, 8, 18–25.

Griffiths, M.D., Wardle, J., Orford, J., Sproston, K. and Erens, B. (2009). Sociodemographic correlates of internet gambling: findings from the 2007 British Gambling Prevalence Survey, *CyberPsychology and Behavior*, 12, 199–202.

Grun, L. and McKeigue, P. (2000). Prevalence of excessive gambling before and after introduction of a national lottery in the United Kingdom: another example of the single distribution theory, *Addiction*, 95, 959–966.

Gupta, R. and Derevensky, J.L. (1998). Adolescent gambling behavior: a prevalence study and examination of the correlates associated with problem gambling, *Journal of Gambling Studies*, 14, 319–345.

Hannum, R.C. and Kale, S.H. (2004). The mathematics and marketing of dead chip programmes: finding and keeping the edge, *International Gambling Studies*, 4, 33–47.

Hansen, M. and Rossow, I. (2008). Adolescent gambling and problem gambling: does the total consumption model apply?, *Journal of Gambling Studies*, 23, 135–149.

Heather, N. and Robertson, I. (1983). *Controlled Drinking*, London: Methuen.

Heilizer, F. (1964). Conflict models, alcohol, and drinking patterns, *Journal of Psychology*, 57, 457–473.

Herman, R. (1976). *Gamblers and Gambling: Motives, Institutions and Controls*, Lexington, Mass: Lexington Books.

Hickey, J.E., Haertzen, C.A. and Henningfield, J. E. (1986). Simulation of gambling responses on the addiction research center inventory, *Addictive Behaviors*, 11, 345–349.

Hirschi, T. (1969). *Causes of Delinquency*, Berkeley, California: University of California Press.

Huggins, M. (2007). Betting, sport and the British, 1918-1939, *Journal of Social History*, (Winter) 283–306.

Hyman, M. (1979). The Ledermann curve: comments on a symposium, *Journal of Studies on Alcohol*, 40, 339–347.

Ibánez, A., Blanco, C., de Castro, I.P., Fernandex-Piqueras, J. and Saiz-Ruiz, J. (2003). Genetics of pathological gambling, *Journal of Gambling Studies*, 19, 11–22.

Jacobs, D.F. (1989). Illegal and undocumented: a review of teenage gambling and the plight of children of problem gamblers in America, in H.J. Shaffer, S. Stein,

B. Gambino and T. Cummings (eds.) *Compulsive Gambling: Theory, Research and Practice*, Lexington, Massachusetts: Lexington Books.

Jacobs, D.F. (1993). Evidence supporting a general theory of addiction, in W.R. Eadington and J.A. Cornelius (eds.) *Gambling Behavior and Problem Gambling*, Reno: University of Nevada.

Jaffe, J. (1992). Current concepts of addiction. In C.P. O'Brien and J. Jaffe (Eds), *Addictive States*. New York: Raven Press.

Jaffe, J. (1977). Tobacco Use as Mental Disorder: the Rediscovery of a Medical problem, in *Research on Smoking Behavior* in M. Jarvik, J. Cullen, E. Gritz, T. Vogt, and L. West (eds.) National Institute on Drug Abuse Research Monograph 17, U.S. Dept of health, Education and Welfare, NIDA, Rockville, Maryland.

Jahoda, G. and Cramond, J. (1972). *Children and Alcohol: a Developmental Study in Glasgow*, London: HMSO.

James, W. (1891). *The Principles of Psychology, Vol. 1*, London: Macmillan.

Janis, I. and Mann, L. (1977). *Decision-making: a Psychological Analysis of Conflict, Choice, and Commitment*, New York: Free Press.

Jellinek, E. (1960). *The Disease Concept of Alcoholism*, New Jersey: Hillhouse.

Johanson, E.E., Duffy, F.F. and Anthony, J.C. (1996). Associations between drug use and behavioral repertoire in urban youths, *Addiction*, 91, 523–534.

Joseph, M.H., Young, A.M.J. and Gray, J.A. (1996). Are neurochemistry and reinforcement enough – can the abuse potential of drugs be explained by common actions on a dopamine reward system in the brain?, *Human Psychopharmacology Clinical and Experimental*, 11, S55–S63.

Kassinove, J.I. (1998). Development of the gambling attitude scales: preliminary findings, *Journal of Clinical Psychology*, 54, 763–771.

Kassinove, J.I., Tsytsarev, S.V. and Davidson, I. (1998). Russian attitudes toward gambling, *Personality and Individual Differences*, 24, 41–46.

Kerr, J., Kinsella, R., Turley, C. and Barnard, M. (2009). Qualitative follow-up of the British Gambling Prevalence Survey 2007. National Centre for Social Research, Prepared for The Gambling Commission.

Kingma, S. (2004). Gambling and the risk society: the liberalisation and legitimation crisis of gambling in the Netherlands, *International Gambling Studies*, 4, 47–67.

Knapp, T.J. (1997). Behaviorism and public policy: B.F. Skinner's views on gambling, *Behavior and Social Issues*, 7, 129–139.

Koo, J., Rosentraub, M.S. and Horn, A. (2007). Rolling the dice? Casinos, tax revenues, and the social costs of gaming, *Journal of Urban Affairs*, 29, 367–381.

Korn, D., Gibbins, R. and Azmier, J. (2003). Framing public policy towards a public health paradigm for gambling, *Journal of Gambling Studies*, 19, 235–256.

KPMG (2000). *The Economic Value and Public Perceptions of Gambling in the UK*. Report for Business In Sport and Leisure.

Krishnan, M. and Orford, J. (2002). Gambling and the family from the stress-coping-support perspective, *International Gambling Studies*, 2, 61–83.

Kurland, A. (1978). *Psychiatric Aspects of Opiate Dependence*, West Palm Beach, Florida: CRC Press.

Ladouceur, R. and Walker, M. (1996). A cognitive perspective of gambling, in P.M. Salkovskis (ed.) *Trends in Cognitive and Behavioural Therapies*, 89–120, New York: Wiley.

Ladouceur, R., Boisvert, J.M. Pepin, M., Lorangere, M. and Sylvain, C. (1994). Social cost of pathological gambling, *Journal of Gambling Studies*, 10, 399–409.

Ladouceur, R., Boudreault, N., Jacques, C. and Vitaro, F. (1999). Pathological gambling and related problems amongst adolescents, *Journal of Child & Adolescent Substance Abuse*, 8, 55–68.

Ladouceur, R., Jacques, C., Sévigny, S. and Cantinotti, M. (2005). Impact of the format, arrangement and availability of electronic gaming machines outside casinos on gambling, *International Gambling Studies*, 5, 139–154.

Ladouceur, R., Tourigny, M. and Mayrand, M. (1986). Familiarity, group exposure, and risk-taking behaviour in gambling, *Journal of Psychology*, 120, 45–49.

Langer, E.J. (1975). The illusion of control, *Journal of Personality and Social Psychology*, 32, 311–328.

LaPlante, D.A. and Shaffer, H.J. (2007). Understanding the influence of gambling opportunities: expanding exposure models to include adaptation, *American Journal of Orthopsychiatry*, 77, 616–623.

Laybourn, K. (2008). *'There ought not to be one law for the rich and another for the poor which is the case today': the Labour Party, lotteries, gaming, gambling and bingo, c.1900-1960s*, Oxford: Blackwell Publishing.

Leary, K. and Dickerson, M.G. (1985). Levels of arousal in high and low frequency gamblers, *Behavior Research and Therapy*, 23, 635–640.

Legg, C.R. and Booth, D. (eds.) (1994). *Appetite, Neural and Behavioural Bases*, Oxford: Oxford University Press.

Lesieur, H.R. (1984). *The Chase: The Career of the Compulsive Gambler*, Rochester, Vermont: Schenkman.

Lesieur, H.R. (1990). Working with and understanding Gamblers Anonymous, in *Working with Self-Help*, T.J. Powell (ed.) Silva Spring, Maryland. National Association of Social Workers, NASW: USA Press.

Lesieur, H.R. and Rosenthal, R.J. (1991). Pathological gambling: a review of the literature (prepared for the American Psychiatric Association Task Force on DSM-IV committee on disorders of impulse control), *Journal of Gambling Studies*, 7, 5–39.

Lester, D. (1994). Access to gambling opportunities and compulsive gambling, *The International Journal of the Addictions*, 29, 1611–1616.

Leventhal, H. and Cleary, P. (1980). The smoking problem: a review of the research and theory in behavioral risk modification, *Psychological Bulletin*, 88, 370–405.

Light, R. (2007). The Gambling Act 2005: regulatory containment and market control, *Modern Law Review*, 70, 626–653.

Littler, A. and Fijnaut, C. (eds.) (2007). *The Regulation of Gambling: European and National Perspectives*, Leiden: Martinus Nijhoff (See chapters by Arendts; Huls; and Verbiest).

Livingstone, C. (2005). Desire and the consumption of danger: electronic gaming machines and the commodification of interiority, *Addiction Research and Theory*, 13, 523–528.

Livingstone, C. and Woolley, R. (2007). Risky business: a few provocations on the regulation of electronic gaming machines, *International Gambling Studies*, 7, 361–376.

Lobo, D.S.S. and Kennedy, J.L. (2009). Genetic aspects of pathological gambling: a complex disorder with shared genetic vulnerabilities, *Addiction*, 104, 1454–1465.

Lorenz, V.C. and Yaffee, R.A. (1984). Pathological gambling: medical, emotional and interpersonal aspects, paper presented at Sixth National Conference on Gambling and Risk Taking, Atlantic City, New Jersey, December.

Lorenz, V.C. and Yaffee, R.A. (1988). Pathological gambling: psychosomatic, emotional and marital difficulties as reported by the spouse, *Journal of Gambling Behavior*, 4, 13–26.

Lubman, D.I., Yücel, M. and Pantelis, C. (2004). Addiction, a condition of compulsive behaviour? Neuroimaging and neuropsychological evidence of inhibitory dysregulation, *Addiction*, 99, 1491–1502.

Lund, I. (2006). Gambling and problem gambling in Norway: what part does the gambling machine play?, *Addiction Research and Theory*, 14, 475–491.

Lund, I. (2007). Lessons from the grey area: a closer inspection of at-risk gamblers, *Journal of Gambling Studies*, 23, 409–419.

Lund, I. (2008). The population mean and the proportion of frequent gamblers: is the theory of total consumption valid for gambling?, *Journal of Gambling Studies*, 24, 247–256.

Macleod, J., Hickman, M., Bowen, E., Alati, R., Tilling, K. and Smith, G.D. (2008). Parental drug use, early adversities, later childhood problems and children's use of tobacco and alcohol at age 10: birth cohort study, *Addiction*, 103, 1731–1743.

McCusker, C.G. and Gettings, B. (1997). Automaticity of cognitive biases in addictive behaviours: further evidence with gamblers, *British Journal of Clinical Psychology*, 36, 543–554.

McCusker, C.G., McClements, R. and McCartney, U. (1995). *Cognitive bias for addiction-related stimuli*, paper presented at the London Conference of the British Psychological Society, December.

McMullan, J. and Perrier, D. (2007a). The security of gambling and gambling with security: a rejoinder, *International Gambling Studies*, 7, 377–382.

McMullan, J. and Perrier, D. (2007b). The security of gambling and gambling with security: hacking, law enforcement and public policy, *International Gambling Studies*, 7, 43–58.

Madden, G.J. Ewan, E.E. and Lagorio, C.H. (2007). Toward an animal model of gambling: delay discounting and the allure of unpredictable outcomes, *Journal of Gambling Studies*, 23, 63–83.

Markland, J. (2007). A New Zealand commentary, *International Gambling Studies*, 7, 235–237.

Marotta, J., Cornelius, J. and Eadington, W. (2002). *The Downside: Problem and Pathological Gambling*, Reno: Institute for the Study of Gambling and Commercial Gaming (see chapters by Horvath and Pierce; Hallebone).

Marshall, D. (2005). The gambling environment and gambler behaviour: evidence from Richmond-Tweed, Australia, *International Gambling Studies*, 5, 63–83.

Messerlian, C., Derevensky, J. and Gupta, R. (2004). A public health perspective for youth gambling, *International Gambling Studies*, 4, 147–160.

Meyer, G., Hayer, T. and Griffiths, M., (Eds.) (2009). *Problem Gambling in Europe: Challenges, Prevention, and Interventions*. New York: Springer (see Chapters by Druine; Linnet; Jaakkola; Meyer and Hayer; Demetrovics; Croce et al; Goudriaan et al; Götestam and Johansson; Dzik; Lupu; Becoña; Jonsson and Rönnberg; and Häfeli).

Miers, D. (1996). The implementation and effects of Great Britain's national lottery, *Journal of Gambling Studies*, 12, 343–373.

Miers, D. (2004). *Regulating Commercial Gambling: Past, Present, and Future*. Oxford: Oxford University Press.

Minihan, M. (1967). *Dostoevsky: His Life and Work by Konstantin Mochulsky*, Princeton, New Jersey: University Press.

Mohsin, A. and Lockyer, T. (2008). Hamilton, New Zealand: divergent attitudes when the casino came to town, *Cornell Hospitality*, 49, 163–176.

Moore, S.M. and Ohtsuka, K. (1999). Beliefs about control over gambling among young people, and their relations to problem gambling, *Psychology of Addictive Behaviors*, 13, 339–347.

Moran, E. (1970). Gambling as a form of dependence, *British Journal of Addiction*, 64, 419–428.

Moran, E. (1987). *Gambling Among Schoolchildren: The Impact of the Fruit Machine*, London: The National Council on Gambling.

Munafò, M. and Albery, I. (eds.) (2006). *Cognition and Addiction*, Oxford: Oxford University Press (see chapters by Albery et al; Field; McCusker).

Myerson, A. (1940). Alcohol: a study of social ambivalence, *Quarterly Journal of Studies on Alcohol*, 1, 13–20.

National Lottery Commission. Annual reports and accounts 2007/2008. London: The Stationery Office.

National Research Council, National Academy of Sciences, Committee on the Social and Economic Impact of Pathological Gambling (1999). *Pathological Gambling: A Critical Review*, Washington DC: National Academy Press.

Newman, O. (1972). *Gambling: Hazard and Reward*, London: Athlone Press.

Niaura, R., Goldstein, M. and Abrams, D. (1991). A bioinformational systems perspective on tobacco dependence, *British Journal of Addiction*, 86, 593–597.

Nower, L. and Blaszczynski, A. (2006). Impulsivity and pathological gambling: a descriptive model, *International Gambling Studies*, 6, 61–75.

O'Brien, C.P., Childress, A.R., McLellan, A.T. and Ehrman, R. (1992). A learning model of addiction, in C.P. O'Brien and J.H. Jaffe (eds.), *Addictive States*, New York: Raven Press, 157–178.

Ocean, G. and Smith, G.J. (1993). Social reward, conflict, and commitment: a theoretical model of gambling behavior, *Journal of Gambling Studies*, 9, 321–339.

O'Connor, J. (2000). An investigation of chasing behaviour, unpublished PhD thesis, University of Western Sydney, Macarthur.

Oei, T.P., Lin, J. and Raylu, N. (2008). The relationship between gambling cognitions, psychological states, and gambling: a cross-cultural study of Chinese and Caucasians in Australia, *Journal of Cross-Cultural Psychology*, 39, 147–161.

Orford, J. (1985). *Excessive Appetites: a Psychological View of Addictions*, Chichester: Wiley (1st ed.).

Orford, J. (1992). *Community Psychology: Theory and Practice*, Chichester: Wiley.

Orford, J. (2001a). *Excessive Appetites: a Psychological View of Addictions*, Chichester: Wiley (2nd ed.).

Orford, J. (2001b). Addiction as excessive appetite, *Addiction*, 96, 15–31.

Orford, J. (2008). *Community Psychology: Challenges, Controversies and Emerging Consensus*. Chichester: Wiley.

Orford, J., Griffiths, M., Wardle, H., Sproston, K. and Erens, B. (2009). Negative public attitudes towards gambling: findings from the 2007 British Gambling Prevalence Survey using a new attitude scale, *International Gambling Studies*, 9, 39–54.

Orford, J., Morison, V. and Somers, M. (1996). Drinking and gambling: a comparison with implications for theories of addiction, *Drug and Alcohol Review*, 15, 47–56.

Orford, J., Natera, G., Copello, A., Atkinson, C., Mora, J., Velleman, R., Crundall, I., Tiburcio, M., Templeton, L. and Walley, G. (2005). *Coping with Alcohol and Drug Problems: The Experience of Family Members in Three Contrasting Cultures*. London: Routledge.

Orford, J., Sproston, K., Erens, B., White, C. and Mitchell, L. (2003). *Gambling and Problem Gambling in Britain*. London: Brunner-Routledge.

Orford, J., Wardle, H., Griffiths, M., Sproston, K. and Erens, B. (2010a). The role of social factors in gambling: evidence from the 2007 British Gambling Prevalence Survey, *Community, Work and Family*, 13, 257–270.

Orford, J., Wardle, H., Griffiths, M., Sproston, K. and Erens, B. (2010b). PGSI and DSM-IV in the 2007 British Gambling Prevalence Survey: reliability, item response, factor structure and inter-scale agreement. *International Gambling Studies*, 10, 31–44.

Palmer, R. and Mahoney, E. (2005). Winners and losers: Segmenting a casino loyalty programme, *International Gambling Studies*, 5, 271–287.

Parke, J. and Griffiths, M. (2004). Gambling addiction and the evolution of the 'near miss', *Addiction Research and Theory*, 12, 407–11.

Patford, J. (2007). The yoke of care: how parents and parents-in-law experience, understand and respond to adult children's gambling problems, *Australian Journal of Primary Care*, 13, 59.

Peller, A.J., LaPlante, D.A. and Shaffer, H.J. (2008). Parameters for safer gambling behaviour: examining the empirical research, *Journal of Gambling Studies*, 24, 519–534.

Peltzer, K. and Thole, J.M. (2000). Gambling attitudes among black South African university students, *Psychological Reports*, 86, 957–962.

Petry (2001). Substance abuse, pathological gambling, and impulsiveness, *Drug and Alcohol Dependence*, 63, 29–38.

Petry, N.M. (2006). Should the scope of addictive behaviors be broadened to include pathological gambling?, *Addiction*, 101, Suppl. 1, 152–160.

Plomin, R., DeFries, J. and Loehlin, J. (1977). Genotype-environment interaction and correlation in the analysis of human behaviour, *Psychological Bulletin*, 84, 309–322.

Pomerleau, O.F. and Pomerleau, C.S. (1989). A biobehavioral perspective on smoking, in T. Ney and A. Gale (eds.) *Smoking and Human Behavior*, Chichester: Wiley.

Potenza, M.N. (2006). Should addictive disorders include non-substance-related conditions?, *Addiction*, 101, Suppl. 1, 142–151.

Rachman, S. and Teasdale, J. (1969). *Aversion Therapy and Behaviour Disorders: an Analysis*, London: Routledge & Kegan Paul.

Raeburn, J. and Herd, R. (2003). Gambling and public health: a workplan. Prepared for the Problem Gambling Committee as a joint venture between Hapai Te Hauora Tapui Ltd and The Problem Gambling Foundation of New Zealand.

Reid, R.L. (1986). The psychology of the near miss, *Journal of Gambling Behavior*, 2, 32–39.

Reith, G. (1999). *The Age of Chance*, London: Routledge.

Reith, G. (ed.) (2003). *Gambling: Who Wins? Who Loses?*, New York: Prometheus (see chapters by Reith; Eadington; Grinols; McMillen; Stitt et al; Rose; Volberg; McNeilly and Burke).

Reuter, P. (2009). Ten years after the United Nations general assembly special session (UNGASS): assessing drug problems, policies and reform proposals, *Addiction*, 104, 510–517.

Robinson, T.E. and Berridge, K.C. (1993). The neural basis of drug craving: an incentive-sensitization theory of addiction, *Brain Research Reviews*, 18, 247–291.

Rogers, P. (1998). The cognitive psychology of lottery gambling: a theoretical review, *Journal of Gambling Studies*, 14, 111–134.

Room, R., Turner N.E. and Ialomiteanu, A. (1999). Community effects of the opening of the Niagara Casino, *Addiction*, 94, 1449–1466.

Room, R. (2004). Disabling the public interest: alcohol strategies and policies for England, *Addiction*, 99, 1083–9.

Rose, G. and Day, S. (1990). The population mean predicts the number of deviant individuals, *British Medical Journal*, 201, 1031–1034.

Rose, I.N. (1991). The rise and fall of the third wave: gambling will be outlawed in forty years, in W.R. Eadington and J.A. Cornelius (eds.) *Gambling and Public Policy: International Perspectives*, Reno: University of Nevada.

Rosecrance, J. (1988). *Gambling Without Guilt: The Legitimation of an American Pastime*, Pacific Grove, California: Brooks/Cole.

Rosenthal, R. (1987). The psychodynamics of pathological gambling: a review of the literature in T. Galsk (ed.) *The Handbook of Pathological Gambling*, Springfield, Illinois: Charles C Thomas.

Rosenthal, R. and Lesieur, H.R. (1992). Self-reported withdrawal symptoms and pathological gambling, *The American Journal on Addictions*, 1, 151–154.

Sachs, J. (2005). *The End of Poverty: How We can Make It Happen in Our Lifetime*, London: Penguin.

Scholes, S., Wardle, H., Sproston, K., Erens, B., Griffiths, M. and Orford, J. (2008). Understanding non-response to the British Gambling Prevalence Survey 2007. London: National Centre for Social Research, prepared for the Gambling Commission.

Scott, C.K. and Dennis, M.L. (2009). Results from two randomized clinical trials evaluating the impact of quarterly recovery management checkups with adult chronic substance users, *Addiction*, 104, 959–971.

Searles, J. (1988). The role of genetics in the pathogensisis of alcoholism, *Journal of Abnormal Psychology*, 97, 153–167.

Shaffer, H.J. and Hall, M.N. (1996). Estimating the prevalence of adolescent gambling disorders: a quantitative synthesis and guide toward standard gambling nomenclature, *Journal of Gambling Studies*, 12, 193–214.

Shaffer, H.J., LaBrie, R., Scanlan, K.M. and Cummings, T.N. (1994). Pathological gambling among adolescents: Massachusetts Gambling Screen (MAGS), *Journal of Gambling Studies*, 10, 339–362.

Shaffer, H.J. (1996). Understanding the means and objects of addiction: technology, the internet, and gambling, *Journal of Gambling Studies*, 12, 461–469.

Shaffer, H.J., LaBrie, R.A. and LaPlante, D. (2004). Laying the foundation for quantifying regional exposure to a social phenomenon: considering the case of legalized gambling as a public health toxin, *Psychology of Addictive Behaviors*, 18, 40–48.

Shaffer, H.J., LaPlante, D.A., LaBrie, R.A., Kidman, R.C., Donato, A.N. and Stanton, M.V. (2004). Toward a syndrome model of addiction: multiple expressions, common etiology, *Substance Abuse Column*, 12, 367–374.

Sharpe, L., Tarrier, N., Schotte, D. and Spence, S.H. (1995). The role of autonomic arousal in problem gambling, *Addiction*, 90, 1529–1540.

Sher, K.J. (1991). *Children of Alcoholics: A Critical Appraisal of Theory and Research*, Chicago: University of Chicago Press.

Smith, G., Hodgins, D. and Williams, R. (eds.) (2007). *Research and Measurement Issues in Gambling Studies*, San Diego: Academic Press (see chapters by Reith; Slutske; Parke and Griffiths, Toneatto and Nguyen; Abbott; Petry and Weinstock; Williams et al; McMillen; Wood and Williams; Grinols; Borrell and Boulet; Pierce and Miller).

Southwell, J., Boreham, P. and Laffan, W. (2008). Problem gambling and the circumstances facing older people: a study of gaming machine players aged 60+ in licensed clubs, *Journal of Gambling Studies*, 24, 151–174.

Sproston, K., Erens, B. and Orford, J. (2000). *Gambling Behaviour in Britain: Results from the British Gambling Prevalence Survey*, London: The National Centre for Social Research.

Squires, P. (1937). Fyodor Dostoevsky: a psychopathographical sketch, *Psychoanalytical Review*, 24, 365–388.

Stekel, W. (1924). *Peculiarities of Behaviour: Wandering Mania, Dipsomania, Cleptomania, Pyromania and Allied Impulsive Acts,* English Publication 1938, London: Bodley Head (trans. J. van Teslaar).

Stewart, S.H. and Zack, M. (2008). Development and psychometric evaluation of a three-dimensional gambling motives questionnaire, *Addiction*, 103, 1110–1117.

Storer, J., Abbott, M. and Stubbs, J. (2009). Access or adaptation? A meta-analysis of surveys of problem gambling prevalence in Australia and New Zealand with respect of concentration of electronic gaming machines, *International Gambling Studies*, 9, 225–244.

Strong, D.R., Daughters, S.B., Lejuez, C.W. and Breen, R.B. (2004a). Using the Rasch model to develop a revised gambling attitudes and beliefs scale (GABS) for use with male college student gamblers, *Substance Use and Misuse*, 39, 1009–1020.

Strong, D.R., Breen, R.B. and Lejuez, C.W. (2004b). Using item response theory to examine gambling attitudes and beliefs, *Personality and Individual Differences*, 36, 1515–1529.

Tanasornnarong, N., Jackson, A.C. and Thomas, S.A. (2004). Gambling among young Thai people in Melbourne, Australia: an exploratory study, *International Gambling Studies*, 4, 189–203.

Tiffany, S.T. (1990). A cognitive model of drug urges and drug-use behavior: role of automatic and nonautomatic processes, *Psychological Review*, 97, 147–168.

Trevorrow, K. and Moore, S. (1998). The association between loneliness, social isolation and women's electronic gaming machine gambling, *Journal of Gambling Studies*, 14, 263–284.

Tse, S., Wong, J. and Kim. H. (2004). A public health approach for Asian people with problem gambling in foreign countries, *Journal of Gambling Issues*, 12, 1–15.

Tse, S., Abbott, M., Clarke, D., Townsend, S., Kingi, P. and Manaia, W. (2005). Why people gamble. Report to the Health Research Council of New Zealand.

Turner, N.E., Ialomiteanu, A. and Room, R. (1999). Checkered expectations: predictors of approval of opening a casino in the Niagara community, *Journal of Gambling Studies*, 15, 45–70.

Van Lancker, J. (1977). Smoking and Disease, in M Jarvik, J. Cullen, E. Gritz, T. Vogt, and L. West (eds.) *Research on Smoking Behavior,* National Institute on Drug Abuse Research Monograph 17, US Dept. of Health, Education and Welfare, NIDA, Rockville, Maryland.

Velleman. R. and Orford, J. (1999). *Risk and Resilience: Adults who were the Children of Problem Drinkers*, Reading: Harwood.

Verdejo-García, A., Lawrence, A.J. and Clark, L. (2008). Impulsivity as a vulnerability marker for substance-use disorders: review of findings from high-risk research, problem gamblers and genetic association studies, *Neuroscience and Biobehavioral Reviews*, 32, 777–810.

Vitaro, F., Ferland, F., Jacques, C. and Ladouceur, R. (1998). Gambling, substance use, and impulsivity during adolescence, *Psychology of Addictive Behaviors*, 12, 185–194.

Vitaro, F., Arseneault, L. and Tremblay, R.E. (1999). Impulsivity predicts problem gambling in low SES adolescent males, *Addiction*, 94, 565–575.

Vong, F. (2007). The psychology of risk-taking in gambling among Chinese visitors to Macau, *International Gambling Studies*, 7, 29–42.

Walker, M.B. (1992). *The Psychology of Gambling*, Oxford: Butterworth-Heinemann.

Walters, G.D. and Contri, D. (1998). Outcome expectancies for gambling: empirical modeling of a memory network in federal prison inmates, *Journal of Gambling Studies*, 14, 173–191.

Wardle, H., D'Souza, J. and Farrell, N. (2009). *Gambling Behaviour*, Ch 11 in the report of the 2007 Adult Psychiatric Morbidity Study, the Health and Social Care Information Centre, Social Care Statistics.

Wardle, H., Sproston, K., Orford, J., Erens, B., Griffiths, M., Constantine, R. and Pigott, S. (2007). *British Gambling Prevalence Survey 2007*, London: NatCen/Gambling Commission.

Watson, L. and Kale, S.H. (2003). Know when to hold them: applying the customer lifetime value concept to casino table gaming, *International Gambling Studies*, 3, 89–101.

Weatherburn, D. (2009). Dilemmas in harm minimization, *Addiction*, 104, 335–339.

Welte, J.W., Wieczorek, W.F., Barnes, G.M., Tidwell, M. and Hoffman, J.H. (2004). The relationship of ecological and geographic factors to gambling behaviour and pathology, *Journal of Gambling Studies*, 20, 405–423.

Welte, J.W., Barnes, G.M., Wieczorek, W.F., Tidwell, M.O. and Hoffman, J.H. (2007). Type of gambling and availability as risk factors for problem gambling: a tobit regression analysis by age and gender, *International Gambling Studies*, 7, 183–198.

West, R. (2006). *Theory of Addiction*, London: Blackwell and Addiction Press.

White, N.M. (1996). Addictive drugs as reinforcers: multiple partial actions on memory systems, *Addiction*, 91, 921–949.

White, C., Mitchell, L. and Orford, J. (2001). *Exploring Gambling Behaviour in Depth: a Qualitative Study*. London: National Centre for Social Research.

Whyte, K.S. (1999). Analysis of the national gambling impact study commission act, *Journal of Gambling Studies*, 15, 309–318.

Willig, C. (2001). *Introducing Qualitative Research in Psychology: Adventures in Theory and Method*, Buckingham, UK: Open University Press.

Winters, K.C. and Rich, T. (1998). A twin study of adult gambling behavior, *Journal of Gambling Studies*, 14, 213–225.

Wise, R.A. (1994). A brief history of the anhedonia hypothesis, in C.R. Legg and D. Booth (eds.) *Appetite, Neural and Behavioural Bases*, Oxford: Oxford University Press, 243–263.

Wood, R.T.A. and Griffiths, M.D. (2004). Adolescent lottery and scratchcard players: do their attitudes influence their gambling behaviour?, *Journal of Adolescence*, 27, 467–475.

Wray, I. and Dickerson, M. (1981). Cessation of high frequency gambling and withdrawal symptoms, *British Journal of Addiction*, 76, 401–405.

Zaranek, R.R. and Lichtenberg, P.A. (2008). Urban elders and casino gambling: are they at risk of a gambling problem?, *Journal of Aging Studies*, 22, 13–23.

Zeigler, D.W. (2009). The alcohol industry and trade agreements: a preliminary assessment, *Addiction*, 104, Suppl. 1, 13–26.

Zhonglu, Z. and Dongmei, Z. (2007). A profile of lottery players in Guangzhou, China, *International Gambling Studies*, 7, 265–280.

Zola, I.K. (1963). Observations on gambling in a lower-class setting, *Social Problems*, 10, 360.

Zucker, R.A. (2008). Commentary: Anticipating problem alcohol use developmentally from childhood into middle adulthood: what have we learned?, *Addiction*, 13, Suppl. 1, 100–108.

Index

Note: Page numbers in italics refer to tables and figures.